From Industrial to Legal
Standardization, 1871–1914

Legal History Library

VOLUME 7

Studies in the History of Private Law

VOLUME 3

The titles published in this series are listed at brill.nl/lhl

From Industrial to Legal Standardization, 1871–1914

Transnational Insurance Law and the Great San Francisco Earthquake

By

Tilmann J. Röder

Translated by

Frederik Heinemann

MARTINUS
NIJHOFF
PUBLISHERS

LEIDEN · BOSTON
2012

Cover illustration: Policy of the Californian insurance company Fireman's Fund from 1905. The company W. J. Sloane & Co. from San Francisco insured itself against fire damages of up to US $ 10,000 for an annual premium of US $ 86. After the catastrophe, the Fireman's Fund compensated for the damage. Source: Fireman's Fund Archive. Courtesy of the Fireman's Fund Insurance Company, San Francisco.

This book is printed on acid-free paper.

Library of Congress Cataloging-in-Publication Data

Röder, Tilmann J.
   From industrial to legal standardization, 1871–1914 : transnational insurance law and the great San Francisco earthquake / by Tilmann J. Roder.
      p. cm.
   Includes bibliographical references and index.
   ISBN 978-90-04-21237-4 (hardback : alk. paper)
1. Insurance policies—History—20th century. 2. Standardized terms of contract—History—20th century. 3. Earthquake insurance—Law and legislation—United States—History—20th century. 4. Fire insurance—Law and legislation—United States—History—20th century. I. Title.
   K1241.R63 2012
   346'.08609—dc23

                                                                              2011035426

This publication has been typeset in the multilingual "Brill" typeface. With over 5,100 characters covering Latin, IPA, Greek, and Cyrillic, this typeface is especially suitable for use in the humanities. For more information, please see www.brill.nl/brill-typeface.

ISSN 1874-1793
ISBN 978 90 04 21237 4 (hardback)
ISBN 978 90 04 21463 7 (e-book)

This translation was funded by Geisteswissenschaften International—Translation Funding for Humanities and Social Sciences Germany. A joint initiative of the Fritz Thyssen Foundation, the German Federal Foreign Office, and the German Publishers & Booksellers Association.

Originally published as *Rechtsbildung im wirtschaftlichen >>Weltverkehr<<: Das Erdbeben von San Francisco und die internationale Standardisierung von Vertragsbedingungen (1871–1914)* ©Vittorio Klostermann, Frankfurt am Main 2006.

MIX
Paper from
responsible sources
FSC® C008919

PRINTED BY AD DRUK BV - ZEIST, THE NETHERLANDS

CONTENTS

LIST OF TABLES

LIST OF ABBREVIATIONS

Generally known abbreviations (such as vol.) are not included in the following list.

ADHGB	*Allgemeines Deutsches Handelsgesetzbuch* ('General German Commercial Code')
AGB	*Allgemeine Geschäftsbedingungen* ('general business conditions')
Ass.	Assurance
Assn.	Association
AVB	*Allgemeine Versicherungsbedingungen* ('general insurance conditions')
avv.	*avvocato*
cif	cost, insurance, freight
C.I.I.	*Concordato Italiano Incendio* ('Italian Concordat of Fire Insurance Companies')
Civ.	*tribunal civil* (French 'civil court')
Co.	Company
Cologne Re	*Kölnische Rückversicherungs-Gesellschaft* / *Kölnische Rück* (today's Gen Re)
Comm.	*Commissario* (Italian 'Commissioner')
CVDI	*Centralverband Deutscher Industrieller* ('central federation of German industrialists')
Dept.	Department
Dem.	Democratic Party (California)
Diss.	Dissertation
DJZ	Deutsche Juristen-Zeitung
F.O.C.	Fire Offices Committee
fob	free on board
FUAP	(The) Fire Underwriters' Association of the Pacific
G.	Gesellschaft
Habil.	Habilitation
HZ	Historische Zeitung
Hon.	Honorable (American judge's title)
ICC	International Chamber of Commerce
I.L.	Independent League (California)

ILA	International Law Association
Ins.	Insurance
J.	Justice (English judge's title)
KR	(in footnotes) *Kölnische Rückversicherungs-Gesellschaft* (Cologne Re)
L. Rev.	Law Review
L.J.	Lord Justice (English judge's title)
LZ	Leipziger Zeitschrift für Handels-, Konkurs-, und Versicherungsrecht
MdR	*Mitglied des Reichstages* ('member of the *Reichstag*')
MP	Member of Parliament (GB)
MR	(in footnotes) *Münchener Rückversicherungs-Gesellschaft* (Munich Re)
M.R.	Master of the Rolls (Vorsitzender des Court of Appeals im britischen House of Lords)
Munich Re	*Münchener Rückversicherungs-Gesellschaft/Münchener Rück* (today's Gen Re)
N.Y.	New York
ÖRev	Österreichische Revue
ÖVZ	Österreichische Versicherungs-Zeitung
RA	*Rechtsanwalt* ('advocate')
RabelsZ	Rabels Zeitschrift für ausländisches und internationales Privatrecht
Rep.	Republican Party (California)
rev.	revisor
RJ	Rechtshistorisches Journal
RGZ	Entscheidungen des Reichsgerichts in Zivilsachen (official collection)
RGBl.	Reichsgesetzblatt
ROHG	[Decisions of the] Reichsoberhandelsgericht ('Imperial Supreme Court for Commerce')
SR	(in footnotes) *Schweizerische Rückversicherungs-Gesellschaft* (Swiss Re)
Swiss Re	*Schweizerische Rückversicherungs-Gesellschaft/Schweizer Rück* (today's Swiss Re)
trans.	translated
U.L.	Union Labour (California)
Vers.-Bank	*Versicherungs-Bank* ('insurance bank')
Vers.-G	*Versicherungs-Gesellschaft* ('insurance company')

vs.	versus
VSWG	Vierteljahreshefte für Wirtschafts- und Sozialgeschichte
VVG	*Versicherungsvertragsgesetz* (German 'Insurance Contract Law')
ZHR	Zeitschrift für Handelsrecht
ZVersWiss	Zeitschrift für die gesammte Versicherungs-Wissenschaft
ZVMEV	Zeitschrift des Vereins Mitteleuropäischer Eisenbahn-verwaltungen

LIST OF REFERENCES AND SOURCES

Archive Documents: List of Locations

BA   Bundesarchiv, Potsdamer Str. 1, 56075 DE-Koblenz

BL   Bancroft Library, University of California, Berkeley, CA 94720–6000, USA

CSL   California State Archives, 1020 "O" Street, Sacramento, CA 95814, USA

FFA   Fireman's Fund Archives, 777 San Marin Drive, Novato, CA 94998, USA

KR/A   General Cologne Re (formerly Kölnische Rückversicherungs-Gesellschaft), Theodor-Heuss-Ring 11/Sedanstr. 8, D-50668 Köln

MR/A   Munich Re (formerly Münchener Rückversicherungs-Gesellschaft), Königinstr. 107, DE-80802 München

StUB   Stadt- und Universitätsbibliothek Frankfurt a.M., Bockenheimer Landstr. 134–13; DE-60325 Frankfurt am Main

SR/FA   Swiss Re (formerly Schweizerische Rückversicherungs-Gesellschaft), Mythenquai 50/60, CH-8022 Zürich

FOREWORD

This book is a translation of my dissertation published in 2006 by Vittorio Klostermann, the dedicated humanities publisher from Frankfurt am Main. Just like the title of the German edition, *"Rechtsbildung im wirtschaftlichen Weltverkehr. Das Erdbeben von San Franciso und die internationale Standardisierung von Vertragsbedingungen (1871–1914)"*, the English title tries to put the main elements of my research in a nutshell. However, this has once again proven impossible. I hope that the book will find its readers among the legal historians and legal theorists, researchers studying the development of the insurance business or the perception of risk and disaster, and those interested in the standardising impact of the industrial revolution on human culture in general. I have updated this edition by including the literature available by September 2011.

The German version was awarded the prize *"Geisteswissenschaften International—Preis zur Förderung der Übersetzung geisteswissenschaftlicher Literatur"* by the Fritz Thyssen Foundation, the German Publishers' and Booksellers' Association and the Federal Foreign Office of Germany. The award included financial support for the cost of this translation, aiming at the worldwide dissemination of the German humanities research. I cordially thank the donors as well as the jury which defined "humanities" wide enough to accept a dissertation which was originally handed in at the Law Faculty of Frankfurt's Goethe University. I am deeply grateful to Vittorio E. Klostermann and his colleagues Anastasia Urban and Christina Müller who proposed the book for the award and dedicated much of their time to this project for over two years, as well as to Rosanna Woensdregt, Hylke Faber and Marti Huetink of Brill Publishers who helped me during this marathon, notably the editing process, until I held the printed result in my hands. I am equally grateful to the series editors Remco van Rhee, Dirk Heirbaut and Matthew C. Mirow, who accepted this publication into the present book series.

The translator deserves special attention. Frederik Heinemann did not just translate this book. He studied the works of Giedion, Trakman and Harriman in order to learn the language of the time and transferred sentences into English which I thought were untranslatable. Fritz, I think the worst was *"Die in dieser Hinsicht wichtigsten Klauseln enthalten neben Haftungsbegrenzungen oder-ausschlüssen und Beweislastregelungen auch*

Vertragsstrafen und Verbote, Ansprüche abzutreten", wasn't it? Thank you for mastering this and so many other intractable phrases. This book is also your book.

Before the translation could go to press, Mihan Rouzbehani and Theodor Shulman helped me with the footnotes and annexes and thousands of terrible details. This was a hard and tiring work that took months. I will not forget your patience and commitment. Many thanks.

I dedicate this book to my parents, Hedda and Uwe Röder, who gave me the necessary education and discipline which enabled me to write my dissertation, and to my beloved wife Viktoria Draganova and our daughter Vivien. I thank them for their tolerance when I worked on this study at intolerable times.

Frankfurt, September 2011
Tilmann Röder

INTRODUCTION

THE SUBJECT AND FOCUS OF THE PRESENT STUDY

Did the internationalisation of important branches of business from the 1870's onwards lead to the development of a *lex mercatoria*[1] or similar transnational legal structures? This question formed the starting point for my investigations of the law that was applied in transnational contractual business relationships between 1871 and 1914. The present book is the result of this research.

At first glance, an autonomously created international business law in the nineteenth and early twentieth centuries seems hardly conceivable. The law of Nation States—especially their commercial and civil law codes and the international private law that refers to them—would scarcely seem to allow for the non-governmental formation of law. But reality apparently looked different for large parts of economies entering into the process of industrialisation. In comparison to the needs of business under the dynamics of rapid fundamental changes, national law became the victim of a 'cultural lag'.[2] Neither legislatures, administrative bodies nor judiciaries were successful in keeping up with economic developments. On the international level, the situation was even worse. Frequently, national negotiations on multilateral agreements or the establishment of common arbitration tribunals dragged on for decades. Thus, businessmen themselves updated contract law. At the same time, they adapted the regulations to their own interests as profit-oriented participants in market activities. A central instrument was the 'general conditions of contracts'[3] that they drafted themselves and that, to a large degree, regularly took precedence over national law. These 'general conditions' developed into a general phenomenon that in the course of the nineteenth century—

---

[1] The English term 'law merchant' is used synonymously.

[2] Ogburn 1964, 86.

[3] The German term is *Allgemeine Vertragsbedingungen*. Legal scholars distinguish between general terms and conditions of business which must be introduced to the individual agreements made between parties and general contracts existing in standardised pre-printed forms which do not need to be expressly approved. This distinction is irrelevant for the purposes of this study.

according to the thesis of this study—dominated international business relations from the 1870's onwards in a large part of the business world.

The first part of the present study will discuss the creation and expansion of general business conditions in the national economies and in the beginning world commerce. The term 'standardisation' will serve as an analytical category. The decision in favour of this rather technical term is based on two reasons. Firstly, the standardising of contractual texts points to functionally important parallels between technical and legal standardisation. Both phenomena appear at the same time in history and develop simultaneously. They are also structurally so similar that they can be regarded as a uniform appearance. At the beginning of the industrial revolution, standardisation extended to many fields in all countries, developed rapidly within a few decades and eventually dominated the resulting industrial culture.

Secondly, the concepts of the formation of norms developed by legal theorists do not offer an alternative to the category of standardisation, as they do not live up to the historical development of the complex pre-formulated contract conditions that spread on the national and international level. Of course, specific business conditions did achieve the quality of legal norms, for example, when they received State approval or when their enforcement within a legal system seemed likely. Moreover, from the perspective of systems theory it could then be ascertained that their code value be allocated in the relevant discourses as lawful or unlawful.[4] However, in numerous cases, this classification is questionable. Many of the pre-formulated contract texts were regarded as not legally relevant by their users. Other contract forms did not really make an appearance in practice—for example, in court. Only hypothetically was it possible here and there to determine whether a legal norm had emerged or not. An exclusive examination of the general business conditions as products of the formation of legal norms would contradict the contemporary discourses and must be open to the accusation of being ahistoric. The category of 'standardisation' circumvents these limitations through its wider normative meaning. By directing the focus to the factuality of the business conditions, the concept of standardisation sharpens the view for parallel phenomena in other areas of life.

The survey in Part A of the development of general terms and conditions of business on the national and international level also allows for a

---

[4] Luhmann 1981, 53 *et seq.*; 1993, 69.

better understanding of the case study that follows. Parts B and C discuss how in 1906 and 1907, a specific standard clause in spontaneously activated networks of the insurance business came into existence and how its implementation in national legal codes in the period following was carried out. The results of the efforts at standardisation were determined according to methods of comparative legal analysis and organised by "ideal type"; three chapters deal with the adoption of the standard clause in various legal orders (C.I), their rejection in others (C.II), as well as the absence of a coherent reaction in yet other cases (C.III).

The choice of the 'earthquake clause' in the contracts existing in the fire insurance business to serve as an example of standardised business conditions was made for three reasons: firstly, before 1914, this business branch discussed no other topic so intensively on the international level as the treatment of fire damage caused by earthquakes. This great interest resulted from the experience of the earthquake-fire catastrophe in San Francisco in April of 1906 that drove many insurance companies to the brink of bankruptcy. Secondly, the extant historical material enables the precise reconstruction of a legal change that almost exclusively depends upon the self-organisational activities within a particular branch of business. Thirdly, this example demonstrates the circumstances in which several legal orders succeeded in introducing a standard clause and others failed to do so.

At the end of the investigation, conclusions will be drawn as to the functions, the possibilities and the limitations of international standardisation of the general terms and conditions of business before 1914. Finally, a legal-historical appraisal of the phenomenon of the general terms and conditions of business as a transnational legal structure will be postulated based upon said conclusions.

State of Research and Sources

Few legal scholars have paid much attention to the history of the international standardisation of contracts prior to 1914. The same holds largely true for the origins of the contract law form on the national level.[5]

For this reason, the present investigation mainly relies on primary sources. In the investigation of the changes in the contract conditions in

---

[5] Among the exceptions are Scherner (1992, 42 *et seq.*) and Lammel (1993, 89 *et seq.*).

the fire insurance industry that resulted from the San Francisco earthquake, the 'grey literature'—that is, contemporary publications in the insurance branch—proved especially informative. This also holds true for the historical consequences of the catastrophe in business and science. The journals that were primarily consulted are American, Austrian, French, German and Italian.

Moreover, the correspondence between the directors of the European and American reinsurance and fire insurance companies that discussed and promoted the project of introducing an internationally unified earthquake clause was of major importance. The most important extant source for these materials is the Archives of the Swiss Re in Zurich.

The holdings of the following archives and collections that were additionally consulted in this study are:

> Allianz Versicherungsgesellschaft—Archives, Munich
> Deutscher Verein für Versicherungswissenschaft—Library, Berlin
> Deutsches Bundesarchiv (The Federal Archives), Koblenz
> General Cologne Re—Archives, Cologne
> Institut für Versicherungswissenschaft—Library, Cologne
> Munich Re—Archives, Munich
> Archivio centrale dello Stato, Roma
> Assicurazioni Generali—Archives, Trieste
> Riunione Adriatica di Sicurtà—Archives, Trieste
> The Bancroft Library, Berkeley, Ca.
> California State Archives, Sacramento, Ca.

The historical contextualising of the study arose from the engagement with very different legal, technical and cultural-historical literature. Pride of place is occupied by the published work of Atiyah,[6] Giedion[7] and Berz[8] as well as that of Harriman.[9]

---

[6] 1979. Considering the reality of the practice of contract forms, the work of Hofer (2001) proved to be less useful.

[7] 1948.

[8] 2001.

[9] 1928.

CHAPTER ONE

STANDARD CONTRACT TERMS IN NATIONAL
AND INTERNATIONAL BUSINESS

In his *Mechanization Takes Command* in 1948, the Swiss cultural historian Sigfried Giedion traced the profound influence exercised by industrial production on the life and experiences of the average citizen.[1] For Giedion, culture is a feature of society at large as manifested in such inconspicuous basic commodities as a tin loaf of bread, a product that always looks and tastes the same.[2] To him, the origin and abiding power of this industrial civilisation is mechanisation, an idea that, for this study, requires merely a slight adjustment of the focus on standardisation, since this phenomenon embraces not only technology and business but also the practice of contract law. The perspective changes from the novel means of production to the products themselves and their specific and, at least historically, new features.[3]

1.1. FROM WEAPONS TO CONTRACTS: STANDARDISATION TAKES COMMAND

In 1767, the French Royal Corps of Artillery introduced mass-produced cannon carriages. Its technology was regarded as revolutionary.[4] The production of the carriages radically differed from the traditional procedure that manufactured unique versions of a product. The mark of the Ancien Régime was the serial number that had to be stamped on each individual part of a product, since only these parts fit together.[5] In contrast, the newly developed carriages overseen by their designer, the French General

---

[1] Giedion's book (1948) in part recounts observations that he made during a trip through the United States in 1937.

[2] Giedion 1948, 197 *et seq.*

[3] Compare Vec (2000), a description of the project, 'Law in the Industrial Revolution', launched by an independent group of young scholars at the Max Planck Institute for European Legal History in Frankfurt am Main, Germany. For Michael Stolleis (1999, 37 *et seq.*), the emergence of 'mass society'—which is characterised by mechanisation, standardisation and ideologisation—is the beginning of a new epoch.

[4] Rosen, 'Le Système Gribeauval et la Guerre Moderne', *Revue Historique des Armées 2, 3* (1975); Jobe et al. 1981.

[5] Berz 2001, 20.

Jean Baptiste Vaquette de Gribeauval (1715–1789), all had the same design and shape and were thus interchangeable. Presumably, contemporary observers recognised in this military innovation the possible beginning of a technological revolution, for they characterised the equipment not just descriptively as carriages—*affûts Gribeauval*—but rather as *système Gribeauval*.[6]

A few years later, the French engineer Honoré Blanc designed an infantry weapon that consisted entirely of intricately uniform and interchangeable components. The *modèle 1777* promised to solve a central problem of military logistics: whereas up to that point, defective weapons had to be sent to a remote manufacturer for repair, damaged parts could now be replaced right on the battlefield. Blanc succeeded in convincing his customers; his weapons remained in use well into the nineteenth century in all the armies of Europe and the United States.[7]

The principles of the *système Gribeauval* and the *modèle 1777*—making use of uniform and interchangeable parts—were products of the eighteenth century. They were consistent not only with the spirit of rationalism and the French enlightenment but also exactly matched the systems of knowledge current in the seventeenth and eighteenth centuries. For here and there, the category of 'identity' moved to the centre of belief, replacing the thought paradigm of the 'similarity' of things.[8] In the new order of the age of mechanisation, 'identity' meant two things: the first was that all the individual parts having the same form were subject to the same technical standards. Thus it appeared that they could be manufactured in absolute uniformity. The second was that all individual parts followed one common standard.[9] Only in this way could they function as a unit. As a bearer of identity, the technical norms came into existence after uniform parts were manufactured and machines having the same function were installed. In the French cannon carriages and weapons, a new technological development was launched. It led to the industrial mass production of standardised goods.

Even in Gribeauval's and Blanc's time, conditions were ripe for standardisation's triumphant march through Europe and North America. This

---

[6] The system was named after its designer, General Jean Baptiste Vaquette de Gribeauval (Frontard, 'Histoire de la norme', *La normalisation technique, Culture technique* 29 [1994], 19 *et seq.*).

[7] Berz 2001, 18.

[8] Ibid., 27 *et seq.*

[9] Ibid., 37.

process continued for decades. By means of the exclusion of corporative organisations from the sphere of the regulation of technology, an opportunity was created for new norms. It soon became apparent that the losers in this development were the guilds and crafts organisations. The winners were the large established manufacturers, often with sovereign privileges and State capital behind them. For them, the investment involved in developing their own technical norms paid off, since they were set up to produce large amounts of goods of a similar type.

The general restraint of sovereign States in the area of standardisation was also important. Their governments stimulated the new business and technical developments by supporting the natural sciences,[10] breaking up traditional regulatory monopolies and finally guaranteeing freedom of trade.[11] As stakeholders in the technical standardisation, they entered the fray only in a few key areas in which it was important to secure their sovereignty and to create uniform living conditions.[12] The military economy, the transport system and communications technology were of utmost importance.[13] The establishment of measurement and currency units also resulted through laws and ordinances.[14] In other areas, State institutions intervened in business activities only selectively for the sake of technical standardisation. This only changed in World War I.[15] Private stakeholders used this freedom extensively and created widespread complexes of norms.[16]

The entry of standardisation into technology between the eighteenth and the nineteenth centuries is not an isolated phenomenon. A similar development began at the same time in the field of law. The stakeholders are known from the sphere of standardisation. Large companies and sovereign States that were engaged in business activities began to establish

---

[10] Musgrave 1999, 98 *et seq.*

[11] An example drawn from Prussia: Vogel 1983, 135 *et seq.*

[12] Vec 2003, 44.

[13] Koch, 'Studien über Telegraphenrecht', *ZHR 4* (1861), 348 *et seq.*

[14] Hawtrey 1992, 1.

[15] In 1901, the Engineering Standards Committee was established in England. In reaction to the pressure created by the war economy, the 'German Standards Committee' (*Deutscher Normenausschuß*) was formed in 1917, and the French *Commission Permanente de Standardisation* followed in 1918. In the USA, several organisations involved with normalisation and three government departments united in 1918 under one umbrella organisation (Galland 2001, 7; Berz 1995, 222).

[16] Two examples from the margins of technology demonstrate the dissimilarity of these processes. Standardisation at the time was not practiced by State institutions, but rather by the administrations of the railway (Bartky 2000, 19 *et seq.*; Dohrn-van Rossum 1992, 318 *et seq.*). Other standards simply emerged: for example, the 'Qwerty'-typewriter keyboard at the Remington Arms Company (Beeching 1990, 41; Liebowitz/Margolis 1990, 1–21).

individual contract relations on the footing of uniform, pre-printed contract forms.[17] The variety of the forms of these contracts was extensive. They ranged from individual conditions printed on letterheads—for example, that of the jurisdiction—to the widespread standard form contracts. From the point of view of technology, it was the standardisation of a specific print media that was important. They helped to reduce the amount of written correspondence and to avoid errors based upon sloppy handwriting; in short, they economised office organisation.

The legal dimension of the phenomenon was equally, if not more important. Standard form contracts were useful in the drawing up of large numbers of contracts that had the same contents as individual contracts. Many simply reproduced the regulations of statutory law or of generally recognised legal customs. This group includes the many standard forms that were used by notaries public, estate agents, chambers of commerce, stock exchange associations, government agencies and other institutions operating neutrally between contract partners.[18]

Other bodies of rules supplemented the legal stipulations, modified them or created essentially new standard form contracts. In addition, numerous individual clauses were added as well as—more on the periphery—the so-called international commercial terms, that is, abbreviations in which foreign business people and shippers consolidated the contents of their contracts. This group is, from the point of view of legal history, especially interesting. In Germany, the term 'general business conditions' (*Allgemeine Geschäftsbedingungen*) became widely accepted by the end of the nineteenth century.[19] At the same time, business practice repeatedly coined special terminology that stayed in vogue for several years or, in some cases, decades. For example, the contract conditions operative in railway companies were called '*Reglements*' ('regulations') up to the turn of the century. Similarly, the terminological history proved parallel in other countries that entered industrialisation in the course of the nineteenth century. In part, the designations directly corresponded to the German terminology, for example *standard business terms, conditions générales, contrats types* and *condizioni generali* (*di contratto*). In French

---

[17] Raiser 1935, 26 *et seq.*

[18] According to Raiser (1935, 24), forms used by notaries public and pre-prints of individual contracts only fulfilled a 'security function'.

[19] The term was used by large banks in Berlin from the 1880's onwards. The dominant information in 'standard business terms' was originally of a commercial and technical nature common to banks (Koch 1932, 33).

theory of law, the term coined by Raymond Saleilles,[20] *contrat d'adhésion*, prevailed in the first three decades of the twentieth century before being adopted in other legal systems influenced by the French tradition and then into the Anglo-American systems.[21] Whatever the terminology— *Allgemeine Geschäftsbedingungen, contrats d'adhésion* or *contracts of adhesion*—and whatever the systematic interpretation of them by contemporary legal scholars may have been, the designated phenomena had the same functions in practice.

Standard business terms were, as the terminology implies, *standards*; they shared the function of technical norms. The basic principles of standardisation known in the world of technology—the existence of objective standards and the uniformity of the standardised objects—reappear in the context of trade. Businesses and institutions that made use of standard terms of business could assume that all of the contracts concluded by their representatives coincided in all aspects regulated by the standard terms. The identical character of the texts seemed to guarantee the exact conformity with the individual contracts—or at least provided the appearance of a uniformity that was sufficient for trade.

And what is standardisation? From the variety of different descriptions and definitions of this term, it is clear that a lack of uniform agreement bridging individual empirical disciplines prevails.[22] But from our historical distance, it is possible to derive a generic concept that embraces all of the various meanings of the term.

Standardisation appears at the turn of the nineteenth century as a novel cultural technology.[23] It involves a strategy for the organisation

---

[20] Saleilles 1901, 229.

[21] Above all, Patterson ('The Delivery of a Life-Insurance Policy', Harvard L. Rev. 33 [1919], 198 *et seq.*) and Kessler ('Contracts of Adhesion: Some Thoughts About Freedom of Contract', Columbia L. Rev. 43 [1943], 629 *et seq.*) enabled the transfer.

[22] The term 'standardisation' is treated differently in technology, business and science. In technology, a distinction is drawn between technical standardisation—that is, standardisation of parts; and typification—that is, standardisation of the total product; and programming—the standardisation of production and administration procedures. In the field of trade, the term is used to refer to meeting certain specifications of quality. Additional uses of the term, usually modified to suit the specific field, can be found in psychology, linguistics, statistics and other empirical disciplines. See 'standardization' in the *Encyclopedia Britannica* (1962), vol. 21, 307; *Standardisierung* in *Brockhaus*, 20th ed. (1998), vol. 21, 10.

[23] In a similar vein, Miloš Vec (2000, 47 *et seq.*) characterises Giedion's 'mechanisation' as a 'collective pattern'. Georges Canguilhem (1994, 180 *et seq.*), Michel Foucault (1975, 152 *et seq.*) and other writers have pointed out that the logic of standardisation of people and the principle of technical standardisation converge. Well-known examples are the control and discipline existing in institutions such as schools, the military, mental institutions,

of complex processes and procedures. It is primarily employed to solve quantitative problems such as the mass production of goods or the implementation of new infrastructure installations. In its origins, standardisation is thus not only closely related to the technical and business changes that ushered in the industrial revolution in Europe and North America, but also with the demographic consequences of a strong growth in population. Standardisation can be considered a novelty because in contrast to older organisational strategies, its aim is to achieve uniformity in almost scientific consistency.[24] In this respect, it differs from harmonisation.

In addition to the designation of a specific cultural technology, the term 'standardisation' invokes the concrete processes of its application. In the same way that screws and their threads are standardised, contract forms and their contents are standardised as well. To standardise a screw is obviously to make it identical to all other screws in having a definite character; likewise, standardising a contract is to make it the same as all other contracts in its class.

All processes of standardisation appear—at the risk of initial oversimplification—to be divided into two phases: developing a standard, and then implementing it. Closer observation, however, demonstrates that most of the processes are more complex. Thus, considerations as to the introduction of a standard often shape its initial phase, for example by including institutions whose recognition is necessary for the later success of the standard. Should problems arise during the introduction of a standard, it will in all likelihood have to be modified. In addition, the maintenance of generally recognised or binding authoritative regulations is only successful if these are regularly adapted to changes in external conditions. In this sense, the American engineer Norman S. Harriman aptly describes standardisation as a dynamic process involving origin, maintenance and additional development of norms.[25]

---

prisons and the world of work in industrial societies. The similarities of all these strategies lie primarily in the focus upon norms (or normality) and standards as well as on their concentration on the production of (mass) identity (Ewald, 'Norms, Discipline, and the Law', *Representations 30* (1990), 138–161; Link 1999, 129, 191 *et seq.*, 205).

[24] Vec (2003, 8 *et seq.*) works with a broader concept of 'standardisation' and finds numerous examples of pre-industrial processes of standardisation.

[25] 1928, 79 *et seq.*

1.2. CONTRACT TERMS AND CONDITIONS IN INDIVIDUAL COUNTRIES

1.2.1. *The Beginnings of Standardisation in Technology and Law*
(ca. 1770–1830)

The term *proto-standardisation* coined in French studies of standardisation is well suited, in addition to characterising the history of technology, for application to a historical phase that stretches from the end of the early modern period up to the middle of the nineteenth century. In this period, standardisation comes into its own in various fields.[26]

The latest scholarly investigations locate the origins of technical standardisation in the military economy. It possibly began in the first half of the eighteenth century with the production of pieces of uniforms in accordance with specified clothing sizes. The process was facilitated by patterns that established the standards.[27] In addition, French weapons manufacturers achieved a still higher degree of technical precision, and with the *modèle 1777*, standardisation spread internationally. In the United States, its principles were applied by 1800 to the production of looms, sewing machines, typewriters, printing presses and watches as well as other production procedures.[28]

Private insurance companies became the pioneers in the field of contract law.[29] Geographically, England can be identified as the point of origin of the widespread practice of using mass-produced contracts. In the eighteenth century, the entire English insurance industry worked according to the principle of maximising profits, whereas on the continent, State insurance systems and mutual companies still dominated.[30] The English so-called 'insurance offices' thus endeavoured to negotiate the maximum number of contracts. Not only the goal of increasing profits but also the idea of spreading risk as widely as possible, called the 'law of the large number' in business, sparked these efforts. For a variety of reasons—also to maintain control over the contracts generated—, the English insurance

---

[26] In the phase called 'proto-standardisation', the principles of exchangeability and sameness gradually prevail. It ends when the technical norms begin to produce sufficient compatibility beyond the boundaries of the individual products and manufacturers (Galland 2001, 6).

[27] As of the mid-eighteenth century, Prussian military uniforms were cut according to normalised measurements and sizes following a pattern (Krause 1983, 175 *et seq.*, 189 *et seq.*).

[28] Berz 2001, 31 *et seq.*

[29] Kessler, Columbia L. Rev. 43 (1943), 631 *et seq.*

[30] Trebilcock 1985, 1 *et seq.*

societies based all of the individual contracts on identical contract terms.[31] An additional industry that at an early period worked with the principle of the standard business terms was the transport business.[32]

The origins of this practice did not depend merely upon a specific business climate. As with technology, law also provided the opportunity to formalise contracts necessary for private stakeholders. Around 1770, the idea of the freedom of contract became common among English jurists.[33] As judges, lawmakers and civil servants, they campaigned for the dismantlement of the restrictive estate and mercantile economic constitution.[34] As a consequence, the bond between civil law and the social status of the legal subject was removed. Jurists replaced it with the elaboration of the contract's contents through the parties to the contract themselves. They found support in the representatives of classical national economics. Thus, the English path to 'liberty of contract' is just as intimately connected with the name of the national economist Adam Smith[35] as with that of the judge Lord Mansfield.[36] Hence, freedom of contract, whatever the status of any economy, became a central feature of laissez-faire economic and political ideology.

The transformation of civil law 'from status to contract'[37] was adopted a little later in other legal orders. Primarily in Europe and North America, statutory restrictions fell by the wayside[38] and permitted the slow development of an independent law of contract.[39] The maxim of private autonomy corresponded to the trust that middle class society placed in the free manifestation of the will of the individual in legal dealings[40] and towards social self-organisation. In accordance, the freedom of contract reached a position of importance in English and Anglo-American common law,[41] in the French codes,[42] and in the formal-deductive civil law system of the

---

[31] Supple 1970, 81 *et seq.*, 103 *et seq.*

[32] About 1800, for example, haulage companies in England and France (Atiyah 1979, 557; Pohlhausen 1978, 55 *et seq.*). Coing (1989, 537) also emphasises the importance of the general terms and conditions in these two branches.

[33] Atiyah 1979.

[34] Ibid., 226.

[35] Smith 1776.

[36] Atiyah 1979, 120 *et seq.*, 194 *et seq.*

[37] The formulation is Maine's (1861/1954, 100).

[38] Klapisch 1991, 34, 41.

[39] Will 1994, 30, 33.

[40] Called 'will theory' by legal scholars.

[41] Pound, 'Liberty of Contract', *Yale Law Journal 18* (1909), 454, 456 *et seq.*; Will 1994, 28.

[42] *Code civil des Français* (1804), *Code de procédure civile* (1806) and *Code de commerce* (1807). The *Code civil* was in effect, among other places, in the Kingdom of Italy as of 1806, in the Confederation of the Rhine as *Badisches Landrecht* as of 1810, furthermore in parts of

German Historical School.[43] The development of the opportunity for an autonomous elaboration of contracts offers a parallel to the breakup of the guilds' regulation monopolies in technology.

The history of the policies of the first private fire insurance companies active in Germany provides a concrete example of the spreading of the practice involving preformulated contracts. The origin of these companies was to be found in London. In 1786, the English Phoenix Assurance Company established a branch office in Hamburg.[44] Previously, the city senate had decided to loosen the monopoly of the public *Hamburger Brandkasse* ('Hamburg fire society') and to permit private insurers to offer supplementary insurance.[45] With great success, the *Londoner Phoenix zu Hamburg* offered its *Propositiones für auswärtige Versicherungen* ('propositions for foreign insurance') to the public.[46] These conditions differed radically in their clarity and intelligibility from all standard form contracts that had been used in Hamburg up to this point.[47] This precision in the formulation of the conditions contributed to the establishment of the London Phoenix company as the first internationally active insurance company in Germany. In the ensuing decades, numerous insurance companies were guided by these 'propositions'. In 1812, a businessman by the name of Averdick, a former employee of London Phoenix, formed the *Berlinische Feuerversicherungs-Anstalt* and offered contracts that were similar to those of the English company.[48] In 1819, the policies of the *Berlinische* and *Londoner Phoenix zu Hamburg* together influenced the first conditions adopted by the *Leipziger Feuerversicherungs-Anstalt*.[49] Here too,

---

Poland, Luxemburg, Holland and Belgium as well as—drastically modified—in Romania as of 1863, in Portugal as of 1867 and in Spain as of 1888/89.

[43] In Germany, no unified code of civil law, but rather a trans-territorial jurisprudential discourse existed in the nineteenth century. In the 1850's, Austrian jurisprudence became a part of the German Historical School.

[44] Trebilcock 1985, 187 *et seq.*

[45] Ebel 1936, 57 *et seq.*

[46] Dating from the 9th of December 1790, in part cited in the introduction to Ziegler (1905 I, 11 *et seq.*).

[47] Cf. the following older, by far less systematic contract conditions used by Hamburg-based mutual companies and the *Hamburger Brandkasse: Fewer Contract* [from the 3rd of December 1591, made between a brewery owner and one hundred additional owners] *Füer Ordnung und Contract der Achtentich* [80] *vereinigten Eigendohmer* [*Hamburger Ordnung von 1620, Vertrag von 1622*]; *Professionelle Ordnung einer specialen Feuer-Cassa* [*Hamburg 1720, die General Feur-Cassa ergänzender Gegenseitigkeitsverein*]. All reprinted in: Ebel (1936, 66 *et seq.*, 69 *et seq.*, 85 *et seq.*).

[48] Ziegler 1908, 22 *et seq.*

[49] In addition, they influenced the five Hamburg underwriting companies (Ziegler 1908, 2).

Hamburg businessmen played a leading role just as they did in Gotha,[50] where in 1820 the *Feuerversicherungs-Anstalt für den deutschen Handelsstand* originated.[51] These and additional companies, among them some based abroad, expanded their business activities throughout Germany. Insofar as they employed contract terms that in part corresponded to and in part were actually identical to these contract terms, these companies contributed significantly to the development of fire insurance law in Germany.[52]

The observation of the early processes of standardisation in technology and law highlights several additional points of congruence. In both areas, it is striking that the processes were decentralised in the beginning.[53] Technical norms or the contents and wording of contracts are initially harmonised within individual companies or institutions. Only selectively do additional alignments follow, for example when particular stakeholders copy the contract clauses or technical norms from partners or competitors. Such measures can, of course, start a comprehensive harmonisation of the respective material.[54]

Most successful regulations become valid in the sense of being generally recognised without institutional sanctions. Their mere application creates normative effects. The exact circumstances governing success in an individual case—be it the market power exercised by specific users, the consensus of everyone involved or other matters—have nothing to do at all with their applicability and standing. Law is a means of standardisation only where the State becomes a stakeholder.[55]

1.2.2. *Intensification of the Mass Phenomenon (ca. 1830–1870)*

Standardisation developed into a mass phenomenon around the middle of the nineteenth century.[56] This development accompanied the beginning of industrialisation in the large European and American economic

---

[50] Ibid.
[51] Carl Weisse was the guiding spirit in the founding of the Leipzig company; Friedrich Wilhelm Arnoldi was instrumental at the Gotha company (Ziegler 1908, 1).
[52] Ibid., 2.
[53] Harriman 1928, 24.
[54] A graphic example is offered by insurance law (Duvinage 1987, 54).
[55] With reference to the technical standardisation, Vec 2003, 22 *et seq.*
[56] This is as true for technical standardisation as for the use of contract forms (Kessler, Columbia L. Rev. 43 (1943), 631 *et seq.*).

areas.[57] Whole commercial branches underwent a complete reorganisation in this phase. Included in the process were the production and handling of raw materials such as cotton, coal and iron ore, the trade and the transport industries as well as the newly emerging service sectors including insurance and banking. The organisational model of the emerging national economies was the public company that permitted the immense accumulation of capital and expansion of business activity.[58]

Large companies organised their production and business procedures with the aid of standardisation. In the process, the regulations increasingly exceeded the boundaries of the individual companies. Complex projects were impossible to manage in both technical and legal matters without the mutual cooperation of both business partners, as the realisation of railway transport demonstrates. Different companies participated in the construction of the railway cars and the railway networks and had to coordinate their technical norms with each other or adjust to those of a company in charge of a given project. In a similar fashion, adjustments to the standard form contracts were necessary. Occasionally, the contract terms of the railway companies clashed with firms responsible for maintenance of the railway networks, and sometimes with those of other transport companies. Moreover, companies in many countries had to pay attention to strict statutory regulations. In the case of transport that crossed national boundaries, these parallel but different regulations could result in an unmanageable confusion.[59] For these reasons, the companies involved began to bring their contract terms into line with each other. The general business conditions spread throughout national economies 'like an epidemic' in the middle of the nineteenth century.[60] Besides the general insurance terms[61] and the railway regulations for passenger and goods transport,[62] new standard form contracts increasingly appeared: sea transport contracts and bill of lading terms for the shipping business,[63]

---

[57] That is, during the respective take-off phases (Rostow 1960; Cameron, 'A New View of European Industrialization', *The Economic History Review 38* (1985), 1 *et seq.*).

[58] Micklethwait and Wooldridge 2003, 55 *et seq.*, 79 *et seq.* Coing (1989, 575) also emphasises the importance of stock as an instrument of finance—in addition to the other bearer bonds, especially industrial obligations.

[59] The *ZVMEV* reported repeatedly on these problems. See in this context the memoir by de Seigneux/Christ 1875.

[60] Raiser 1935, 42.

[61] Laband, *ZHR* 17 (1873), 476 *et seq.*

[62] Senckpiehl 1909, 20; Goldschmidt, 'Die Haftungspflicht der Eisenbahnverwaltungen im Güterverkehr', *ZHR 4* (1861), 569 *et seq.*

[63] Eucken 1914; Senckpiehl 1909, 20.

standard-form contracts for shipping companies,[64] acquisition and package-shipping terms and conditions for haulage companies,[65] postal regulations,[66] payment and delivery terms and conditions of wholesalers,[67] factory and work statutory ordinances,[68] standard labour contracts[69] and stage-engagement forms,[70] bearer bonds, bank regulations and standard business terms in banks,[71] terms of sale in bookstores,[72] 'lottery plans' of state lotteries, reading-circle and subscription terms.[73] These models were adhered to by—insofar as their economic situations permitted—landlords,[74] warehouse and hotel owners, even architects, engineers, economists,[75] artists[76] and many others.[77]

The scale and the contents of the standard form contract depended primarily on the interests of the users and varied accordingly. Basically, they included the important rights and obligations of the contract partners as well as sanctions resulting from breaches of contract.[78] Moreover, they frequently specified the duration of the contract, the possibilities for premature termination of the contractual relationship, and modalities

---

[64] Eucken 1914, 63 et seq.

[65] Senckpiehl 1909, 20; Isaac 1928; Schwartz 1932.

[66] Vec 2004, col. 237.

[67] Brunn 1956, 3; Michel 1932, 2.

[68] Laband, 'Die Handelsusancen', ZHR 17 (1873), 476 et seq.; Koehne 1901, 7 et seq.

[69] Examples in Lotmar 1902, vol. 1, 227 et seq., especially 229, fn. 1: Formularverträge der Wiener Lohnarbeiterinnen ('contract forms for female employees in Vienna') and Musterarbeitsverträge des Verbandes zur Verbesserung der ländlichen Arbeitsverhältnisse im Gebiete des landwirtschaftlichen Centralvereins der Provinz Sachsen ('standard work contracts for rural workers in Saxonia').

[70] 'Stage-engagement form contract' of the Federation of the German Theatre of 1845, reprinted in Opet 1897, 467–476; Bühnenengagenmentsformular für Nichtvereinsbühnen ibid, 476–480.

[71] Koch 1932, 32. Banks maintain different conditions, for example, savings and loan associations, Nußbaum 1913.

[72] Wächter, 'Das Rechtsverhältnis zwischen dem Verleger und dem Sortimentsbuchhändler über die à Condition gegebenen Artikel', ZHR 2 (1859), 505 et seq.

[73] Laband, ZHR 17 (1873), 476 et seq.

[74] Brückner 1902, 200; Michel 1932, 2; Raiser 1935, 20.

[75] Michel 1932, 2.

[76] Opet 1897, 495–500.

[77] An exception is the trade practiced by warehouses with consumers in the so-called 'detail business'. Despite the huge extent of commerce, no general terms and conditions were adopted until after World War I (Senckpiehl 1922, 10).

[78] Rabel (1936, 38 et seq.) lists, for example, 'especially the characteristics of the goods, the place and dates of their departure or arrival, means of payment, distribution of the costs among the parties, the responsibilities and liabilities at departure, insurance, documentation, the transfer of risk and the exemption from acts of God, strikes and the like, finally the proof of lading or prevention thereof as well as the certifications of quality and weight, in addition to the calculation of due-dates and so on' (trans.).

for resolving conflicts. In view of the means of conflict resolution, a jurisdiction was generally specified if the contract was of relatively minor financial significance, whereas in larger cases a process of arbitration was agreed upon.[79] The recourse to autonomous mechanisms for dispute settlement was especially widespread in wholesale trade and in purely business areas of the service sector, such as in maritime insurance and reinsurance.[80] This tendency can be explained as stemming both from a low level of trust in the ability of the law to adjudicate the commercial facts of a case and from the desire to save costs and time.[81]

Many standard form contracts went beyond the needs of individual contractual relationships in their specifications. For example, German, Austrian and Italian bank conditions regulated all of the existing business models without consideration as to what degree they would be relevant in a particular case.[82]

The reasons for the vigorous spread of standardised contract texts as of the middle of the century are at present shrouded in mystery. Scholars—mainly legal sociologists—have been seeking explanations for this phenomenon since the 1920's.[83] Many of these authors believe to know definite motives in the authors and the users of standard business terms that are, unfortunately, not accessible to proof. Others argue too vaguely and on an ahistoric basis.[84] For instance, it cannot suffice to explain the standardisation of the contents of contracts with a mere reference to rationalisation[85] as long as both processes are not considered as necessary historical processes. It is more conducive to begin with examining the functions that standard form contracts—and standards generally—fulfil.

---

[79] Raiser (1935, 41) also makes this observation.

[80] Krause 1930, 89, 93, 119.

[81] Rabel 1936, 46; Cramer 1922, 26 *et seq.*

[82] Blanket general terms and conditions of business in banking were common primarily in Germany, Austria and Italy, occasionally in Switzerland and the Netherlands. In Russia, Scandinavia, England, France and the United States of America, banks preferred to issue conditions relevant to specific types of business transactions (Koch 1932, 35 *et seq.*).

[83] Some particularly excellent writings on this matter are Raiser 1935; Kessler, Columbia L. Rev. 43 (1943), 629 *et seq.*; Bonell 1976; Pohlhausen 1978.

[84] This is conspicuous in the legal commentary of the 1920's and 1930's. Authors deal with the historical emergence of this phenomenon, however, only in passing; for example Großmann-Doerth, 'Der Jurist und das autonome Recht des Welthandels', *Juristische Wochenschrift, 58. Jahrgang* (1929), 3447 *et seq.*; Löning, 'Autonomes Recht der Wirtschaft', *Mitteilungen des Jenaer Instituts für Wirtschaftsrecht 20* (1930), 13 *et seq.*; and Koch 1932.

[85] Brunn (1956, VII, 1, 32), for example, does exactly this.

Every standard serves in the first instance as 'a definite basis of reference or comparison'.[86] The participants in each case know or can easily find out what the designations *inch, metre, modèle 1777, MG08/15, Condizioni generali di polizza delle Assicurazioni Generali di Trieste* or the abbreviations *Fob Rio de la Plata* and *Cif Hamburg* in international transport contracts mean.[87] Thus, standards enable and simplify certain kinds of communication. Moreover, they allow for the creation of stable and verifiable relationships. An additional function of standards is the generation of compatibility.[88] In this context, numerous examples can be found in technology, from simple connective systems such as screws and threads[89] to industrial products that can be assembled and complex systems of electrical appliances that function on the basis of compatible connections, cable capacities and frequencies. In a similar fashion, standard form contracts bind business stakeholders to definite goals. To be sure, State statutory regulations offer norms that can be drawn upon as the basis of individual contracts. But it is precisely these regulations that for a variety of reasons the users of standard form contracts look to evade.

Against the background of the functions of standards described above, three attempts to explain the vigorous spread of the practice of using standard form contracts appear plausible: firstly, to increase the efficiency and thus the economic potential of a company; secondly, to profit from having drafted the contracts oneself; and, thirdly, to facilitate international business activities.

As to the first point, there is no denying that standardising contracts helped reduce a firm's overhead. The legal sociologist Ludwig Raiser[90] correctly alludes to the advantages of using standardised contracts in reducing a firm's business costs. On the one hand, the uniformity of the standard

---

[86] Harriman 1928, 24.

[87] Foreign businessmen and shippers understood that the goods had to be delivered at the place of departure (Rio de la Plata) by the consignor 'free on board' and that the consignee had to bear the costs, insurance and freight to the consignee destination (Hamburg). Conflicts arose primarily with the question as to who had to bear which risks. *Cif* (cost, insurance, freight) and *fob* (free on board) are verifiable from the middle of the nineteenth century onwards. On the use of this and other contract formulas see Inhulsen, 'Die Cif-Klausel', *Monatsschrift für Handelsrecht und Bankwesen* (1908), 100; Disconto-Gesellschaft Berlin 1913; Mittelstein 1918, 5 *et seq.*

[88] Harriman (1928, 6) believes that in the historical period of the publishing system ('cottage period'), the desire for interchangeability of materials, parts and multiple parts led to the idea of standardisation.

[89] A well-known example is the standardisation of screws and threads by engineers such as the Englishmen Joseph Whitworth (Vec 2006, 305 *et seq.*).

[90] 1935, 18.

form contract reduced the red tape normally required to handle contracts. On the other hand, its uniformity simplified the appraisal of the different stipulated obligations and claims. It is likely that exceeding a critical mass of contractual relationships would have made their supervision virtually impossible. This holds especially true for the insurance business, for while non-contractual elements form the subject of economic transactions in other branches—say in the wholesale wine business or the commodities market where fluctuating prices constitute the risk—, insurers only know the 'risk' of a contractual object once its description is contractually fixed. To them, standardisation of contracts meant the creation of uniform contractual subject matter.

Secondly, the opportunity it provided to deviate from existing contract types and develop new ones was of great importance. Precisely in particularly dynamic economic phases, the regulatory interests of business constantly varied[91] to a degree of which the existing national law fell short. Its regulations appeared as antiquated, unbalanced or ineffectual for other reasons to the business stakeholders.[92] The discrepancy that arose can be characterised by the term "cultural lag" coined by the American legal historian William Ogburn.[93] The business world compensated for the law's 'cultural lag'[94] by means of the standard business terms that it authored itself.[95] In this manner, new types of contracts repeatedly arose in the nineteenth century.[96] Some of these were later on introduced into law, providing a further reason for regarding standardisation of contract terms as a practice of continually updating the law.[97]

---

[91] Kessler, Columbia L. Rev. 43 (1943), 629 *et seq.*

[92] Goldschmidt, *ZHR 4* (1861), 570; Will 1994, 37. Koch (1932, 4) justified the exclusion of liability clauses used by large banks as 'protective measures' against immoderate financial risks that arose from legal liability and explained them as 'the result of bad experiences derived from lawsuits'.

[93] Ogburn (1964, 86) explains the term he coined thus: 'A cultural lag occurs when one of the two parts of culture which are correlated changes before or in greater degree than the other part does, thereby causing less adjustment between the two parts than existed previously'.

[94] The German term *Kulturelle Verspätung* was coined by Vec (2002, 127).

[95] In a similar sense Neubauer (1990, 132) speaks of a 'law-representative function' of the general terms and conditions of contract.

[96] Pappenheim (1915, 295) writes 'There are important contract types that are embellished in carefully advanced development of general conditions in the most intricate details about which the scholarly legal literature knows nothing, although they represent the legal order for an entire field-commanding form of business'.

[97] On the banking industry see Koch 1932, 4, 10; for insurance see Lammel 1993, 102. The law governing railway transport originated in contract practice before it was integrated into the State body of laws; compare Senckpiehl 1909, 21. The dynamics of the development

In the process of developing their own standard form contracts, their authors fully exploited the communicative potential in the standard business terms that standardisation offered. Standard form contracts were well suited to express the necessary terms of an agreement.[98] However, they were also suited to conceal the actual intentions of the contract's authors. Wherever the standard form contracts became common in the nineteenth century, abuses became known. The insurance companies took advantage of their contractual partners by concealing unfair conditions behind cryptic formulations and irrelevant explanations. The contemporary expression 'fine print' indicates that large parts of the population had negative experiences. When bilked contractual partners sued to obtain the expected coverage, they often had to be satisfied with the reply that they had entered into the contract on their own free will and must now accept conditions that objectively contradicted the apparent contractual purposes.[99] Of course, many drafters of standard form contracts were not the least interested in a just balance of the contractual partners' rights and obligations. Whoever made use of the standard business terms most often attempted to shift the economic risks in any business deal entirely onto their prospective contractual partners. The standard business terms offered anyone who was capable of enforcing them in a contract the opportunity of translating their economic superiority into an unbalanced contractual relationship.[100] In this respect, Ludwig Raiser must be agreed with in his recognition that the definitive mark of the standard business terms is the exercise of economic power.[101]

---

of new contract types increases in the twentieth century. At the same time, the underlying business relationships became increasingly more complex—for example, in leasing, factoring and franchising—and for this reason, legislatures as a rule refrained from codification (Martinek 1992–1993, vol. 1–3).

[98] Koch (1932, 9 *et seq.*) emphasises this aspect. Farny ('AVB unter dem Gesichtspunkt der Produktbeschreibung', *Zeitschrift für die gesamte Versicherungswirtschaft* 1975, 169 *et seq.*) speaks of a 'product-descriptive function'.

[99] In the United States, this problem became known through 'wildcat' insurance companies, by definition shady companies that during the expansion of the fire insurance industry in the West swindled farmers out of their money with dodgy policies (McIntosh 1954, 5).

[100] In this respect, the most important clauses in the standard contracts also contained, in addition to restrictions on or exclusions from liability and regulations on onus of proof, contract penalties and prohibitions against transferring insurance benefits (Michel 1932, 46).

[101] In Raiser's study (1935, 26), the 'function of increasing power' carries the central importance as a feature of one-sided contract terms; Saleilles (1901, 229), Kohler, 'Bezugsverträge und §138 BGB', *Archiv für bürgerliches Recht* 31 (1908), 249 *et seq.* and Pappenheim

A third argument that explains the spread of the practice of standard form contracts is the advantages they offered in international business activities. In this constellation, different legal systems necessarily came into contact with each other. In the case of conflict, their collision frequently led to legal vagaries, as it was unclear which legal system would be applied in resolving the disputes. This aspect plays a role even before the internationalisation of business, for example in the legally fragmented German Confederation and the Swiss Confederation.[102] As of 1870, it became increasingly obvious that national statutory regulations were not sufficient for the needs of international business activity. This deficiency especially applied to international private law, which was so unpopular among practicing businessmen because it had the reputation of entailing uncertain results.[103] The business stakeholders required clarity as to which legal system had authority in cases of conflict. The creation of their own contractual bases offered a simple solution. Standard clauses and standard contracts could serve the interests of the business community from different states and business and legal systems. In addition, the participants were able to restrict the appeals to state jurisdiction by means of arbitration agreements.[104] Thus, the branches succeeded in removing conflicts from the sphere of the States' influence.[105]

The biased allocation of economic risks in the standard form contracts frequently led to friction between the party authoring the contract and the other interested party. The most virulent conflicts arose when the user of the standard form contracts was a member of either a monopoly or a cartel.[106] For this reason, the complaints of businessmen against the contractual terms of the railways, whose services they were dependent

---

(1915, 292 et seq.), who had included the specific problems of the world economy, had arrived at a similar position.

[102] Wieacker 1981, 577, 589.

[103] Scherner 1992, 43; Ruck 1934, 331; Meyer 1992, 17, 35 et seq., 75. The criticism of international private law did not cease in the twentieth century; see, for example, Rabel 1936, 36.

[104] Entire branches submitted to compulsory arbitration to the exclusion of State court jurisdiction, for example the international silk trade in the framework of the New York Silk Association (Ishizaki 1928, 276). Nevertheless, it happened that despite the exclusion of State jurisdiction, parties that had lost in arbitration approached the courts. It is assumed, however, that this move could be damaging to a company's reputation within the branch of business to which it belonged and would only be ventured upon in special circumstances.

[105] Cramer's demonstrations (1922, 26 et seq.) provide a good example.

[106] That is, as a so-called 'conditions cartel', often strengthened by price tariffs and quota fixing of the sales volume (Raiser 1935, 17, 27 et seq.).

upon, became more numerous in the middle of the nineteenth century.[107] At this time, important steam-engine railways crisscrossed England and the United States, France and Belgium, and Germany, Switzerland and Russia. In these countries, economic associations and State institutions attempted to restrain the transporters with varied success. The legal handling of the railway regulations moved into the centre of international conflicts with respect to the standard form contracts. This derived from the fact that clients of the transport companies—similar to the situation in the insurance business—were not simply merchants, but rather drawn from the public at large. Moreover, State institutions were probably especially interested in the railways due to its importance for the military infrastructure.

A glance at the discourse in the various countries around 1860 shows how closely these problems resembled each other. For the first time since the inception of the standard form contract, significant restrictions upon freedom of contract threatened a business branch. For this reason, the scope in which the terms of contract had been able to unfold up to then was endangered.

In England, where railway technology had become widespread the first, jurists had long been able to rely upon entrenched positions.[108] Railway managements had been enjoying freedom of contract and could to a large extent limit their liability.[109] For just under a century, however, liberal court practices had chipped away at the rigorous principles governing the common carrier.[110] Around 1860, the major issue in disputes was to convince courts that the controversial terms had been adopted in the individual contracts.[111] The simple acknowledgement of the contract partners that their rights had been curtailed was sufficient to achieve this end.[112] In addition, judges had to be convinced that exclusionary clauses

---

[107] Examples in Pohlhausen 1978, 1 *et seq.*

[108] Contemporary scholars confirm this, especially the most important on the English legal situation, Shelford 1845.

[109] Smith 1855, 319 *et seq.* The Railway and Canal Traffic Act of 1854, sec. 7, simply prohibited the standard exclusion of the liability for diligence for damages to transported animals and goods through transport companies. The law did not apply to damage to luggage and passengers. According to the Carriers Act of 1830, sec. 6, exclusions by means of 'special contract' were also permissible in the transport of goods (Atiyah 1979, 558).

[110] Redfield 1854, 234.

[111] Will 1994, 84; on English legal practice following the legislation of 1854, see 47 *et seq.*

[112] Redfield 1854, 270 *et seq.*

were 'just and reasonable',[113] but they did not undertake to control the contents of the standard form contracts.[114] In addition, English judges explicitly refused to take into consideration the problem of monopolies in their decisions. In a characteristic dictum, Justice Erle explained: 'The notion that customers of railways require protection on account of incapacity to resist oppression, is not more true than the notion that, against a large protection of its customers, railway companies stand in the need of every aid the law can afford'.[115] Least of all did the English judiciary become engaged with the arguments involving public policy. These represented to them from time immemorial 'a very unruly horse, and when once you get astride it you never know where it will carry you. It may lead you from the sound law'.[116] English judges consistently maintained this course in the decades that followed.

The position of American jurisprudence differed from English common law only in nuances.[117] However, American courts of law tended to hand down stricter decisions on the question of inclusion than did the English courts in that the American courts at least required definite signs of agreement with the restrictions on liability.[118] In addition, individual American civil law judges began to take into consideration the aspect of public policy in their decisions as from around 1860.[119] This trend was the harbinger of a change that in the following decades led to a systematic control of the contents of standard business conditions.

---

[113] The Railway and Canal Traffic Act 1854, sec. 7, established this yardstick. The regulation was pushed through in the legislative process despite a suggestion by Lord Brougham that the standard conditions of business should be generally subject to challenge (Will 1994, 44 *et seq.*) because of the dishonest coercion they exerted.

[114] However, exclusions of 'wilful misconduct' in the standard conditions of business were not permissible according to general law governing freight carriers. This also held true for the United States (Redfield 1854, 274; Bennett and Shelford 1855, 713).

[115] Decision by Justice Erle J., M'Manus vs. Lancashire & Yorkshire Railway Co. (1859), in: Hurlstone & Norman's Reports, Exchequer, vol. 4, 327, 346 and English Reports 157, 865, 873. Will (1994, 40 *et seq.*) argues that alternatives in the sense of a critical handling of monopolistically constituted business terms have been applied in common law.

[116] A famous formulation by J. Burroughs in Richardson vs. Mellish (1824), 2 Bingham's Reports, Common Pleas 229, 252.

[117] In the middle of the 1850's, however, the appearance of specifically American monographs on railway law indicated the development of independent positions, especially Redfield (1854) and Bennett (1855), a special edition for the United States of Shelford's English monograph of 1845.

[118] However, it was also sufficient in the United States to display the conditions in the office of the railway company.

[119] For example, a New York court discussed in some detail the danger of delivering the defenceless public to the will of the railway company (Redfield 1854, 274; Bennett and Shelford 1855, 713).

In France, a tradition of adjudication had been practiced since the beginning of the nineteenth century that refused to recognise the validity of unfair liability exclusions with arguments that were conversant with real practices[120] and that were upheld by the Paris Court of Cassation. The judges had found in favour of a shipper whose cargo—a mirror— had been shattered in the course of transport by coach. Two arguments put forward by the judges countered the refusal of the haulage company to compensate the loss on the grounds that it had excluded all liability in the bill of lading (*lettre de voiture*). First, the contract conditions had not been signed by the sender, who persuasively maintained that he had not had any knowledge of any exclusion. Second, the exclusion of liability would have had no force because of the unfairness of the conditions even if the sender had had cognizance of their existence.[121] These considerations were transferred by the French civil courts to the standard form contracts.[122] They also accepted the argument that unfair restrictions on liability injure *ordre public*.[123]

In Germany, the railway regulations also contained sweeping liability exclusions. Legal practice and legal scholarship agreed almost unanimously that these contract conditions overrode other legal stipulations.[124] The regulations of the State railways were treated as State legal norms. If the railway was privately owned, it was important, in the words of the Berlin historian of commercial law, Levin Goldschmidt, 'to respect the private autonomy of the company. The regulations, tariffs, and schedules required no law to confirm them nor management structures to accept them. The contracts that were drawn up in accordance with them are completely in force as long as they do not absolutely conflict with restrictive or prohibitive laws or public decency'.[125] As in the other countries, the question of the inclusion of controversial conditions in the individual

---

[120] Judgement Catalogne vs. Mérillon, 28.12.1805 (1807), col. 138 *et seq.*

[121] Judgement Catalogne vs. Mérillon, 21.1.1807 (1807), col. 141 *et seq.*

[122] Zink 1860, 609; Alauzet 1868, 361. The legal enforcement of the complete liability led to special tariffs for valuable transports (Alauzet 1868, 382).

[123] Evidence in Pohlhausen 1978, 55 *et seq.*

[124] Special regulations on liability existed in Prussian law (Law on the Railway Companies of 3 November 1838, liability for the result and liability of loss through fortuitous event in §25) and Austrian law (Railway Work Rules as of 16 November 1851). Subsidiarily, the respective law affecting commerce and general civil law applied. Only the Prussian Rhine Province law, which was heavily influenced by French law, enforced the prohibition of comprehensive liability exclusions as stipulated in §25 of the Prussian Railway Law for a number of years (Pohlhausen 1978, 51 *et seq.*).

[125] Goldschmidt, *ZHR 4* (1861), 589.

contracts assumed great importance. In general, a 'proper publication' of the conditions was regarded as sufficient.[126] If such was lacking, the presumed knowledge by the other contract party of the liability limitation was adequate for its application.[127]

Since a change in the legal practice was not in sight, the chamber of commerce had tried to include its criticism of the contract practice of the railway companies into the negotiations on the introduction of a general German commercial code since the 1850's. However, they achieved no measurable success. In the first drafts, their interests were taken into consideration, but the proposed compelling stipulations were once again withdrawn.[128] The law introduced by the German States between 1861 and 1863 only insignificantly reduced the freedom of contract of railway companies.[129] In 1860 Switzerland, the demands for increasingly more compelling legislation or supervision by regulative agencies went nowhere.[130]

It is clear that at this time the principle of freedom of contract was widely accepted. Everywhere jurists took pains to avoid infringements of the sphere of the private and autonomous form of contracts. In following this very formal perspective, the majority of them—with the sole exception of French legal scholars—refused to recognise the problem that 'freedom' of contract in the reality of mass-produced standard form contracts could deteriorate to a mere formulaic fiction. The freedom to determine the contents of contracts had become, at least in parts of the business world, a privilege enjoyed only by the economically dominant stakeholders. The more big business or cartels dominated their branches, the easier they

---

[126] For example, by means of the inscription on the contract documentation, that is, the bill of lading, baggage voucher, transport voucher, animal tags (*Viehzettel*), passenger ticket or announcement (Goldschmidt, *ZHR 4* [1861], 584); on other jurisdictions, see Pohlhausen 1978, 81 *et seq.*

[127] Goldschmidt, *ZHR 4* (1861), 594 *et seq.* This principle also applied outside of transport law; Laband, *ZHR* 17 (1873), 476 *et seq.*

[128] In its first reading, a provision was passed in the form of Article 339 that declared the law of liability of the transporter to be compulsory law (Lutz 1858–66, vol. 2, 827 *et seq.*). In the second reading, this condition was restricted to simple waggoners (Lutz 1858–66, vol. 23, 1230 *et seq.*).

[129] §18 of the introductory provisions of the *Allgemeines Deutsches Handelsgesetzbuch* (*ADHGB*, 'General German Commercial Code') underscored the obligation of the contractor to negotiate freight contracts. Articles 422–431 defined the contract terms that were to be regulated. Limitations of liability and other controversial terms of the regulations found explicit legal recognition (Art. 427, para. 1, no. 1); *Preussische Gesetzessammlung* (corpus juris) 1861, 449 *et seq.*; Introductory Act of 24 June 1861; *Österreichisches Reichsgesetzblatt* 1863, no. 1 (*Einführungsgesetz* ['Introductory Act'] of 17 December 1862).

[130] The critical writings of Vogt (1859, 38 *et seq.*) form an exception.

could cut off the discussion of the contracts' substance and unilaterally dictate their terms. The straightjacket into which their contract partners were constrained found clear expression in the American term 'take-it-or-leave-it contract'.[131] Those ignorant of the law accepted these conditions possibly because of indifference or trust in the good sense of the conditions they did not understand. Their decision made prior to agreeing to the contract evaporated into a 'more or less voluntary engagement with an experience that in its legal consequences could not be anticipated but merely understood as typical'.[132] But even those who recognised the imbalance of the contract terms were forced to enter into these economically essential business relationships in full consciousness of their drawbacks.[133]

1.2.3. *Institutionalisation and State Control (ca. 1870–1914)*

The changes in standard form contracts and the juristic discussion of mass contracts became noticeable at the beginning of the 1870's. This period is relevant for the emerging industrialised societies in a similar fashion. In various countries, practice and discourse began to coalesce. Primarily, this merging was due to the wave of internationalisation that in the following years comprised numerous more or less industrialised economies and brought them together in an incipient world economy.[134]

In the phase of 'proto-standardisation,' standardisation had originated in contract contents within individual firms and led to a harmonisation of the regulations in many branches. In the following decades, the boundaries of the individual companies were exceeded; this development continued after 1870. From now on, associations and cartels increasingly took over standardisation. This instrumentalisation was accompanied by a professionalisation of the insurance industry. The stakeholders began to carefully prepare the introduction of new standard form contracts with the aim of improving the odds of success. In order to avoid later friction, they integrated the largest possible number of groups with vested interests in the process of standardisation.[135] They kept their eyes on the

---

[131] Kessler, Columbia L. Rev. 43 (1943), 630.
[132] Raiser 1935, 17 *et seq.*
[133] Ibid., 20; Koch 1932, 1; Kessler, Columbia L. Rev. 43 (1943), 630.
[134] The studies in Harley 1996 provide an overview.
[135] Standards that were agreed upon among the groups taking part secured compromises. This is a conclusion that Harriman (1928, 74, 97) also reaches in his discussion of technical standardisation.

standard form contracts introduced into practice and maintained a certain flexibility in order to prevent the regulations from becoming too fixed. For 'overstandardisation', as this tendency in technical standardisation was termed,[136] entailed two dangers. The first lay in the prevention or delay of necessary innovations,[137] and the second in the more difficult adaptation to local conditions—for example in foreign markets. The affected technical norms or standard form contracts lost their compatibility.[138]

It should be observed in passing that the parallel developments of technical and legal standardisation did not cease after 1870. Up to World War I, both underwent very similar processes of change.[139] Standardisation entered the twentieth century as one of the dominant structural features of industrialised society.

The increased development after 1870 intensified the legal policy question of modern private law with respect to boundaries of private autonomy that could protect the weaker participant in commerce. The answers occupied a broad spectrum, from the liberal ideal of complete market freedom to the socialist call for broad nationalisation.[140] Most industrial countries still exercised cautious reservation. But slowly, the willingness to more or less intensive guiding intervention began to emerge.

In 1870 England, the changes that manifested themselves were so strong that Patrick S. Atiyah interpreted this period as the beginning of the end of freedom of contract.[141] Justifiably, he criticised scholars for having overlooked 'the extent of Parliamentary and Governmental interference, the vast mass of legislative intervention with freedom of contract and the free market'.[142] But Atiyah's thesis must be countered by the observation that parliamentary laws and administrative regulations only had a modest influence on the common law of the nineteenth and early twentieth century. They were designed at the most to close loopholes

---

[136] Harriman 1928, 85.

[137] Ibid.

[138] Compare the discussions by Rabel 1936, 42 et seq.

[139] In technology, the changes could be described by means of the keywords 'institutionalisation', 'professionalisation', and 'internationalisation' (Harriman 1928, 79 et seq.; Vec 2003, 38 et seq.).

[140] Repgen 2001, 26 et seq., 68 et seq., 83 et seq.; investigated in Hofer 2001 from a historical point of view.

[141] Atiyah (1979, 569 et seq.) dates the period of freedom of contract in England from 1770 to 1870.

[142] Ibid., 234. In this opinion, he differs from a series of historians he cites, from Albert V. Dicey (1905) to Eric Hobsbawm.

and to correct egregious mistakes in judge-made law.[143] In the meantime, the English judiciary attempted to separate statutory from contract law in order to preserve freedom of contract as the highest maxim of private law :[144]

> Everything which did not fit the scheme of the free market, or of the general principles of contract law which were based on the free market, was simply defined as not being part of the contract law, but some other special rules—company law, or factories legislation, or building regulation, or sanitary laws, or licensing requirements, or any one of a hundred other different branches of social or economic activity. The law of contract became increasingly pure at the very same time that the volume of regulatory law was increasing.[145]

Still believing in a 'pure' contract law, English House of Commons lawyers and especially those in the House of Lords energetically opposed each and every attempt to counteract biased liability limitations or exclusions with the open control of contents.[146] However, they developed special rules on the inclusion and interpretation of exclusion clauses that in the twentieth century were so extensively applied that a covert control of contents can be spoken of.[147] This practice began in the middle of the 1870's with the so-called 'ticket cases', a comprehensive group of decisions governing the contract conditions printed on the passenger tickets of railway companies.[148] A decision from 1877 became the leading case.[149] Afterwards,

---

[143] Laws were restrictively interpreted and regarded as not susceptible to analogy (Klapisch 1991, 42).

[144] Typical were the remarks directed to his colleagues among the judges by Sir George Jessel (M.R.): '[...] if there is one thing more than another which "public policy" requires, it is that men of full age and competent understanding shall have the utmost liberty in contracting, and that their contracts, when entered into freely and voluntarily, shall be held sacred and shall be enforced by Courts of Justice' (1875). Law Reports 19 Exchequer Cases 462. Jessel established the principle of the 'sanctity of contract'.

[145] Atiyah (1979, 236) follows the deliberations of Friedman, 1965, here.

[146] Will 1994, 20.

[147] Ibid., 21.

[148] Ibid., 23, 75 et seq., 90 et seq. As late as 1869, English judges ruled that liability exclusions unknown to a banking customer were nevertheless valid because he should have expected them: Cockburn J. in: Zunz vs. The South Eastern Railway Co. (1869), in: Law Reports (First Series) 4 Queen's Bench 539, 544. The case of Henderson vs. Stevenson (1875) ushered in the change in that the judges required a railway company to produce the precise proof that it had expressly cited their exclusion clause to a subsequently injured party. Law Reports (First Series) 2 English and Irish Appeals, 470.

[149] Court of Appeal, Parker vs. The South Eastern Railway Co. (1877), in: Common Pleas Division 2, 416 et seq.

liability limitations were only valid if the user of passenger tickets had been aware of these conditions or had verifiably been made aware of them.[150]

In a sense, these rules on the 'reasonable sufficiency of notice' led contract law back to the foundations of traditional common law that had been virtually eliminated by the homemade contracts employed by business as a contractual basis. The judges turned standard business conditions back into exceptions which the parties should be aware of when entering into an agreement.[151] The courts did not go any farther until the middle of the twentieth century.[152]

In the same period, the willingness to limit freedom of contract in order to balance economic and social differences was growing in the United States. The American branch of common law detached itself in this question from the legal system of the mother country. Prominent jurists such as Roscoe Pound supported this process.[153]

Private law courts advanced further in the direction of general control of the contents of standard form contracts. The legislatures of many individual States planned even deeper inroads into the freedom of contract. However, most of the laws protecting weaker contract parties were never implemented,[154] for a considerable part of the American social legislation was declared invalid by American courts, including the Supreme Court, with reference to the right to freedom guaranteed by the Fourteenth Amendment to the American Constitution.[155] The protection of the freedom of contract was considered a problem of constitutional law in the United States, in contrast to England, Germany and France.[156] Nevertheless, in some areas the legislators succeeded in effectively intervening in the dealings between unequal contract partners. For example, as of 1881,

---

[150] Decisions made by Lord Justice Mellish: Court of Appeal, Parker vs. The South Eastern Railway Co. (1877), in: Common Pleas Division 2, 423.

[151] Will 1994, 90.

[152] Ibid., 100 et seq., 126 et seq.

[153] In a 1909 study, Pound characterised the concept of the freedom of contract as 'a fallacy to everyone acquainted at first hand with industrial conditions'. Pound demanded a change in legal practice. This essay is credited with having a pioneering influence in American legal history (Horwitz 1992, 34).

[154] The laws primarily affected labour law: the setting of minimum wages and maximum hours of work, protection of working women (Klapisch 1991, 41).

[155] Pound (*Yale Law Journal 18* (1909), 466 et seq.) described some of the cases.

[156] Klapisch 1991, 42.

several States defined the permissible subject matter in 'standard policy' fire insurance contracts.[157]

In France, a phase of business liberalism began at the beginning of the 1860's and continued into the 1880's. The breakthrough of the freedom of will in private law doctrine was of great importance. Liberalisation primarily meant the abolition of State supervision of the public companies and the nullification of the limitations of freedom of contract in labour and commercial law.[158] However, beginning in the middle of the 1880's, the business policy slowly changed to one characterised by interventionism. Individual, widespread types of contracts became regulated by law.[159] This change primarily affected transport law. The tariffs and conditions of the transport firms became subject to licensing requirements. In response, however, the railway companies expanded their exclusionary clauses. The civil courts—*tribunaux civils*—recognised these liability limitations. In their opinion, the burden of proof in cases of tortious liability lay in any case with the dispatcher.[160] Finally, 1895 saw the rise of political protest against the liability exclusions and the argument that they infringed the freedom of contract.[161] Obviously, sensitivity to the problem of standard form contracts was growing.[162] Ten years later, exclusionary clauses were legally prohibited.[163] Case law only became favourable to the dispatcher in 1911.[164]

French insurance law was not legally regulated before World War I; the homemade contract conditions remained the insurance companies' most important source of law.[165]

In Germany, the founding of the Empire in 1871 resembled the breaking of a dam for mass contract law. The wave of cartel agreements and start-ups of foundations on the national level completely changed the business

---

[157] In 1873, Massachusetts was the first state to introduce a standard policy that starting in 1881 became obligatory (Hardy 1913, 21).

[158] Halpérin 1996, 143.

[159] Ibid., 257.

[160] For example, in the decision Civ. 10 novembre 1884 (*Recueil Siery* 1885/1, 129).

[161] A campaign waged by the radical Member of Parliament Rabier (Halpérin 1996, 261).

[162] In the philosophy of law, it was primarily Saleilles who contributed to the development of a critical theory of the standard form contracts, which according to his doctrine fundamentally differ from the traditional contracts (Saleilles 1901, 229).

[163] Halpérin 1996, 261.

[164] Judgements Civ. 21 novembre 1911, Civ. 27 janvier 1913 and Civ. 21 avril 1913 (*Recueil juridique et critique Dalloz* 1913/1, 249).

[165] Halpérin 1996, 153, 260.

structure.[166] These lobbies energetically supported the introduction of standard business terms.[167] Around the turn of the century, the standard form contract dominated—as in the other important industrial states— the legal reality in manufacturing and heavy industries, wholesale, the transport business, the insurance business and other branches.[168]

When by the middle of the 1870's the euphoria of the foundation of the Empire had evaporated and a recession begun, this contract practice became a centre of criticism. Socialist, petty bourgeois and conservative forces scourged them as harmful consequences of inordinately large con- centrations of business power. Moderate demands were aimed at legal limitations on freedom of contract and reinforcement of State supervi- sion. More radical voices demanded the nationalisation of entire branches of commerce, especially the railway and the insurance businesses.[169] The government of the Reich followed suit in one point: between 1876 and 1909, it placed the railway in State ownership.[170] In other matters, from the 1869 edition of the German Commerce Code and the *Gewerbeordnung* from the same year up to the Civil Code of 1896, legislation oriented itself on private business, freedom of contract and individual contracts.[171] Only a few sections contained mandatory provisions for the protection of eco- nomically weaker contract partners.[172] In 1896, the commercial law scholar Karl Adler rather dejectedly remarked: 'When legislation becomes incon- venient for the stock market, as currently, then the conferences between jurists and bank people begin and the results are new business conditions

---

[166] Blaich 1979, 3, 5 *et seq.*
[167] Raiser 1935, 27.
[168] Ibid., 28.
[169] Examples are Wagner 1870; Mohl 1876; Wagner 1883. Documentation on the debate on the insurance business can be found in Tigges 1985, 69 *et seq.*
[170] Private autonomy of the railways for all practical purposes ended in 1870 when the North German Confederation elevated the company regulations of the 'German Railway Industry Association' (*Norddeutsche Bund die Betriebs-Reglements des Vereins deutscher Eisenbahnverwaltungen*) to the level of law. The participating States thus subjected the pri- vate and autonomously created contract type to their legal principles (Senckpiehl 1909, 21). The nationalisation of the railways occurred successively between 1871 (Alsace-Lorraine) and 1909 (Wilhelmi, 'Staat und Staatseisenbahn', *Archiv für Eisenbahnwesen 73* (1963), 377 *et seq.*).
[171] Repgen 2001, 68 *et seq.*, 83 *et seq.*, 504.
[172] The contemporary literature cites the Law for the Protection of Labourers of 1891, the Amendment to the State Supervision of Industry of 1891—in which the use of general factory and work orders were not regulated but rather prescribed—the hire-purchase act of 1894, the law on the private law relationships in domestic shipping of 1895, the Order for Seamen of 1902 and the law of insurance contracts of 1908. See the critical remarks to this legislation in Ehrlich 1899, Lotmar 1902, 231 *et seq.* and Pappenheim 1915, 295 *et seq.*

and practices that, completely or partially, thwart the influence of the law'
(trans.).[173] The control of the mass contract practice by the government
tended to favour the users of standard business terms. The control could
be brought into play at two points: at the uptake of the business activity,
and during the entrepreneurial activity itself. The largest amount of attention was paid to fire and life insurers, whose services were demanded by
a wide range of the population.

Until 1870, the insurer required a licence to operate a business. The
standard insurance terms had been subject to approval as a part of the
business plans. But a considerable liberalisation occurred with the amendment of the stock corporation law in 1870.[174] For registration in a commercial trade register or a similar administrative recording agency, it now was
sufficient to fulfil a few formal prerequisites. Only in the case of a violation of the law did the supervision of the business transactions intervene.
Thus, the inspection of the contents of insurance conditions on the part
of the regulatory agencies completely disappeared.[175]

The government of the Reich did not depart from this course until the
turn of the century. Only with the advent of the Insurance Industry Regulation of 1901 was the system of licensing and substantial state supervision
reinstated. For the enforcement of the law a central authority, the *Kaiserliches Aufsichtsamt für Privatversicherung* ('Imperial Supervisory Agency
for Private Insurance'), was established. Under its leadership, interested
parties in the insurance industry and insurance companies brought all
contractual bases up to date in a combined effort. The regulatory office
hardly ever permitted exceptions to these standard conditions.

Despite the nationalisation of the railways and the partial supervision
of the insurance business, it must not be denied that freedom of contract for large parts of the business world was not curtailed. Thus, Raiser
was justified in declaring that legislation left the solution of the pending
problems to case law.[176] Still, the beginnings of an independent judicial

---

[173] Adler 1897, 78.
  [174] *Gesetz betreffend die Kommanditgesellschaften auf Aktien und die Aktiengesellschaften*
of 11 June 1870, *Bundesgestzblatt des Norddeutschen Bundes*, 375; as imperial law: *Gesetz
betreffend die Kommanditgesellschaften auf Aktien und die Aktiengesellschaften* of 22 April
1871, *RGBl.* 1871, 87.
  [175] And thus the result was a combination of the normative system in the permission
process and a formal State supervision. On the concept see Wenzel 1901, 10 *et seq.*
  [176] Raiser 1935, 18.

policy could be observed here.[177] On the one hand, standard business terms were understood as *lex contractus* ('the law of contract'), that is, as an expression of consensual will of the parties.[178] On the other hand, the Supreme Court for Commerce[179] did not recognise the legal force of all of the clauses while interpreting contracts.[180] Without finally closing the book on will theory, judges relied upon the innate rationality of any given business and the 'reasonable will of honest parties' and decided 'in accordance with fairness and good will' (trans.).[181] In 1881, the First Civil Senate of the Imperial Court started inspecting the validity of standard form contracts in their totality when the suspicion of abuse of a monopoly position arose.[182]

The developments of the standard contracts in the individual countries described above provide the background for the spread and standardisation of the standard business terms in international business relations.

1.3. Contract Terms in a Global Economy

1.3.1. *The Internationalisation of Business (1871–1914)*

At the beginning of the 1870's, the forces of internationalisation increasingly affected the more or less widely industrialised countries of Europe as well as of North America and Japan.[183] Business conditions were

---

[177] Ogorek, 'Privatautonomie unter Justizkontrolle. Zur Rechtsprechung des Reichsoberhandelsgerichts (1870–1879)', *ZHR* 150 (1986), 87 *et seq.*; Lammel 1993, 115.

[178] In the decision of the *Reichsoberhandelsgericht* (*ROHG*, 'Imperial Supreme Court for Commerce') 11 (1873), 271, 273, for example, it was decided that the judge was 'not authorised on the basis of considerations of fairness to disregard the application of contracts and on the same grounds to submit them to correction; in fact it is his duty strictly to enforce the law of the contract that the contracting parties have entered into, no matter how severe, as long as nothing illegal is specified'.

[179] Between 1871 and 1879 the highest civil law authority.

[180] For example, it declared certain contractual penalties as inadmissible: decision *ROHG* 11 (1873), 271 *et seq.*

[181] Decision *ROHG* 4 (1871), 63 *et seq.* and *ROHG* 1 (1870), 154 *et seq.*, cited in Ogorek, *ZHR* 150 (1986), 103.

[182] *Reichtsgericht* decision *RGZ* 3 (1881), 319 *et seq.* As of about 1888, the first senate declared that unfair contract clauses were contrary to public interest and null and void if the consumer had no chance to enter into an equivalent contract with another contractor at more favourable conditions: decision *RGZ* 20 (1888), 115 *et seq.* The second senate later agreed with this interpretation: decision *RGZ* 83 (1913), 319 *et seq.*

[183] For the insurance industry, see Pearson/Lönneborg, 'Regulatory Regimes and Multilateral Insurers before 1914', *Business History Review* 82, no. 1 (2008), 59 *et seq.*, and Borscheid/Umbach, 'Zwischen Protektionismus und Globalisierung—Die internationale

favourable all over the world. Europe, with the exception of some internal conflicts and the crisis in the Balkans, was enjoying a wave of peace following the Franco-Prussian War. North America had also found tranquillity following the Civil War (1861–65). Even Japan had opened its market after the rise of the Meiji Dynasty.[184] But above all, the industrial revolution created economic and technical conditions that enabled economic expansion into the most remote regions of the world.

The economic power of the industrial States mainly originated in the steady increase of production through progressive improvements in production methods. This economic system could only be maintained through an expansion of the markets and the increase of the imports of raw materials.[185] This was one of the reasons for the imperialist expansion that began in 1875. By 1914, a dozen European countries, the United States of America and Japan had divided up among them a quarter of the earth as colonies. In addition, if the territories that depended on the imperialist countries as protectorates, dominions or through trade, leasing, friendship or protection contracts are taken into consideration, the economic influence of the Europeans, Americans and Japanese comprised about 85% of Earth.[186] Only in the context of this notion is the statement sustainable that the greatest part of Earth can be included in the network of the first world economy.[187] Of course, the economic exchange in the large regions outside of Europe and North America was also increasing. The yearly trade volume between China, Japan and India grew even faster than that of the total world trade.[188] Nevertheless, from the perspective of the imperialist countries, the economic peripheries remained unimportant as independent economic systems. At the most, they were only interesting in their future development as possible markets.[189]

Versicherungswirtschaft vor dem Ersten Weltkrieg', *Jahrbuch für Wirtschaftsgeschichte* 49, no. 1 (2008), 207 *et seq.*

[184] Pohl 1989, 40, 66.

[185] Ibid., 123 *et seq.*

[186] Said 1994, 42.

[187] However, in consideration of the development of the gross national product and the national income, the colonies were de facto never really integrated into the European-North Atlantic economy (Hobsbawm 1999, 27 *et seq.*).

[188] The yearly growth rate was 5.4% compared to 3.4% (Sugihara 1986, 709 *et seq.*; Lewis 1981, 11).

[189] See Reisinger 2001, 215 for additional references.

Table 1. Share of the continents in world foreign trade. Kenwood and Lougheed 1992, 79 *et seq.*[190]

	1875/76	1913
Europe	67%	62%
USA	9.5%	13.2%
Asia	13%	11%
Latin America	5.4%	7.6%
Africa	1.9%	3.7%
Oceania	3.4%	2.4%

Table 2. Share of the global export trade (gross national product). Krugman, 'Growing World Trade: Causes and Consequences', *Brookings Papers on Economic Activity 1* (1995), 327 *et seq.*[191]

Year	1850	1880	1913	1950	1973	1985	1993
Quota	5.1%	9.8%	11.9%	7.1%	11.7%	14.5%	17.1%

In total, international trade between 1880 and 1919 is estimated to have multiplied by a factor of twenty-five.[192] In so doing, a world economic system of unprecedented complexity developed. By 1913, the world export quota had grown to a level that was only achieved again in 1973 following the economic collapse between the two world wars. Similar numbers are also available for the service sector.[193]

1.3.2. *Adjustment of Contract Bases to Economic Internationalisation*

Through numerous measures, the stakeholders attempted to technically and legally facilitate the increasing international exchange of raw materials and industrial products, capital, services and people. Often, standardisation that up to then had enabled economic trade within the individual countries was questioned. In part, solutions were achieved through compromise, i.e. mutual adaptation. Where this was not possible, new

---

[190] Kenwood and Lougheed 1992, 79 *et seq.*

[191] Table: World Merchandise Exports as Percentage of GDP in Percent (merchandise trade measured as the average of exports and imports), Krugman, 'Growing World Trade: Causes and Consequences', *Brookings Papers on Economic Activity 1* (1995), 327 *et seq.*

[192] An estimated number; Reisinger 2001, 213.

[193] For example, the insurance industry had achieved a level of internationality by 1913 that was only re-established by the middle of the 1970's (Borscheid, 'Internationalisierung der deutschen Versicherungswirtschaft 1870–1945', *VSWG* 88 (2001), 311 *et seq.*).

standards replaced old ones that were abandoned in favour of 'world trade'.[194]

As previously on the national level, the States did not leave all matters to the self-organisation of business and technology. Through international contracts, they primarily regulated matters that could not be functionally handled on the level of the individual States and even established international interstate institutions, the so-called administrative unions.[195] In Germany, these included surface and sea transport, contemporary communications technology, metrical units, time zones and control of epidemics.[196] In these areas, international law evolved into an international 'law of cooperation'.[197]

Table 3. International Standardisation through International Law.
Knipping 1996, 148 *et seq.*[198]

1865	Creation of an International Telegraphic Union[199]
1874	Creation of the general postal service: Freedom of transit, uniformity of postal rates, waiver of sharing of postal rates. Membership of all States including colonies within three decades[200]
1875	International telegraph contract of St. Petersburg: deregulation of the telegraph for private exchange and regulation of the international service industry[201]
1875	Paris Metre Convention: unification of the metric system[202]
1881	Phylloxera-Convention: Regulation of the international trade with agricultural products[203]
1883	Paris Union was established by the Convention for the Protection of Commercial Property: reciprocal guarantee of invention patents, patterns and models, factory and trade markets in the convention countries[204]

---

[194] Contemporaries termed the international exchange of goods, services and capital 'world trade'; Meili, 'Die durch den Weltverkehr und die moderne Verkehrstechnik hervorgerufene Ausweitung des Rechtsgebiets und ihre Folgen für das juristische Studium', *Archiv für Rechts- und Wirtschaftsphilosophie 3* (1909), 595 *et seq.* On the internationalisation of technical standards, see Harriman 1928, 84, and Lage 1922, 89 *et seq.*, 133 *et seq.*

[195] Vec 2006, 21–164.

[196] Martitz 1906, 453.

[197] Wolfrum 1995, 1242 *et seq.*

[198] See Knipping (1996, 148 *et seq.*) for reprints of some of the following agreements.

[199] Paris Contract of the 5th/7th of May 1865; Martitz 1906, 450; Koch, *ZHR 4* (1861), 358 *et seq.*

[200] Martitz reports (1906, 450) that the regulations applied areas of 1,3 billion inhabitants.

[201] Boas 1912, 13.

[202] Treaty of Berne of October 9, 1874; Martitz 1906, 450.

[203] Treaty of November 3, 1881; Martitz 1906, 453.

[204] 20th of March 1883, Martitz 1906, 450 *et seq.*

Table 3 (*cont.*)

1883/84	Conferences of Rome and Washington: establishment of time zones[205]
1885	Expansion of the International Telegraph Agreement of St Petersburg to include the telephone service[206]
1886	International Berne Convention for protection of works of literature and art[207]
1886	Berne Convention for the technical units in the railways and the guaranteed sealing devices of transport cars to guard against customs fraud[208]
1890	Berne Convention for the creation of a transport union of member states with unitary transport laws[209]

The compliance with these agreements was monitored by numerous 'commerce organisations' and 'world unions'.[210] In 1906, the trade lawyer Karl Gareis named the *Bureau international des administrations télégraphiques*, the *Bureau de l'Union postale universelle* and the *Office central des transports internationaux* as the central agencies, all of which were located in Berne, as well as the Paris *Bureau international des poids et mésures* and the Brussels *Bureau de l'Union internationale pour la publication des tarifs douaniers*.[211]

The lists demonstrate that from the point of view of the international community, the regulation of 'administrative and technical' questions had priority. The law of contract, on the other hand, affected few international contracts. A concerted standardisation in this area—at least in Europe—can be spoken of only for central European law governing railway transport. Here, the problems had been notorious since the middle of the nineteenth century. At the State borders, the change in haulage contractors and in transports law had a similarly inhibiting effect on transport as did the differing gauges on the technical level. In addition, many transports never reached their addressee, such as the famous books from Lausanne that never reached the Dutch King and caused three lawsuits.[212] The Swiss

---

[205] Vec 2003, 43.
[206] Boas 1912, 13.
[207] Knipping 1996, 231 *et seq.*
[208] 15th May 1886, followed by three additional conferences up to 1913 with additional agreements (Haustein 1953, 11; Martitz 1906, 450).
[209] 14th October 1890; Martitz 1906, 450.
[210] See the discussion in Vec 2006, 21–164.
[211] Gareis 1906, 113.
[212] The shipment was intended for the King of the Netherlands, *Chateau de Loo à Apeldoorn près Geldern* (via Basel and Krefeld in the Rhineland); after three days, it arrived in Krefeld, then at a Count v. Loo at the Castle Loo near Geldern in the Lower Rhineland.

lawyers de Seigneux and Christ provided the impetus for an internationally unified regulation of the railway regulations.[213] Since numerous States had already curtailed the private autonomy of the law of transport, only a regulation based upon international law seemed a realistic alternative to the stakeholders.[214] The implementation in the member States was monitored by the above-mentioned *Office central des transports internationaux*. In addition, the agency provided a court of arbitration for internationally contested cases.[215] Within a decade, the member States arranged for an adaptation of the international transport regulations to international rules.[216]

The success of the Berne Convention of 1890 provided a fresh impetus for the legal utopia of a unified international commercial law. In 1906, the international jurist Ferdinand von Martitz predicted that the agreement formed 'the promising beginning of the development of a world business law' (trans.)[217] But the creation of standardised contractual bases for the railway transport business represented an exception. For the most part, the harmonisation and standardisation of the law of contracts was left up to business itself. Instead of creating a 'world business law' in the form of standardised contractual bases, States restricted themselves to improving the framework conditions for international legal relations. At the Hague Conferences of 1893, 1894, 1900 and 1904, approximately fifteen European countries and Japan agreed upon the first joint regulations of international private law.[218]

The influence of these national activities, however, remained limited for the most part. Much stronger were the initiatives of non-State stakeholders that contributed to an adaptation of the contract bases to the reality of world commerce. These processes of harmonisation and standardisation

---

Finally, it arrived at the proper addressee twenty days later. The lawsuits involved the sender against the Swiss Western Railway; the Western Railway sued the Swiss Central Railway, and the latter sued the State Railway of Baden. The legal costs of 1881 francs were far greater than the value of the shipment (*ZVMEV* [1878], 756).

[213] 'Memoir of de Seigneux and Christ' (*Denkschrift von de Seigneux and Christ*), *ZVMEV* (1874), 881, 904; De Seigneux 1875.

[214] *Convention internationale concernant le transport des marchandises*; the Law of Passenger Transport Contract was only instituted following World War I (Haustein 1953, 13).

[215] The court of arbitration was set up on the basis of Article 57, para. 1, no. 3, of the International Agreement of 1890; the Code of Procedure was based upon a resolution of the Federal Council of Switzerland (Eger 1909, 499).

[216] In Germany, the Railway Transport Regulation of October 16, 1899 exactly corresponded to the International Agreement and went into effect with the new legislation on the 1st of January 1900 (Senckpiehl 1909, 22).

[217] Martitz 1906, 450. The German term introduced by Martitz is *Weltverkehrsrecht*. Gareis expressed himself in a similarly optimistic fashion (1906, 95). They made use of concepts from the 1880's (Cohn 1888 and Zitelmann 1888).

[218] Kegel 1995, 170 *et seq.*

developed differently and discontinuously. Political impulses for business activities were not necessary;[219] it was sufficient that new regulations
were regarded as necessary. At the same time, it did not matter whether
the respective matter was already legally regulated on the national level,
whether here and there standard business conditions existed or whether
there was a lack of regulation. In all of these cases, the above mentioned
cultural lag between business and law can be observed in this context.
Repeatedly, the stakeholders were concerned with the creation of up to
date contract bases that corresponded to their needs and beliefs.

Whether for the most part a concerted regulation was lacking in the
non-State standardisation process, as the commercial law historian Karl
Otto Scherner believes,[220] can only be resolved through the investigation
of the individual procedures. These are, however, not easy to discover—
which is rather attributable to a lack of records than to a lack of such procedures. Nevertheless, 'grey literature' reveals which particular commerce
branches especially aimed at an international harmonisation of their
contractual contents. At issue are branches that were actively engaged
in 'world commerce' and whose contractual practices traditionally were
based upon standard form contracts. The insurance and the transport
industries were especially active and played leading roles through the
spread of mass contracts on the individual State level.[221] But also other
branches such as overseas trade created numerous standard contracts,
standard clauses and contract formulas for international business.

Table 4. International Standardisation of Contract Terms and Conditions
(Selected Examples). Sources see footnotes mentioned in the table.

1850's	Adaptation of the contract formulas *fob* and *cif* in long-distant transport[222]
as of 1853	Adaptation of the *Allgemeiner Plan Hamburgischer Seeversicherungen* ('Hamburg Standard Form of Maritime Insurance Policies') in Denmark, Sweden, Norway[223]
1863	Standard clauses and Charters for the Mediterranean and Black Sea Freight Committee[224]
1864	Agreement on the York-Antwerp Rules at the initiative of the

---

[219] Scherner 1992, 43.

[220] Ibid.

[221] Coing 1989, 537.

[222] The *cif* clause is first mentioned in an English judgement in 1862. In France and
Germany, it became common after the war in 1870–71 (Mittelstein 1918, 5).

[223] Scherner 1992, 76.

[224] Published in the 'Shipping and Mercantile Gazette' (21st March, 1863); Eucken
1914, 64.

Table 4 (*cont.*)

	International Law Association: standard regulations on the large losses that by virtue of the agreement of the parties can be included in individual contracts.[225]
1868	Model contracts and standard conditions of the Association of Grain Merchants of the Hamburg Grain Exchange[226]
after 1868	Standardisation of the bill of lading conditions for sea transport between Europe and the USA through the Transatlantic Shipping Conference[227]
1870	First conditions for futures trading on the New York Cotton Exchange[228]
1872	Harmonisation of the contract terms for valuables insurance through the *Internationaler Verband zur Transportversicherung von Post- und Eisenbahnsendungen* ('International Post and Railway Transportation Insurance Association')[229]
1875	A new *Bremer Seeversicherungs-Police* ('Maritime Insurance Policy of Bremen'), written in consultation with the *Internationaler Transportversicherungsverband* ('International Transport Insurance Federation', ITVV), as well as the standardisation of steamboat transportation bill of lading clauses[230]
1877	Model contracts and standard conditions of London Corn Trade Association[231]
1878	Negotiations on the World Post Congress in Paris on common policy conditions for consignment insurance[232]
1881	Adoption of a River Transportation Policy by the Rotterdam Stock Exchange at the initiative of the ITVV[233]
1883	Standard export conditions for silk traders from Yokohama[234]

---

[225] The York-Antwerp Rules were revised many times, among others in 1877 and 1890 (Bousquet 1906, 14 *et seq.*).

[226] Cutrera 1926; Kahn 1961, 21 *et seq.*

[227] Eucken 1914, 66.

[228] The futures trading conditions of the Liverpool Cotton Association followed in 1873, the conditions of the traders in New Orleans in 1880, the *Coton Usages, Contrats et Règlements* of Le Havre in 1882 (Kühlmamn 1909, 3).

[229] Berckum, 'Die Valorenversicherung', *ZVersWiss* 7 (1907), 469.

[230] *Annalen des gesamten Versicherungswesens* 1874, 397.

[231] Schwob 1928.

[232] Report in *Masius' Rundschau* 1878, 368 *et seq.*

[233] Koch 1999, 26.

[234] So-called *Yokohama Kiito Urikomi-donya Moshiawase-Kisoku* (*Réglementation entre les commissionaires et leurs commettants pour la vente des soies grèges à Yokohama*) (Ishizaki 1928, 82). The contract conditions for the international import of silk were used by, among others, the Silk Association of America, the French *Union des marchands de soie* and the Zurich *Seidenindustrie-Gesellschaft* (Ishizaki 1928, 20 *et seq.*, 56 *et seq.*)

Table 4 (cont.)

1890	Berne agreement: international law agreement on the standardisation of railway transport law in the majority of European countries[235]
1890	Formation of the 'International Catastrophe Federation of the Accident Insurance Companies' by German, Austrian, Swiss and Russian companies[236]
1893	Common Insurance Conditions offered by a group of insurance companies based in Belgium, Germany, the Netherlands, Austria, and Switzerland to travellers to the World Exhibition in Chicago (the so-called 'World Police')[237]
1895	Formation of the *Mitteleuropäischer Seereise-Unfallversicherungs-Verband* (MSUV, Central European Sea Voyage Accident Insurance Association), and agreement on standard contract conditions[238]
after 1895	ITVV policies for the insurance of river transports on the Rhine and East German rivers[239]
1897	Agreement on standard contract conditions for the *Mitteleuropäischer Seereise-Unfallversicherungs-Verbandes*, 'for the popular conducted tours to the orient and the north'[240]
1900	Agreement on the Harter Act clause for maritime insurance contracts through the ITVV: exclusion of liability in the event of culpable cause of damage through the captain or a crew member[241]
1904	Standard contract conditions of the German-Netherlands grain contracts[242]
1905	Standard charter conditions of the Baltic and White Sea Conference[243]
1906	Contract conditions of the Bremer cotton stock exchange that at this time all German, Austrian and Swiss traders and spinners were members of[244]

---

[235] Treaty of October 14, 1890; Gareis 1906, 110.

[236] 26 Borscheid 1990, 440.

[237] *Annalen des gesamten Versicherungswesens* 1893, 32 *et seq.*

[238] *Masius' Rundschau* 1895, 290.

[239] Moldenhauer, 'Binnenversicherung', in: Manes, *Versicherungslexikon*, 1st ed. (1909), col. 271–294.

[240] Note in *ZVersRW* 3 (1897), 889.

[241] 'Bericht von der Internationalen Conferenz der Seeversicherer in Paris', *ÖVZ* 1900, 305 *et seq.*

[242] Hirsch 1929, 111; Michel 1932, 3.

[243] The activity of the confederation extended beyond the designated seas. The first contract form affected the coal imports from England (Eucken 1914, 65).

[244] Cramer 1906.

Table 4 (*cont.*)

1907–1912	Standard earthquake clauses for fire insurance policies
about 1907/08	Cartel conditions of the companies engaged in transport from England to Australia; standard conditions also used by shipping associations for transport from China to England, from Europe and New York via Panama to the West Coast of the USA as well as from New York or New Orleans to West Indian ports[245]
1908	Agreement on contract bases between the Belgian *Fabrikantenverband* ('Belgian factory owners association') and the association of German warehouses and department stores[246]
1911	General ITVV conditions for river transportation insurance contracts[247]
1911	Standard La Plata Clause for maritime insurance contracts[248]
1912	Publication in three languages of the court of arbitration clauses of the International Federation of Cotton Spinners and Weavers Association[249]
1912/1913	Joint recommendation of the ILA and the See-Casco-Commission of the ITVV as well as the clauses designated by Shipping Gazette for sea insurance policies that applied to wood transport from the USA[250]

This list clearly shows the evolution of very different contractual structures. In some areas, the stakeholders reached agreements on comprehensive standard form contracts. This was achieved in the domestic/inland shipping industry and in the trade with agricultural products that was conducted via international stock exchanges. In other areas, the stakeholders agreed on clauses that were relevant only for individual, one-off and limited problems; the maritime insurance business offers many examples of this phenomenon. Widespread standard form contracts simply had no relevance here because all the contracts were negotiated on an individual basis. Nevertheless, maritime insurers looked for common solutions in specific problem situations. Thus, in Paris in 1911, the 150 members of the International Association of Maritime Insurers discussed the

---

[245] Eucken 1914, 66.
[246] Michel 1932, 3. frequently
[247] Koch 1999, 26.
[248] Könige 1912, 144.
[249] *Internationaler Verband der Baumwollspinner- und Weber-Vereinigungen* ('International Federation of Cotton Spinners and Weavers Association'), Board of Arbitration Clauses (1912).
[250] *Mitteilungen der Internationalen Vereinigung der Seeversicherer* ('Publications of the International Union of Maritime Insurers') 1 (1912–1914), 79.

problem of the financial losses suffered in large fires in the warehouses at the Rio de la Plata, in Buenos Aires and in Montevideo. Finally, they reached agreement on a standardised limitation of the storing risk through the so-called 'La Plata Clause': 'The insurance risk ends with the arrival of goods in a storage facility, warehouse, shed or private storage facility, in any case, however, ten days after the arrival of the respective goods' (trans.).[251]

The existence of international branch organisations turned out to be helpful. For example, there was a constant need for a standardisation and updating of the contractual bases in the transport and the transport insurance business. The International Transport Insurance Federation established in 1874 frequently seized the initiative. Many of its reforms led—such as the list above clearly shows—to a successful implementation of new regulations.

Attentive contemporaries also recognised the enormous significance of the organisational structures for the non-State development of law. In 1906, a group of business officials and jurists established a 'Foundation for Internationalism' especially for the support and stimulation of the movement towards internationalisation.[252] In The Hague office of the Foundation, the 'Review of Internationalism' was established and published in English, French and German. However, no more than three editions were published during 1907. At the same time, the scholarly judicial world began to show an interest in 'the modern non-State international associations and congresses and international law'. Under this title, the German Professor Wilhelm Kaufmann examined the origin of 'international autonomous norms'. The listing and characterisation of the different participants alone filled eight pages of his study.[253] The American Simeon E. Baldwin[254] and the Austrian Alfred H. Fried conducted similar studies.[255]

On the other hand, only a few standardisation processes seem to have succeeded without a minimum of central supervision. For example, it seems that the contract formulas *cif* and *fob* spread widely and quickly

---

[251] Könige 1912, 144.

[252] Wehberg, *ÖVZ* 1910, 89–90.

[253] Kaufmann 1908, 419 *et seq.*, 424–431.

[254] Baldwin, 'The International Congresses and Conferences of the Last Century as Forces Working Toward the Solidarity of the World', *American Journal of International Law* 1 (1907), 565 *et seq.*, 808 *et seq.*

[255] Fried often wrote about the international creation of associations, e.g. in the *Revue für Internationalismus* 1907, 40 *et seq.*

through simple use; oddly enough, more is not known about them than
that they have been in use since the middle of the nineteenth century.[256]

The large variety of contents, forms and participants not only reveals
tendencies towards a differentiation of the law, but also towards the sepa-
ration of law and State. This analysis alone does not identify the emergence of a new legal order. Apparently, the process of fragmentation still
remained the most important.

The reasons for the development of international or transnational law
structures still remain unclear. Scherner believes that the 'economically
efficient requirement for a legal standardisation' was 'virtually compulsory' in the case of transboundary services (trans.). In his examination
of the process of standardisation in railway, bank and insurance law, he
primarily points to the desire for equal treatment and legal clarity.[257] The
following investigation of the insurance companies' standardised exclusion of liability for earthquake-induced fire damages shows, however, that
the motives of the proponents and adversaries of international standardisation of standard business terms were far more complex.

---

[256] Mittelstein 1918, 5 *et seq.*
[257] Scherner 1992, 43.

CHAPTER TWO

THE EARTHQUAKE CLAUSE IN FIRE INSURANCE CONTRACTS
THE DEVELOPMENT OF A STANDARD (1906–1907)

Every process of standardisation is unique. Despite the features it shares
with other instances of standardisation, each process evolves differently, be
it through the rigid channels of existing institutions or through the spontaneous development of flexible networks. This diversity is increased by the
variety in the goals set by the different efforts at standardisation as well
as by the external conditions that can influence their course and success.
The example of the earthquake clause readily demonstrates this variety.

The earthquake clause was a regulation in the standard form contract
of the fire insurance business with which insurers excluded liability for
fire damages caused by earthquakes. It was developed in Europe after the
earthquake in San Francisco in April, 1906, and introduced into many business areas. Mostly, it supplanted older, less complex exclusion clauses.

In the first instance, the earthquake clause reflected the economic and
judicial experiences of the insurance companies in San Francisco. The
specific conditions that influenced its development include, in addition,
the different estimates of the possibility of additional and similar damages. An anomaly lies in the sharp disjunction between the phases of the
origin and implementation of the clause. Finally, the success and failure
of its introduction depended upon very different, specific relationships in
the given business areas.

2.1. The Aftermath of an Earthquake

2.1.1. *A Paradise for Fire Insurers*

At the beginning of the twentieth century, fire insurers considered the
West Coast of the United States of America a goldmine. Since the turn
of the century, 'the fire insurance business on the whole of the Pacific
coast and especially in California proved to be extremely favourable' and
yielded 'considerable profits' for the companies involved (trans.).[1] These

---

[1] 'Das amerikanische Pacific- und kalifornische Feuerversicherungsgeschäft in den letz-
ten 6 Jahren', *ÖVZ* 1906, 122.

estimates by an Austrian insurance newspaper relating to 'the America business' were generally shared in Europe and the United States.[2]

California especially deserved its reputation; there, insurers achieved an average premium of almost 1%.[3] Between 1901 and 1905, more than 61% of this income remained for business operations and reserves after all compensation payments had been subtracted. This result was notably higher than the quotas achieved in the entire 'Pacific Coast Department'[4] (58%) or in the United States as a whole (56.19%).[5] In metropolitan San Francisco, where about two-thirds of all buildings were insured against fire, the insurers managed to retain an amazing 73% of the premium income after making all damages payments.[6] In an international comparison, these results were extraordinary.[7]

The low damage quotas were considered to be the success of a policy of urbanisation that had taken the danger of fires into consideration after the fires in Chicago (1871) and Boston (1872) and again in Baltimore (1904).[8] Many architects and engineers had begun to turn away from using wood as a building material and to work with fireproof materials.[9] Insurers offered financial incentives to home owners to promote the installation of protective fire walls and sprinklers. Politicians in large cities made sure that water reservoirs for fire fighting and subterranean pipelines were connected to fire hydrants. They enlarged their fire departments and provided them with state-of-the-art equipment.[10] San Francisco, whose fire

---

[2] *Berliner Börsen-Courier*, cited in 'Die Erdbebenkatastrophe in San Francisco und die Feuer-Versicherungs-Gesellschaften', *ÖVZ* 1906, 111 *et seq.; The Times*, cited in 'Die Erdbebenkatastrophe in San Francisco und die Feuer-Versicherungs-Gesellschaften', *ÖVZ* 1906, 112; 'Pressemitteilung der Berlinischen Feuer', *ÖVZ* 1906, 309; 'Die Katastrophe von San Francisco', *ÖRev* 1906, 104; Lock, 'Amerikanische Feuerversicherungsmethoden und Bedingungen', *Insurance World*, October 1906, trans. in *Der Versicherungsfreund*, 1 November 1906, 1.

[3] *The Times*, cited in *ÖVZ* 1906, 112; Ziegler 1905, 34.

[4] This term for the American West Coast complies with a classification by the United States Insurance Supervisory Agencies.

[5] However, in the United States, 35% of the income from premiums was used for general expenses ([Note] in *La Semaine*, 4 November 1906, 8).

[6] Calculation based upon the figures offered by the American *Coast Review*, cited in *ÖVZ* 1906, as well as [note] in *La Semaine*, 4 November 1906, 7. The damage adjuster R. K. Mackenzie (1907) cites a damage quota of 28.7% for 1881–1902.

[7] Compare the figures in Ziegler (1905, 34): the average in North America was 10%, in Norway 4.5%, Sweden 4%, Austria-Hungary 3%, Germany 2.1%.

[8] Lock, *Insurance World*, October 1906, trans. in *Der Versicherungsfreund*, 1 November 1906, 1.

[9] Marks, The San Francisco story—April 18–21 (1909).

[10] Lock, *Insurance World*, October 1906, trans. in *Der Versicherungsfreund*, 1 November 1906, 1. The so-called "Brauseapparate", i.e. automatic fire-extinguishing systems, were called *sprinklers* in the USA.

department consisted of almost six hundred men and had thirty-eight large steam-powered pumping engines and fifteen reserve engines, was regarded as a pioneer in fire fighting. The maintenance of this force cost the city of 450,000 inhabitants more than $800,000 a year.[11] The citizens of this 'booming and up-and-coming trade centre on the Pacific coast'[12] could, however, easily afford this luxury; many of them had grown rich from the forty-niner gold rush, others with fruit and vineyards, and in the meantime, the Pacific overseas trade had reaped large amounts of wealth.[13] In the face of these positive developments, it was forgotten that the city for the most part consisted of wooden buildings and that it had been afflicted by large fires in the course of its young history.[14] Many experts saw these improvements as by no means sufficient.[15]

The prospect of generous profits had enticed many insurance businesses to move to California. At the beginning of 1906, 114 fire insurance companies were competing against each other.[16] The share of the California companies was very small at 5.2%,[17] while the other American companies also held no more than just over 50% of the market. Correspondingly high, on the other hand, was the share of foreign companies.[18] Since the days of the gold rush, British fire insurance had dominated the scene. In 1905 in San Francisco alone, the London Assurance Corporation received $87,719 in premium payments. This sum insured goods to the value of about $8 million. Thus, a European company occupied the leading

---

[11] *Financial Chronicle*, cited in *ÖVZ* 1906, 35; Mackenzie 1907.

[12] *ÖVZ* 1906, 111.

[13] Mackenzie 1907.

[14] McIntosh 1954, 3, 6; 'Monuments to Insurance' in *Fireman's Fund Record* (April 1906) (Archives 4-1-3-4-59, 0411).

[15] A study by the National Board of Fire Underwriters in 1905 had concluded that the water supply from hydrants would not be sufficient in the case of a big fire catastrophe. The Chief Engineer of the San Francisco Fire Department, Dennis Sullivan, had been demanding more money for improvements for years (Bronson 1997, 21). An anonymous critical report appeared at the end of October 1906 in *The Times*. Compare Lock, *Insurance World*, October 1906, trans. in *Der Versicherungsfreund*, 1 November 1906, 1.

[16] 39th Annual Report of the Insurance Commissioner of the State of California for the year 1906, 5.

[17] Ibid., 10.

[18] At the beginning of 1906, American companies in California insured property for a total of $476,627 million (56.6%) and non-American companies for a total of $365,703 million (43.4%) (*ÖVZ* 1906, 111). The American companies received 72.3% of all premiums ($1,164 million), the foreign companies 27.7% ($446,5 million; pounds sterling calculated in US dollars); [Note] in *La Semaine*, 4 November 1906, 7.

position in the most important metropolis on the West Coast.[19] The share
of the German insurance companies in the California market had, following the withdrawal of some companies, shrunk to about 6%.[20] Nevertheless, they still occupied the third place behind the American and British
companies.

2.1.2. 'San Francisco is gone'

For the residents of San Francisco, most of them presumably still in bed
at 5:12 a.m. on the 18th of April, 1906, a tremendous roar announced the
onset of an earthquake registering 8.3 on the Richter scale. The earthquake hardly lasted a minute but had devastating effects. Whole streets
lined with houses broke apart. One of the first fatalities was the Comman-
dant of the city fire department, Dennis T. Sullivan, whose loss severely
impeded the beginning of the rescue and fire-fighting efforts.[21] Likewise,
the engineer on duty in the central city electric plant was severely injured
during the first tremors, which meant that for a quarter of an hour the
electricity in the electric mains continued to flow, 'wrecking havoc' (trans.)
through short circuits.[22]

Adding to the disastrous consequences of the quake, the modern
infrastructure of the city collapsed in unexpected ways. San Francisco
was crisscrossed with electric, gas and water mains. After the quake, gas
streamed out of burst mains and ignited on errant sparks in the air. At
least thirty-two separate fires broke out. At the same time, the water supply failed. The city was supplied with three 30- to 44-inch cast iron pipes,
all of which were destroyed. The fire department and the city inhabitants
were forced to watch helplessly while the fire swept through the centre of
the city and developed into a raging inferno of destruction while millions
of gallons of water seeped away into the marshy ground surrounding the
city.[23] A few hours later in another part of the city, the 'Ham and Eggs'
fire erupted as a cook tried to fix breakfast on a damaged stove. This fire

---

[19] The most important American insurance company, the Fireman's Fund, locally collected $77,608 in premiums payments in the same year (*ÖVZ* 1906, 111 *et seq.*).

[20] Hagen, 'San Franzisko und die Feuerversicherung', *DJZ* 1906, col. 741.

[21] Report of the Committee of Five to the 'Thirty-five Companies' on the San Francisco
conflagration, April 18–21, 1906. (1907—BL), 11.

[22] Mackenzie (1907) assumed that the city of Oakland, which suffered damages from
the earthquake similar to those in San Francisco, escaped a disaster because the electricity
was immediately cut off.

[23] The city engineer T. Woodward testified in court in the case *Levi Strauss Realty Comp.
vs. Transatlantic* that 10 million gallons of water (45,000 m^2) had been lost ([Note] in *La*

could not be put out either. South-westerly winds drove the flames further into the city. In the meantime, 300,000 to 400,000 people tried to flee the city.

That same Thursday night, a third wall of fire originated in the Alcazar Theatre. Here, a soldier had knocked over a petroleum lamp, and neither the fire-fighting team nor the army, which in the meantime had taken control of the city, was able to put out the blaze or prevent a fourth major conflagration in Leroy Place. Until the afternoon of the 20th of April, the flames burned on when suddenly the wind turned and drove the fire back into the already fire-ravaged quarters. In the meantime, one of the water mains had been repaired, and with water, dynamite and artillery fire, the flames were finally brought under control.[24]

All in all, a scene of total destruction developed in the aftermath of the quake: 'For miles and miles there was nothing but shaky brick walls and twisted steel rods covered by darkness at night and shrouded in clouds of dust by day'.[25] The number of the dead was and remains uncertain.[26] Only the suburbs in which an additional 100,000 people lived remained unscathed.[27] Jack London, who had been in the destroyed quarter and in the midst of the fires, wrote in a famous eyewitness report: 'Not in history has a modern imperial city been so completely destroyed. San Francisco is gone. Nothing remains of it but memories... Its industrial section is wiped out. Its business section is wiped out. Its social and residential section is wiped out. The factories and warehouses, the great stores and newspaper buildings, the hotels and the palaces of the nabobs, are all gone. Remains only the fringe of dwelling houses on the outskirts of what was once San Francisco'.[28] The area destroyed by the flames measured about 3,000 acres on which about 28,000 houses had stood. Four-fifths of the value of personal wealth was destroyed. In material terms, no previous destruction had ever reached this dimension.

Semaine, 2 December 1906, 6; Mackenzie 1906; *San Francisco Chronicle*, 14 May 1906, and the report of the findings of the official investigation cited in *ÖVZ* 1906, 313.

[24] On the unfolding of the catastrophe, Kennedy 1908. Isolated fires broke out on the 23rd of April. 'The Earthquake at San Francisco', *The Times*, 24 April 1906.

[25] Mackenzie, cited in 'Erdbeben und Brände in San Francisco im April 1905' [sic], *Der Versicherungsfreund*, 20 April 1907, 7. Only a quarter of the Western Addition as well some isolated mansions could be saved.

[26] Since then, the estimate is 3,000 dead. Hansen, 'Who perished', *The Virtual Museum of the City of San Francisco* (http://www.sfmuseum.net/perished/index.html).

[27] Mackenzie 1907.

[28] London, 'The Story of an Eyewitness', *Collier's Weekly*, 5 May 1906.

Within a few hours, the news of the disaster was telegraphed all over the world.[29] Everywhere, this news reached insurance companies whose representatives in California had concluded contracts involving enormous risks, among them life insurance policies, fire insurance policies as well as policies as reinsurers.[30] In light of the extent of the damages in San Francisco, the news went down like a bomb. Despite the scientific recognition of the risk of a major conflagration in San Francisco,[31] insurance companies had regarded the chances of it actually happening as highly unlikely. The *Financial Chronicle* succinctly characterised the situation shortly after the disaster: 'In a twist of fate and due to the earthquake, the entire valuable equipment failed in the hour of the greatest need and the city was reduced to an utterly defenceless community, thus throwing all the calculations of the fire insurance industry completely out of the window'.[32]

2.1.3. *The Worldwide Aftershocks in the Insurance Business*

The city's government and private citizens already began to plan the rebuilding of the city during the clean-up work.[33] San Francisco was to arise out of its own ashes, regain its former magnificence but be more fire-proof.[34] The emergency care of the citizens who had been made homeless and the clearing work were paid for with State monies and donations.[35] The reconstruction of destroyed private property, on the other hand,

---

[29] Kahn, 'The San Francisco disaster—honest and dishonest insurance'. Speech in the House of Representatives, June 28, 1906, 3.

[30] The first telegrams that arrived at *Helvetia* have been preserved as copies from April 20, 1906. MR/A E-25 running no. 51 (Helvetia/San Francisco Schäden/I).

[31] For example, the critical study by the Board of Fire Underwriters of the Pacific, 'On percentage co-insurance and the relative rates chargeable therefore; also on the cost of conflagration hazard of large cities' (1905), was known.

[32] *Financial Chronicle*, cited in ÖVZ 1906, 135 (The quotation was re-translated into English).

[33] The coordination and leadership was taken over by the Building Trade Council and a reconstruction committee that had organised itself. 'Zur Katastrophe in San Francisco', *ÖRev* 1906, 140, with reference to *New Yorker Staats-Zeitung*, 9 May 1905; 'The Work of Relief. Splendid Contributions', *The Daily Telegraph*, 21 April 1906, 9; 'Preparing to Rebuild the City', *The Tribune*, 24 April 1906, 7.

[34] Christy 1906; Loewenthal, 'Die Erdbebenkatastrophe in St. Francisco und die Feuer-versicherungsgesellschaften', *Der Versicherungsfreund*, 1 May 1906, 2.

[35] President Theodore Roosevelt explicitly rejected offers of help from abroad, which was harshly criticised in insurance circles (*ÖRev* 1906, 111). On the policy of donations, see Strupp 2004, 151 *et seq.*

was the responsibility of each of the afflicted.[36] Since many of these were insured against fire damage, the citizens of San Francisco expected that the insurance companies would make good on their complete losses.

Even the vague conception of the dimensions of the destruction reported to have occurred caused considerable anxiety in the international insurance business community. Some daily newspapers managed to heighten uncertainty with rash reports on the extent of the fire damage and involvement of the individual companies.[37] The shareholders were the first to react. Even as the fires were still smouldering, the price of shares for insurance companies on the American East Coast,[38] in England and on the European continent collapsed. The insurance lawyer and publicist Ludwig Fuld from Mainz reported on 'panic-stricken selling on the part of shareholders' (trans.).[39] The investors feared the loss of their stock value, the no-show of their anticipated dividends and, a worst-case scenario, the demand for remargining accounts in order to raise the basic capital of their companies.[40]

The *New York Herald*, the *London Review* and the Austrian *Versicherungsfreund* published the first reliable reports on the possible losses in San Francisco while the fire was still raging. The *Herald* estimated the insured losses at $250 million;[41] the *Review* arrived at a larger sum of $300 million.[42] Thus, the question was raised how the fire and reinsurance companies would react to the damage claims for the losses suffered in the fire.[43]

The fire insurance companies involved reacted immediately. On the 21st of April, the representatives of sixty companies met in Oakland on

---

[36] Phelan, Finance Committee of Committee for Rebuilding of San Francisco, Ca., Rebuilding of San Francisco. With Special Reference to Ways and Means for Reconstructing the Private Edifice (1906—BL).

[37] 'Die Erdbeben Katastrophe in St. Francisco und die Feuerversicherung', *Der Versicherungsfreund*, 20 April 1906, 6; Prange, 'Die Erdbebenkatastrophe in San Francisco und die deutsche Feuerversicherung', *Feuerversicherung und Feuerschutz* 1906, 107.

[38] Reports in *The New York Times*, 26 April 1906.

[39] Fuld, 'Feuerversicherung und Erdbeben', *ÖVZ* 1906, 121; similarly Prange, *Feuerversicherung und Feuerschutz* 1906, 107. On the stock market losses between 1905 and 1907 see the list of the companies involved in the indemnification of damages in San Francisco in the annexe. Many of the companies not involved in California realised profits (Fischer, 'Organisation und Verbandsbildung in der Feuerversicherung', *Zeitschrift für die gesamte Staatswissenschaft / Ergänzungsheft XXXVIII* [1911], 101).

[40] *ÖRev* 1906, 111; Hagen, *DJZ* 1906, col. 741; 'Zur Lage in San Francisco', *ÖVZ* 1906, 216.

[41] *The New York Herald*, European Edition (Paris), 21 April 1906, 2.

[42] The *Review*, cited in *Der Versicherungsfreund*, 20 April 1906, 6.

[43] *ÖVZ* 1906, 111.

Table 5. Development of the price of shares of English Insurers on the London stock exchange. *The Times*, cited in *ÖVZ* 1906.[44]

Name	17.4.1906	21.4.1906	Losses
Atlas (London)	£ 7½	£ 6,–	–20%
Commercial Union (London)	£ 92½	£ 83½	–9.73%
Liverpool, London & Globe (Liverpool)	£ 53,	£ 44,–	–16.98%
London & Lancashire Fire (Liverpool)	£ 36,–	£ 29,–	–19.49%
London Assurance Corp. (London)	£ 74,–	£ 61,–	–17.57%
North British and Mercantile (Lo.)	£ 45,–	£ 40½	–10%
Northern Assurance (Aberdeen)	£ 89,–	£ 84½	–5.06%
Norwich Union Fire (Norwich)	£ 127½	£ 124½	–2.35%
Phoenix (London)	£ 42,–	£ 32½	–22.6%
Royal (Liverpool)	£ 56,–	£ 47,–	–16.07%
Royal Exchange (London)	£ 32 ½	£ 305,–	–5.13%
Sun (London)	£ 14,–	£ 12½	–10.71%
Union Assurance Society (London)	£ 25½	£ 22,–	–13.73

San Francisco Bay and announced that 'only losses attested to in the proper way by the institutions involved by virtue of their conditions and thus liable for compensation' (trans.) would be paid for.[45] According to a report of the *San Francisco Examiner*, the companies intended to indemnify claims for 25% of the damages.[46] Another paper wrote that the fire insurance companies had committed themselves to pay as much as '75 to 80 million dollars in order to demonstrate their willingness to the afflicted population' (trans.).[47]

These dispatches and rumours provoked vigorous reactions. The California representatives of the insurance companies saw themselves open to attacks from two sides: the insured feared that they had been deprived of their legitimate demands for complete indemnity. At the same time, the

---

[44] Source of the calculations: *The Times*, cited in *ÖVZ* 1906, 112; similar data in 'Further Decline in Insurance Shares', *The Financial Times*, 24 April 1906, 1.

[45] *Der Versicherungsfreund*, 1 May 1906, 2. According to Hagen (*DJZ* 1906, col. 741), the meeting took place on April 22, 1906.

[46] *The San Francisco Examiner*, cited in 'Die Schadensliquidation von San Francisco', *ÖRev* 1906, 271. *The Examiner*, however, was notorious for its populist, not always truth-loving, reporting: '*The Examiner* has been the chief sinner against common sense and ordinary justice' ('Underwriters are Making Good Progress', *The Coast Review*, April 1906, 190 b).

[47] *Der Versicherungsfreund*, 20 April 1906, 6.

directors in the distant head offices of the insurance companies refused to honour any and all compensation promises. Their reinsurers, they maintained, would 'lodge a protest against such generous act of accommodation as a show of loyalty towards their shareholders' (trans.).[48] Especially the Europeans did not feel responsible to make reimbursements for damages from an earthquake catastrophe[49] and quickly came up with arguments. Some argued that the insurers had not been willing to accept the risk of an earthquake when concluding the contracts and therefore could not be made responsible retroactively.[50] Others argued in the interests of the shareholders and the other insured parties. In addition, neither German nor English companies could be responsive to the 'unjustified demands of the Americans' (trans.) without coming into conflict with the supervising agencies in their own countries.[51] Americans and French also joined the warning chorus.[52]

To mollify public opinion, the insurers published press releases in their home countries and unhesitatingly made statements about the possible participation in the damages.[53] Many referred to earthquake clauses used in San Francisco. Others declared that possible losses were covered by profits, reserve funds and saving reserves—even when these were imaginary.[54] Even completely uninvolved companies butted in,[55] probably because they feared being drawn into the maelstrom of a stock market crash.

---

[48] Ibid.

[49] Ibid., for example, spoke of a *force majeure*.

[50] Fuld, *ÖVZ* 1906, 121; [Note] in *La Semaine*, 21 October 1906, 7.

[51] Hagen, *ÖVZ* 1906, 216, 235; *The Times*, cited in *ÖVZ* 1906, 135; 'Kulanz und Versicherungsbedingungen', *Wallmann's Versicherungs-Zeitschrift*, 9 September 1906, 2217 *et seq.*; 'Insurance Losses at San Francisco', *Pall Mall Gazette*, 24 April 1906; Fuld, 'Ersatzpflichtige und nicht ersatzpflichtige Feuerschäden in San Francisco', *ÖVZ* 1906, 122.

[52] [Note] in *La Semaine*, 26 August 1906, 6. The American damage adjuster Greely declared publicly: 'In the laws under which the fire insurance companies are organised and licensed, there is nothing about a voluntary distribution of the company's funds' (trans.). *ÖRev* 1906, 271.

[53] Examples in *ÖVZ* 1906, 112, 122 *et seq.*, 319; *Der Versicherungsfreund*, 1 May 1906, 2. 'Die Beteiligung der einzelnen Gesellschaften an den Schäden in San Francisco', *ÖVZ* 1906, 122 *et seq.*; 'Die Hamburger Versicherungsgesellschaften und San Francisco', *ÖVZ* 1906, 319.

[54] For example, the *Helvetia*, the *Aachener & Münchener* and the *Münchener Rück* companies made legitimate declarations. The *Transatlantische* (Hamburg) and the *Norddeutsche Feuer* (Hamburg) companies, on the other hand, declared that possible liabilities were covered through their own capital or reinsurance, but went bankrupt a few months after that (*ÖVZ* 1906, 112, 319).

[55] For example, the *Magdeburger Feuerversicherungs-Gesellschaft* ('Magdeburg Fire Insurance Company') *ÖVZ* 1906, 112.

The public relations work delivered the desired results. By the end of April, the *Österreichische Versicherungs-Zeitung* (*ÖVZ*) stated that tempers had 'calmed down a bit'.[56] Every day, newspapers like the Californian *Coast Review*, the *New York Times*, the *Economist*, the *London Times* and the *Frankfurter Zeitung* published information about the business of the individual companies in San Francisco and corrected the erroneous reports of other papers.[57]

However, the opinion began to prevail that the legal situation was too unclear in order to precisely estimate the liability for compensation. The insurance companies in California had used such different policy conditions whose interpretation was so varied that reliable prognoses were difficult to make.

2.1.4. *The Beginning of Damage Settlements*

In the meantime, the representatives of the insurance companies had begun with the settlements of the insured damages in San Francisco. Like the insured, they faced considerable problems. In many cases, the insurance policies had been destroyed in the fire, which made the establishment of the insurance claims more difficult. It was even worse when it turned out that an insurance company had lost its records.[58]

The companies sent so-called damage regulators to San Francisco in support of the local representatives. These became the first generation of adjusters for large damages.[59]

The adjusters organised themselves in small or large groups in order to coordinate their work in difficult cases. In the centre was the 'Committee of Fifteen on Adjustments' under the direction of Horace F. Atwood.[60] In

---

[56] *ÖVZ* 1906, 111.

[57] Manes summarised matters, 'Haftung der Versicherungsanstalten bei Erdbeben', *Masius' Rundschau* 1906, 163; *ÖVZ* 1906, 111.

[58] *Hamburger Nachrichten*, cited in *ÖVZ* 1906, 230; *ÖVZ* 1906, 235; [Note] in *La Semaine*, 23 September 1906, 6. An American company reported to the Münchener Rück that fortunately it possessed duplicates of the files in the company's central office (23 April 1906, Springfield Fire & Marine an MR/N.Y. Office, Copy MR/München, MR/A E-25 running no. 5 (Damage/San Francisco).

[59] By 1904, after the fire in Baltimore and the hurricane disaster on the West Coast of the United States, some of them had been authorised to settle claims. 'Der Bericht eines Schadensliquidators in San Francisco', *ÖVZ* 1906, 319.

[60] The establishment of this committee was agreed upon at the meeting of the local insurance representatives on the 21st of April (Report of the special committee of the Board of Trustees of the Chamber of Commerce 1906, 14).

a 'general adjustment office'[61] they set up themselves, Atwood and fifteen additional experts coordinated the liquidation of damages in which more than five companies were involved.[62] Their goal was to reach the quickest, most discrete and most economical agreements possible with the insured parties. In order to achieve reductions in the claims during the negotiations, the adjusters conducted extensive research on the unfolding of the catastrophe. They looked for eyewitnesses and collected photographs that documented earthquake damage to the buildings.[63] From these sources and reports from the fire departments they put together a report that included all the accessible information on all the houses in every block in the city.[64] This labour paid off: on the average, the insurers were able to reduce the amount of the claims paid out to the insured by over 26%.[65] On the basis of this success, the majority of insurance agencies oriented themselves at the regulation practice of the 'Committee of Fifteen' and sought their cooperation.[66]

In the beginning of May, Atwood reported rapid progress.[67] Based upon the *New Yorker Staats-Zeitung*, the news reached Europe that according to reports issued by insurance companies, the compensation for insurance claims on fire damages was expected very soon.[68] But the semblance that the catastrophe could be easily resolved without massive conflict was deceptive.

---

[61] Report of the Committee of Five to the 'Thirty-five Companies' on the San Francisco conflagration, April 18–21, 1906. (1907—BL), 12.

[62] Report of the special committee of the Board of Trustees of the Chamber of Commerce 1906, 12; *Westliche Post*, 10 July 1906; Mackenzie 1907.

[63] 'Photograph Proofs of Earthquake Losses', *The Coast Review*, June 1906, 231; Bament 1906 (1973), 91.

[64] Mackenzie 1907.

[65] *Westliche Post*, 10 July 1906; 'Die Versicherungs- und Entschädigungssummen in San Francisco', *Der Versicherungsfreund*, 1 August 1906.

[66] *ÖRev* 1906, 177; *ÖVZ* 1906, 319; Mackenzie 1907.

[67] *ÖVZ* 1906, 195.

[68] In addition, the *Staats* reported that this news was received on all sides with great enthusiasm—even from the banks that endeavoured to financially accommodate the numerous impoverished citizens of San Francisco. At the same time, the insurance companies had conceded the authority to begin the work of clearing up in districts devastated by the quake and subsequent fires, so that the 'policy owners' could rescue what remained beneath the debris without having to fear endangering their claims for compensation (*ÖRev* 1906, 140, with reference to *New Yorker Staats-Zeitung*, 9 May 1905).

2.1.5. *Points of Conflict in Material Law*

Soon, the substantive law[69] began to create significant problems for both the insurance providers and the injured parties. In many individual cases, it turned out that the legal bases offered no unequivocal solution to ambiguous damage claims. Even those on the scene could not always form a reasoned judgement of the situation. And for the European observers, the legal situation seemed even more 'chaotic'.[70] Nevertheless, they tried to cobble together a composite picture out of the numerous individual bits of information.[71] These contemporary investigations of the contractual problems in California acquired an importance somewhat later that cast a shadow far beyond the question of the regulations of damage claims. The points of conflict recognised at the time thus directly led to the development of a standard clause for the exclusion of earthquake damages.

In California, the pluralistic legal source doctrine of the common law had been in force since a decision of the State Supreme Court in 1888.[72] Solutions to legal conflicts involving insurance disputes were primarily to be found in concrete agreements sanctioned by contracts. Here, lawyers struck pay dirt. Insurance companies amply relied upon freedom of contract and based their differing policies upon the contracts.[73] Eight different formulations alone to cover the regulations governing the consequences of earthquakes were counted.[74] Clashes with state law were not to be expected, since the State of California—in contrast to other states in the union[75]—had up to then scarcely regulated the material law of insurance.

---

[69] Substantive law is law that establishes rights and obligations between individuals.

[70] *Berliner Tageblatt*, 6–7 June 1906, cited in *Feuerversicherung und Feuerschutz* 1906, 126.

[71] The most successful in this endeavour was Manes, *Masius' Rundschau* 1906, 161.

[72] Taught in California, among others, by the influential lawyer Prof. John N. Pomeroy and approved by the California Supreme Court in Sharon vs. Sharon 1888. Börner 2000, 134.

[73] Manes, *Masius' Rundschau* 1906, 161; compare Manes' articles in *Der Tag*, 22 April, 26 April and 29 April 1906.

[74] Best's *Insurance Report*, cited in *The Review*, 17 August 1906. The reliability of this exclusion clause was derived both from the principle of the freedom of contract and the Civil Code, sec. 2628. The regulation reads: 'If a peril is specifically excepted in a contract of insurance, a loss, which would not have occurred but for such peril, is thereby excepted; although the immediate cause of the loss was a peril which was not excepted'.

[75] Other states prescribed the wording of obligatory contractual bases, e.g. the New York Standard Fire Insurance Policy. See in detail: Fire Insurance Law Chart. Summary of Special State Laws etc. (1903).

When lack of clarity as to the interpretation of the insurance conditions remained, lawyers had to rely upon case precedents in California or other common law courts. But up to then, no decisions as to the entire range of earthquakes and fire insurance existed.[76] Until the Supreme Court would render decisions on the San Francisco damages, only the California Civil Code of 21 March 1872 could offer any guidance.[77] Two French court decisions that came close to the issue were cited in the European press, but ignored in California.[78]

The damages to property that resulted from the San Francisco earthquake can be divided into four groups. Relatively uncommon were damages that were caused (1) by the tremors alone or only by (2) the fire in isolation. Generally, the claims adjusters were forced to determine damages that had been caused by (3) both in equal proportions. The fourth group consisted of the remaining damages that had originated in other causes, especially through detonations laid by authorities and gas explosions.

2.1.5.1. *Pure Tremor Damage*

Pure tremor damages, that is, damage to buildings without the addition of fire damage, were not covered by insurance.[79] There was complete agreement on this point since insurance contracts clearly only insured against fire damage.

2.1.5.2. *Damage Equally Caused by the Collapse of Buildings and Fire*

There was, however, vehement discord about insured buildings and objects that first were damaged by the quake's tremors and then were ravaged by the firestorm. Most of the 28,000 destroyed buildings met their

---

[76] 'Earthquake Clause Policies', *The Coast Review*, May 1906, 214.

[77] The Civil Code included in Title XI some general rules on the replacement obligation of the insurer in case of damage. The part on fire insurance (Title XI, Chapter III, §§2752–2756) mentions no additional relevant conditions on replacement obligations; nor do any other statutes or reports from the state of California.

[78] The Paris magazine *L'Argus* cites two decisions that the Paris *Tribunal de la Seine* reached after a major eruption of Mont Pelée on the island of Martinique. In this case, the fire insurance company, Lancashire, successfully defended itself with an exclusion clause that exempted damages caused by a volcano (grounds for the decision in *L'Argus*, 23 August 1903). In the other case, a suit against Lancashire was also denied. They had used a policy without an exclusion clause, but were able to prove that the insured objects had already been destroyed by the force of the volcanic eruption before the fire had reached them (grounds for the decision in *L'Argus*, 2 August 1906). The *ÖVZ* 1906, 265 cited the clause from the first case and spoke of a 'precedent'.

[79] Greely, cited in *ÖRev* 1906, 271; *Weekly Underwriter*, cited in *ÖVZ* 1906, 148.

destruction in this order. Later investigations have established that about 5,000 buildings had completely collapsed after the earthquake before the fire reached them.[80]

To what degree the insurance provider was responsible for damages depended upon the wording of the policy. And sometimes this wording led to serious problems for the insurance providers.

Most of the affected insurance companies had patterned their policies after the exemplar of the New York Standard Fire Insurance Policy. These policies had been used by numerous companies in San Francisco whose central offices were located in the state of New York, as well as by additional American and British firms.[81] The so-called 'fallen building clause' was an integral part of these conditions: 'If a building or any part thereof fall, except as the result of fire, all insurance by this Policy on such building or its contents shall immediately cease'.[82] This fallen building clause had been formulated by fire insurance providers just before the turn of the century in order to defend themselves against the widespread and deceptive practice of insured parties who set fire to dilapidated buildings after they had collapsed and then tried to collect the insurance money.[83] After the San Francisco disaster, it was beyond dispute that this clause could be used to adjudicate the combination of earthquake and fire damage. But what actual circumstances were covered by the fallen building clause?

According to the consensus in American jurisprudence at the time, a collapsed building that had suffered total destruction lost all of its value as an insurable object and no longer enjoyed contractual protection.[84] For this reason, the fallen building clause then assumed independent importance when an insured building had only partially collapsed ('any part thereof'). Even in these cases, the protection of the insurance was considered to have expired immediately. The previous court decisions, however,

---

[80] Thomas and Witts 1871/1980, 221.

[81] Presumably, some one hundred insurance companies used this or a similar policy. Compare the list of the damaged San Francisco companies in the annex; Sofonea 1973, 34.

[82] Cited in Whitney 1906, 39.

[83] Mackenzie 1907; A. M. Best Co. 1907, 13.

[84] Nave vs. Home Mutual Insurance Co. (Supreme Court of Missouri) is considered to be a *leading case*. Manes (*Masius' Rundschau* 1906, 216) cites and comments upon the explanations in Bennett's Fire Insurance Cases (1872, 88) and in Wood's commentary (1906).

offered little clarity as to how extensive the partial damages had to be.[85] The San Francisco cases thus offered a twofold potential for conflict. Not only could the state of the buildings before the outbreak of the fires be debated,[86] but also whether the proven damages caused by collapsing buildings were sufficient to cause the termination of the insurance coverage.

A considerably smaller group of insurance companies carried earthquake clauses.[87] These clauses exempted the companies from the obligation to pay compensation for damages that could arise from earthquakes and other disasters. In San Francisco, a total of five different formulations were used,[88] the most often used perhaps being: '[The company insures] against all direct loss or damage by fire, except caused directly or indirectly by invasion, earthquake, insurrection, riot, civil war or commotion, or military or usurped power, or by order of any civil authority'.[89] Thus, the clause was designed to exclude an insurer's responsibility when the causes of fire damage could be traced back to the earthquake or one of these other events. The problem that confronted the insurance provider and the insured party was to determine this direct or indirect causality in individual cases.

Strictly regarded, the earthquake could not actually cause any fire damage, since earthquakes themselves—in contrast to volcanic eruptions— could not generate any sources of fire. In this respect, the formulation

---

[85] Mackenzie (1907) states that at least an 'integral or extensive portion of the building' must have collapsed or that the damage must have considerably affected the appearance of the entire building. The incorrect report of *The Coast Review* ('If Any Part Fall', June 1906, 231 *et seq.*) that there was no court decision on the collapse clause shows the unreliability of information current at the time.

[86] Prange, *Feurversicherung und Feuerschutz* 1906, 107; *ÖRev* 1906, 104, 111.

[87] See the annexed list of San Francisco insurance companies paying damages suffered by clients in the earthquake.

[88] Whitney 1906, 37 *et seq.*

[89] Cited in Whitney 1906, 38; see Manes, *Masius' Rundschau* 1906, 161 *et seq.* A second widespread clause read: 'This Company shall not be liable for loss caused directly or indirectly by invasion, insurrection...; or for loss or damage occasioned by or through any volcano, earthquake [...]; or by neglect of the insured to use all reasonable means to save and preserve the property at and after the fire or when property is endangered by fire in neighbouring premises; or (unless fire ensues, and, in that event, for the damage of fire only) by explosion of any kind...' (Whitney 1906, 37). This clause was used by Indemnity, Norwich Union, Providence (Washington), Williamsburg City. Very similar clauses were used by Aachen-Munich, Alliance (London), Commercial Union (London/New York), German Alliance (New York), German American, New Hampshire, New Zealand, Palatine (London), Phoenix (Hartford), Rhine & Moselle (Strasbourg) (Whitney 1906, 40); Fuld, *ÖVZ* 1906, 121. Two additional especially inclusive clauses are printed in *ÖVZ* 1906, 265.

'caused directly' was open to dispute. The insurers argued that all the sources of fire in insured buildings that occurred at the time of the tremors and because of their effects were directly caused by the earthquake. This definition encompassed some dozens of fires that had been triggered on the morning of the 18th of April, 1906, by turned-over stoves, cracked fireplaces or upset candles, short circuits and gas explosions.[90] Most of the buildings were destroyed in the fire storms that engulfed one house after another, street for street, and lasted several days. In the opinion of the fire insurers, these damages stood in indirect causal relationship to the earthquake.[91]

Especially vexing was the determination of the cause of damages when the fires broke out hours or days after the earthquake and could not be extinguished.[92] The 'Ham and Eggs' fire and the conflagration that erupted in the Alcazar Theatre are famous examples. The insurer argued that these damages were also indirectly caused by the earthquake.[93]

Not all of the insurance providers had expressly excluded themselves from all directly and indirectly caused damages. Many earthquake clauses excluded only the directly caused damages stemming from earthquakes or spoke very generally about an exclusion from the dangers from earthquakes.[94] Whether the insurer was liable for indirectly caused consequences of the earthquake on the basis of these policies could only be determined through interpretation. German and French observers pointed to section 2628 of the California Civil Code[95] which equated indirect and direct causality. They argued that by 'power of the law' every earthquake clause included all damages that were connected to the earthquake.[96] At the same time, they suffered from a misunderstanding based upon the differences between the continental European legal systems and common law. Whether the Civil Code was introduced into the finding of justice or not depended alone upon whether jurists regarded the recourse to its stipulations as necessary. The legal force of the Civil Code that the

---

[90] [Note] in *La Semaine*, 9 September 1906, 7.

[91] Ibid.

[92] Fuld, *ÖVZ* 1906, 121.

[93] *Berliner Lokal-Anzeiger*, cited in *ÖZV* 1906, 112.

[94] *ÖVZ* 1906, 234.

[95] Civil Code, sec. 2628: 'If a peril is specifically excepted in a contract of insurance, a loss, which would not have occurred but for such peril, is thereby excepted; although the immediate cause of the loss was a peril which was not excepted'.

[96] [Note] in *La Semaine*, 23 September 1906, 6; *Berliner Tageblatt*, 6/7 June 1906, cited in *Feuerversicherung und Feuerschutz* 1906, 126.

Californian legislature of 1872 for all intents and purposes had imputed to it in a European sense had long before the turn of the century been overturned by the practices of the Supreme Court.[97] The simple existence of section 2628 of the Civil Code by no means meant that this proviso also had to be applied.

The combination of fallen building clauses and earthquake clauses was regarded as the safest clause combination.[98] To be sure, the fallen building clause in combination with a well formulated earthquake clause had no independent meaning, but it could reinforce the argument of the insurer.

Loewenthal's assertion that insurance policies without any exclusion clauses existed remains unsupported by any specific examples.[99] In addition, problems arose when the clauses contained contradictory formulations that led to the insurer's original meaning's being turned against them.[100]

2.1.5.3. *Pure Fire Damages*

Those insurance providers whose contracts contained earthquake clauses could at best be released from responsibility for the few buildings that had been exclusively damaged by fire.[101] All other cases were subject to compensation.[102]

2.1.5.4. *Damages from Explosions, Blasting, and Sundry Causes*

There remain some important types of cases that likewise had to be solved on the basis of policy conditions, case law and the civil code. One of them concerned the many damages to buildings that were caused by explosions

---

[97] Börner 2000, 134; Gray, 'E pluribus unum? A Bicentennial Report on Unification of Law in the United States', *RabelsZ 50* (1986), 116.

[98] A. M. Best Co. 1907.

[99] Loewenthal, *Der Versicherungsfreund*, 1 May 1906, 1. Specific examples could not be found.

[100] The clause used by North German (New York), a subsidiary of the Hamburg company *Norddeutsche Feuer*, stipulates for example: 'The Company shall not be liable for loss caused by invasion, insurrection [...]; or (unless fire ensues, and, in that event, for damage by fire only) by explosion of any kind or from any cause, or the bursting of a boiler, or earthquake, or hurricane [...]'. Whitney 1906, 39 *et seq.*

[101] The problems of interpretation discussed in the section above were also to be solved in this context.

[102] *ÖVZ* 1906, 111; *ÖVZ* 1906, 134. The Civil Code, sec. 2626, supported this principle of liability: 'An insurer is liable for a loss of which a peril insured against was the proximate cause; although a peril not contemplated by the contract may have been a remote cause of the loss [...]'.

of the city's gas mains.[103] In the other cases, insurance providers, injured parties and city officials disputed who was responsible for the damage to buildings as the result of the creation of firebreaks by detonations placed by well-meaning fire fighters.[104] It was certain that the insurers were going to have to pay compensation for insured objects that suffered damages as a result of efforts to save them, based upon a recognised principle of insurance law which section 2627 of the Civil Code makes clear: 'An insurer is liable where the thing insured is rescued from a peril insured against, that would otherwise have caused a loss, if in the course of such rescue the thing is exposed to a peril not insured against, which permanently deprives the insured of its possession, in whole or in part; or where a loss is caused by efforts to rescue the thing insured from a peril insured against'.

Damages caused by gas explosions, like the damages caused by collapsed buildings, were generally excluded in contract clauses.[105] However, if the earthquake caused an explosion that led to a fire, the fire damages could be seen as indirect consequences of the earthquake. Thus, the earthquake clause could also apply here.[106] American judges had already reached judgements in earlier and similar cases, but these decisions could not be subsumed under a single category. The German insurance scholar Alfred Manes cites no fewer than four diverging opinions reached by American courts from the four volume work on insurance contractual law by J. A. Joyce.[107]

The detonations of buildings and large sections of streets by San Francisco officials to create firebreaks provided less controversy. Although all insurance companies had excluded damages caused by civil or military authorities,[108] American jurisprudence had repeatedly decided that the liability for objects that had been detonated to protect an additional spread of fire could not be excluded.[109] In this respect they agreed with California law as the passage from the California Civil Code quoted above defines it. The insurance providers protested that they were being forced to

[103] Manes, *Masius' Rundschau* 1906, 161.
[104] 'Liability for Dynamited Buildings', *The Coast Review*, May 1906, 214. The fire fighters and the army had allegedly demolished many buildings in the wealthy housing districts with dynamite blasting and artillery fire.
[105] Examples in Whitney 1906, 37 *et seq.*; Manes, *Masius' Rundschau* 1906, 162.
[106] But see Prange, *Feuerversicherung und Feuerschutz* 1906, 107.
[107] Manes, *Masius' Rundschau* 1906, 162; Joyce 1897.
[108] *The Coast Review*, May 1906, 214.
[109] Manes, *Masius' Rundschau* 1906, 161; Vance 1904.

compensate for, in the words of an insurance agent in a German newspaper, 'the in all respects unprofessional and inexpert dynamiting and
detonating by authorities of large street blocks that were thus not only
useless but additionally dangerous and destructive'.[110] But the opinions
rendered by American courts conformed to the internationally recognised principles of insurance law according to which damages caused by
measures designed to prevent or reduce danger had to be compensated
for without consideration of their success, as long as they were commensurate with the circumstances.[111] In the meantime, the Californian *Coast
Review*[112] pointed out to its readers that the buildings affected would have
been total write-offs in any case. For this reason, the fire insurance providers recognised that the damages resulting from dynamite explosions had
to be compensated for[113]—'no matter what the policy terms in this regard
specified'.[114] Only isolated voices such as the *Weekly Underwriter* continued to gainsay this viewpoint.[115]

Already at the beginning of May 1906, the fire and reinsurance providers
were forced to admit that the legal problems were more serious than they
had expected previously. The analysis of the situation in substantive law
demonstrated how disadvantageously their own contractual regulations
could work out in practice in cases of earthquake damage. Many companies faced enormous losses; others could not even put a figure on their
liabilities because they did not know to what degree they were obligated
to honour their claims. A summary of the financial situation was not easily made because of the unmanageable variety of the conditions. It must
be assumed that many an insurance provider recognised soon after the

---

[110] *ÖVZ* 1906, 234. Detonations to combat fires had a tradition in San Francisco, but
were controversial in other parts of the United States. The *ÖVZ* (1906, 134) cites American
experts, such as the Chief of the fire department in New York, who rejected dynamite detonations to fight fires, and the 'Fire Commissioner' Hugh Brunner: 'The detonations perhaps
would have a beneficial effect if dynamite could create level open surfaces, but instead of
razing a building completely, they mostly simply fragment them so that the houses then
provide easier prey for the flames than intact ones' (trans.). Similarly critical remarks are
made by the *Mining and Scientific Press* 1906.

[111] Hagen, *DJZ* 1906, col. 743.

[112] *The Coast Review*, May 1906, 214.

[113] Whitney 1906, 26.

[114] The Head of the Royal Exchange took the view that his company was not liable for
damages resulting from detonations, but that refusing to make payments could not be
defended in law (*ÖVZ* 1906, 195). Other companies instructed their claims adjusters to stick
to the conditions specified in the contracts (*ÖVZ* 1906, 134).

[115] *ÖVZ* 1906, 148.

earthquake the advantage to be gained from the introduction of unitary and, for the company, favourable regulation.

In light of the initial court cases, the parties reckoned that several years would pass by the time all claims had been adjudicated.[116]

2.1.6. *Attempts to Reach Out-of-Court Settlements*

2.1.6.1. *Insurers Seeking Alliances*

In May 1906, numerous disputes between the insurance providers and the insured disabused those people in the business who had harboured notions of a peaceful resolution of the difference between the two groups. Although the first companies began to pay out claims, they were forced to swim against the harsh and icy currents of public opinion ebbing back and forth in the San Francisco Bay Area. Since their conference in Oakland, they were suspected of having devised a clever strategy to swindle the injured parties out of their rightful compensation. At the same time, the insurers' camp was by no means unified.

While it was clear to all the insurance companies that none of them could simply refuse to pay compensation without endangering the entire industry in the United States,[117] the European companies nevertheless intensified their course against the assumed 'accommodating' practice of regulating claims. On the 30th of April, 1906, the representatives of twenty continental European reinsurance companies, acting at the instigation, among others, of the Swiss Reinsurance Company, Swiss Re, convened in Frankfurt, Germany, to discuss the situation in San Francisco.[118] They came from Germany, Austria-Hungary, Italy, Denmark, Switzerland, Russia and France.[119] Their cooperation was based upon a spontaneous organisation of its members in a branch that up to this time had never met together. The conference assumes major importance in the history of the earthquake clause because the assembled company representatives

---

[116] A practitioners' assessment, *ÖVZ* 1906, 134.

[117] Hagen, *DJZ* 1906, col. 741; [Note] in *La Semaine*, 21 October 1906, 7.

[118] SR/FA A9.0–29/gray file/unbound material.

[119] Taking part were *Badische Rück- und Mitversicherungs-G., Erste Böhmische Rück, Europa, La Fondiaria, Hamburg, Hamburg-Bremer Allgemeine Rück, Kölnische Rück, Minerva Retrocessions- und Rückversicherungs-G., Münchener Rück, Nordisk, Nye Danske, Oberrheinische, Prudentia, Rheinisch-Westfälische Rück, Rossija, Salamandra, Schweizerische Rück, Skandinavia, Societé Anonyme de Réassurances contre l'Incendie.* While some companies are not represented in the archived documents, others are listed: *Gladbacher Rück, Skandia, Süddeutsche Rück, Westdeutsche, Wiener Rück.* Drafts and letter samples, SR/FA A9.0–30/loose material.

not only reached operative agreements on the regulation of damages, but also made strategic decisions as to the future earthquake danger policy. Chapter 3.2.6 will deal with these.

The reinsurance providers had agreed upon a resolution that they sent to the fire insurance companies involved in the negotiations in San Francisco a few days later. In this resolution, they demanded a narrow interpretation of the cumbersome contracts. Benefits of the direct insurers paid to the injured parties for which a 'compelling legal commitment' did not exist would not be honoured by the reinsurers.[120] This communication was published three weeks later in the leading insurance journals.[121] This step was extraordinary, since no branch within the insurance industry valued discretion more than the reinsurers did.[122] Their decision to exercise collective pressure on their contract partners was intended to demonstrate to the international public how alarmed they were. An additional reason for the means of the open letter was the lack of other opportunities to exert influence upon the regulatory practices of the fire insurance providers.[123] Unrestricted involvement in the regulations of individual cases was not possible. Only when lawsuits between the direct insurer and the injured party were being conducted could the reinsurer exert specific rights enjoyed by the direct insurer (that is, all objections and rejoinders accruing to the direct insurer). In addition, the terms of the policy determined the obligation of the reinsurer to the direct insurer who had made the contract in the first place.[124] Neither earthquake clauses in the reinsurers' contracts nor the agreement to provide benefits to the

---

[120] SR/FA A9.0–30/unbound material.

[121] 'Zur Katastrophe in San Francisco (Erklärung von 20 europäischen Rückversicherungsgesellschaften, Frankfurt a.M. den 30.4.1906)', *Masius' Rundschau* 1906, 226 *et seq.*; *Der Versicherungsfreund*, 20 May 1906, 5 *et seq.*; *Zeitschrift für Versicherungswesen*, 23 May 1906.

[122] The trust that the primary insurers paid the reinsurers was based on this bond of discretion, since the former confided internal information about its business to the latter that under no circumstances should ever be leaked to a third party. It proved to be correspondingly difficult for the authors outside this loop to write about the branch. The legal historian Victor Ehrenberg (1885, 2 *et seq.*) describes this difficulty in a Festschrift for Georg Beseler which he wrote on behalf of the legal faculty in Rostock.

[123] The legal situation of the reinsurers was 'legally not very advantageous' according to Hagen (*DJZ* 1906, col. 742). The contracts made by the reinsurers presented contemporary jurists with considerable problems, since in this branch—where disputes were almost exclusively resolved through written legal opinions and courts of arbitration—, there was a dearth of case law, relevant legal norms and even standard contracts (Ehrenberg 1885, 4 *et seq.*; Hanzlik 1911, 4 *et seq.*, 30 *et seq.*).

[124] This was often explicitly expressed in the reinsurers' contracts and was, in the opinion of some authors, also valid as customary law (Ehrenberg 1885, 59 *et seq.*, 109 *et seq.*;

injured parties only in the case of an agreement between direct insurers and reinsurers was sufficient to breach this accessory relationship.[125] The reinsurers were not even able to mount a defence against *ex gratia* payments, since the decision as to damage claims lay in the absolute discretion of the chief insurer.[126] The procedure adopted by the reinsurers was however also remarkable because there was no reason to regard their existence as threatened in any way.[127] At issue for them was merely to limit their own losses in good time.[128] The pressure yielded results, and the conduct of the reinsurers influenced the settlement statistics of the fire insurers in San Francisco.[129] Many a company was unable to achieve an economic settlement through the reinsurers because they carried out their threat and stubbornly refused to pay compensation.[130]

Whether the Frankfurt declaration of the reinsurers had reached the British fire insurance providers when they met in London on the 2nd of May 1906 is not certain.[131] They could well have independently advocated the undertaking of a similar policy. In London, all of the fire insurance offices active in San Francisco were represented. Almost all had used the fallen building clause in San Francisco, but only three (Alliance, Commercial

---

Rau 1899, 47; 'Nachklänge von San Francisco', *Masius' Rundschau* 1906, 385. May [1882, 10] represents an opposing point of view; Vivante 1899, 397).

[125] Hagen, *DJZ* 1906, col. 741.

[126] Hagen (*DJZ* 1906, col. 741) cites relevant German case law; also Loewental, *Der Versicherungsfreund*, 1 May 1906, 1; Loewenthal, the owner and chief editor of the journal *Der Versicherungsfreund*, thus corrected the view expressed in the previous edition of the journal that the reinsurers had no obligation to provide indemnification in the case of *ex gratia* payments. The *ÖVZ* (1906, 111 *et seq.*) adopted his viewpoint.

[127] This was already apparent at the time of the conference in Frankfurt. The American fire insurance companies were traditionally not completely in agreement with the reinsurers and had enlisted their services as little as possible. In addition, a great number of reinsurance companies were involved in fire insurance in San Francisco, and many of them had referred parts of their portfolios to their retrocessionaires—the reinsurers of the reinsurers—, so that the risks had been spread widely. In the reinsurers' contracts in San Francisco, the issue was primarily a model of excess liability insurance in which the reinsurer bore responsibility that went beyond certain contractually determined maximums of the fire insurance providers. The insurance providers were, in part, obligated by law in this matter. Appraisals of the situation can be found in Manes, *Masius' Rundschau* 1906, 163; Loewenthal, *Der Versicherungsfreund*, 1 May 1906, 1 *et seq.*; Mackenzie 1907. On reinsurance providers in the United States, Jahn 1912, 58.

[128] Experience shows that the reinsurers achieved worse results in the reinsurance of fires than the chief insurers. Compare the statistics for 1881–1906 in Moldenhauer, 'Rückversicherung', in Manes, *Versicherungslexikon*, 1st ed. (1909), col. 1045.

[129] *ÖVZ* 1906, 195; *ÖVZ* 1906, 208 *et seq.*; Whitney 1907, 15.

[130] Mackenzie 1907.

[131] But likely since letters in central Europe were delivered within two to three days and telegrams reached their destination within hours.

Union and Norwich Union) had made use of an earthquake clause. The delegates agreed to proceed very restrictively in regulating damages and to reject claims that seemed invalid.[132]

However, the London explanation served merely to mollify the British public and the reinsurers on the continent. In the United States, the British insurance representatives behaved very differently. The issue there was not to defend themselves against damage claims but rather to increase their market share in San Francisco and California at large.[133] The British companies willingly compensated damage claims[134] and advertised in American trade journals that enough money was available to compensate claims.[135] They could afford to be obliging, since nowhere in the world did fire insurance providers command the vast resources available to British companies.[136] The strategy worked, for after a few weeks the Chairman of the Royal Exchange reported to his general assembly that British companies enjoyed special popularity on the American West Coast.[137]

Most of the other companies maintained a rigid course in opposition to the injured parties. In doing so, they produced a storm of outrage that continued into October of 1906.[138] The injured parties mobilised all their might in order to force their opponents to make comprehensive payments for damages. The *Weekly Underwriter* described the situation from the perspective of the insurance provider:

> Thus two parties... stand in opposition to each other. On the one side the insurance companies who desire to pay no compensation besides actual fire damages, and on the other side the angry and noisy insured who insist

---

[132] They especially emphasised the collapse and detonation damages. The resolution was supported by the three more favourably situated companies with respect to their own position ('Earthquake and Fire in San Francisco', *The Coast Review*, June 1906, 236; 'San Francisco und der Standpunkt der englischen Feuerversicherungs-Gesellschaften', *ÖVZ* 1906, 158; 'Die englische Gesellschaften und der Brand von San Francisco', *ÖRev* 1906, 132; *Los Angeles Times* 8 May 1906).

[133] That is why the CEO of the London & Lancashire explained in a general meeting: 'The battle is to the strong, and those who can deal with this occurrence without flinching are the companies which will gain the most benefit from what has taken place' ('London and Lancashire Meeting', *The Financial Times*, 26 April 1906, 5).

[134] The Commercial Union had already explained on May 2, 1906 that it would pay damages if the business interests demanded it even in the absence of a legal obligation. (*ÖVZ* 1906, 158).

[135] *ÖRev* 1906, 132.

[136] Supple 1970, 218.

[137] *ÖVZ* 1906, 195. *The Economist* (1 June 1907) praised the strategy in a similar vein: '[...] a splendid advertisement for the British fire offices'.

[138] Mackenzie 1907.

that everything will be paid and are supported by a hostile daily press that demands wherever possible the immediate incarceration of all insurance executives and the eventual expulsion of all non-compliant insurance companies from California (trans.).[139]

H. F. Atwood, the head of the committee for the investigation of damages in San Francisco, reported that if one listened to the injured, one was forced to believe that a fire storm alone was behind all the damages in San Francisco and that the Richter scale had not moved a pip on the day in question: 'Of two thousand injured parties scarcely twenty will admit that they suffered earthquake damages'(trans.).[140] In California and the United States, it became common, according to a report of a claims adjuster in San Francisco,[141] to designate the disaster not as an earthquake but rather as a *conflagration*. The entire business community of the destroyed city, its inhabitants, the press, the insurance supervision agency and other administrative bodies up to and including the political leadership surrounding Mayor Eugene E. Schmitz and the governor George C. Pardee maintained this party line idiom.[142] Finally, the California Congressman Julius Kahn maintained in the United States House of Representatives that the earthquake had not inflicted any damages outside of a few older districts with dilapidated houses.[143] Greeted by the applause of the assembled congressional representatives, he announced that by the end of the year he would publish the names of the companies unwilling to pay compensation in the *Congressional Record*.

The damage liquidator Otto E. Greely interpreted these procedures as part of a conscious strategy, supported in his view by the Chamber of Commerce and the 'propertied classes' of San Francisco,[144] to retell the story of the disaster so as to blacken the reputations of the insurance providers. His speculation has been substantiated by recent scholarship.[145]

---

[139] Cited in 'Die schwierige Lage der Feuerversicherungs-Gesellschaften in San Francisco', *ÖVZ* 1906, 202.

[140] Atwood, cited in *ÖVZ* 1906, 195.

[141] *ÖVZ* 1906, 318; [Note] in *La Semaine*, 15 July 1906, 5.

[142] *ÖVZ* 1906, 195, 202, 318.

[143] Kahn, 'The San Francisco disaster—honest and dishonest insurance'. Speech in the House of Representatives, June 28, 1906, 3.

[144] *ÖVZ* 1906, 318.

[145] Massive business interests that did not exclusively aim at the avoidance of reductions on the part of the insurance companies formed the basis for the reinterpretation of the disaster's history. For companies like the powerful Southern Pacific Railroad, the issue was to maintain the most favourable business atmosphere on the West Coast. For this purpose, the public had to be persuaded that the danger of earthquakes on the Pacific

The massive campaign had the desired effect, to the disadvantage of the insurance companies.[146] If the liquidators wanted to negotiate any deductions, they were forced to deal with the 'new' history.[147]

This change in the situation destroyed the hopes of the insurance providers to arrive at a rapid and favourable regulation of damages.[148] The adjusters attempted to document the destructive effects of the earthquake by introducing eyewitness accounts, referring to the earliest newspaper articles,[149] presenting their collection of photographs, and examining the tremors and destruction of individual buildings by means of scientific methodology.[150] At the same time, the directors of the insurance companies began to recognise that the differences of opinion concerning the obligations of the insurance providers must be eliminated and their future conduct coordinated. On the 31st of May, 1906, the representatives of eighty-seven American, fifteen British, six German insurance companies and one company each from Austria, Sweden and New Zealand[151] met behind closed doors in the offices of the Phoenix Insurance Company in Brooklyn, New York.[152] They discussed the proposal to reimburse 75% of the insured damages and to reject 25% of the earthquake-caused damages. Sixty-one of the 111 companies present adopted the proposal, since it seemed to them to greatly facilitate the settlement of the damages, to speed up the work and to reduce the large costs of ascertaining the

---

coast was minor (Hansen and Condon 1989, 108 et seq., 112, 120; Strupp 2004, 165 et seq.; Steinberg 2000, 27 et seq.).

[146] Leading seismologists still claimed years later that research on earthquake dangers was impossible because of the manipulation of public opinion (Lawson 1911, 1 et seq.; Branner 1913; compare Hansen and Condon 1989, 109 et seq., 120).

[147] La Semaine (26 August 1906, 6) reports that among the first 2,000 claimants to testify under oath against one company, not a single one of them admitted to having suffered earthquake damages.

[148] Manes, Masius' Rundschau 1906, 162.

[149] Whitney 1906, 22.

[150] ÖVZ 1906, 202, 246, 313; The Weekly Underwriter, cited in ÖRev 1906, 177.

[151] The criterion for the choice of the foreign companies was apparently the existence of a separate place of business in the United States. At least nine of the invited companies did not accept the invitation. The names and the votes of the participating companies can be found in the table listing the companies playing a role in the San Francisco disaster in the Annexe.

[152] Reports of the New York Conference: 'Die Abschätzungsbasis der Schäden in San Francisco', ÖRev 1906, 159; Mackenzie 1907; 'Die zur Ordnung der Versicherungsschäden in San Francisco vereinbarten Regeln', Der Versicherungsfreund, 20 July 1906; ÖVZ 1906, 202, 319.

damages. In addition, these companies agreed upon common guidelines for the regulation of claims.[153]

Eighteen of the companies abstained, and thirty-two voted against the 'New York Agreement'. The latter group demanded that each obligation be completely met and each individual case handled according to its specific circumstances. The point of orientation should not be the proven damages, but rather the former value of the insured property stated in the policy. Here, deductions, termed in American parlance 'deductions from the face of the policy',[154] could be made. Without being explicit, the companies in opposition announced a policy of complete indemnification of the claims of the insured parties.[155] Many of these companies were able to replace the damages without any problems and hoped to advertise their companies in the bargain. They were regarded in business circles in San Francisco as 'old, substantial companies with a reputation for honourable, straightforward methods'.[156] Others had not included in their policies sufficient earthquake clauses and in any event had no hope of reaching viable compromises with their insured clients.[157]

The insurance representatives in New York failed to create a permanent and sustainable agreement. On the 31st of May, they left open the possibility to hold additional deliberations. But the next morning, the Californian newspapers reported extensively on the results and the details of the meeting. The local press—in contrast to the *New York Times*, which praised the proposal of the companies offering 75%[158]—derisively dubbed the companies striving to achieve the 75% results the 'six-bits companies'.[159] The other companies willing to pay compensation were termed 'dollar for

[153] Report of the Committee of Five to the 'Thirty-five Companies' on the San Francisco conflagration, April 18–21, 1906. (1907—BL), 12 *et seq.* German trans. in *ÖRev* 1906, 159; more detailed in *Der Versicherungsfreund*, 20 July 1906, 1 *et seq.* as well as of 1 June 1907, 1 *et seq.* (Insurance Press). Partial French trans. [note] in *La Semaine*, 1 July 1906, 6.

[154] Whitney 1906, 26.

[155] This apparent generosity largely depended on the fact that the buildings in San Francisco were underinsured. On the average, 60% of the value was insured, 40% uninsured and also not covered by coinsurance (Mackenzie 1907; Whitney 1906, 26; 'Buildings Underinsured', *The Coast Review*, May 1906, 208).

[156] Whitney 1906, 21.

[157] [Note] in *La Semaine*, 5 August 1906, 7.

[158] The New York Times, however, praised the suggestion of the "six bits-companies", cited in *ÖRev* 1906, 177.

[159] A twist, of course, of the derogatory expression for something of little value, a 'two-bit' operation worth only twenty-five cents.

dollar companies' because of their willingness to pay a dollar in compensation for every dollar insured.[160]

The insurance providers' faith in a discreet treatment of their positions was dashed, and acute disgruntlement soon developed between the companies with divergent positions.[161] The insurers, however, still hoped that agreement might be reached in the negotiations conducted by their California representatives. By cable, the branch directors received the New York decisions[162] and met on the 7th of June 1906 in San Francisco. But here too, differences of opinion largely disturbed the proceedings.[163] And thus, the death knell sounded for the prospects of a common-cause procedure of the insurers.

2.1.6.2. *The Escalation of the Conflicts over Damages*

In mid-June 1906, the situation in San Francisco was more complicated than ever.[164] Each insurance company set up its own regulations for claims settlements.[165] The thirty-two 'dollar for dollar companies' left the 'General Adjustment Bureau'. On the 21st of June, they and three other companies opened their own claims office in the famous Ferry Building in San Francisco, and on the 10th of July a 'Committee of Five' moved into the building in order to regulate the large damages of the thirty-five companies.[166] In the same building, the San Francisco Chamber of Commerce had also set up an office just after the earthquake.[167] The shared roof symbolised the growing symbiosis between the companies that desired to render full compensation and their creditors.

From this point on, four classes of insurance companies can be distinguished in terms of claims settlements. The first group comprised the thirty-five companies who desired to settle claims in a comprehensive manner. They claimed responsible for about half of the total amount of damages in San Francisco, some 42,077 claims; however, some of the companies had issued merely a small number of contracts.[168] The second group consisted

---

[160] Mackenzie 1907.
[161] ÖVZ 1906, 319; Whitney 1906, 20.
[162] ÖRev 1906, 159.
[163] Mackenzie 1907.
[164] Prange 1906, 107.
[165] Mackenzie 1907; Whitney 1906, 21.
[166] Report of the Committee of Five to the 'Thirty-five Companies' on the San Francisco conflagration, April 18–21, 1906. (1907—BL), 15 *et seq.*
[167] San Francisco Chamber of Commerce, Annals (1909), 27.
[168] Marks, The San Francisco story—April 18–21 (1909); ÖVZ 1906, 216; *The New York Times*, cited in ÖRev 1906, 177.

of companies that did not want to pay any more than they felt obligated to pay according to their own estimates. Some maintained this position because they were financially weak and were forced to demand payments from their shareholders in order to raise capital without weakening their financial situation, others because they did not recognise an obligation greater than the one that they had contracted to pay.[169] The third group of companies attempted to compensate the damages in every way possible and to use all of their resources in order to ensure that business operations continued to function.[170] In many cases, this was only attainable if the insured parties agreed to accept unfavourable settlements and thus helped to maintain the solvency of their insurers. Thus, some of the smaller, and even the larger, insurance companies could survive, among them the severely damaged Fireman's Fund.[171] The other companies were either already bankrupt[172] or put off the compensation payments and thus merely delayed their inevitable bankruptcy.[173] About a third of the small companies in this group were severely damaged.[174]

In the meantime, the disputes in San Francisco became more and more frequent. The attempts of alleged injured parties to swindle insurance providers caused problems.[175] The California insurance commissioner, E. Myron Wolf, thus issued the warning to the insured parties that 'this kind of behaviour simply provides unethical insurance companies with the pretext for short-changing honest insured parties' (trans.).[176] He recommended that they would be better advised to demonstrate solidarity with the affected community of the insured.[177]

The insured followed the insurance commissioner's recommendation. The services of lawyers and notaries public who promised, for a fee, to achieve recognition of the claims of the insured enjoyed increasing popularity. The insurance providers, on the other hand, were suspicious of

---

[169] Agreeing [note] in *La Semaine*, 26 August 1906, 6.
[170] Fuld, 'Nochmals die Erdbeben in Amerika und die Versicherungsgesellschaften', *ÖVZ* 1906, 307 *et seq.*
[171] *ÖVZ* 1906, 276; Mackenzie 1907.
[172] For example, the Security Fire: *ÖVZ* 1906, 208 *et seq.*
[173] A. M. Best Co. 1907; Atwood cited in *ÖVZ* 1906, 195; [Note] in *La Semaine*, 2 December 1906, 6.
[174] [Note] in *La Semaine*, 16 December 1906, 6.
[175] *ÖVZ* 1906, 208 *et seq.*, 216; [Note] in *La Semaine*, 16 September 1906, 6.
[176] Statement to the *Insurance Record*, cited in *ÖVZ* 1906, 235.
[177] [Note] in *La Semaine*, 4 November 1906, 8.

the 'eyewitness factories' (trans.) in which the injured parties allegedly obtained every sworn evidence they required.[178]

The Californian press added fuel to the fire. Above all, the *San Francisco Examiner* pilloried the insurance providers who proved uncooperative.[179] Reports circulated that individual insurance representatives and adjusters were threatened with lynching.[180] The insurance commissioner increased the pressure on the companies, demanded information on all their obligations and threatened those who opposed his demands with the cancellation of their licenses.[181]

At the same time, the number of complaints in insurance industry journals against the city and the federal authorities increased and alleged that government officials were interfering unduly in the settlement activities[182] and were even helping the insured to defraud the insurance companies.[183] The insurance providers regarded a telegram from Governor Pardee and Mayor Schmitz addressed to all the involved companies as the peak of this audacity. In this telegram, the politicians demanded comprehensive replacement benefits to be paid to the injured parties and alleged that the earthquake had only caused serious damage in a very few cases.[184] As a result, many companies refused to cooperate with government officials wherever they could.[185]

2.1.6.3. *The Preparation for Juridical Disputes*

By the end of June, a little light had penetrated the darkness of the antagonists' positions. New estimates of the financial situation had become known. On the 30th of June, the New York Superintendent of Insurance

---

[178] Mackenzie, cited in *Der Versicherungsfreund*, 20 May 1907, 1. The *Hamburger Nachrichten* reported on these 'claims settlement offices', as cited in *ÖVZ* 1906, 230, 208 *et seq.*

[179] *The Examiner* is cited in *ÖRev* 1906, 270 *et seq.*; [Note] in *La Semaine*, 29 July 1906, 6, speaks of a *campagne de haine*.

[180] *ÖVZ* 1906, 319.

[181] Wolf threatened to recommend this action to the regulatory officials in other states. (*The Weekly Underwriter*, cited in *ÖRev* 1906, 177; Whitney 1906, 23 *et seq.*; [Note] in *La Semaine*, 4 November 1906, 8 (according to a report of the *London Times*). [Note] in *La Semaine*, 23 September 1906, 6, describes how the Insurance Commissioner from Nevada, Davis, threatened the London & Lancashire with the removal of their license because the company had treated poor insurance clients worse than their wealthier clients.

[182] *ÖVZ* 1906, 195, 208 *et seq.*

[183] For example, officials had refused to specify how much they had taken from private warehouses to take care of the population that insured businessmen later declared destroyed by fire (*ÖVZ* 1906, 246).

[184] 'Governor's and Mayor's Joint Telegram', *The Coast Review*, June 1906, 244 *et seq.*

[185] [Note] in *La Semaine*, 26 August 1906, 6; *ÖVZ* 1906, 208 *et seq.*

published an official study of the total amount of damages. He fixed the
sum of the anticipated damages at about $133 million.[186] Earlier fears of
the insurance branch now appeared to have been exaggerated. The news
that many American companies had already paid a quota of 75% was
greeted with enthusiasm. English insurance providers, it was reported,
had completely reimbursed their insurance claims.[187]

Two weeks later however, attentive observers could compare the statistics of the New York insurance commissioner with those from San Francisco. A projection of the 'Committee of Fifteen on Adjustments' arrived at
the figure of $100 million for the business district in San Francisco alone.[188]
The figures from New York were thus cast into doubt. An estimate by the
journal *Insurance Record* placed the total claims of the insured at $296
million.[189] If additional deductions of about 25% could be achieved, the
damages still amounted to $219 million. The reinsurers, therefore, had to
anticipate absorbing more than one-third of these costs.[190]

Slowly, the economic situation began to clarify. But those involved and
observers alike sensed that numerous legal battles were still in the offing.[191]
This impression was based upon the experiences shared by the 'six-bit
companies'. Many of the insured parties refused to relinquish a quarter

---

[186] The reports in the European press on the statistics presented by the New York
authorities were very conflicting. Cf. 'Die Versicherungsschäden in San Francisco', *ÖRev*
1906, 208; '113 Millionen Dollars [sic] Versicherungsverluste in San Francisco', *ÖVZ* 1906,
158; *Berliner Tageblatt*, 6/7 July 1906.

[187] *ÖRev* 1906, 208; Greely, cited in *ÖRev* 1906, 271. [Note] in *La Semaine*, 11 November
1906, reported, however, while citing the *Insurance Press*, that the Commercial Union, Palatine, Alliance and Norwich Union regulated between 50% and 75% of the claims against
them.

[188] The statistics from the beginning of July included 166 concluded damage claims
from the 1,221 cases registered with the Committee in the business quarter in San
Francisco. The total insured value comprised about $19 million, from which $5 million
(over 26%) were deducted ('Die Versicherungs- und Entschädigungssummen in San
Francisco', *Der Versicherungsfreund*, 1 August 1906 with reference to the *Westliche Post*, 10
July 1906 and *ÖVZ* 1906, 235).

[189] *ÖVZ* 1906, 235; 'Zur Lage von San Francisco', *ÖRev* 1906, 226.

[190] Results of a projection based upon the figures from sixty-nine fire insurance
companies:

Gross damages of the 69 companies	$167,129,063
Saved or not damaged	$24,094,455 (14.4% of the gross damages)
Remainder (net damages)	$143,034,608
Share of the direct insurers of the net	
damages	$91.650.948 (64.1% or 54.8% of gross damages)
Share of the reinsurers of net damages	$51,383,660 (35.9% or 30.8% of gross damages)
Premiums of 69 Companies (1905)	$2,010,591

Source: *ÖVZ* 1906, 246; all above monetary figures are in US dollars.

[191] Atwood, cited in *ÖVZ* 1906, 195; *Weekly Underwriter*, cited in *ÖVZ* 1906, 202.

of the insured damages because they hoped to reach more beneficial settlements by going to court. However, the insured whose houses had been severely damaged by the earthquake were more prepared to reach settlements.[192]

The establishment of the 'Policyholders' Protective League' on June 26, 1906, announced an additional intensification of the confrontation between the insurance providers and their clients.[193] This organisation encouraged its members to take legal action against the insurance companies and supported them in doing so.

The Policyholders' League united the economic power of the largest companies and most important organisations in San Francisco.[194] Each of the insured could become a member; the founding members commanded assets of about $100 million.[195] They elected Henry Weinstock as their chairman.[196] The economic organisation provided all the other trustees.[197]

Table 6. The Trustees of the Policyholders' League. 'The Policyholders' League', *The Adjuster* 33, August 1906, 64 *et seq.*[198]

Trustee at Large	Colonel Harry Weinstock (Weinstock, Lubin & Co.)
Merchants' Association	Andrew Carrigan (Dunham, Carrigan, and Hayden Co.)
	Albert Dernham (Buckingham & Hecht)
Chamber of Commerce	Charles H. Crocker (H. S. Crocker & Co.)
	Rudolph Taussig (Louis Taussig & Co.)
Merchants' Exchange	James D. Phelan (Mutual Savings Bank)
	F. W. Van Sicklen (Dodge, Sweeney & Co.)
San Francisco Board of Trade	Charles Holbrook (Holbrook, Merrill & Stetson)
	Joseph D. Grant (Murphy, Grant & Co.)
Manufacturers' and Producers' Association of California	Frederick W. Dohrmann (Nathan-Dohrmann Co.)
	A. S. Barbaro (Italian-American Bank)

---

[192] *ÖVZ* 1906, 216.

[193] It already received unusual attention at its establishment. The internationally read daily newspaper *Journal of Commerce* published two articles about it in its edition of 27 June, 1906, 13.

[194] A memorial writing respectfully speaks of the league as an 'organization of the merchants and capitalists of San Francisco' (Record of the Fireman's Fund Insurance Company in the San Francisco disaster of April 18th–21st, 1906 (1907—BL), 6). Similarly, Whitney 1906, 41.

[195] 'Policyholders' Plan', *The Journal of Commerce*, 27 June 1906, 13.

[196] Ibid.

[197] Ibid.

[198] Ibid; 'The Policyholders' League', *The Adjuster* 33, August 1906, 64 *et seq.*

Table 6 (*cont.*)

San Francisco Clearing-House Bank) Association[199] Associated Clearing Bank of San Francisco	Charles K. McIntosh (San Francisco National Joseph A. Donohoe (Donohoe-Kelly Banking Co.) R. M. Tobin (Hibernia Savings and Loan Society) George A. Storney (Mutual Savings Bank) John U. Calkins (Mechanics' Savings Bank)

In the first days of August, the Policyholders' League announced its programme that had been agreed upon by its trustees and adopted in its by-laws. The first five goals were:

1. To induce insurance companies to make prompt adjustments.
2. To investigate, discuss and report upon any company's declining liability on technical and legal grounds, and to organize incorporations of trusteeships to collect such claims in the courts.
3. To ascertain whether companies actually require time in which to pay in full, and if so to arrange on behalf of policyholders for such payment.
4. To secure by suit or otherwise from insolvent insurance companies the best possible results for policyholders.
5. To give public endorsements to all insurance companies that treat San Francisco fairly in the present calamity....[200]

The Protective League desired to react flexibly in response to the economic situation and the insurance companies' willingness to pay compensation. With this strategy, it largely contributed to the survival of the Californian company Fireman's Fund.[201]

The Policyholders' League identified their main opponents in Germany and Austria.[202] In fact, the *Österreichische Phönix* ('Austrian Phoenix',

---

[199] The Clearing-House Association was regarded as 'the strongest financial institution on the Pacific Coast, representing with their combined capital hundreds of millions of dollars'. Its support of the Policyholders' League was of great importance because it and the banks such as the Associated Clearing Bank of San Francisco had provided advance financing for the rebuilding of the city. At the same time, it represented policyholders of great importance, for the banks had concluded many fire insurance policies prior to the earthquake for mortgaged buildings in order to protect themselves against the loss of their securities ('Coast Notes' (according to *Insurance World*), *The Adjuster* 33, August 1906, 69).

[200] *The Adjuster* 33, August 1906, 65; 'Policyholders' Protective League/ Board of trustees: statement of purposes', *The Journal of Commerce*, 4 August 1906, 13.

[201] Report of the special committee 1906, 41 *et seq.* (*Fireman's Fund Archives*: 4-1-3-4-42; 0408).

[202] [Note] in *La Semaine*, 26 August 1906, 6.

Vienna), the Strasbourg company *Rhein & Mosel* ('Rhine & Moselle', Strasbourg) and the *Transatlantische* (Transatlantic) and *Norddeutsche Feuer* ('North German Fire') Company from Hamburg refused to pay compensation in marked obstinacy.[203]

2.1.7. *Court Cases and Settlements*

Many insurance providers believed right from the beginning that in view of the substantive legal situation, they were by no means obligated to pay compensation. They expected that their legal position would be confirmed in courts of law.[204] For this reason, they sometimes rejected the claims of injured parties in a rough-and-ready manner. Thus, the New York company Williamsburg City Fire returned all the damage files to their insured parties with references to their earthquake clause. Its refusal was based on the expectation that the other insured parties would insist on equal treatment according to the initial compensation of individual insured parties. In its readiness to defend its legal position in courts of law, the company was aware of the support of several important American and European institutions that also counted on court verdicts to clarify the legal situation.[205]

By the summer of 1906, few court cases had actually been filed. In August, the Policyholders' League announced that they would be taking up the first cases against German and Austrian companies.[206] On September 20, 1906, some 150 court cases were pending against American and foreign insurance companies according to the French insurance journal *La Semaine*.[207] By 1909, their number had grown to several hundred.[208] Statistics are lacking on the empirical relationship between the resolution of conflicts in and out of court and on the subject matter of the actions and the results. The low number of court cases in relation to the 90,000 cases of damages is remarkable.[209] However, comparable cases were often

---

[203] 'Geschäftsbericht des Kaiserlichen Aufsichtsamts für Privatversicherung für das Jahr 1906' (Business report of the Imperial Supervisory Agency for Private Insurance for 1906), *Stenographische Berichte über die Verhandlungen des Reichstags, XII. Legislaturperiode, I. Session, Anlagen*, no. 503, 2666 *et seq.*

[204] 'Zur San Francisco-Katastrophe', *ÖRev* 1906, 130.

[205] [Note] in *La Semaine*, 5 August 1906, 7.

[206] [Note] in *La Semaine*, 23 September 1906, 6.

[207] [Note] in *La Semaine*, 14 October 1906, 6.

[208] *Journal of Commerce*, 11 May 1909, cited in MR/A E-25 running no. 54 (Helvetia/San Francisco Schäden/RA Kisskalt II).

[209] Whitney 1906, 52. Bament (1973, 88) and Marks (The San Francisco story—April 18–21 [1909]) speak of a figure of over 100,000 cases.

adjudicated in class-actions suits. Behind the few hundred cases, many more additional individual conflicts were hidden.

In Europe, little was known about the court cases and the settlements in California. The readers of insurance journals learned of only some of the more spectacular cases.[210] However, a fire insurance provider remarked to the *Daily Express* that the court costs would be the highest in the history of the insurance business.[211] This observation led the German insurance legal expert Otto Hagen to advise the insurance providers to give in.[212] Whether the companies nevertheless obtained more favourable results in court than predicted, as Otto Greely conjectured—he was convinced that insurance providers had paid damages that they would have avoided had they gone to court[213]—is uncertain. Equally unproven remain the charges stemming from Europe that judges lacked independence and objectivity.[214] In order to counter such accusations, the Court of Appeals Judge William W. Morrow mandated that the insurance cases be tried in courts outside of San Francisco.[215] Nevertheless, the important trial involving the California Wine Association against the Commercial Union was handled before the Superior Court of the State of California 'in and for the City and County of San Francisco'.[216]

---

[210] In Europe, only the quality European journals and the *Journal of Commerce*, whose edition reached the continent after a delay of a few days, were read regularly.

[211] *ÖVZ* 1906, 148.

[212] Hagen, *DJZ* 1906, col. 744 *et seq.*

[213] *ÖVZ* 1906, 313.

[214] The article 'San Francisco und die Feuerversicherungs-Gesellschaften' reports of the "pressure that the Californian insured exert through the compliant American courts", *Der Versicherungsfreund*, 1 December 1906, 5 *et seq.*; Mackenzie declared, "[...] an appeal to State courts is useless," and, "insurance companies will not find justice in California at this time." R. K. Mackenzie, cited after: 'Erdbeben und Brände in San Francisco im April 1905 [sic!]', *Der Versicherungsfreund*, 1 June 1907, 3; similar: Fuld, 'Nochmals die Erdbeben in Amerika und die Versicherungsgesellschaften', *ÖVZ* 1906, 307 *et seq.*; Laband, article in the *DJZ* of 1 August 1908, reprinted in *Der Versicherungsfreund*, 20 August 1907, 6; statement of the chairman of the Royal Exchange in *ÖVZ* 1906, 195; Sofonea, Londra, Amburgo, San Francisco: tre sinistri „storici", 34.

[215] *ÖVZ* 1906, 265.

[216] California Wine Assn., et al. vs. Commercial Union Ass. Co., et al., Testimony, vol. 1, file 1, 1 *et seq.* In addition, 'neutral' juries also rendered decisions against insurance companies, for example, against the Connecticut Fire, which in a Santa Rosa court case had succeeded in having a number of farmers without any direct interest in San Francisco appointed as jury members (*The Policy-Holder*, 20 May 1908/*Weekly Underwriter*, copy in: MR/A E-25 running no. 53 [Helvetia/San Francisco Schäden/RA Kisskalt I]).

2.1.7.1. *Law of Evidence and Levels of Review: Steps in Favour of the Injured Parties*

In the courts, considerable difficulties arose in clarifying the judicially relevant facts of a case. The insured had to prove that they had concluded a contract with the sued company and that fire damages that corresponded to the promised coverage had, in fact, occurred. These aspects, however, appeared not to have created any problems, for no cases in which the insured could not provide any evidence have come to light. The courts were happy with *prima facie* evidence. This meant that sworn evidence of the injured parties and circumstantial evidence based upon official investigations were generally sufficient.[217] The waiver of complete proof stemmed from the experience that a lot of evidence usually went lost in the case of fires.[218]

The insurance companies could in return object to the claims for indemnification. These objections had to receive the judge's recognition as admissible exceptions. At this point, the problems in substantive law were dealt with, especially questions regarding the validity and interpretation of the specific clauses of exclusion. If the court recognised a clause as valid, the insurance company had to provide the proof of the claimed facts of the case that corresponded to the clause. Here, a higher degree of evidence was required than the factual basis for a writ offered by the injured party. If the contract covered fallen building clauses, it was most important to prove how much of the building had already collapsed before the fire broke out. The same question also arose when no fallen building clause had been agreed upon but when the company wanted to claim deductions from the amount insured, and when damages from explosions had occurred. In the case of the earthquake clauses, it was essential to prove the causality between the earthquake and the fire damages.[219] The decision as to whether the facts submitted by the company were sufficient to prove the case in court was a matter for the jury to decide. Finally, the plaintiff could offer counter-evidence that was then dealt with. It was at this point that the judge then made his decision.[220]

---

[217] Hagen, *DJZ* 1906 col. 744; Mackenzie 1907.

[218] Complete proof was called *conclusive evidence*, which was more difficult to provide than prima facie evidence, for the former required witnesses, objects or documents (Mackenzie 1907).

[219] Mackenzie 1907; [Note] in *La Semaine*, 11 November 1906, 8.

[220] This interplay can be followed through two levels of jurisdiction in the case of the California Wine Association, et al., vs. the Commercial Union, et al. Transcript of the trials

In the cases in San Francisco, the legal requirements for the proof of alleged facts upon which juries were required to base their decisions did not deviate from existing law. A judge of the United States Circuit Court thus declared to his jury of twelve: '[…] the defendant must [not] prove such fact to a demonstration or absolute certainty, but only to a degree of proof as produces conviction of unprejudiced mind'.[221] It was thus sufficient that the persuasive power of the prima facie evidence be exceeded by the defendants, the insurance companies. But herein lay the structural disadvantage for the defendant in comparison to the plaintiff. Most of the cases were decided in favour of the plaintiff because the insurance provider failed to provide evidence contrary to the appearance of a specific state of affairs. Only in a few cases did the ruins offer proof as to the process of the destruction. Eyewitnesses were required, but by this time, the inhabitants of the burned out parts of the city were scattered to the four winds, and as victims of the disaster, they were not always willing to testify against other injured parties.[222]

A year after the earthquake, the amount of court proceedings pending in the Californian courts had reached its peak. Many cases were about to reach culmination in the trial courts. In this situation, the Californian legislature granted the insurance commissioner the authorisation to curtail legal disputes. In an amendment of the Political Code of the 8th of March, 1907,[223] he was permitted to revoke the license of foreign companies that appealed a case originating in the jurisdiction of the state court in California to the United States Circuit Court.[224] Such a restriction of the stages of appeal had earlier applied in California[225] and received the highest recognition in case law.[226] Then, the protection of the insured against unreasonably long judicial procedures had been the main issue, but now,

---

in suits against the Commercial Union Assurance Company, Ltd., London: mss., and its subsidiary, the Commercial Union Fire Assurance Company, New York (1908–1910), Bancroft Library.

[221] Judge Hon. William C. Van Fleet, Statement The Court, in: California Wine Assn., et al. vs. Commercial Union Ass. Co., et al., Testimony, vol. 6, 1685.

[222] Mackenzie 1907; Marks, The San Francisco story—April 18–21 (1909); Whymper, cited in Supple 1970, 248.

[223] *Partial recodification of the insurance laws of the State of California* 1907, chapter 119.

[224] *Partial recodification of the insurance laws of the State of California* 1907, chapter 119/ Political Code Article XVI, §608.

[225] Political Code, sec. 595; amended, Statutes 1873–74, 8; 1877–78, 13. *Insurance Laws of the State of California* 1904, 7.

[226] Harrigan vs. Home Life Insurance Company, 128 Ca. 539, *Insurance Laws of the State of California* 1904, 8.

some observers believed that fears that the court practice favouring the insured up to this point would be reversed were decisive.[227]

The first of three companies whose license the Insurance Commission Myron E. Wolf revoked was the Commercial Union of London mentioned above. The same fate soon struck the Palatine of London and the Williamsburg City Fire of Brooklyn, New York.[228] The three companies, in appealing to the Circuit Court, had taken an enormous financial risk, as they represented some of the largest insurers in San Francisco, and they had lost.

2.1.7.2. *Cases Involving Damages Caused by Partial Building Collapse*

In most of the damage cases, the injured parties declared that their property had survived the earthquake without any damages. The insurance adjusters had, of course, believed few of these claims, but they were hardly ever able to refute them.[229] In view of the difficulty in proving their cases, most of the insurance companies adopted a conciliatory manner and attempted to settle out of court by negotiating reductions in the compensation for earthquake damages.[230]

Apparently, only six large companies succeeded in court in being released from their compensation obligation in isolated cases on the basis of the fallen building clause. The companies were able to prove that the fires had broken out after the collapse of the buildings.[231] In the process, a casuistry relating to the fallen building clause developed that had been non-existent up to then.[232]

2.1.7.3. *Cases involving Fire Damage*

Just shortly after the earthquake, the *Coast Review* had expressed doubt that cases based upon the earthquake clause could be won:

---

[227] *La Semaine* expresses this presumption in its issue 4 November 1906, 8.

[228] [Note] in *La Semaine*, 1908, 24, mentions an open letter from the English Counsel on the matter.

[229] Seiler 1942, 28.

[230] *ÖVZ* 1906, 134.

[231] Seiler 1942, 28.

[232] A. M. Best Co. (1907, 13) speaks of a '"material portion" of the insured building' that must collapse: 'A falling of a chimney or plastering cannot be considered as the falling of a substantial or material part of a building. The original intent of this clause was to provide against claims arising from the collapse of buildings because of structural weakness, and the Courts discriminate between buildings which fall because of some inherent weakness and those which are demolished by some outside agency'.

How would the defendant 'quake' company prove that an earthquake
caused the fire? In a very few instances fire started immediately after the
quake; but in the course of the three days many fires were started in widely
separated places. These fires were not caused directly or indirectly by the
quake; certainly no defendant company would prove that they were ... Fires
were started by accident, firebugs and by pyromaniacs.

Nor can it be proved that, with few exemptions, any 'loss' was due directly
or indirectly to the quake's total destruction of the water supply, for until
the very last there was some water, and streams of water were thrown on
the flames in many localities.[233]

The prediction made by the *Coast Review* turned out to be correct. Most
of the legal action involving the earthquake clause ended with decisions
against the insurance companies, as these were unable to offer evidence
of a causal relationship between the earthquake and the individual fire
damages.

The principle of the *prima facie* evidence discussed above also applied
to the question of the cause of the damages. Circumstantial evidence or
even a corresponding oath of the injured party[234] was thus sufficient to
prove that the fire in the city had caused the specific damages.[235]

Courts accepted the various earthquake clauses that were offered in
rebuttal by the insurance companies as acceptable objections.[236] Nevertheless, some cases ended before the admission/acceptance of the counter-evidence because the judge's interpretation of the clauses differed
from that of the insurers. For example, Judge Whitson of the United States
Circuit Court expressed the view in the case of T. I. Bergin vs. Commercial Union[237] that it was irrelevant whether the quake had destroyed the
water mains and thereby made the extinguishing of the fire impossible.
The lawyers for the insurance company had attempted to demonstrate
an indirect causality between the earthquake and the damages. Whitson,
however, declared that the wording of the stipulated earthquake clause
did not cover the indirect causation of damages.[238]

---

[233] 'Earthquake Clause Policies', *The Coast Review*, May 1906, 214.
[234] Mackenzie 1907.
[235] Hagen, *DJZ* 1906, col. 744.
[236] Drumm, 'Die Beweislast bei der Erdbebenklausel in den deutschen Feuerversicherungsverträgen', *ZVersWiss* 7 (1907), 374 *et seq.*
[237] Court proceedings of 15 January 1907; Mackenzie 1907. Compare Wise's statement
(Defendant Commercial Union) in California Wine Assn. vs. Commercial Union F. I. Co.,
Testimony, vol. 1, 14.
[238] Judge Whitson is cited as stating: 'I cannot help thinking that the words "direct or
indirect loss or damages" refer to the direct or indirect loss or damages that were caused by
the fire and not to possible disruptions in facilities that are designed to extinguish fires'. At

Neither did the representatives of the Williamsburg City Fire succeed in persuading the judges of their interpretation of the earthquake clause. The company had argued up to the highest court of appeal, the Ninth U.S. Circuit Court of Appeals, in favour of its interpretation that in view of the exclusions in its policy it was not liable '[for loss] caused directly or indirectly by invasion, or for loss or damage by or through any volcanoes, earthquakes, hurricanes etc....'.[239] In the specific case, the damages had originated after the fire from another house had jumped to the insured building.[240] The court decided that the exclusion of 'indirectly caused damages' referred solely to a case of invasion, for otherwise the words 'direct or indirect' in connection with the case of an earthquake would have to have been repeated.[241]

The number of cases that failed on the basis of the differences in interpretation of the earthquake clause was limited. Judges generally recognised the clause as relevant and simply required the insurance companies to demonstrate the alleged causality between earthquake and fire damages,[242] which the insurers almost always failed to do.

In the extensive materials that are still extant from the case of the California Wine Association vs. the Commercial Union, the causality problem is especially well documented. The California Wine Association, a group in control of the California wine business,[243] had its most important production outlet in South of Market in San Francisco, where the first fires following the earthquake broke out. The California Wine Association suffered a loss of $90,000 in one of its wine cellars, and the trial, commencing on the January 3, 1908, was held in the Superior Court of the State of California, the Honourable Frank J. Mirasky, Judge, presiding.[244] The insurance company defended itself with reference to the earthquake clause: '... the insurance

---

issue was the first trial in which this relationship was tested, and the case was important as a precedent. The decision of the appellate court was expected in May of 1907, but before it could be made the Insurance Commissioner revoked the license of the Commercial Union of London (Mackenzie, cited in *Der Versicherungsfreund*, 20 May 1907, 2).

[239] 'Zur Erdbebenklausel in der Feuerversicherung', *ÖVZ*, 5 December 1908, 335.

[240] [Note] in *La Semaine*, 1908, 808.

[241] *ÖVZ*, 5 December 1908; [Note] in *La Semaine*, 1908, 808. Judge Van Fleet had arrived at a similar decision in the lower court ('Earthquake Clause Was Not Good', *The Coast Review*, November 1907, 637; 'Quake Ruling of Judge Van Fleet Upheld', *The Coast Review*, October 1908, 1039).

[242] Mackenzie 1907; [Note] in *La Semaine*, 11 November 1906, 8.

[243] Peninou and Unzelman 2001, 76 *et seq.*, 92.

[244] California Wine Assn. vs. Commercial Union F. I. Co., Testimony, vol. 1, file 1, 1 *et seq.*

company shall not be liable for loss which was caused directly or indirectly by earthquake'.[245] The lawyer for the Commercial Union, Miller, announced that he would prove that the earthquake had caused not only the considerable damage to the city's infrastructure but also the actual outbreak of the fires.[246] The statements of witnesses for the parties on the course of the fire comprised about 3,000 pages in five volumes and was produced and argued in thirty-four hearings. The court finally decided in favour of the plaintiff. With the aid of new lawyers, the Commercial Union risked the appeal to the U.S. Circuit Court, where the presiding Judge, the Honourable William C. Van Fleet, presided. The case was adjudicated in connection with twenty-four other damages that had originated at the same place in a similar fashion.[247] The evidence that the lawyers of the Commercial Union presented to the jury[248] filled an additional six volumes with more than 1,600 pages.

After the hearing of evidence on July 9, 1910, Judge Van Fleet once again summarised the principles of the causality doctrine for the jury. The jury had to deliver a decision in each of the individual twenty-five cases that had been argued.[249] Van Fleet began by pointing out that it was important whether a fire was caused directly or indirectly by the earthquake.[250] In both cases, the liability would be null and void for the respective insurer. A sufficient causality, according to his explanation, existed when the earthquake was a *proximate cause* of the resulting damages.

In California, the common law that applied in such cases distinguished between *proximate cause* and *remote cause* in the sense of a primary cause and an intermediate cause. Van Fleet explained these terms at some length:

---

[245] 'Opening Statement Defendant', California Wine Assn. vs. Commercial Union F. I. Co., Testimony, vol. 1, file 1, 8.

[246] 'Opening Statement Defendant', California Wine Assn. vs. Commercial Union F. I. Co., Testimony, vol. 1, file 1, 12.

[247] Statement Van Ness (Counsel California Wine Assn., plaintiff), California Wine Assn., et al. vs. Commercial Union Ass. Co., et al., Testimony, vol. 1, 1 *et seq.* The locations were: in the proximity of Bluxome/5th, 4th/Brannan; 3rd between Brannan and Townsend. Statement Sutro (Counsel California Wine Assn., plaintiff), California Wine Assn., et al., vs. Commercial Union Ass. Co., et al., Testimony, vol. 1, 3.

[248] Statement Miller (Counsel Commercial Union, defendant), California Wine Assn., et al., vs. Commercial Union Ass. Co., et al., Testimony, vol. 1, 10 *et seq.*

[249] Statement The Court, California Wine Assn., et al. vs. Commercial Union Ass. Co., et al., Testimony, vol. 6, 1696 *et seq.*

[250] Statement The Court, 1683.

By a 'proximate' cause is here meant that from which the event naturally followed without the intervention of any intermediate cause... When the proximate cause of an effect has been ascertained, the law ceases to inquire further, and attributes the effect exclusively to such a cause.

The proximate cause is not necessarily the last occurrence in point of time. It is that occurrence which produces an unbroken chain of events down to the loss in question so linked together as to form one continuous whole....

When, however, there are two causes of a loss, which are concurrent in point of time, and the damage done by each cannot be distinguished, the predominant, efficient one is regarded as the proximate cause of such loss.[251]

In the explanations that followed, Van Fleet enhanced the doctrine of causality with numerous examples in which the earthquake was presented as a *proximate cause* of fire damage. The point of origin for his imaginary chain of causes was the assumption that the earthquake could itself have caused a fire, say, through knocked over gas lamps and short circuits.[252] But it could also be considered a *proximate cause* of fires if these fires did not begin during or directly after the disaster.[253] His example was a fire that had developed 'uninterruptedly from building to building, from block to block'—until it reached the insured property. Not each and every building must have caught fire in the process; some of them could, for example, have been left out by flying sparks.[254] Even official measures such as detonations would not interrupt the causality in the sense of a *proximate cause*, Van Fleet explained.[255] He classified accidental explosions that caused fires similarly.[256]

The deliberations of the judge are remarkable because he expressed viewpoints that were very close to the notions embraced by the insurance companies on the controversial terrain of earthquake causality. Van Fleet impressed on his jury that in its deliberations it should take into consideration all the circumstances in determining whether it was dealing with a *proximate cause* or a *remote cause*, including the distance of the cause of a fire from the place of destruction, the amount of time between

---

[251] Statement The Court, 1683 *et seq.*
[252] Statement The Court, 1684.
[253] Statement The Court, 1690.
[254] Statement The Court, 1691.
[255] '[...] the fire caused by such official act is to be considered as part of the original fire [...]', Statement The Court, California Wine Assn., et al. vs. Commercial Union Ass. Co., et al., Testimony, vol. 6, 1686 *et seq.*
[256] Statement The Court, 1689 *et seq.*

the outbreak of the fire and the fire damage to the insured property, the force of the wind and its direction. Unusual winds should not prematurely be recognised as intermediate, independent causes, since they could be a consequence of the conflagration that was caused by the earthquake, that is, a part of the causality that could be traced back to the earthquake.

He offered only one example in which the earthquake was not a proximate cause:

> The earthquake may have produced conditions but for which the loss may not have occurred, such, for example, as the destruction of the City's water supply or its fire alarm system; but if you find that the loss in any case was directly caused by fire, the peril insured against [...], then in such case the plaintiff is entitled under the admitted facts to a verdict, notwithstanding it appears that the earthquake produced conditions remotely contributing to that loss.[257]

Van Fleet did not mention an aspect that could have benefitted the insurance companies, an aspect that involved a special liability regulation in the Civil Code that dealt with the law of insurance. Pursuant to section 2628, the liability for damages that depended upon contractually determined causes—such as earthquakes—was cancelled so far as these causes turned out to be a *sine qua non* condition of the specific damages:

> Sec. 2628. If a peril is specifically excepted in a contract of insurance, a loss, which would not have occurred but for such peril, is thereby excepted; although the immediate cause of the loss was a peril which was not excepted.

This section could clash with the principles of liability explained by Van Fleet and which also formed part of the Civil Code.[258] In San Francisco, the fire was frequently recognised as the proximate cause of the damages. However, the earthquake could nevertheless have operated as a *conditio sine qua non* in the sense defined in section 2628 with the legal consequence that the liability was then negated.

The insurance companies also did not include section 2628 in their legal arguments, an omission that could be attributed to the fact that at the beginning of the twentieth century, jurists had deliberately turned

---

[257] Statement The Court, 1683.

[258] Sec. 2626: 'An insurer is liable for a loss of which a peril insured against was the proximate cause; although a peril not contemplated by the contract may have been a remote cause of the loss; but he is not liable for a loss of which the peril insured against was only a remote cause'.

their backs on the codified law of the Civil Code.[259] Also, the applicability of section 2628 had perhaps been denied in earlier cases. In any event, the contradictions inherent in sections 2626 and 2628 were only resolved decades later.[260]

Van Fleet's jury deliberated until June 11, 1910. The foreman of the jury declared that they had reached a verdict in only one of the twenty-five cases:[261] 'We have reached a verdict in one case only and disagreed on all the rest, and we have realized some little time past that it is absolutely futile to attempt to reach a verdict in any other cases'.[262] Judge Van Fleet persuaded the jury to attempt a verdict. Within one day, the twelve jurors reached a unanimous decision on all of the cases and on Sunday June 12, 1910, handed over two packages to the bailiff, one for the plaintiff and one for the defendant. The decisions are not known, but it can be assumed that they were decided in favour of the plaintiffs, that is, against the insurance companies. The legal battle between the California Wine Association and their insurance companies finally ended in the Supreme Court with a victory for the damaged company.[263]

Van Fleet's discussion of causality shattered the lopsided picture that the insurers later painted of the court cases in California. In their presentation, they had failed in their defence against the damage claims solely because of the inflexible restrictions on presenting evidence even though, they argued, the causality between the earthquake and the fire damages had been obvious.[264] The proceedings against the Williamsburg City Fire and the Commercial Union,[265] the *Rhein & Mosel*,[266] the *Transatlantische*

---

[259] Gray, *RabelsZ 50* (1986), 116.

[260] In 1963, the California Supreme Court decided that the *conditio sine qua non* in section 2628 never could be a 'remote cause' and that the 'immediate cause' be understood as the chronologically closest cause ('efficient proximate cause doctrine'); Sabella vs. Wisler (17 January 1963), 377 P.2d, 889 (California 1963).

[261] That case was California Wine Ass. Vs. Palatine (File no. 14,400); Statement The Foreman, California Wine Assn., et al. vs. Commercial Union Ass. Co., et al., Testimony, vol. 6, 1706 *et seq.*

[262] Statement The Foreman, 1706.

[263] Peninou and Unzelman 2001, 101.

[264] Drumm, *ZVersWiss 7* (1907), 374 *et seq.*; Witzleben, 'Die Erdbebenklausel in den Feuerversicherungsverträgen', *ZVersWiss 7* (1907), 380; Mackenzie 1907; Fuld, *ÖVZ* 1906, 307 *et seq.*

[265] Some were mentioned in Statement Sutro (Counsel California Wine Assn., plaintiff), California Wine Assn., et al. vs. Commercial Union Ass. Co., et al., Testimony, vol. 1, 6.

[266] [Note] in *La Semaine*, 26 August 1906, 6; 'Reminiszenzen an die San Francisco-Katastrophe vom Jahr 1906', *ÖRev* 1910, 336.

as the direct insurer as well as Lloyds Underwriters (London)[267] and the *Transatlantische* as reinsurers[268] were caught in the spotlight of international attention. Almost all of the verdicts went against the insurance companies.[269]

On May 10, 1909, the U.S. Circuit Court for the first time sentenced a company to pay damages after a lengthy discussion of the earthquake clause. The court found that the relevant fire had not been caused by the earthquake. The *Journal of Commerce* wrote that the verdict was significant for several hundreds of cases.[270]

2.1.7.4. *Court Cases and Settlements Abroad*

Some of the foreign companies had already made it known a few months after the earthquake that they would not yield to even the highest judicial authorities in the United States. The companies that most vehemently followed this policy were the *Transatlantische* Insurance Company, the *Norddeutsche Feuer* Insurance Company and the *Hanseatische* Fire Insurance Company (Hamburg),[271] the *Rhein & Mosel* (Strasbourg) and its reinsurer, the *Helvetia* (St. Gallen), as well as the *Österreichische Phönix* (Vienna). The representatives of the injured parties reacted with the announcement that they would be filing legal actions in the registered home offices of these companies in the event that the companies did not have sufficient deposits in the United States. This fear turned out to be justified.[272]

As a result, lawyers adopted a variety of legal measures to gain the damages that their clients had been guaranteed by American courts. They sued the American insurance supervision authorities for paying out the deposits of the fire and reinsurers. They employed political pressure in order to get the companies to compromise. They sued the companies at their

---

[267] Alliance (London) vs. Lloyds Underwriters ([Note] in *La Semaine*, 21 October 1906, 7).

[268] Hanover Fire vs. Transatlantic (*ÖVZ* 1906, 265; [Note] in *La Semaine*, 11 November 1906, 8; *ÖRev* 1906, 248.

[269] Sofonea 1978. The *DVZ* (3 October 1907) reports on the verdict of a jury in the U.S. Circuit Court that served as precedent for rejecting the lawsuit against Alliance (London).

[270] Journal of Commerce, 11 May 1909; compare MR/A E-25 running no. 54 (Helvetia/San Francisco Schäden/RA Kisskalt II).

[271] The case of Levi Strauss Realty Co. Vs. Transatlantic, in which numerous prominent witnesses testified, was especially spectacular (*La Semaine*, 2 December 1906, 6).

[272] Apparently, some of the companies had no deposits in the United States ('Insurance Situation in San Francisco', *The Journal of Commerce*, 17 July 1906, 13; [Note] in *La Semaine*, 2 December 1906, 6).

headquarters in Germany, Austria and Switzerland for the enforcement of the judgements obtained in the United States; and they sued the companies again in Europe for damages according to their contracts.

The confiscation of the funds belonging to the insurance companies required to pay compensation was basically successful.[273] As a result, two companies threatened with bankruptcy, *Transatlantische* and the *Norddeutsche Feuer* Insurance Company, ceased to do business in the United States.

Highly interesting was a dispute between a group of injured parties around the lawyer L. A. Redman and the *Rhein & Mosel* and the *Helvetia* Insurance Company, both of which had concluded direct fire insurance contracts prior to the earthquake disaster. Confronted with the demands for compensation, the *Helvetia*'s board of directors stated that it desired to withdraw from the United States insurance market. They transferred their entire portfolio to the *Rhein & Mosel*. However, to maintain their stake in the lucrative business on the Pacific Coast, they immediately took on 95% of this risk in reinsurance and included the Munich Reinsurance Company and the Cologne Reinsurance Company in this undertaking.[274] While the *Rhein & Mosel* Insurance Company—that is, the front man— was being sued in California,[275] the *Helvetia* demanded in 1906 that its fire insurance deposit in New York be returned, since it was no longer directly active in the United States.[276] The insured immediately attempted to get at this deposit[277] as well as at the claims outstanding against *Helvetia*'s retrocessionaires. In addition, a law firm endeavoured to confiscate the New York deposit of the Munich Re and the Cologne Re as of September 1907.[278] This approach as well as one sensational lawsuit against *Helvetia* as a reinsurer of the *Rhein & Mosel*[279] constituted the lawyers' attempts

---

[273] *ÖVZ* 1906, 265; [Note] in *La Semaine*, 23 September 1906.

[274] 'Aufsichtsamt und Cautionen—ein aktueller Beitrag', *DVZ*, 21 June 1908, 357 *et seq.*; 11 September 1906, *MR/A* E-25 running no. 52 (Helvetia/San Francisco Schäden/III).

[275] 11 September 1906, written communication from Redman to Superintendent Francis Hendricks (1906).

[276] *DVZ*, 21 June 1908, 357 *et seq.*

[277] 11 September 1906, written communication of Redman to Superintendent Francis Hendricks, Albany (New York) (copy MR), MR/A E-25 running no. 52 (Helvetia/San Francisco Schäden/III); 18 November 1906 written communication of Otto Kelsey to Helvetia (copy MR), MR/A E-25 running no. 52 (Helvetia/San Francisco Schäden/III).

[278] 5 September 1907 KR to MR (copy of a telegram von Kremer, German American, to KR), MR/A E-25 running no. 52 (Helvetia/San Francisco Schäden/III); undated file entry, MR/A E-25 running no. 52 (Helvetia/San Francisco Schäden/III).

[279] The case Brandenstein vs. Helvetia was characterised as a 'test case' *AnnVW*, 21 August 1907; compare MR/A E-25 running no. 52 (Helvetia/San Francisco Schäden/III).

to define the unclear relationship between the directly insured and the reinsurers to the benefit of the injured parties. However, they were aware that their position stood in contrast to the positions that not only insurance companies[280] but also legal scholars adopted.[281] The Superintendent of Insurance for the State of New York did not agree with them and successfully resisted the attack on the deposits of the *Helvetia* Company and their retrocessionaires.[282]

In Europe, the injured parties counted on public pressure at first. Individual injured parties registered complaints against the involved companies with the German regulatory agency.[283] Others turned to the government[284] and sent representatives across the Atlantic who were supposed to negotiate with the companies locally. They found support in San Francisco in the person of the German Consul Bopp[285] and at the German-American Association of California, who in their concern about the 'faith in German probity' (trans.) published open letters on behalf of the injured parties.[286]

In November of 1906, representatives of the policyholders in Germany and Austria, considered 'decent citizen and lawyers from San Francisco'

---

[280] 'Reinsurers not subject to garnishee', *Insurance Monitor* 1906, 393; 14 October 1908 expert opinion from Kisskalt for MR, MR/A E-25 running no. 54 (Helvetia/San Francisco Schäden/RA Kisskalt II).

[281] The insecurity of the lawyers for the injured parties becomes apparent from a written communication from the American lawyers that managed to find its way via Grossmann (Helvetia) to the Munich Re Group (*Münchener Rück*). This communication cited 'May on Insurance, sec. II' and 'Philipps on Insurance, sec. 382' for the opposing side, MR/A E-25 running no. 52 (Helvetia/San Francisco Schäden/III).

[282] 18 September 1907 KR to MR, MR/A E-25 running no. 52 (Helvetia/San Francisco Schäden/III); the case John J. Tierney vs. Helvetia vor dem U.S. Circuit Court: 29 October 1907, Superintendent of Insurance an Hon. Clinton MacDougall, U.S. Marshall for Northern District of New York (copy MR), in: MR/A E-25 running no. 52 (Helvetia/San Francisco Schäden/III); explanation of the Superintendent of Insurance, Otto Kelsey, New York, to the MR, a confiscation of its deposit was not allowed, 18 November 1907 note MR, in: MR/A E-25 running no. 54 (Helvetia/San Francisco Schäden/RA Kisskalt II). The results of the suit against Helvetia are not known.

[283] 'Geschäftsbericht des Kaiserlichen Aufsichtsamts für Privatversicherung für das Jahr 1906', *Stenographische Berichte über die Verhandlungen des Reichstags, XII. Legislaturperiode, I. Session, Anlagen*, no. 503, 2666 *et seq.*; *Der Versicherungsfreund*, 20 November 1906, 5 *et seq.*; 'Feuerversicherungs-Aktiengesellschaft Rhine & Moselle, *Berliner Börsenzeitung*, 12 January 1906; compare MR/A E-25 running. no. 51 (Helvetia/San Francisco Schäden/I).

[284] 'Zur "Frisco-Katastrophe" ', *Der Versicherungsfreund*, 1 December 1906, 4.

[285] [Note] in *La Semaine*, 2 September 1906, 7.

[286] Explanation of the German-American Federation of California, 1 October (addressed to the Emperor, the Chamber of Commerce and the mayors of all German cities, the German-American National Federation of the United States, and all German newspapers with the request for publication), printed in *Der Versicherungsfreund*, 1 December 1906, 5 *et seq.*

(trans.),[287] entered the fray.[288] The mayor of San Francisco, Eugene E. Schmitz, personally accompanied them. The representatives had power of attorney to conduct the negotiations, convene an international arbitration panel or proceed through the German legal system.[289] Their declared goal was to recover $7 million, a sum derived from various amounts.[290] In order to achieve this purpose, they conducted negotiations with the insurance companies and instituted proceedings in 1906. In addition, Schmitz and the representatives of the insured attempted to have the Supervisory Agency for Private Insurance use means of coercion against the companies unwilling to cover their debts[291]—if necessary, even the revocation of permission to conduct business. They argued that the companies had broken their 'obligations owed to the State of California' (trans.). The officials showed considerable understanding for the position of the injured parties. However, they did not see themselves in a position to intervene and could only advise the insurance companies to cooperate with the insured parties in San Francisco in reaching settlements or in cases that went to court.[292]

This recommendation was followed chiefly by the *Transatlantische* Insurance Company which found itself in an especially unfortunate legal position. It had been sued in the district court of Hamburg for damages and was only able to base its defence on the fallen building clause.[293] An expensive hearing of the evidence as to how long before the outbreak of the fire portions of the insured buildings had collapsed was yet to begin. In this situation, the board of directors in the company accepted a settlement that included the liquidation of the company.[294]

---

[287] 'Geschäftsbericht des Kaiserlichen Aufsichtsamts für Privatversicherung für das Jahr 1906', *Stenographische Berichte über die Verhandlungen des Reichstags, XII. Legislaturperiode, I. Session, Anlagen*, no. 503, 2668 *et seq.*; named were Oscar Sutro, Frederick W. Dohrmann, William Thomas and councellor Cullinan ([Note] in *La Semaine*, 18 November 1906, 8; 'Die Kalamitosen von San Francisco als Kläger in Europa', *ÖRev* 1906, 280.

[288] 'Die Hamburger Feuerversicherungs-Gesellschaften und San Francisco', *ÖVZ* 1906, 319; [Note] in *La Semaine*, 16 September 1906, 6; *Handel und Industrie*, cited in *Der Versicherungsfreund*, 1 January 1906, 4.

[289] [Note] in *La Semaine*, 18 November 1906, 8; source: *Gazette de Francfort*.

[290] [Note] in *La Semaine*, 18 November 1906, 8; *ÖRev* 1906, 280.

[291] [Note] in *La Semaine*, 21 October 1906, 7; 18 November 1906, 8.

[292] Business report of the Imperial Supervisory Agency for Private Insurance for 1906, *Stenographische Berichte über die Verhandlungen des Reichstags, XII. Legislaturperiode, I. Session*, file, no. 503, 2668 *et seq.* From a rescript of the Regulatory Agency to injured parties, cited in *Der Versicherungsfreund*, 20 November 1906, 5 *et seq.*

[293] *ÖRev* 1906, 248; *Der Versicherungsfreund*, 1 December 1906, 4.

[294] 'Geschäftsbericht des Kaiserlichen Aufsichtsamts für Privatversicherung für das Jahr 1906', *Stenographische Berichte über die Verhandlungen des Reichstags, XII. Legislaturperiode, I. Session, Anlagen*, no. 503, 2667 *et seq.*

Five other companies that defended themselves by means of the earthquake clauses proved to be less obliging. The financially precarious *Norddeutsche Feuer* Insurance Company obligated itself to recognise the decisions in test cases and to exempt the other insured parties from the burden of adjudicating each case.[295] A corresponding trial ran before the district court of Hamburg. The court decided that the earthquake clause was unclearly formulated in the critical passage,[296] and on January 11, 1907 required the company to pay damages.[297] Several months later, the *Norddeutsche Feuer* Insurance Company followed the *Transatlantische* into bankruptcy.[298]

The district court in Hamburg decided the legal dispute between Don Juan Coheen vs. Hanseatic Insurance Company to the contrary. Here, the judges recognised the earthquake clause as a valid objection and rejected the claim.[299]

The cases against the *Rhein & Mosel*,[300] the *Helvetia*,[301] and the *Österreichische Phönix*[302] went on for years. After 1907, the insurance industry and

---

[295] The Rhine & Moselle Insurance Company allowed for the preclusionary deadlines to be exceeded. 'Geschäftsbericht des Kaiserlichen Aufsichtsamts für Privatversicherung für das Jahr 1906', 2669 *et seq.*

[296] At issue was the exclusion of damages indirectly caused by earthquakes. Declaration of the North German Fire Co., cited in *ÖRev* 1906, 280; approx. February 1907, expert opinion Kisskalt for MR, MR/A E-25 running no. 54 (Helvetia/San Francisco Schäden/RA Kisskalt II); the wording of the clause is printed above in chapter 3.1.5.2, fn. 100.

[297] 'Geschäftsbericht des Kaiserlichen Aufsichtsamts für Privatversicherung für das Jahr 1906', *Stenographische Berichte über die Verhandlungen des Reichstags, XII. Legislaturperiode, I. Session, Anlagen*, no. 503, 2667 *et seq.*

[298] 'Geschäftsbericht des Kaiserlichen Aufsichtsamts für Privatversicherung für das Jahr 1906', 2666 *et seq.*

[299] Kisskalt to MR, 17 October 1907 MR/A E-25 running no. 54 (Helvetia/San Francisco Schäden/RA Kisskalt II).

[300] The firm of A. G. Spalding & Bros. (San Francisco) initiated the first suit against the Rhine & Moselle at the end of 1906, 24 December 1906 Helvetia to MR, MR/A E-25 running no. 51 (Helvetia/San Francisco Schäden/I). The lawyers of the insurer company estimated their prospects of defending against the claims as very favourable because of the clearly worded exclusion clause (approx. in February 1907, expert opinion of the RA Kisskalt for MR, MR/A E-25 running no. 54 (Helvetia/San Francisco Schäden/RA Kisskalt II). The fires that caused the damages, however, had broken out long after the earthquake; the issue was, among others, the Alcazar Theatre fire (*La Semaine*, 26 August 1906, 6). The regional court of Strasbourg announced a decision for the 12th of January 1911 (*ÖRev* 1910, 336).

[301] 24 November 1908 Kisskalt to MR (copy), E-25 running no. 54 (Helvetia/San Francisco Schäden/RA Kisskalt II); 17 October 1907 Kisskalt to MR, MR/A E-25 running no. 54 (Helvetia/San Francisco Schäden/RA Kisskalt II).

[302] Arguing before the commercial court, the editor of the *San Francisco Bulletin* demanded damages for his publishing house that had still been intact twenty-four hours after the earthquake ([Note] in *La Semaine*, 16 December 1906, 6). In the cases Jakob Stern vs. the Austrian Phoenix and Levi Strauss & Co. vs. Austrian Phoenix at the beginning of

legal journals only reported cases whose goal was to obtain the enforcement of the judgements obtained in California.[303] Prominent jurists such as Paul Laband and Josef Kohler published essays on the problem. They agreed that the California court decisions could not be enforced in Germany, because at the time of the California court decisions, no German verdicts would have been enforceable in California.[304] At the beginning of 1909, the *Reichsgericht* concurred with this view and rejected a court order containing an enforcement judgement.[305]

2.1.8. *The Earthquake Balance Sheet: The View from the International Insurance Business*

By the end of 1906, the major portion of the more than 90,000 insured and registered fire damage claims had been settled. At that point, the insurance companies were in a position to provide a well-grounded estimate of the consequences of the earthquake for their industry. At a conference in Glasgow on February 4, 1907, the damage adjuster Robert K. Mackenzie

---

1908, extensive witness hearing were begun (Court files of the Austrian Phoenix in copies, MR/A E-25 running no. 53, Helvetia/San Francisco Schäden/RA Kisskalt I).

[303] The most important cases of this kind were mounted against the Rhine & Mosel Company and the Transatlantic in 1907 ('Das deutsche Reichsgericht über die San Francisco-Urteile', *ÖRev* 1909, 125; July 1907, *MR/A* E-25, no. 51 (Helvetia/San Francisco Schäden/I).

[304] This point of view is based upon §328, no. 5, of the German Code of Civil Procedure (*Deutsche Zivilprozeßordnung*). The change in the California Code of Civil Procedure of March 11, 1907 did not retroactively help the lack of reciprocity. An scholarly debate developed on this problem: Fuld, *ÖVZ* 1906, 307 *et seq.*; Kisskalt, 'Die Vollstreckbarkeit kalifornischer Urteile in Deutschland', *LZ* 1907, col. 689 *et seq.*; Marcuse, 'Die Vollstreckbarkeit amerikanischer Urteile in Deutschland', *LZ* 1908, col. 220 *et seq.*; Kisskalt, 'Ein Nachspiel zur Katastrophe von San Francisco', *Das Recht* 19 (1907); Laband, 'Zum Entwurf des Vereinsgesetzes', *DJZ*, 1 August 1908, 871; H. T. [Tarnke], 'Anerkennung und Vollstreckung kalifornischer Urteile in Deutschland', *AnnVW* 1907, 733 *et seq.*; *APrivVers.* 6, 99; Neumeyer, *DJZ* 12, 1193; Kohler, 'Aenderung des Zwischenstaatsrechts in Bezug auf die Vollstreckungsklausel', *DJZ* 1908, col. 276. The Munich Re commissioned several expert opinions on the matter, among others from W. Kisskalt, on Pro *et seq.* Seuffert and the American law firm Underwood, Van Horst & Hoyt. Opinions and correspondence in MR/A E-25 running no. 53 (Helvetia/San Francisco Schäden/RA Kisskalt I). Between April and July of 1907, director Thieme (MR) and Kisskalt aimed at changing the German Code of Civil Procedure, consulted with the speaker of the imperial government for the insurance industry, Privy Councillor Oegg, and devised petitions that were sent to, among others, the Imperial Chancellor; correspondence and drafts, MR/A E-25 running no. 53 (Helvetia/San Francisco Schäden/RA Kisskalt I).

[305] At issue was presumably the case of Canepa and Pierson vs. Transatlantic. The district court in Strasbourg had already rejected all lawsuits petitioning for enforcement of the California decisions in the judgement of May 21, *MR/A* E-25 no. 53 (Helvetia/San Francisco Schäden/RA Kisskalt I); Das deutsche Reichsgericht über die San Francisco-Urteile, *ÖRev* 1909, 125.

put a figure of at least $300 million on the totality of damages.[306] Other contemporary estimates ranged from $350 million to $1 billion.[307] According to the present state of our knowledge, the total costs of the material damages can be set at $400 million.[308] In Mackenzie's estimate, the insurance industry paid out between 235 and 265 million dollars to cover damages.[309] This estimate seems realistic in the light of the total risk accepted in San Francisco.[310]

Never before had a comparably large compensation been paid. It roughly corresponded to the sum of the surplus funds of all the companies that compensated for damages in California or—using another contemporary comparison—to the profit of the entire American fire insurance industry for several decades.[311] Altogether, there were at least 243 companies directly or indirectly involved in paying compensation.[312] According to the calculations of the insurance expert Albert W. Whitney, compensation for about 80% of the insured value was paid,[313] possibly even more.[314] This percentage was very high compared to the settlements of earlier fire disasters in the United States. For this reason, Whitney explicitly stated in

---

[306] Mackenzie reported on the 4th of February, 1907 to the *Versicherungs- und Aktuar-Sozietät* in Glasgow on his experiences in San Francisco (Mackenzie 1907).

[307] One estimate was $350 to 500 million: *The Commercial and Financial Chronicle*, 19 October 1907; another was $500 million: 'Schätzung einer deutschen Rückversicherungs-gesellschaft', cited in *ÖVZ* 1906, 235; similarly, Fuld, *ÖVZ* 1906, 121 *et seq.*; $1 billion: 'Report of the Committee of Five to the "Thirty-five Companies" on the San Francisco conflagration', April 18–21, 1906, (1907—BL), 11; $350 million represented in 1906 about 1.3% of the American GNP and $500 million about 1.8% (Odell and Weidenmier 2001, 2).

[308] Later, the American civil engineer J. R. Freeman put the figure of $420 million on the total damages. $20 million was the amount of the damages directly caused by the earth-quake and $400 million the amount of the damages caused by fire (Freeman 1932, 663).

[309] Mackenzie 1907. At least $280 million: *ÖVZ* 1906, 235; similarly, Fuld, *ÖVZ* 1906, 121 *et seq.*

[310] My own projection: the premium income in San Francisco was $2.99 million in 1905. This means that given an average premium of about 1%, the property insured had a total value of $300 million. The largest part of this property (my own estimate: property worth $280 million) was destroyed; about 86% of the insured property, that is over $240 million, was replaced.

[311] A total loss of $180 million is commensurate with the profits of the fifty years prior to the earthquake (that is, 3% of the total of premiums equalling $6 billion) according to Whitney's calculation in 'Report of the special committee' 1906, 54 *et seq*. According to Mackenzie's estimate, the fire destroyed the profits of thirty-five years within three days (Mackenzie 1907).

[312] A. M. Best Co. 1907, 6. The official statistics took less than half of these 243 companies into consideration (*ÖVZ* 1906, 319).

[313] Whitney 1906; Mackenzie 1907.

[314] On the basis of the damage table of sixty-nine companies printed above, the quota is 85.6%. See also the table 3.1.6.3, fn. 190.

Table 7. Method of Payment Adopted by 77 Fire Insurance Companies
in Settling the San Francisco damages. Whitney 1906.[315]

Payment Percentage[316]	American Companies	British Companies	'Colonial' Companies	all Companies
100% cash	3	2	—	5
99%	3	1	—	4
98%	13	8	1	22
95–98%	—	1	—	1
90–95%	7	1	—	8
75–90%	20	2	—	22
56–75%	1	3	—	4
50–56%	2	—	—	2
40–50%	2	—	—	2
30–40%	1	—	—	1
Small Dividends	1	—	—	1
Paying by Instalments	1	—	2	3
Discretion of the Adjuster	1	—	—	1
No Payment	1	—	—	1
Totals				77

his study for the San Francisco Chamber of Commerce that he regarded the rights of the insured as altogether upheld.[317] However, the settlement results of the individual companies in part differed widely.

The international spread of the losses among the fire insurance companies can be gauged from the statistics published in the London *Times*. Accordingly, 65.3% of the net damages were suffered by American companies, 34.4% by the foreign fire insurers.[318] The percentage of the reinsurers is known from another damage balance sheet: it amounted to 36% of the net damages suffered by the direct insurers.[319]

By the beginning of 1907, fifteen of the ninety American insurance companies and four of the fifteen continental European companies involved

---

[315] Ibid.

[316] Payment of 95%–99% followed in exchange for discounts of 1–5% immediately.

[317] After the Chicago fire in 1872, the insured had received compensation for 50% of their losses, in Baltimore (1904) even 90%—however, without allowing for the earthquake damages. Whitney's study is based upon the settlement of about 10,000 damage claims (Whitney 1906).

[318] The Times, cited in [note] in *La Semaine*, 4 November 1906, 8.

[319] According to the statistics on the settlement of sixty-nine companies, the primary insurers bore 54.8% of the gross damage costs and the reinsurers 30.8%. The recovered values amounted to a percentage of 14.4%. See the table in chapter 3.1.6.3, fn. 190.

in earthquake settlements had filed for bankruptcy.[320] Many other companies—among them only one British firm—had to supplement their share capital in order to compensate for their losses, the sole means of guaranteeing the continuation of business activities.[321] Thus, a portion of the damages was spread among the many thousand shareholders whose financial shares in the companies had already suffered considerable losses immediately after the earthquake.

British companies were the most easily capable of assuming their large portion of the damages, as they possessed the largest financial reserves.[322] Many of them belonged to the 'dollar for dollar' companies or benefitted from the good reputation that British fire insurance companies earned in settling damage claims. In 1907, the business volume of the 'dollar for dollar' companies grew an average of 87% in comparison to 1905, while the development in other companies stagnated.[323]

In view of this balance, the impression of the insurance jurist Hagen that the fire insurance business had 'been shaken to the roots' is understandable.[324] The disaster influenced the world economy far beyond the insurance industry and finally led to the international financial crisis of October 1907.[325]

2.2. THE REACTIONS OF THE INSURANCE INDUSTRY

After the disaster in San Francisco, many of the insurance companies who had been directly or indirectly affected tried to protect themselves against the economic consequences of a similar occurrence in the future. Their reactions differed greatly, which is only partly attributable to the fact that the situation the insurance companies faced after the earthquake was greatly heterogeneous. The dissimilarity also stemmed from the differences

---

[320] Mackenzie 1907.

[321] Ibid.; *The Spectator*/[Note] in *La Semaine*, 28 October 1906, 6.

[322] Mackenzie, 1907.

[323] Calculations based on premium income according to the data collected by Marks, The San Francisco story—April 18–21 (1909).

[324] Hagen, *DJZ* 1906, col. 741.

[325] The transfer of a million Pounds in gold from Great Britain to the United States for the reparation of insured damages as well as measures of the Bank of England to prevent further transfers led to a recession of the US economy in May 1907 and ultimately to the collapse of the financial sector (beginning with the Knickerbocker Trust Corp.), a recession that spread out internationally. Odell and Weidenmier 2001, 11 *et seq.*

in the perception of the disastrous events[326] and in the conception of seismicity. It divided the private insurance industry into separate factions that were already apparent before the end of 1906: one faction of the insurers regarded the fire damages caused by the earthquake as insurable; the other faction did not.

2.2.1. *The San Francisco Disaster: Difference in the Perception of the Events*

What constituted the actual calamity in San Francisco? For the inhabitants of the city, for its economy and its administration, it was the death of thousands of people and the destruction of almost all the material wealth through the firestorm. On the other hand, in the perception of the insurers, 'San Francisco' became a synonym for an economic disaster. The contemporary statements from insurance companies show that many regarded the entire political situation in California, including the behaviour of the injured parties, city officials and the courts as part of the disaster.

Accordingly, the opinions on the causes of the events also diverged. The inhabitants of San Francisco adopted the reinterpretation that made the earthquake disappear as a central factor and replaced it with the firestorm. It is to be assumed that most of them did not consciously embrace this change, but rather that they accepted it more or less passively from the propaganda disseminated by economic organisations and the media. An exception is the Chinese population, a part of which believed that the anger of the earth dragon Day Loong had descended upon the city.[327] In a similar fashion, fundamentalist Christian groups interpreted the events as God's punishment.[328]

In the discourse within the insurance industry, the earthquake received a lot of attention, chiefly for two reasons. Firstly, most companies were interested in countering the damage claims of their insured parties with substantive objections. These objections were most convincingly based upon the effects of the earthquake. Secondly, the investigation of the causes of the damages belonged to the rudiments of the insurance industry. After the disaster of San Francisco, it became clear within the international community of the insurance business that each company

---

[326] For the perception of natural disasters see Groh, Kempe, Mauelshagen 2003, 11 *et seq.*, as well as Massard-Guilbaud 2001, 9 *et seq.* A sociological approach to the phenomenon of disaster has been profitably exploited by the legal historion Luminati (1995, especially in 15 *et seq.*).

[327] Pan 1995, 34 *et seq.*

[328] Kurzman 2001, 89 *et seq.*

would have to reconsider its future business policies and practices. For this reason, the management and directors were forced to grapple with the dangers and risks that had manifested themselves in San Francisco.

In this analysis, however, different points of emphasis became apparent. In the American contribution to the discourse, the San Francisco disaster tended to take on the nature of an anthropogenic occurrence. The *Journal of Commerce* published, for example, a series of statements in which the question of fire safety in American metropolises was front and centre. The authors—managers of large insurance companies, chiefly Henry Evans[329]—demanded improvements in the urban building codes and infrastructure. The European insurance circles, on the other hand, paid little attention to this aspect, and for them, the earthquake did not move one jot away from the centre of their deliberations.

2.2.2. Danger or Risk? Differences in the Perception of the Possible

The differences between the American and the European view of the events in San Francisco found a continuation in the question as to how earthquakes were to be assessed as a catalyst of city fires. Could earthquakes be integrated into the fire insurance business? That is, were they risks open to scientific determination, mathematical calculation and economical management? Or did earthquakes represent incalculable sources of danger that the fire insurer should do best to avoid? The answer to this question was of central importance for the future policy of the insurance business.

A strict semantic difference between 'danger' and 'risk' does not precisely correspond to the period's pragmatic meaning of the terms.[330] The difference is helpful, however, in the examination of the different perceptions of earthquakes, as it exposes a hidden line of demarcation between the later advocates and opponents of an exclusion clause. 'Dangers' were perceived as situations in which damaging occurrences loomed large. Up until the early modern period, the estimate of dangers depended upon

---

[329] 'The Earthquake Clause', *The Journal of Commerce*, 25 January 1907, 13.

[330] The term 'risk' and its cognates in other languages became current in the sixteenth century in Romance languages and in the nineteenth century in German-speaking areas. 'Risk' means the possibility that a pattern of behaviour entails drawbacks, but the exact meaning varies. The term is often synonymous for 'danger' and 'hazard', Rammstedt 1992, col. 1046 with references. Differing meanings are cited, for example, in *Grand Dictionnaire du XIX. Siècle* (1875), vol. 13, 1230 (colloquial language, insurance and legal jargon); *Enciclopedia universal ilustrada europeo-americana* (1926), vol. 51, 531 (only colloquial language). The *Enciclopedia Italitoa* (1936), vol. 14, 420 *et seq.* elaborately explains 'risk' in the contexts of economics and the mathematics of insurance.

experiences that were acquired haphazardly, seldom in the accompaniment of systematic examination. As a consequence, the chances of learning about the probability of the occurrence of specific events had been rather slim.[331]

This changed in the eighteenth century. Mathematicians, natural scientists and economists began to research the causes and development of particular events and the frequency of their occurrences. Their interests were aimed at natural phenomena, the mortality of certain population groups and similar subjects.[332] With the aid of the calculation of probability, they succeeded in reducing the uncertainty about the future occurrence of these kinds of events.[333] This technique was applied in State administrations and in the insurance industry that at the same time was pervading broad areas of life.[334]

These systematic investigations of damage-causing events transformed 'dangers' into 'risks'. Risks differ from dangers in that the uncertainty of the occurrence of threatening events (a danger) is replaced by the certainty of a definite probability (a risk). Risks—in contrast to dangers—are susceptible to calculation. Precisely for this reason, they could become contractual matters in the insurance business.[335]

The risk-paradigm spread to all societies involved in the process of industrialisation. At the beginning of the twentieth century, it became an indispensable foundation for the private and State insurance systems, business financing, economic calculation and other areas.[336]

The discussions among the insurers of the danger or the risk of earthquake-caused firestorms ran parallel to their discussions of the causes of the San Francisco disaster. They moved along two axes: that of technology

---

[331] The theory of probability originated in the Renaissance. Its principles were developed between 1700 und 1760 (Bernstein 1996, 3 et seq.; Daston 1988).

[332] A precondition of this kind of investigation was the decline in metaphysical interpretations of natural phenomena that becomes apparent in the seventeenth century (Massard-Guilbaud 2001, 21; Kempe 2000, 155 et seq.).

[333] See, for instance, Rosenhaft 2010, 16 et seq. and Pearson 2010, 75 et seq. who identify the third quarter of the 18th century as the critical period in the development of proto-insurance.

[334] Bernstein 1996, 86 et seq.; Supple 1970, 3 et seq.

[335] The notion of 'risk' used here, which places this concept in the historical context of the origin of the modern period, corresponds to that used by Bernstein (1996, 1 et seq.). It differs from the concept in modern sociology shaped by decision theory and which emphasises the anthropogenic character of risks. This limitation does not appear to be useful for historical research; but see Sieferle 2004.

[336] Its clear index is the broad spreading of life insurance among all population groups in Europe and North America, an expansion that also includes other populations in the regions of the world whose life styles were oriented upon Europe.

and that of seismology. American insurance companies for the most part sought technical solutions. Numerous learned journals published informed reports that considered the construction method, architecture, and infra-structure of large cities.[337] The questions they posed were directly influ-enced by the California disaster: which buildings withstood a firestorm reaching temperatures of 1,000 or 2,000 degrees? Which windows, doors and roofs permitted the penetration of the fire into the buildings and how did it spread?[338] Was the San Francisco redwood moistened by sea breeze actually as fire-resistant as stone, as was repeatedly stated?[339] Should the steel and cement used in skyscrapers be applied in the construction of all buildings[340] or did these buildings precisely collapse in the fire?[341] Had the lessons from the fire disasters in Chicago and Baltimore been paid atten-tion to[342] or had construction not become safer?[343] Would stricter building codes help?[344] And how could earthquake-safe buildings be constructed?[345] Numerous commissions examined these and other questions. The most important studies originated as public contracts.[346] Some additional studies were made for fire insurance companies,[347] civil engineers[348] and architects.[349] The attention devoted to the technical questions on the

---

[337] Whitney observed that contending against shoddy building practices was an uphill battle ('indifference of the American people to the enormous annual fire-loss') and demanded in view of the San Francisco disaster a reorientation of thinking (Whitney 1906, 53 et seq.).

[338] A report cited in Der Versicherungsfreund, 1 September 1907, 3 (source: Insurance Press).

[339] Mackenzie 1907.

[340] A commission appointed by the Secretary for the Interior reports on the 'magnifi-cent proof of its resilience', cited in Insurance Press/Der Versicherungsfreund, 1 September 1907, 3). Mackenzie (1907) cites a similar appraisal by the Committee of the Twenty.

[341] An opinion expressed by an engineer, J. S. Sewell and cited by Mackenzie (1907). See also Atwood, ÖVZ 1906, 195.

[342] Lock, Insurance World, October 1906, trans. in Der Versicherungsfreund, 1 November 1906, 1.

[343] As cited in Insurance Press/Der Versicherungsfreund, 1 September 1907, 3.

[344] A question cited in the Secretary's report, 3.

[345] A building method, which, according to Geschwind (2001, 29 et seq.), was promoted.

[346] Report of the Sub-Committee on Statistics (1907—BL); Municipal Report on the San Francisco Earthquake and Fire of April 1906 (1907); Insurance Press/Der Versicherungsfre-und, 1 September 1907, 3; Sewell, Soulé and Humphrey, 'The San Francisco Earthquake and Fire of April 18, 1906 and their effects on structures and Structural Materials', USGS bulletin no. 324 (1907).

[347] Reed (1906—BL); Report of the Committee of Five to the 'Thirty-five Companies' on the San Francisco conflagration, April 18–21, 1906. (1907—BL).

[348] San Francisco Association of the American Society of Civil Engineers, Reports, Pro-ceedings of the American Society of Civil Engineers, March 1907.

[349] Notes on the Californian Earthquake. Reports by the State Board of Architects, and by the Home Fire Insurance Co. Ills., Eng. Rec. May 19, 1906. The Structural Association

rebuilding of San Francisco could create the impression that the danger of uncontrolled fires was being reduced.[350] But this appearance was deceptive, for even in San Francisco no sustainable changes were made following the discussion.[351]

However, the insurance companies did not extend their confidence to the same degree. Neither Europeans nor Americans were happy with technical solutions alone. In order to learn whether earthquakes were predictable or at least could be estimated on a scale of probability, the insurance industry looked for scientific understandings on seismicity. Could the risk of disaster be calculated for the cities on the American West Coast and in other regions?

At the turn of the century, the probability of the occurrence of seismological events was chiefly estimated by relying on historical statistics. In 1906, the internationally recognised French seismologist Fernand de Montessus de Ballore published an up-to-date compilation that was immediately printed in the insurance journal *La Semaine*:[352]

Table 8. Earthquake Statistics (1856–1906) by Montessus de Ballore.
[Note] in *La Semaine*, 23 December 1906, 8.

Region	Number of Tremors	Region	Number of Tremors
Italy (minus Sicily)	27,672	Portugal	2,656
Japan	27,562	Holland and North Germany	2,326
Greece	10,306	Java	2,155
South America	8,081	New Zealand	1,925
Mexico	5,586	Antilles	1,704
Asia Minor	4,451	British Isles	1,139
USA and Pacific Coast	4,467	Atlantic Coast	937
Sicily	4,331	India	813
Switzerland	3,895	Scandinavia	646
Central America	2,739	Russia	258
East India	2,561	Africa	179
France	2,793	Australia and Tasmania	83
		Total	130,000

of San Francisco, founded in reaction to the earthquake, also commissioned comparative studies on the building methods and earthquake- and fire-safety of individual buildings.

[350] Lock, Insurance World, October 1906, trans. in Der Versicherungsfreund, 1 November 1906, 3.

[351] Of the 20,000 new buildings that were constructed in the following three years, only 1,700 conformed to the new safety regulations devised by city officials. These regulations were later relaxed (Strupp 2004, 159).

[352] [Note] in *La Semaine*, 23 December 1906, 8.

On the other hand, the causes of earthquakes were still a matter of uncertainty. Scientists had been investigating such different factors as air pressure and temperature, the aurora borealis, exploding meteors and sun spots, magnetism, electricity and electromagnetic voltage for decades.[353] The theory that the gravitational pull of the moon triggered 'tidal waves of the imagined molten core of the earth' (trans.)[354] appeared to be supported by statistics.[355] Many authors believed the collapse of large underground cavities as the consequence of gas pressures in the core of the earth or of sudden transformation of large amounts of water into steam to be more plausible.[356] Another scientist believed that the tremors of the earth resulted from its 'continuous vibrations that naturally originated from the parts of the earth where the largest movement develops, i.e. at the equator, and spread from there to the poles accompanied by electric currents' (trans.).[357] Since this process developed slowly, volcanic eruptions and earthquakes could be predicted.[358]

After the San Francisco disaster, many of these theories and speculations became very popular[359] and spread among insurance companies on the European continent. The French professional journal *L'Argus* revived the old saw connecting seismological and meteorological phenomena.[360] The German business paper *Handel und Industrie* entertained the notion that volcanoes provide a 'safety valve' (trans.) for Earth—and only for the moment did not actually provide protection from earthquakes.[361]

In view of these uncertainties, the impression that reliable statements about future earthquakes were impossible to make apparently hardened among continental European companies. To them, earthquakes were incalculable risks.[362] It seemed more likely that 'we are at the

---

[353] Roth, who rejected the theory, 1882, 5, 28 *et seq.*; Brauns (1913, 156 *et seq.*) took no position; galvanism was taken to mean electromagnetic pressure.

[354] Falb 1869, 5; Roth 1882, 10 *et seq.*

[355] Schmidt 1875; Falb, Roth and Schmidt relied on the hypothesies of the seismologist Alexis Perrey, who beginning in 1841 had published over 4,000 studies on earthquake statistics.

[356] Roth 1882, 29.

[357] Röttger 1889, 8.

[358] Ibid., 13.

[359] Brauns 1913, 156 *et seq.*

[360] *L'Argus*, cited in *Der Versicherungsfreund*, 1 October 1906, 1; Röttger 1889, 32 *et seq.*

[361] 'Noch immer Erdbebengefahr', *Handel und Industrie*, cited in *Der Versicherungsfreund*, 20 January 1907, 4.

[362] Compare the statement of the reinsurers in 'Zur Katastrophe in San Francisco', *Masius' Rundschau* 1906, 224 *et seq.* Hagen points out that pertinent regulations in the

present... living in a period of seismological and volcanic changes that make predictions and calculations for the future simply impossible' (trans.).[363]

The explanations offered by the damage regulator Robert Mackenzie, who in his talk before the British insurers at the beginning of 1907 also spoke about the causes of the San Francisco earthquake, struck quite a different tone. He knowledgeably described how the seismic shock of April 18, 1906 overcame geo-technical restraints along the San Bruno Fault[364] that extended deeply beneath the earth's surface and ran from north to south along the continental coast.[365]

Mackenzie's explanations brought his listeners up to date on the latest state of seismological research in the United States.[366] Just a few weeks after the earthquake, American periodicals such as *National Geographic*,[367] *Scientific American*,[368] *Popular Science Monthly* and the *Journal of Geology* had published well-researched analyses of the event.[369] American scientists assumed that tectonic earthquakes—in contrast to volcanic

---

Swiss and German VVG draft were lacking; this refutes the notion of the existence of a general principle (Hagen, *DJZ* 1906, col. 742; Ruttke, 'Die Versicherung gegen Erdbeben und andere unmessbare Gefahren', *Mitteilungen für die öffentlichen Feuerversicherungs-Anstalten* 1909, 237 *et seq.*; Liebig 1911, 87).

[363] Not even the earthquake zones could be geographically differentiated from the safe regions (*Handel und Industrie*, cited in *Der Versicherungsfreund*, 20 February 1907, 4; similarly *Der Grenzbote*, 21 June 1906 and 'Zur Frage der Deckung von Erdbebenschäden', *Berliner Börsen-Courier* 92, 24 February 1915, supplement, 1–2).

[364] Which is now known as the San Andreas Fault; Ellsworth (1990, 159 *et seq.*) summarises current knowledge on the earthquake of 1906.

[365] Mackenzie 1907.

[366] Mackenzie's explanations agreed, for example, with the basic assumptions made by Dutton (1904) and in contemporary earthquake catalogues by Holden (1898) and Mac Adie (1907).

[367] Ransome (U.S. Geological Survey), 'The Probable Cause of the San Francisco Earthquake', *The National Geographic Magazine*, May 1906, vol. XVII, no. 5.

[368] 'The San Francisco Earthquake', *Scientific American*, 19 May 1906, 419 *et seq.*

[369] Published in Jordan's collection 'The California Earthquake of 1906' (1907): Jordan, 'The Earthquake Rift of April, 1906' (reprint from *Popular Science Monthly*); Branner, 'Geology and the Earthquake' (reprint from *Out West*); Derleth, Jr., 'The Destructive Extent of the California Earthquake. Its Effect Upon Structures and Structural Materials Within the Earthquake Belt'; Gilbert, 'The Investigation of the California Earthquake' (summary of current research at the time, reprint from *Popular Science Monthly*); Taber, 'Local Effects of the California Earthquake of 1906' (reprint from *The Journal of Geology*); Omori, 'Preliminary Note on the Cause of the California Earthquake of 1906' (reprint from *Bulletin of the Imperial Earthquake Investigation Committee of Japan*); Fairbanks, 'The Great Earthquake Rift of California' (reprint from *Bulletin of the California Physical Geography Club*, October 1907).

earthquakes, a distinction that was generally recognised[370]—such as that in San Francisco were related to orogeny.[371] Some researchers had even expressed their fears on the future danger to California. The geologist Frederick L. Ransome, for example, claimed that in view of the geological structure of the Pacific coast, serious seismic disruptions remained probable. However, he wrote: 'That San Francisco will rise beautiful and triumphant from ruin no one who knows California can doubt. Earthquakes are a risk that will be accepted by the people in the future with as little hesitation as in the past'.[372] Similarly optimistic, the Japanese seismologist Fusakichi Omori expressed: 'Future studies in various phenomena connected with the movements of the earth's crust might perhaps tend to advance our knowledge respecting the problem of the prediction of great earthquakes, which are often preceded by what may be called "foreshocks". In the meanwhile, and always, it will be necessary to build houses and other structures strong enough to resist earthquake shocks, a problem which presents no great difficulties'.[373] However, most important for the insurance business was the estimate of experts that following the abatement of the geotectonic pressures, many decades, perhaps even a century, would elapse before the next earthquake in California.[374]

The contrast between these coherent positions held by American experts—of course, explanations already outdated by contemporary scientific standards were also being spread in the US[375]—on the causes of the earthquake and the uncertainties of the continental European authors described above is striking. Americans and the British could view the possibility of an earthquake as a calculable risk.[376] The state of the information on the European continent, however, was insufficient for such an estimate.[377]

This knowledge gap between the continents grew even larger, as earthquake research was significantly strengthened in the United States.

---

[370] Gilbert in Jordan 1907.

[371] Ransome, *The National Geographic Magazine*, May 1906, vol. 17, no. 5, with reference to John Milne and Andrew C. Lawson; similarly Gilbert, in Jordan 1907.

[372] Ransome, *The National Geographic Magazine*, May 1906, vol. 17, no. 5.

[373] Omori, in Jordan 1907.

[374] Mackenzie 1907; Derleth, in Jordan 1907, 100 *et seq.*; Jordan, in Jordan 1907, 55.

[375] Dean, 'The San Francisco Earthquake of 1906', in: *Annals of Science 50* (1993), 511 *et seq.*; Thomas and Witts 1871/1980, 167 *et seq.*, 219).

[376] Opinions on the matter were, however, by no means unanimous, not even within the individual insurance companies (Trebilcock 1998, 277 *et seq.*).

[377] Mackenzie's remarks were also published in German in 1907, but represented only one of several different opinions recorded there.

In California, Governor Pardee authorised a commission to investigate the disasters of the April 18, 1906.[378] The other institutions involved in increased earthquake research were California universities,[379] the U.S. Geological Survey,[380] the U.S. Weather Bureau,[381] and the U.S. Coast and Geodetic Survey.[382] The Japanese government also sent scientists to California as part of the Imperial Earthquake Investigation Committee.[383] One year after the disaster, the American geologist Warren Upham concluded in London that the earthquake of 1906 had given research an 'enormous boost' (trans.).[384] Four years later, the Seismological Society of America, which originated in the investigative committee headed by A. C. Lawson, was founded.[385]

2.2.3. San Francisco, Valparaiso, Kingston: The Global Dimension

While the insurers intensively dealt with the situation in California, additional earthquakes demonstrated the global extent of the seismic danger to them. On August 16, 1906, an earthquake measuring 8.6 in intensity on the Richter scale destroyed the Chilean provinces of Talca and Valparaiso, 'the opulent, flourishing pearl called Chile lying in the midst of paradise'.[386] In the port city of Valparaiso, two violent tremors caused parts of the business quarter and the affluent quarter to collapse. On the same day, several apartment buildings burned down. More fires, including in other cities in the region, followed on the 17th, the 20th and the 21st of August. Valparaiso, one of the largest cities in the Republic of Chile with a population of 125,000 people, was almost completely destroyed.

---

[378] Report of the State Earthquake Investigation Commission, vol. 1, 1–vol. 2 (1908–1910).

[379] John C. Branner (Stanford) 1913; Stephen Taber (Stanford University); and Charles Derleth, Jr. (University of California) published studies in Jordan, ed., 1907).

[380] Studies published by Ransome and Gilbert.

[381] Marvin, 'The Record of the Great Earthquake Written in Washington by the Seismograph of the U. S. Weather Bureau', *The National Geographic Magazine*, May 1906, vol. 17, no. 5, 296.

[382] Bauer and Burbank, 'The San Francisco Earthquake of April 18, 1906, as Recorded by the Coast and Geodetic Survey Magnetic Observatories', *The National Geographic Magazine*, May 1906, vol. 17, no. 5, 298.

[383] The Imperial Earthquake Investigation Committee headed by Prof. F. Omori.

[384] Undated newspaper article (ca. 1907) in *Sammlung von Erdbebenberichten aus der Presse*, StUB Frankfurt.

[385] Byerly, 'History of the Seismological Society of America', *Bulletin of the Seismological Society of America 54* (1964), 1723 *et seq.*

[386] *ÖRev* 1906, 213.

In the following months, the insurers experienced their second 'San Francisco'. Once again, the stocks for the insurance companies active abroad plummeted on the international stock markets. Only after reassuring reports did the market prices return to normal.[387] In addition, the extent of the total damages did not approach that of San Francisco. Nevertheless, they were estimated to be 'abnormal' among insurance companies.[388] Soon it became known that the most affected companies were Chilean and English.[389] Many of the other foreign insurers, among them a few German companies, had withdrawn from the country shortly before the misfortune.[390] The anxiety was especially justified for those companies that had already lost their reserves in San Francisco.[391]

At first, domestic and foreign insurers refused, based on their exclusion clauses, to pay any indemnity for losses.[392] At a meeting in London on October 12, 1906, the European companies involved adopted a policy of non-payment. They also instructed their representatives in Valparaiso to pursue this policy.[393] Some companies had excluded the earthquake danger with a simple clause: 'this policy does not insure against loss or damages caused by a volcano, earthquake, hurricane or other eruptions, tremors, atmospheric natural events'.[394] The Austrian insurance journal *Österreichische Versicherungs-Zeitung* also reported, however, on the following comprehensive regulation, which it translated into German:

> Excluded dangers:...the coverage does not include the destruction or damage caused by fire that results from a) a subterranean fire, earthquake, volcanic explosion, hurricane or other natural events or b) as the result of an enemy attack, insurgency, rioting, etc., etc., unless the insured can demonstrate that the destruction or damage did not originate in these events (trans.).[395]

---

[387] Besides Chilean companies, those chiefly affected were English and, to a lesser extent, German (*ÖRev* 1906, 213; 'Die Erdbebenkatastrophe von Valparaiso', *ÖVZ* 1906, 252 *et seq.*).

[388] *ÖVZ* 1906, 252 *et seq.*

[389] *ÖVZ* 1906, 252; 'Désastre du Chili', *La Semaine*, 26 August 1906, 6.

[390] Among others, the *Hamburg-Bremer* Fire Insurance Company, *Magdeburg* Fire Insurance Company, the *Transatlantische* Fire Insurance Company, State Fire. The reason was a two-year-old regulatory law that came into effect at the end of 1905 and that was regarded as repressive (*La Semaine*, 9 September 1906, 6 *et seq.*; *L'Argus*, cited in *Der Versicherungsfreund*, 1 October 1906, 2; *ÖVZ* 1906, 252; *Feuerversicherung und Feuerschutz* 1906, 227).

[391] *ÖVZ* 1906, 252.

[392] For example, the director of the Atlas Insurance Company; *La Semaine*, 9 September 1906, 6; *ÖVZ* 1906, 259.

[393] Herzog n.d., 269.

[394] Ibid.

[395] *ÖVZ* 1906, 252; Mackenzie 1907.

Observers praised the shifting of the burden of proof at the end of the last clause. The *ÖVZ* predicted that 'no courts existed, even in America, that in view of the clear wording and sense of this agreement on the payment of earthquake damages would decide that companies were obligated to pay damages for fires that resulted from the earthquake, whether they were caused directly or indirectly' (trans.).[396] And yet problems arose. Some significant fires broke out days after the earthquake. The insurers had to anticipate resistance if they refused payment for damages that originated later.[397] For this reason, they attempted to regulate these damages with settlements that covered up to 50% of the damages.[398]

On November 4, 1906, *La Semaine* reported that the estimates of all damages had been concluded. This report shows that the reductions from the insured sums lay between 25% and 50%.[399] But the information of the French paper was not completely accurate. One month later, the *ÖVZ* delivered the surprising news that the English insurance companies had by no means included exclusion clauses involving earthquake fire-damage in their Chilean policies.[400] Moreover, they were—in contrast to earlier statements—no better protected than in San Francisco. Now, the British insurers were prepared to take their chances in court. It is possible that they invoked the fallen building clauses. The *ÖVZ* remarked, rather pessimistically by this point, that the courts would, just as in California, side with the injured parties and decide against the insurance companies— even if the policies contained clearly formulated earthquake clauses.[401] Nothing further was reported on the decisions arrived at by Chilean courts. The total amount that was paid by foreign companies finally amounted to less than $10 million.[402]

The third city following San Francisco and Valparaiso to be destroyed by an earthquake was Kingston (Jamaica) on January 19, 1907. At this time, some 46,000 people lived in the port town of the British colony. Here

---

[396] *ÖVZ* 1906, 252.

[397] Witzleben, *ZVersWiss* 7 (1907), 384.

[398] Herzog (n.d., 269) reports that they were successful in this endeavour.

[399] Some 50% in the case of buildings that had totally collapsed during the earthquake; 25% if the buildings were destroyed in the conflagration directly after the earthquake; 25% if they were so damaged by fire that they had to be torn down (*La Semaine*, 4 November 1906, 6).

[400] Report in *ÖVZ*, cited in *Feuerversicherung und Feuerschutz* 1906, 227.

[401] *Ibid.*

[402] See the table in the annexe on the companies involved in compensation for fire damages in Valparaiso. *La Semaine* (9 September 1906, 6) estimated the total damages at—a doubtful—1.24 billion francs ($245 million) and those in the less seriously damaged city Santiago at 10 million francs ($1.96 million).

also, fires that lasted for days followed the quake and destroyed numerous insured buildings.[403] The total damages were estimated at up to $12.5
million—an amount that exceeded the yearly export income of the entire
island. The London parliament granted a financial emergency aid package
amounting to $4.75 million.[404]

As in the two cities previously decimated, an especially large number
of British insurance companies had insured against fires in Kingston. And
they had used the same policies as in Valparaiso.[405] At first, the British
companies refused to make good on their coverage. By mid-May, a number of British managers began 'to confer on whether it was "advisable" to
pay the damages in Kingston' (trans.).[406] Apparently, not all of the companies decided to follow this course; those who continued to refuse to pay
damages probably lost all their cases. The last cases were decided in the
autumn of 1907 by the judicial council of the London Privy Council as the
highest court.[407] In addition, it became known that a German company had
refused to pay compensation on the grounds of an exclusion clause, but a
Jamaican court ruled against the company.[408] In Kingston, the direct insurers and reinsurers paid out approximately $5 million in compensation.
In the cases where matters landed in court, they also had to assume the
high court costs. On the average, they were merely able to reduce payments by 15% through negotiation.[409]

At this juncture, internationally active insurance companies in three
American countries were busy dealing with earthquake-related fire damages. The replacement obligations in Chile and Jamaica were financially
not comparable to those in California. However, 'Valparaiso' especially
quickly became a buzzword next to 'San Francisco' for the powers that

---

[403] Contempory reports were provided by Hall 1907; Treves 1908; Hall Caine 1908; *The
Jamaica Gleaner* (ed.), Geography and History of Jamaica, 24th ed. (1995).

[404] Lobdell 1993, 15 *et seq.*

[405] Mackenzie 1907.

[406] 22 April 1907 Simon to Gruenwald, SR/FA A9.0–32/yellow file folder (correspondence chiefly from Cologne Re 10/1906–8/1907), 2 *et seq.* The director of the Swiss Re Charles
Simon conjectured that they would pay, 'since they had paid in San Francisco and did not
want to treat the compatriots in Kingston worse than the Yankees in California'.

[407] Herzog n.d., 270; Lobdell 1993, 15 *et seq.*; 'Feuerschaden durch Erdbeben', *Der Versicherungsfreund*, 10 September 1907, 8.

[408] Those insured by Aachener & Münchener Fire Insurance Company were able to
prove that the fires had broken out prior to the earthquake (Herzog n.d., 270).

[409] Herzog n.d., 270; Lobdell 1993, 15 *et seq.; Der Versicherungsfreund*, 10 September
1907, 8.

demanded a blanket exclusion of earthquake risks from all fire insurance contracts.[410] A quotation from the *Zeitschrift für die gesamte Versicherungswissenschaft* captured the atmosphere of those involved:

> The insurance industry all over the industrialised world has been shaken to its very foundations by the repeated earthquake disasters in the last few years, and, we need to be clear on this matter, less directly by the large losses suffered by providing damage costs than indirectly by the uncanny perception that the clauses designed by the insurer to exclude the risk of earthquakes from fire insurance have proven in practice to be insufficient for this purpose (trans.).[411]

2.2.4. *Radical Thought Experiments*

Despite the perception of a previously scarcely considered cause of fire disasters that for some insurance companies in the United States and Europe became a threat to their very existence, no discussion developed as to the basic distribution of the burden posed by earthquake-caused fire disasters. Comments on the total economic system of assuming and distributing risks assumed merely a peripheral status.

The insurance industry suggested two solutions. Both were intended to protect the commercial insurance business from the consequences of financial disaster. For an increase in what had already been experienced was thoroughly imaginable: 'Such a disaster occurring in New York or London would certainly wipe out the strongest establishments of these great metropolises that practice their business there, and the entire mercantile community would be deprived of the protection so necessary to their existence' (trans.).[412] For this reason either 'national sources of aid' had to be provided for the handling of earthquakes[413] or it was a 'matter for the inhabitants of these so devastated areas themselves to form reciprocally functioning institutes that would offer them aid in the event of such dreadful natural disasters [...]' (trans.).[414] Other voices demanded the socialisation of the insurance industry for protection against natural disasters. Governor Pardee countered that the amounts of compensation that had been paid in San Francisco by domestic and foreign insurers

---

[410] For example, Fuld, *ÖVZ* 1907, 307 *et seq.*
[411] Witzleben, *ZVersWiss* 7 (1907), 378.
[412] Mackenzie 1907.
[413] Gröppler (1910, 60) refers to the United States.
[414] *L'Argus*, cited in *Der Versicherungsfreund*, 1 October 1906, 2 *et seq.*

could not be raised by his state. Socialisation, moreover, meant the end of the international character of the insurance business.[415]

The Europeans, who in remote regions such as California and Chile had to pay damages in the millions, engaged in more intense debates on the 'internationalism' of the insurance business. The broad spreading of the risks in San Francisco had protected nine out of ten companies from breaking down under the burden of the claims.[416] But at the same time, the circles of the economically affected had become highly visible. It was not just the shareholders of individual companies that were involved in the indemnification, but also those of the reinsurers, the retrocessionaires and other fire insurance companies that had assumed the coinsurance or had signed *surplus lines*.[417] The collapse of the American insurance company Traders alone had affected twenty additional companies.[418]

In Germany, the President of the *Deutscher Feuerversicherungs-Schutzverband* ('German Association for the Protection of the Fire Insured'), Otto Prange, polemicised the most against the urge of many insurers to go abroad. The director was not mainly concerned with an international equalisation of risks, as Alfred Manes in *Der Tag* had written:[419]

> In fact it started around ten years ago to be part of the bon ton in the German insurance industry to present oneself as an 'international businessman' whose own four walls had become too confining and required one to cross the big pond and take up residence for weeks and months in New York and other places in the United States and set up second-to-none enterprises (trans.).[420]

But they lacked sufficient knowledge of the local conditions. Prange conceded that the fire insurance business had acquired 'certain internationality' (trans.) as a coincidental business development; everything else he regarded as 'empty phrase-making' (trans.).[421]

His rival Manes, the director of the *Deutscher Verein für Versicherungswissenschaft* ('German Insurance Science Association'), made no direct

---

[415] Whitney, cited in Mackenzie 1907.

[416] See the annexe for a list of companies involved in compensation in San Francisco.

[417] *ÖRev* 1906, 104. Surplus lines insurance is coverage that is unavailable through admitted carriers but can legally be placed with eligible non-admitted companies. These surplus lines companies may be located in other states or countries.

[418] Hagen, *DJZ* 1906, col. 741.

[419] Most likely an article in *Der Tag* on 22 April, 26 April or 29 April, 1906.

[420] Prange, *Feuerversicherung und Feuerschutz* 1906, 106.

[421] Ibid.

response. Instead, in an essay on the handling of the San Francisco damages by German companies, he adopted the standpoint of German fire insurance policy holders, who could argue that they also bore some of these costs that accrued to German companies through fires abroad. 'This argument is, of course, not completely unfounded', wrote Manes, 'but it cannot by any means stand as a criticism of the German companies. The internationalisation of the insurance business is ... today an absolute necessity, if for no other reason than that without such a development, the reinsurance that the entire private insurance business necessarily relies upon would be impossible' (trans.).[422] Thus, just as Germans bore part of the costs for foreigners in the case of compensation payments, the same principle applied in return. The security of a company was by no means increased if it retreated to the national level. Moreover, Manes wrote, that the German insurance business operated in a prudent manner abroad.[423]

Ludwig Fuld also warned the European companies against withdrawing from the American market as they had done after the Chicago fire. He recommended that policy holders pay heed to the worldwide exclusion of earthquakes and other natural events on the part of their insurers.[424]

Swedish and French observers made similar remarks. The Swedish journal *Gjallarhornet* reminded critics of insurance business internationalism of the last violent earthquake on the west coast of their own country, which geologists had traced back to a submarine earthquake in Skagerrak or Kattegat, and warningly asked:

> What would be the consequences of the earthquake if it had been even more intense, had destroyed Gothenburg or the rest of the coast cities, perhaps even Christiania [i.e., Oslo], and been followed by great fire damages? ... There is no reason for the Swedish insurance business to claim any qualitative superiority to foreign businesses ... How will we therefore maintain the demand that the fire insurance business operate only within the area that lies, so to say, in front of one's nose? It would be bad for us if foreign insurers were to come up with such an idea in reference to our country' (trans.).[425]

---

[422] Manes, *Masius' Rundschau* 1906, 165; Liebig (1911, 79 *et seq.*) makes a similar argument.
[423] Manes, ibid.; Liebig, ibid.
[424] Fuld, 'Feuerversicherung und überseeisches Geschäft', *ÖVZ* 1907, 45.
[425] *Gjallarhornet*, cited in 'Internationalität des Feuerversicherungsbetriebes', *ÖVZ* 1906, 168.

In view of the San Francisco experiences, *L'Argus* even advised its readers in the head offices of French insurance companies to enter the American market in order not to miss out on the opportunity.[426]

In the insurance business, a retreat from the earthquake-endangered zones of or the rest of the world was seldom seriously considered.[427] Only a few heavily damaged European companies gave up their business activities in the United States.[428] Despite the disaster, the region remained one of the most lucrative markets in the world.[429] At the same time, the readiness among the fire insurance companies at home or abroad to reinsure themselves was growing. Companies that had concentrated on the Californian market expanded their business activities to other states.[430] Others increased their stock capital[431] or merged with stronger companies in order to be able to maintain their business with joint capital.[432] The enthusiasm for the New World, whose economic boom could yield profits even on this side of the Atlantic, was unbroken.

In the opinion of the insurers, solutions to the problem of the earthquake-induced fire damages had to be found within the existing system. In this sense, a German author recommended an international cooperation between the fifty largest private insurance companies in the world for the handling of natural disasters and suggested in addition that the internationalisation of the business be followed by an international law of supervision.[433] Manes even went one step further and saw the time come for a real 'earthquake insurance'.[434] But the suggestions that aimed at fundamental changes in the insurance system were soon forgotten. Thus, it

---

[426] *L'Argus*, cited in *Der Versicherungsfreund*, 1 October 1906, 2.

[427] *Handel und Industrie*, cited in *Der Versicherungsfreund*, 20 February 1907, 4.

[428] [Note] in *La Semaine*, 11 November 1906, 7; the *Allianz* also considered taking this step ('Eine Fusion in der Feuerversicherung', *ÖVZ* 1906, 309).

[429] Accompanied by applause, the Director of the Munich Reinsurance Company, for example, declared at the end of 1906 at a general shareholders' meeting of his company that he desired to remain in the lucrative American market (*Wallmann's Versicherungs-Zeitschrift* 1907, 630; *DVZ* 1907, 4, and *AVW* 1906, 32; compare 'Nachklänge von San Francisco', 'Erklärung der Münchener Rückversicherungs-Gesellschaft', printed in *Masius' Rundschau* 1906, 385).

[430] For example, the California from San Francisco.

[431] For example, the Munich Re Group by 9% ([Note] in *La Semaine*, 18 November 1906, 7).

[432] For example, the *Süddeutsche Feuer* with *Allianz* (*ÖVZ* 1906, 309).

[433] *Geheimer Justizrat Schmersahl* in *Der Tag*, cited in *Der Versicherungsfreund*, 1 March 1909, 4. Compare Blum, 'Die Umlage der Katastrophenschäden bei Katastrophenverbänden', *ZVersWiss* 13 (1913), 94 *et seq.*

[434] Manes, *Masius' Rundschau* 1906, 167 *et seq.* Insurance against damage due to earthquakes was offered in the USA as of 1916. Steinberg 2000, 377.

remained up to the private insurance industry to take the necessary steps within the framework of its own possibilities.

2.2.5. *The Initial Consequences in the Crisis Regions*

In order to compensate for the losses and generate new profits, the fire insurance companies in the United States had resorted to drastic measures. They behaved similarly in the other dangerous regions.

In May 1906, the first of these measures was the increase by 25% of the fire insurance premiums along the coast of the Pacific Ocean and in all other endangered business centres.[435] In August, the rates in the eastern states for normal risks increased by 10% and those for especially high risks by 20%. This tendency continued throughout the United States[436]—a 'consoling side' of the disaster, remarked one insurer, since the premium rates had disintegrated prior to the disaster.[437] The economic pressure of higher premiums was designed, in addition, to stimulate building owners to increase their fire safety in order to be downgraded into more favourable risk classes.[438]

Many businesses limited their business engagements in San Francisco and reviewed their maximums for other large cities.[439] Many reduced the commissions for their representatives.[440] In doing so, they punished the mistakes of the local agents; for, in part, the San Francisco losses were so high because many of the insurance agents had not cancelled contracts for which premiums had not been paid for months at a time.[441]

This package of measures did not convince everybody enough to legitimise a continuation of the business endeavours in the United States and overseas. In the London *Times* of August 20, 1906, an anonymous author demanded still more restrictive reforms, among them tighter controls on the European companies in the business dealings of their branches overseas, clear reductions in business costs and the introduction of a 'stringent

---

[435] *Der Versicherungsfreund*, 10 June 1907, 1; *ÖVZ* 1906, 134.

[436] [Report] in *Westliche Post*, 10 July 1906.

[437] *ÖRev* 1906, 104.

[438] *Der Versicherungsfreund*, 10 June 1907, 2; Report of a commission mandated by the Secretary of the Interior of the United States, cited in *Der Versicherungsfreund*, 1 September 1907; 3 (source: *Insurance Press*).

[439] [Note] in *La Semaine*, 11 November 1906, 7 (source: *Insurance Press*).

[440] Report of Head of the Royal Exchange, *ÖVZ* 1906, 195.

[441] [Note] in *La Semaine*, 16 September 1906, 6; Mackenzie 1907.

earthquake clause'.[442] This article caused an international stir.[443] Only a few agreed with the criticism of the business practices of the insurers.[444] The most prominent opposing voice was that of Frank Lock, the director of the American branch of the Atlas Assurance Company of London, who prophesied a 'period of prosperity, and not despite San Francisco, but in fact as a consequence of San Francisco' (trans.).[445] He acknowledged certain deficiencies in business practices, but argued that American conditions fundamentally differed from those in Europe. Above all, the large freedom enjoyed by the branch directors was not detrimental, as the directors of the large companies could not monitor their 'incredible global interests' (trans.) without transferring a large amount of decision-making powers to their local directors.

> In every large business, the right and proper delegation of responsibility is the key to success [...] (trans.).[446]

2.2.6. Additional Premiums or an Earthquake Clause?

The decisive points for the fire insurers' and reinsurers' future handling of earthquake and fire damages were set in the course of 1906. The management of the companies had to decide whether they wanted to be responsible or not for this kind of damage in the future. In making this decision, they had to take many factors into account. The particular perception of earthquakes as a danger or a calculable risk was of great importance. In this respect, a widening of the gulf between the Anglophone part of the insurance world and its continental European counterparts became apparent. In addition, the business perspectives in the crisis regions largely influenced the decision.

Taking part in the controversies on the future policy governing earthquake risks were European and North American insurers as well as interested spheres of business, politics and public administration. In Germany and England, whose insurance businesses had been involved to a large extent in the indemnity for losses in California, the discussions attained a high degree of intensity. A strong interest was also noticeable in the

---

[442] *ÖRev* 1906, 226.

[443] *ÖRev* 1906, 226. *Insurance Press* and *Insurance Field* report intense reactions in the United States, cited in *Der Versicherungsfreund*, 1 November 1906, 6.

[444] *ÖRev* 1906, 226.

[445] Lock, Insurance World, October 1906, trans. in *Der Versicherungsfreund*, 1 November 1906, 1.

[446] Ibid, 3.

Netherlands due to the major activities of the Dutch companies overseas. In other countries, well known in part for being prone to earthquakes, such as Italy, the topic was, surprisingly, hardly discussed.

The national discussions were not completely separated from one another. The fire insurance and reinsurance companies informed themselves and each other by means of the international daily press and the insurance trade press, as can be seen by the correspondence between some of the directors involved.[447] The arguments raged back and forth across national borders to such an extent that it truly became an international discourse. At the same time, the exchange of opinions remained too decentralised to allow for the crystallization of common lines of allegiance.

Many of those involved recognised that a new orientation as to the handling of earthquake-induced fire damages was necessary. The alternative to a withdrawal of the companies from all the dangerous zones was either the acceptance of the earthquake risk in exchange for high additional premiums under certain restrictions or the introduction of a strict earthquake clause.[448]

The notion of assuming the earthquake risk encountered serious opposition mainly from reinsurers: 'Earthquakes as well as volcanic eruptions are natural events against which insurance cannot reasonably provide a guarantee, since the risk involved is infinite, while infinite obligations on the part of insurance agencies even for individual areas may not be assumed because in doing so they would expose themselves to the danger of not being able to meet, or only partially meet, the obligations to the insured' (trans.).[449] This statement made to the *Frankfurter Zeitung* formed the basis for one German reinsurance agency's view that the acceptance of the risk of earthquakes represented 'a derring-do mentality'. The compensations paid out in San Francisco corresponded, according to their figures, to a business period of nine hundred years; the premiums appropriate to the earthquake fire risk would accordingly have to be 'exorbitantly high'.[450]

---

[447] Grünwald to Simon, SR/FA A9.0–29/folder III/S.F. 18 April 1906/ (diverse correspondence chiefly with Re 6/1906–6/1907), 183 *et seq.*; 15 September 1906, Simon to Grünwald, SR/FA 1906, 185 *et seq.*

[448] Lock, Insurance World, October 1906, trans. in *Der Versicherungsfreund*, 1 November 1906, 2; *The Adjuster* 33, October 1906, 189 *et seq.*

[449] Cited in *ÖVZ* 1906, 235.

[450] *ÖVZ* 1906, 235; similarly Fuld, *ÖVZ* 1906, 121 *et seq.*

Instead, what was sought was nothing less than the perfect earthquake clause. This strategic goal had already prevailed at the international reinsurance conference on April 30, 1906, in Frankfurt, Germany. In their resolution, the reinsurers had proclaimed it

> desirable, in order that the insured clearly know the situation as well, that in the future, in all policies in any area where it is still lacking, a clause will soon be included that excludes the obligation for compensation for each and every damage that results directly or indirectly from earthquakes and other unanticipated natural events, and that the insurance companies advocate for such a clause not only being adopted in their own policies, but also in the policies of all of the companies working in the same area (trans.).[451]

This rather labyrinthine formulation shows how seriously the reinsurers took their situation. They desired to express the primary issue confronting them in an unmistakable manner: the clarification of the exclusion of disaster indemnity in fire insurance by means of a worldwide introduction of a uniform exclusion clause. Their goal, of course, was standardisation. According to their concept, the first thing to be done was to develop a legally flawless stipulation. Then, fire insurers were to adopt this exact standard in all contracts all over the world. And here, the enormity of the problem becomes apparent. The hopes that relate to this concept correspond to standards' functions. The reinsurers wished to make clear that earthquake damages were contractually excluded. They were hoping for a reduction of their business risks that derived from the uncertainty of the then prevailing state of law. They were thus interested in the improvement of communication in order to create stable circumstances and to save money by means of reducing legal risks.

It is remarkable that all the reinsurers explicitly wanted to do was to clarify their exemption from liability. That is, they did not seek to create such an exemption, but rather assumed catastrophe-induced damages already did not require compensation under the prevailing law. They substantiated this interpretation in their statement by citing the 'everlastingly undisputed business custom'[452] as well as the Austrian and French draft laws that would exclude liability for earthquake damages on the part of insurance companies.[453]

---

[451] 'Zur Katastrophe in San Francisco (Erklärung von 20 europäischen Rückversicherungsgesellschaften)', *Masius' Rundschau* 1906, 227.

[452] Ibid., 225.

[453] The issue was Article 46 of the draft of a French insurance contract law and Article 76 of the corresponding Austrian draft. The reinsurers cited from the motives of the

Numerous fire insurers,[454] scientists and journalists argued similarly.[455] The companies desired to exempt themselves from liability for indirect and direct fire damages by means of a clause 'which the greatest legal nit-picking could find nothing to twist or to jibe at' (trans.).[456] The journal *Handel und Industrie* was optimistic: 'The wording of such a clause will not be easy to find; it must, however, be found and finally will be found if, in fact, it is seriously sought' (trans.).[457] Numerous powers had been working precisely in this direction in 1906. The insurers tackled the various failures of their exclusion clauses. Where did the problems lie? The American, German, Austrian, Chilean and soon, in addition, the Jamaican and British courts repeatedly declared the earthquake clause admissible. The insurers recognised the distribution of the burden of proof as one of the weak points:

> In San Francisco, the insured parties worked with the obvious fact that it was impossible to adduce evidence that the fire that had destroyed an individual property had in reality broken out as the result of the earthquake, and the courts were only too ready to support them in this opinion. It is not to be underestimated how important it is that the burden of proof rests with the insured party (trans.).[458]

Unclear formulations also rebounded unfavourably upon the insurers. For this reason, the exclusion of the earthquake danger was to be expressed more clearly than previously.[459] These insights into the procedural suitability of the earthquake regulations were as important as those into the weak points in substantive law. All of them were taken under close scrutiny in the later development of a new standardised clause.

French draft: '*Les primes sont généralement fixées d'après des statistiques qui servent de base à des calculs de probabilité*', therefore '*incendies causés par des cataclysmes au sujet desquels aucune prévention ne peut être faite, aucun calcul ne peut être établi*' may not be taken into consideration. Cited in *Masius' Rundschau* 1906, 226.

[454] 25 June 1906 Jacobi (Preußische National/Chicago) to SR, SR/FA A9.0–29/Mappe III/S.F. 18 April 1906/ (diverse correspondence mainly reinsurance 6/1906–6/1907), 1 *et seq.; Masius' Rundschau* 1906, 385; 'Stronger Earthquake Clauses Advocated', *The Journal of Commerce*, 12 May 1906, 13.

[455] *L'Argus*, cited in *Der Versicherungsfreund*, 1 October 1906, 2; *Handel und Industrie*, cited in *Der Versicherungsfreund*, 20 February 1907, 4; *The Adjuster* 33, October 1906, 189 *et seq.*; 'Earthquake Clause', *The Journal of Commerce*, 23/24 January 1907, 12.

[456] *Handel und Industrie*, cited in *Der Versicherungsfreund*, 20 February 1907, 4.

[457] Ibid.

[458] Mackenzie 1907.

[459] See reports in *Wallmann's Versicherungs-Zeitschrift* 1 (1907), 630; *DVZ* 1907, 4 and *AVW* 1906, 32.

But the perfect earthquake clause had still not been found. The lack of information led to a confusion of proposals. Thus a German 'expert' recommended the 'Hamburg transatlantic policy' in the *Österreichische Revue* and especially praised its shifting of the burden of proof,[460] the British Mackenzie argued for the South American clause of a British company[461] and the French journal *L'Argus* regarded the French version[462] as the best.[463]

2.3. THE MOTORS OF AN INTERNATIONAL STANDARDISATION OF THE EARTHQUAKE CLAUSE

The international discourse on the handling of the earthquake fire damages in which the insurers engaged had been able to develop within a few weeks because modern print media and the transport infrastructures enabled a wide-ranging interregional communication. From the point of view of the fire insurance branch, it may have sufficed if the individual companies or associations changed their own contract conditions to their discretion. But for the reinsurers, it was important that these changes be uniformly adopted in all business branches.[464] Since they regarded earthquake damage as uninsurable, only the flawless and global exclusion of the fire insurers' liability for earthquake-induced damages could make them feel protected from the kind of disasters they had just experienced. And the pressure increased with the news of each additional earthquake[465] and was strengthened by the growing demand for reinsurance for fire risks in large cities.

---

[460] *ÖRev* 1906, 130.

[461] Mackenzie 1907. A California journal ('Couple of Cast Iron Earthquake Clauses', *The Adjuster* 33, October 1906, 147) made precisely the same argument.

[462] Here, the issue was a simple exclusion clause ('Saint Pierre, San Francisco, Valparaiso', *L'Argus*, cited in *Erdbeben und Feuerversicherung*, *ÖRev* 1906, 231 *et seq.*; *L'Argus*, cited in *Der Versicherungsfreund*, 1 October 1906, 2).

[463] The brilliant exclusion clause for catastrophe damages that the Harvard professor I. M. Kidding had devised after the volcano catastrophe in Martinique in 1902 was overlooked; it was published posthumously by his friend K. Solomon (Kidding, 'A New Exclusion Clause for Fire Insurance Clauses, with special attention to avalanche caused damaged', in *Bahamas Law Review* 1 [1906], 11).

[464] In 1907, a task force emphatically made the importance of 'persuading *all* the companies working in one field of activity to adopt a *unified* clause' clear. (Gruenwald et al. 1907, 4; emphasis in the original).

[465] Insurance journals did not only report on the catastrophes in Chile and Jamaica, but also on additional earthquakes in which it only became clear later that no fire damages had occurred.

The discourse alone did not lead to the desired homogeneous changes in the insurance policies by the fire insurance companies. A consensus on the ideal formulation of an earthquake clause was already impossible due to the mere fact that each specific appraisal was based upon additional information haphazardly put together. On the national level, there were associations or cartels in most countries representing the fire insurance business that could have taken over the relevant decision processes. But on the international level, the appropriate institutions were lacking. The reinsurers likewise lacked organisation. Although almost all of them had met on April 30, 1906 in Frankfurt in order to arrive at a common position, they had not designed structures for the implementation of their demand for an earthquake clause. Just as in other complex processes of standardisation, a minimum of coordination had to be accomplished.

2.3.1. *The Project of the Four Reinsurers*

1.3.1.1. *Origin of the 'Earthquake Commission'*
Precisely two months after the Frankfurt conference, that is, on June 30, 1906, the General Directors of four reinsurance companies met in Munich: Charles Simon of the Swiss Re from Zurich, H. Gruenwald of the Cologne Re from Cologne, and B. Lindner of the Badische Re and Co-Insurance Company.[466] Their host was Carl Thieme, the head of the Munich Re Company, the most important reinsurance company in the world.[467]

The four directors had assembled because of the reports on the obliging payment behaviour of some companies and prepared a new statement of their industry on the San Francisco regulation practice. After consultation with the signers of the resolution of April 30, 1906, Gruenwald sent an admonitory telegram to the 'Union of the American Companies'[468] and to the Union of British Fire Insurance Companies, the Fire Offices Committee[469] in London.[470]

---

[466] Gruenwald to Lindner, Simon, Thieme on April 9, 1907, SR/FA A9.0–32/yellow file folder (correspondence mainly from Cologne Re 1907), 3 *et seq.*

[467] Jahn 1912, 66 *et seq.*

[468] It is unclear which union is referred to. Since the National Board of Fire Underwriters did not deal with the operative business of its members, it is more likely that Gruenwald directed his correspondence to the Board of Fire Underwriters of the Pacific.

[469] On the structure and cartel policy of the F.O.C., see Westall 1984, 130 *et seq.*

[470] The telegram was probably sent on the 4th of July (30 June 1906. Collective writings of the four reinsurers to signers of the entry for 30 March 1906 (from KR, copy to SR), SR/FA A9.0–29/gray bolted file folder/loose material.

Following the meeting in Munich, the four directors continued their informal cooperation on the earthquake question. Simon also included the St. Petersburg reinsurance company Rossija through its Berlin representative Cyon and the director Behre in their activities.[471]

The reinsurers corresponded through letters that could reach their addressees in Central Europe within a day. Pressing matters were communicated by telegram. Their correspondence on the earthquake question thus assumed a high degree of vitality and density. Sometimes Gruenwald and Simon exchanged several letters a day.[472] In addition, the four companies corresponded across the globe with dozens of other reinsurance companies and several hundred fire insurers. They exchanged their views on their own and other positions in the earthquake question and informed each other about the reinsurance and retrocession connections of the companies involved in San Francisco.[473] Moreover, they spent a lot of time travelling to the European business partners and at conferences[474]—suitable occasions to discuss the earthquake question. On July 9, 1906, Simon wrote to his colleague Gruenwald of the Cologne Re: 'When do you think is the proper time in the future for dealing with the earthquake question? I am beginning to feel uneasy about the fact that we are still active with standard clauses in many places on the coast and thus are at the mercy of a new earthquake' (trans.).[475] The 'standard clause' Simon refers to is the fallen building clause, which in San Francisco, according to the views of the insurers, had proven ineffectual. Gruenwald answered him the following day:

> I am prepared at any time to approach the future treatment of the earthquake question. Up to now we have been waiting for the Russian conference, but it is still not known when it is to take place. Therefore, it now seems completely acceptable to me that the transportation conference scheduled to take place on September 20 in Lucerne be made an occasion for the discussion of the matter by the interested reinsurers. It is by no means unlikely that the Russian conference will be combined with the transportation

---

[471] 2 July 1906 Gruenwald to Simon SR/FA A9.0–29/Mappe III/S.F. 18 April 1906/ (diverse correspondence mainly Re 6/1906–6/1907), 5 *et seq.*; 7 July 1906 Gruenwald to Simon SR/FA, 34 *et seq.*

[472] For example, four letters on August 25, 1906, SR/FA, 133 *et seq.*

[473] E.g. 10 July 1906 Gruenwald to Simon, SR/FA 1907, 51 *et seq.*

[474] This is not merely shown by the correspondence; the insurance historian Arps (1968, 128) reports that during this period, Thieme spent around 200 days a year travelling on business.

[475] 9 July 1906 Simon to Gruenwald, SR/FA, 39*ff.*

conference. It would then only be a matter of winning the approval of some of the important companies for the choice of time and the discussion of the matter' (trans.).[476]

Gruenwald had recognised that a reform of the earthquake regulation could hardly succeed without the support of the Munich Re. The reinsurers not only had to develop a concept but also had to gain its acceptance in the fire insurance industry. The more market power they consolidated, the sooner this could be put into practice. Simon's agreement directly followed:

> As to the earthquake question, I gather from a report from the Helvetia delegates[477] that new policies have been made with the entire clause, but with respect to the existing risks we are still stuck with the standard clause.[478] We must answer the question in principle and, of course, for all areas, and I am completely in agreement with your proposal; we must, however, first prepare the question and have the policies sent to us from wherever we do not have them in our records. The transport conference in Lucerne seems quite appropriate. Therefore, take the preliminary steps (trans.).[479]

At this time, the reinsurance companies reappraised the earthquake clauses used by their contractual partners in San Francisco in order to be able to calculate their own losses. Occasionally, they had exchanged copies of these clauses.[480] But the cooperation did not extend any further. The attempts by Simon, Gruenwald and Lindner to persuade other directors of the value of a common policy in the earthquake question did not receive universal acceptance.[481] Despite common interests, the reinsurers remained competitors. At times, not even a common policy with Munich

---

[476] 10 July 1906 Gruenwald to Simon, SR/FA, 51 et seq.

[477] What is meant here is a delegation of insurance officials from the *Helvetia* Company that had gathered information in San Francisco on conditions there.

[478] Simon meant an improved earthquake clause when he spoke of the 'completed clause'. The 'Standard-Clause' is the collapse clause from the New York *Standard Policy*.

[479] 11 July 1906 Simon to Gruenwald, SR/FA A9.0–29/ Mappe III/ S.F. 18.4.1906/ Diverse correspondence, mainly reinsurance 6/1906–6/1907, 54 et seq.

[480] Simon thanked Lindner for sending the Belgian clauses. He reported that he would have 'all of our cedents…provide [him] with the policy conditions for all the relevant contract areas'. He examined and compared these in order to establish their capability for the regulation of earthquakes: 'the French policies also require the same amendments as the Belgian policies should receive' (20 July 1906 Simon to Lindner, SR/FA, 79 et seq.).

[481] Lindner complained to Simon of a lack of collegiality in the entire San Francisco affair (21 July 1906 Lindner to Simon, SR/FA, 81. Simon dispiritedly wrote to Gruenwald that he was not counting on the success of the reinsurers' common action, as they were behaving in such diverse ways (23 July 1906 Simon to Gruenwald, SR/FA, 98 et seq.).

Re seemed to be realistic.[482] Their director Thieme regarded the project of effecting international changes in the insurance conditions with limited enthusiasm.

On July 31, 1906, Gruenwald stirred matters up. He forwarded the following question to Simon:

> Do you not think that it would provide an excellent means of pressure that the direct companies could exploit in their communication with the public if the large majority of the reinsurers cancelled their contracts for the Pacific coast with the stipulation that their continuation would only be approved if firm guarantees for the satisfactory settlement of the earthquake question be established by then? (trans.)[483]

He 'strictly confidentially' reported that he had cancelled the contracts with the Caledonia Insurance Company and the London & Lancashire Insurance Company on the previous day.

> We not only alluded to the necessity of a regulation of the earthquake question, but also to our retrocessionaires' assurances that they would only continue their retrocession if the necessary certainty relating to the earthquake question has been guaranteed. What do you think about this matter? (trans.)[484]

Simon's answer has not been preserved. Gruenwald's unilateral approach was not without its risks for his company, as the fire insurance companies whose policies had been discontinued could find other reinsurers without major difficulties. But he was successful with respect to the Caledonian. The manager in the Edinburgh head office wrote to the Cologne office that they had instructed their New York representatives to insert an earthquake clause into their future American policies.[485]

In the weeks following, Simon, Gruenwald and Lindner succeeded in winning over Thieme for additional cooperation. Three events probably contributed to this. Firstly, the Chilean earthquake of August 16 once again directed the attention of the insurance industry to the problem of the earthquake-induced fire. Nonchalantly, Simon commented: 'Valparaiso [...] comes in handy for us in the earthquake question' (trans.).[486] A little

---

[482] 30 July 1906 Gruenwald to Simon, SR/FA, 111*ff.*; 31 July 1906 Simon to Gruenwald, SR/FA, 115 *et seq.*

[483] 31 July 1906 Gruenwald to Simon, , SR/FA, 118 *et seq.*

[484] 31 July 1906 Gruenwald to Simon, SR/FA, 118 *et seq.*

[485] 10 September 1906 Gruenwald to Simon, SR/FA, 182.

[486] 25 August 1906 Simon to Gruenwald, SR/FA, 133 *et seq.*

later, the reinsurers learned from the *Journal of Commerce* that the use of earthquake clauses was to be made more difficult in California, if not downright forbidden.[487] Finally, the German regulatory agency for private insurance frankly spoke in favour of a general introduction of earthquake clauses and thus supported the position of the reinsurance companies.[488]

On August 30, 1906, the four directors once again met in Munich, this time accompanied by the director of an Innsbruck insurance company, Grossmann. From this point on until the beginning of 1908, they continually worked on the project to introduce a new earthquake clause. They formed an informal committee that they themselves called the Erdbeben-kommission ('Earthquake Commission').[489] As a mark of its involvement, the management of the Munich Re publicly demanded that all companies uniformly insert a 'crystal clear earthquake clause' into their policies 'at least for all well-known earthquake areas' (trans.).[490]

The reinsurers who were part of the Earthquake Commission pioneered the decisive step that gave a home to the polyphonic international discourse on the possible changes in the contractual bases. Self-organisation compensated for the absence of institutions. The structural prerequisites for a process of standardisation had now been created. In the best case, the four directors could succeed in bringing the interested fire insurers and reinsurers across the globe under the same tent and in directing the additional steps leading to a uniform earthquake clause.

2.3.1.2. *Activation of the Global Networks*

At the time of their second Munich conference, the reinsurance directors already had numerous current earthquake clauses at their disposal. Most

---

[487] 13 August 1906 Gruenwald to Simon (holiday letter), SR/FA, 125 and 10 September 1906 Gruenwald to Simon, SR/FA, 182: '[...] it is very clear to me that we will not continue the business on the Pacific coast if an effective earthquake clause cannot be achieved'.

[488] Written communication of the supervisory agency 26/28 August 1906 to all German fire insurance companies and reinsurers, 4 September 1906 Drumm (*Bayerische Versicherungsbank* ['Bavarian Insurance Bank'], Munich) to SR, SR/FA A9.0–32/folder/ correspondence regarding earthquake clause 1906/1907/ *Bayerische Versicherungsbank*, 25 et seq. and 18 September 1906 Simon to *Bayerische Versicherungsbank*, SR/FA, 20 et seq.

[489] Since they did not possess a corresponding mandate for this designation, this was not their official title (3 May 1907 Simon to Gruenwald, SR/FA A9.0–32/yellow folder (correspondence mainly with Cologne Re 1907), 21).

[490] *Masius' Rundschau* 1906, 385; Fuld, *ÖVZ* 1906, 307 et seq.

of the policies came from their home countries[491] and other European business areas.

Table 9. Examples of Earthquake Regulations sent to the *Schweizerische Rückversicherungs-Gesellschaft* ('Swiss Reinsurance Company').
Source see footnote 491.

Date	Sender	Contents
28 July 1906	*Helvetia*	Policies for Switzerland, Vorarlberg and Liechtenstein; Württemberg; Alsace-Lorraine; Hamburg & Bremen; the rest of Germany; Belgium; Constantinople & Alexandria; trans-Atlantic areas; Hamburg Policy for trans-Atlantic areas[492]
29 Aug. 1906	*Bayerische Vers.-Bank*	Policies for their own Dutch business and the Rotterdam and Amsterdam stock exchange policies; also from the Association's business policies for Denmark, Norway and Sweden[493]
2 Oct. 1906	*Baseler Vers.-G*	Policies in German, French, Italian, English, Swedish and Danish[494]
15 Oct. 1906	*Helvetia*	Policy of the *Rhein & Mosel* for the Pacific Coast[495]

---

[491] In the case of the Swiss Re, for example: SR/FA A9.0–32/yellow file folder (correspondence of the Swiss insurance companies) 1, 4 *et seq.* 7 (Helvetia/St. Gallen), 4 *et seq.* (Swiss Mobilar-Fire Insurance Company/Berne), 11 *et seq.* (*Caisses Cantonales d'Assurance*), 14 (*Emmentaler Mobiliar-Versicherungs-Gesellschaft*), 15 *et seq.* (*Baseler Versicherungs-Gesellschaft*), 17 (*Vereinigung kantonaler Feuerversicherungs-Anstalten in der Schweiz*), 20 (*Aargauer Versicherungsamt*), 21 (*République et Canton Neuchâtel/Chambre d'Assurances*), 22 (*Staatskasse des Kantons Solothurn*), 23 (*Brandversicherungs-Anstalt des Kantons Bern*), 24 (*Kanton Thurgau/Assekuranz-Departement*), 26 (*Brandkassa-Verwaltung des Kantons Basel*), 27 (*Hypothekarkanzlei des Kantons Glarus*), 31 (*Brandversicherungsanstalt des Kantons Zug*), 32 (*Steuerkommissariat des Kantons Schaffhausen*).

[492] 28 July 1906 Helvetia an SR, SR/FA A9.0–32/ yellow file folder (correspondence of the *Schweizer Versicherungen*), 3.

[493] 29 August 1906 *Bayerische Versicherungsbank* to SR, SR/FA A9.0–32/folder/ correspondence regarding earthquake clause 1906/1907/ *Bayerische Versicherungsbank*, 26 *et seq.*

[494] 2 October 1906 Baseler Versicherungs-Gesellschaft an SR, SR/FA A9.0–32/ yellow file folder (correspondence of the *Schweizer Versicherungen*), 16.

[495] 15 October 1906 Helvetia an SR, SR, 25.

This collection, however, is insufficient for a systematic examination of the 'earthquake question'. There were still no policies available for many business regions.[496] Existing copies could be out of date. Even with respect to the policies sent in recently, the reinsurers could not know to what extent they were representative of the regions in question. For this reason, the four directors divided up the relevant zones of the earth among themselves at the end of 1906 and each took over the investigation of the zone assigned to him. Later they reported: 'The collection was developed by directly requesting all fire insurance companies—with the exception of those based in the United States and Canada (British North American), whose state of affairs was already well known—to send in the material'.[497]

Table 10. Direct Contacts between the Earthquake Commission and the Fire Insurance Companies.
Source see footnote 498.[498]

Germany	104	Hungary	12
Holland	99	Denmark	11
France	95	Finland	9
Belgium	45	Portugal	8
England	40	Norway	7
Austria	39	Rumania	3
Switzerland	22	Serbia	2
Russia	18	Bulgaria	2
Sweden	18	Greece	1
Spain	18	Turkey	1
Italy	13	Overseas[499]	26
		Totals	593

---

[496] Examples of policies are lacking particularly where the reinsurer was not involved in specific contracts, but had written excess reinsurance contracts that applied to the business of a company in an entire city or region.

[497] Gruenwald et al. 1907, 2.

[498] 26 June 1907 Gruenwald to Simon, Lindner, Thieme, SR/FA A9.0–32/yellow folder (correspondence mainly Cologne Re 1907), 53 *et seq.* The public insurance companies were taken into account but are not included in this list.

[499] The 'trans-Atlantic' areas, according to the archival collection, included, among others, policies from 'Tunisia, Algiers, Egypt, Turkey, Argentina, Brazil, Mexico, Havana, Manila; the Orient, Ile du Réunion, French colonies; Constantinople, Alexandria' (SR/FA A9.0–32/folders and booklets/diverse, 16 *et seq.*).

Simon was responsible for Switzerland and the countries bordering on the Mediterranean from Portugal to Italy.[500] He received numerous submissions as of the end of the year.[501] The reinsurers obtained much more information than merely about the approximately six hundred companies that had been written to. They were successful in activating a virtual network that stretched over all regions of the world in which fire insurance contracts had been concluded. The insurers in the European central administrations regularly sent in more and different copies for the domestic and foreign business markets; they often included the policies of other companies. In addition, there were the known policies of the North American companies and the conditions of the public insurance agencies that were of little interest to the reinsurers.[502]

2.3.1.3. *A Stock-Taking at the End of 1906: International Regulatory Pluralism*

The reinsurers promptly began to put together the information on the earthquake regulations from all over the world into a composite picture of the international legal situation. The results were a colourful mosaic that could be divided into four groups:

1. It had already been known since the earthquake in San Francisco that many North American policies did not contain a single earthquake-related regulation. The fallen building clause of the widely distributed

---

[500] 27 February 1908 Simon to Grünwald, SR/FA A9.0–32/ yellow folder (correspondence Swiss insurance companies)/loose material.

[501] Preserved are, SR/FA A9.0–32/yellow file folder (correspondence Spanish and Portugese insurance companies): 27 July 1906 *Hispañia, Compañia General de Seguros* (5); *"La Polar" Société Anonyme d'Assurances/Bilbao* (6); *Franceso Dresda, General agent in Napoli of La Estrella/Madrid* (7); *La Alborada, Compañía Anónima de Seguras/Vigo* (8); *La Vasconia, Sociedad Anónima de Seguros/Pamplona* (9); *La Estrella, Sociedad Anónima de Seguros/Madrid* (11); *El Día, Compañia Anónima de Seguros/Cartagena* (12); *El Norte, Compañia Anónima de Seguros/San Sebastian* (13); *La Aseguradora Española/Madrid* (14); *La Previsión Española/Sevilla* (15); *Sociadade Portugueza de Seguros/Lisboa* (16); *Erdbebenklausel aus der Police des Phoenix für Spanien* (17); *La Catalana, Compañia de Seguros contra Incendios/Barcelona* (18); *Tagus, Companhia de Seguros/Lisboa* (19); *La Unión y el Fénix Español/Madrid, Policen zu portugiesischem Geschäft* (29); *El Día* to SR, have included an earthquake clause in their policies, convey its wording (31).

[502] The public insurance companies required the support of the reinsurance companies less frequently than did the private companies (statistics in Jahn 1912, 53). Nevertheless, the reinsurers collected the policies and insisted later, for example in Switzerland and Germany, that the public agencies adopt a change in the earthquake regulations.

New York standard fire insurance policy only protected the insurer in a narrow and clearly defined area of application.[503]

2. Simple, indiscriminately formulated earthquake clauses had spread to almost all of Europe as well as to Egypt and the Maghreb. Many European insurers also used them abroad.[504] The clauses excluded, without additional specification, the liability for damages that had been caused by an earthquake. The experiences in San Francisco, Valparaiso and Kingston showed that the liability could be enforced in cases of indirect causality.[505]

3. In more complex clauses, the liability was expressly excluded for fire damages of any kind that directly or indirectly resulted from earthquakes. Such regulations were common in the Levant, in parts of France, in some Balkan states as well as in almost all transatlantic areas.[506] In the United States, only a few companies protected themselves in this manner. Following the earthquake, some companies, to the dissatisfaction of the California public, introduced rather strict earthquake clauses into the newly concluded contracts.[507]

4. The most drastic clauses from the point of view of the insured were those in which the insurance companies excluded themselves from all fire damages that originated 'during' an earthquake. The difficult to prove causal nexus was replaced by the clear chronological interrelationship of the events. In addition, the insurer was able to define the period of time of the earthquake: for some it included the duration of the individual tremors, for others the longer periods of the span between the first and the last tremor. Clauses of this nature were used in Japan.[508] In Europe, they were known from the so-called *Hamburger Börsenpolice* ('Hamburg stock exchange policy').[509]

---

[503] Compare Anonymus, U.S.A. [corpus juris] 1912, 112. The Massachusetts Standard Fire Insurance Policy included neither earthquake nor collapse regulations (Anonymus, 114).

[504] Witzleben, *ZVersWiss* 7 (1907), 380; *Berliner Tageblatt* 6/7 June 1906, cited in *Feuerversicherung und Feuerschutz* 1906, 126. Policies from Germany, Austria, Switzerland, France, Italy, Sweden, England, Spain, Holland and Denmark were mentioned (Herzog n.d., 658; Prange 1906, 106).

[505] Fuld was the only one to hold the opposite opinion (*ÖVZ* 1906, 121).

[506] Witzleben, *ZVersWiss* 7 (1907), 380. The California policies of the British companies Alliance, Commercial Union, Norwich Union as well as the Aachen and the Munich companies ('Zur Ersatzpflicht der Feuerversicherungsgesellschaften bei der Katastrophe in San Francisco', *ÖVZ* 1906, 135; *Berliner Tageblatt* 6/7 June 1906, cited in *Feuerversicherung und Feuerschutz*, 126; Manes, *Masius' Rundschau*, 161).

[507] *ÖVZ* 1906, 265.

[508] Witzleben, *ZVersWiss* 7 (1907), 380.

[509] Gruenwald et al. 1907, 8.

Only a few companies expressly saddled the insured with the burden of proof of the causality between earthquake and fire damage. Examples could be found in Swedish and Japanese policies according to which the injured had to prove that their buildings had not been destroyed by fire during or because of the earthquakes.[510] The insurers made use of different provisos on the exclusion of explosion and detonation damages, whose importance they had recognised long before the great urban disasters, as supporting measures.[511]

This pluralism concerning regulations, only a small minority of which could have definitely excluded liability, could only strengthen the reinsurers' desire to introduce a unitary standard clause. A cultural lag cannot be spoken of here, as it was generally not State regulations that had proven insufficient, but rather the contractual conditions that the fire insurers had devised themselves. Nevertheless, the problem described by Ogburn[512] manifested itself here, that is, the tension between the existing regulations and the needs of the insurance business that had so drastically changed through the experience of the past disasters.

2.3.1.4. *Reinsurers as Legal Comparatists*
The first half of 1907 was spent examining and investigating the earthquake regulations. The reinsurers proceeded in four elaborate working stages. The material they obtained was first organised in folders and notebooks and commented upon following the following system:[513]

1. Name, location of the company
2. Wording of the clause[514]
3. Deficiencies of the clause
4. Comments.

Interesting in this context are the third and fourth categories. The deficiencies of the earthquake clauses were entered in three sub-categories.

---

[510] Witzleben, *ZVersWiss* 7 (1907), 380.
[511] Compare here Manes, *Masius' Rundschau*, 162.
[512] See above, chapter 2.2.2 and fn. 93.
[513] SR/FA A9.0–32/folders and booklets, preserved material on: England, Holland, Greece, Switzerland, Spain, France, Portugal, diverse areas.
[514] Pasted, filled in by machine or hand and partially translated, e.g. SR/FA A9.0–32/folders and booklets/diverse, 5: Danish clause.

This division demonstrates how closely the directors had followed the damage settlements in San Francisco. The rubrics were

a. Deficiencies with respect to the exclusion of indirect damages,
b. Deficiencies in the condition that the burden of proof of the possible allegation of another cause of damage accrues to the insured.[515]
c. Deficiencies in the enumeration of the excluded possibilities.[516]

These problem areas exactly reflected the negative experiences of the fire insurers at the hands of the Californian courts. Many insurers were unable to mount objections to the demands of the insured because their exclusionary clauses were too vaguely formulated. The reinsurers paid attention to this deficiency in the rubrics 'a' and 'c'. At least as important was the observation on the distribution of the burden of proof in rubric 'b', as the few companies that had made use of effective clauses in California almost always failed to prove that the earthquake had caused the damages in the isolated case.

In the fourth category entitled 'comments,' the reinsurers collected current information on the foreign engagements of fire insurance companies. For instance, they knew about the Hispania Company in Barcelona that 'a more precise clause is being prepared'.[517]

From the collection of materials that had been commented upon, the reinsurers developed so-called 'résumés' in which all the important data was summarised according to country.[518] In February 1907, employees of the Cologne Re prepared a country chart in A-3 format that provided

---

[515] For example, in the case of *L'Union*/Paris: The shifting in the burden of proof 'is lacking for volcanoes, earthquakes, tornadoes, hurricanes, cylcones and other meteorological phenomena except lightning' (SR/FA A9.0–32/folders and booklets/Spain, 8).

[516] Here, the focus is aimed beyond the danger of earthquakes at the causes of damages such as landslides, dynamite blasts, volcanoes, hurricanes and other meteorological phenomena. Example of a criticism: 'The clause "the company is not liable for damages that were caused not by fire but by explosions, twisters, hurricanes or heavy gales" makes the exclusion of *fire damages* as a result of such events dubious, and the clause should also include "meteorolog. phenomena of all kinds" '. Damages that originate from demolition recommended by the responsible agencies were also included (commentary on the clause by the Compagnie Belge d'Assurances Générales, Brüssel, policy for Luxemburg, SR/FA A9.0–32/folders and booklets/diverse areas, 13).

[517] SR/FA A9.0–32/folders and booklets/Spain, 5.

[518] Still extant are the résumés from Switzerland, Italy, and Spain (SR/FA A9.0–32/loose material, doc. 2); Russia-Finland (doc. 5), Austria-Hungary (doc. 6), Holland (doc. 7), Denmark (doc. 8), Norway (doc. 9) and Sweden (doc. 10).

an overview of the earthquake regulations all over the world.[519] A part
of the table is a document containing copious commentary.[520] The listing includes a total of 1,087 earthquake regulations. The reinsurers did
not claim that the listing was complete.[521] It was sufficient for them that
they would be able to base their additional decisions upon information
on the largest and most important part of companies from every area of
business.[522]

The reinsurers more from the résumés and the country chart than
the mere knowledge of the international legal situation. This material
included numerous possible solutions to the earthquake problem whose
suitability the reinsurers could compare against the backdrop of current
experiences.

2.3.1.5. *The Perfect Earthquake Clause*

In their work, the reinsurers did not aim at a well-phrased 'ideal type' of
an earthquake clause. At least, no such aim can be found in the extant
records. Instead, they concentrated on precise features that an optimal
solution should possess. This goal is revealed by the often repeated objections to specific regulations and the praise of others. The three pillars of
their clause model derived directly from their criticism of the existing regulations. The perfect earthquake clause would clearly express the exclusion of directly or indirectly caused damages—and, it goes without saying,
'fire damages'—and assign the burden of proof to the injured parties.[523]

---

[519] SR/FA A9.0–32/loose material, doc. 3. The table provided information on all companies active in the respective business areas; the number of those for whom information
was available; the number of those who made use of or did not make use of exclusionary
clauses. In all categories, a distinction was drawn between domestic and foreign stock or
mutual insurance companies and public companies. The country table on the earthquake
clause is dated 'II [probably February] 1907'.

[520] SR/FA A9.0–32/loose material, doc.1.

[521] Gruenwald et al. 1907, 2.

[522] The commentaries in the lists often remark that the companies not represented
from a field of business are 'not of significant importance' (SR/FA A9.0–32/loose material,
doc.1).

[523] Only rarely did the reinsurers criticise additional deficiencies. Thus they noted that
the unclear formulation of the causal connection between the earthquake and the fire
damages in the policy of the Magdeburg Fire Insurance Company for Luxembourg ('the
result of an earthquake') was 'dependent upon the interpretation' (SR/FA A9.0–32/folders
and booklets/diverse areas, 13). A similar criticism was directed at the policy of the Paris
company Confiance and the English company London & Lancashire for Spain (*causados
par*) (SR/FA A9.0–32/folders and booklets/Spain, 8).

Table 11. The Country Table of the Earthquake Commission.
Overview of the Cologne Reinsurance Company
(February 1907, SR/FA A9.0–32/ loose material, doc. 3.).

Area	Public Limited Company		Mutual Association		Public Companies	Extant Material			
						Public Limited Company		Mutual Association	
	Domestic	Foreign	Domestic	Foreign		Domestic	Foreign	Domestic	Foreign
Austria	10								
Belgium	8								
Bulgaria	2								
Denmark	3								
England	35								
Finland	2								
France	33								
Germany	32								
Greece	1								
Holland									
Hungary	4								
Italy	5								
Luxembourg	–								
Monaco	–								
Norway	6								
Portugal	8								
Romania	3								
Russia	13								
Serbia	–								
Spain	15								
Sweden	6								
Switzerland	2								
Turkey	1	>8	–						
	189	206	131	2	81				
Gen. Foreign	120								
Canada	12				1		–		
USA	174				239				

In no phase of their work did the reinsurers significantly depart from this concept. They paid little attention to alternatives[524] such as the 'suspension of the contracts' validity' in the case of an earthquake[525] that was recommended by an Austrian insurance journal. Their abstention from radicalness and simplistic solutions demonstrated the reinsurers' nose for the opposition that the substitution of new regulations for older ones could awake. The suggestions that they wanted to make to the national association of the fire insurance agency on the changes in their policies were comprehensive and restrained at the same time. Since the fire insurers themselves were to formulate the clauses in their own language of business, the wording of the future clauses would, in any event, be different. However, from a legal perspective they had to—at least in a precise implementation—attain the same results in all business areas. The criticism and the suggestions made by the reinsurers constituted a precise description of their solution to the earthquake problem. Their concept aimed at the international introduction of a standard clause and thus, in the words of Ludwig Fuld, at a contribution to the international 'legal equalisation in the field of insurance law' (trans.).[526]

Furthermore, according the fire insurance companies themselves an active role in order to avoid giving them the feeling of interfering in their business was elegant. Still, the reinsurers had to count upon a certain amount of resistance because each change in a policy entailed expenditures of time and money. Nevertheless, the earthquake clauses used in the catastrophe-struck areas had for months been subjected to criticism in insurance journals similar to the one it had received from the reinsurers.[527] That is why they could hope they would have small troubles convincing the insurance companies of the material benefits of the standard clause, provided a general readiness to reform the earthquake clauses existed.

Finally, it is remarkable that in developing their standard, the four reinsurance directors paid no attention to the legal situation in the individual countries. They were able to develop an abstract concept of the earthquake clause because compelling provisions that would have required alternative drafts existed nowhere.

---

[524] 3 May 1907 Simon to Herlitz, SR/FA, 33 *et seq.*
[525] *ÖVZ* 1906, 309.
[526] Fuld, *ÖVZ* 1906, 307.
[527] Compare, for example, *Masius' Rundschau*, 385; Mackenzie demanded in *Der Versicherungsfreund* (20 May 1907, 1 and 2) a 'clear and effective wording for the relevant clause that will protect the company and be just and equitable for the insured party'.

2.3.2. *Opposition in England and the United States*

While the Earthquake Commission pressed on with its examination of the earthquake question, opposition to the exclusion of earthquake-caused damages from the fire insurers' liability was growing in England and the United States.

2.3.2.1. *The United States of America: The Power of Politics and Society*

At the beginning of 1907, it was well known that in several US states, an intervention of the legislative branches threatened to render all of the efforts to introduce an exclusionary clause obsolete. They considered legally obliging the insurance companies to assume liability for earthquake fire damages. In California, where such suggestions had already been made by mid-1906, the plans were even more concrete.[528]

The advocates of State intervention suggested following the example of Massachusetts, New York and other states and to prescribe the wording of the insurers' contracts in the form of *standard policies*. Among the insurance companies, the regulation through standard policies was regarded as a massive attack upon their freedom of contract and a grave interference in the equilibrium between accepted risks and excluded dangers. The American insurance press warned that the legislative interventions could prompt precisely the best and most capable companies to drastically reduce their area of coverage or even cease doing business entirely. The citizens seeking protection by insurance would be the real victims.[529]

The professional insurance world registered the appointment of two commissions from the insurance business whose assignment it was to examine the earthquake question with the according interest. The issue here was to develop common grounds or at least to make the decision between additional premiums and the earthquake clause facing the fire insurance companies easier to arrive at. In addition, they proposed to counter the efforts of state legislatures to achieve standard policies.

---

[528] *Handel und Industrie*, cited in *Der Versicherungsfreund*, 20 February 1907, 4; Mackenzie 1907.

[529] Mackenzie 1907; *Handel und Industrie*, cited in *Der Versicherungsfreund*, 20 February 1907, 4. *Handel und Industrie* believed that the German supervisory agency would force the fire insurers and the reinsurers, by means of direct and indirect pressure, to cease doing business in countries with standard policies. In fact, for example, the *Allianz*—recently merged with the *Süddeutsche* ('South German Insurance Company')—considered leaving the business (*ÖVZ* 1906, 309).

One of these committees was composed of American representatives from the European companies that did business directly or indirectly in the United States and Canada. A meeting was planned for the end of February 1907 in London or Berlin at which they were to report to the general directors.[530] At this conference, the insurers intended to 'protest in the clearest terms the obligatory acceptance of the earthquake risk through law or so-called standard policies'.[531] According to press reports, the American insurers believed that an 'energetic resolution of the prospective conference attended by European companies would bring the California legislature to its senses'.[532] Allegedly, the majority of the American branch directors advocated the adoption of an effective earthquake clause in their policies. However, they recommended allowing the individual companies a free hand in taking on the earthquake risk on the basis of special agreement or in exchange for additional premiums.[533]

The second committee was convened by the Board of Fire Underwriters of the Pacific. At this meeting in February 1907, the general introduction of an earthquake clause was also discussed.[534] Mackenzie believed that the report and the motions adopted by the committee could represent 'long-range significance'[535] similar to the proposals made by the European companies. But the work of both commissions came to naught.[536] The states intensified their legislative preparations for an introduction of *standard policies*. The example of California showed that the fire insurers had temporarily lost all their influence on this process. This situation held especially true for the question of the earthquake exclusionary clause.[537]

2.3.2.2. *Great Britain: The Power of the Market*

In Great Britain, the opposition to the efforts to exclude the liability for earthquake damages from all fire insurance contracts worldwide took on a completely different character. In the United States, the active opposition emanated from the middle of the social fabric—ad hoc associations

---

[530] *Handel und Industrie*, cited in *Der Versicherungsfreund*, 20 February 1907, 4.

[531] Ibid.

[532] Ibid.

[533] Ibid.

[534] 'Now the entire clause matter will be thoroughly discussed in all its details!' Mackenzie, cited in *Der Versicherungsfreund*, 20 April 1907, 1. The association is referred to in the article as 'chamber of the fire insurers on the Pacific coast'.

[535] Mackenzie 1907.

[536] Neither in American nor in European papers did additional reports appear.

[537] See chapter 4.2.2 of this work.

representing the insured, business associations, the press and factions that could ensure for themselves the support of insurance commissioners, governors and other administrative organs.[538] In Great Britain, on the other hand, where regulations in the style of standard policies were virtually anathema,[539] the question of risk bearing was decided within the relatively small setting of forty-four fire offices.[540] Neither political power nor administrative or legislative compulsion was important in Britain, but rather the powers of the market.

It had still been in mid-1906 that the London & Lancashire and the London Assurance had calmed their reinsurers by claiming 'that shortly the British Offices will arrange to take some combined action in the matter'.[541] In fact, the cartel of the English fire insurance industry, the Fire Offices Committee (F.O.C.),[542] had established a sub-sub-committee for the discussion of the earthquake question. Its report was expected from the responsible sub-committee that would then forward a suggestion to the F.O.C.[543]

But two weeks later, Simon received an alarming letter from the director of the Stockholm reinsurance company *Skandia*, Karl Herlitz. He was under pressure from his largest assignee, the powerful Liverpool Royal Insurance Company,[544] which had announced that in the future, it would be assuming the risk of earthquakes in exchange for additional premiums. For the small company *Skandia*, the situation was ominous. Simon also recognized that this venture endangered the project of an international introduction of a unitary earthquake clause. If an insurance company promised to compensate even for earthquake-caused fire damages, it gained a large advantage in comparison to other competitors,[545] who could be forced to follow suit.

---

[538] Ditto.

[539] In English private law, private autonomy enjoyed an especially high degree of significance. See further discussion in chapter 2.2.3 above.

[540] Numbers for 1906 (Emminghaus 1909, 95).

[541] 15 September 1906 Simon to Gruenwald, SR/FA A9.0–29/folder III/S.F. 18 April 1906/ (diverse correspondence mainly reinsurance 6/1906–6/1907), 185 *et seq.*

[542] The F.O.C. had dominated the British fire insurance industry since 1868. Its most important instrument was its premium policy (see Supple 1970, 127 *et seq.*, 217, 282; Cockerell 1976, and Westall 1984, 130 *et seq.*).

[543] 27 February 1907 Hürlimann (Swiss Re) to Simon, SR/FA A9.0–32/folders and booklets/England.

[544] Measured by its premium income, the Royal was the largest British insurance company at the beginning of the twentieth century (Supple 1970, 214).

[545] 3 October 1906 Simon to Gruenwald, SR/FA A9.0–32/yellow file folder (correspondence mainly Cologne Re 10/1906–8/1907), 1. Simon suspected that the California manager

The Royal's announcement became part of the offensive business tactics that many Fire Offices had practiced since the San Francisco disaster. They could afford to compensate for up to 98 to 100 percent of damages. In contrast to most of the American and continental European companies, the British companies had assets that would have sufficed for even more significant disasters at their disposal.[546] And this business policy paid dividends for the companies involved; they had been showing enormous growth in their business volume since the San Francisco disaster.[547] In addition, the British directors had for the most part kept themselves out of the debates on the assumption of the earthquake dangers. Apparently, some of them could imagine insuring against earthquake-induced fire damages in exchange for additional premiums in order to secure their top position in the international fire insurance business.

As long as the Royal was a member of the Fire Offices Committee, it could not alter its policies without the agreement of the other companies.[548] For this reason, it can be assumed that the directors of the Royal were the authors of a written communication that was sent to all members of the Fire Offices Committee at the end of the year. This communication proposed to leave the question whether or not to assume the earthquake and fire risks up to the different offices.[549] This proposal was supported by the following reasons:

a. That there is an appreciable demand for such cover;
b. That the Fire Offices can safely grant it;
c. That by issuing such policies it will be rendered clearer that policies for which the extra has not been paid do not cover the liability.[550]

---

of the Royal was behind this policy: 'I am not surprised that Mr. Rolla-Watt, on the grounds of power politics, is an opponent of such a clause, and I fear that he has henchmen. I regard the question as by no means settled'.

[546] Compare the list in the annexe of the companies involved in compensation of damages in San Francisco. Only one Office, the Regent Fire (Glasgow), experienced difficulties after the Chilean earthquake and had to be liquidated. Compare the table of the companies listed in the annexe involved in damage compensation in Valparaiso.

[547] Compare figures in Marks, The San Francisco story—April 18–21 (1909).

[548] The uniform policy conditions of the F.O.C. 'that contained the known earthquake clause' were obligatory for certain areas in the F.O.C. (10 May 1907 Gruenwald to Simon, SR/FA A9.0–32/yellow file folder [correspondence mainly Cologn Re 10/1906–8/1907], 64 et seq.).

[549] The communication sent to the members of the departments 'home' and 'foreign' is mentioned in the memorandum of 15 February 1907, a copy of which the Swiss Re received on the 4th of May, 1907 (SR/FA A9.0–32/yellow file folder [correspondence mainly Cologne Re 10/1906–8/1907], 44 et seq.).

[550] Thus, another company reported the argumentation; memorandum of 15 February 1907 (copy), SR/FA 1907, 44 et seq.

But not all British companies were prepared to follow this argumentation. On February 15, 1907, the F.O.C.'s office distributed a memorandum to the associated offices in which another cartel member responded to the proposal. The author refuted all three arguments:

The allegation 'that there is an appreciable demand for such cover' was not true; the offices had received few applications since the San Francisco disaster. The offer of the agents of Lloyd's Underwriters to assume the risk in Jamaica had not met increased demand. The authors of this memorandum predicted that the offer to assume the risk would direct the attention to the earthquake problem, thus creating the demand—with consequences for the other companies: 'Offices who do not wish to take this risk will be driven to do so by the competition of those who do'. It was possible that after the experienced sequence of earthquake disasters, calm would reign for a longer period of time 'and the extra rates [would] tend to disappear'.[551]

'That the Fire Offices can safely grant it' had been the second argument. The critics commented that in order to preserve the companies' security, the risk could only be assumed if more than half of the portfolios be forfeited in large cities. The proposal envisaged allowing for the maximum where wood and inferior building construction dominated—'but San Francisco has shown the danger for well-built cities with good Fire and Water Departments (50–100 fires burst out simultaneously)'.[552]

The authors of this memorandum did not directly contradict 'that by issuing such policies it will be rendered clearer that policies for which the extra has not been paid do not cover the liability'. Instead they pointed to the experiences made during the past disasters: '[...] not solved the problem that policy holders will claim that the fire was not caused by earthquake'.[553]

They concluded that the assumption of the earthquake and fire risk was a lottery.

> The only safe course is for the combined British Offices to adopt the strongest Earthquake Clause which can be framed, and to insert it in every policy at home and abroad. It is conceivable that in some cases Banks or others wishing to absolutely secure advances may demand the cover, though at present there is no evidence to this at any extent. They can get such cover perhaps from some Underwriters at Lloyd's, who may by offering it secure a small percentage of other fire business, but this is a trifling evil compared

---

[551] Ibid.
[552] Ibid.
[553] Ibid.

with the incalculable risk which the Fire Offices will incur by adopting a line of action, *the tendency of which is to make all their contracts subject to a liability which the wealthiest of them could not possibly meet.*[554]

This demand for a uniform inclusion of the 'most sharply worded earthquake clause' (trans.) for all areas of business precisely corresponded to the standpoint that the reinsurance branch had taken a few months previously. For the first time, British insurers manifested their adherence to this argumentation.

The arguments of the authors of the memorandum were of purely economic nature. They did not address the question whether the probability of earthquake disasters was calculable. They were satisfied with the following simple prognosis: if some offices assumed the liability for earthquake damages, all others would be required to follow suit, and after such a change of the assumed risks at the latest, the economic consequences of a metropolitan disaster would be incalculable. The warning that even the richest British companies would not be able to honour their commitments had not been mentioned by anyone.

The parties had made their positions on the earthquake dangers clear. Significantly new arguments were not added. At the end of February, the sub-sub-committee of the F.O.C. proposed an earthquake clause. E. Huerlimann, who had travelled to London on behalf of the Swiss Re, reported to Simon that the clause was 'incomplete': the burden of proof rested upon the insurer, and the identification of the excluded damages was unclear. Nothing more happened. Months went by, one meeting of the cartel after another took place without a policy on the earthquake danger becoming any clearer.[555] All they agreed upon was a special permission for the assumption of the risk in Canada.[556] The reinsurers could not know that the members of the F.O.C. wanted to postpone their decision until the pending court cases in San Francisco, Valparaiso and Kingston had been concluded, as the introduction of more stringent earthquake

---

[554] Ibid. Underlining in the original.

[555] Postponements on 22 February 1907 (23 February 1907 McLaren/Guarantee to Simon, SR/FA A9.0–32/folders and booklets/England), on 5 April (27 February 1907 Hürlimann/ Swiss Re to Simon, SR/FA 1907, 4 *et seq.* and 19 April 1907 Alcock/Royal to SR, SR/FA 1907, 1 *et seq.*) and on 10 May 1907 (13 May 1907 McLaren to Simon, SR/FA A9.0–32/yellow file folder/ [correspondence Royal Insurance Co., Liverpool, 15 *et seq.*).

[556] 'British Offices And Earthquake Harzard', The Journal of Commerce, 25 March 1907, 13.

clauses could have been regarded as an acknowledgement that the danger of earthquakes had not been excluded by the previous regulations.[557]

In the meantime, the Royal began to apply pressure on its reinsurers. On April 19, 1907, its General Manager, Charles Alcock, wrote to the Swiss Re that the Royal would be assuming the earthquake fire risk and hoped that the Swiss Re would be following them as a reinsurer. His explanation precisely corresponded with the one in the proposal to the F.O.C.[558] Simon's response was reticent.[559] A few days later, he received a letter from the British Member of Parliament Charles McLaren, who apparently had previously served as a middleman between the Swiss Re and the Royal. McLaren attempted to dispel Simon's misgivings with arguments similar to those employed by Alcock.[560] But Simon could not be convinced. On the same day, he argued in a letter to Gruenwald to resist this 'impertinence' together with Royal's other reinsurers. [561] Gruenwald agreed and took over the coordination of the campaign.[562]

The two directors did not know any of the Royal's other business connections than to *Skandia*.[563] Simon and Gruenwald engaged in correspondence throughout Europe in an attempt to find some. It turned out that the Cologne Re and the American company Phoenix of Hartford had taken over the major share of the Royal's fire insurance business.[564] Other reinsurers involved were Lloyd of Belgium (Brussels—director Engels), *Nordisk Gjenforsikring* ('Northern Reinsurance'; Copenhagen—director P. C. Olsen), *Salamandra* (St. Petersburg—directors Mutzenbecher and Bernard), *Skandia* (Stockholm—director K. Herlitz), and the *Société Anonyme de Réassurance* (Paris—director Spycket).[565] They all had

---

[557] 15 July 1907 McLaren to Simon, SR/FA A9.0–32/yellow file folder (correspondence Royal Ins., Liverpool), 28; 17 July 1907 Royal to SR, SR/FA 1907, 30.

[558] Alcock (Royal) to SR, SR/FA 1907, 1.

[559] Draft of an answer from Simon on the back of Alcock's letter (SR/FA 1907, 1 *et seq.*).

[560] 22 April 1907 McLaren (Guarantee) to SR, SR/FA 1907, 3 *et seq.*, with commentary from Simon in the margin of the letter.

[561] '[...]for the matter is important for the entire profession and we have never been confronted with such an important question', 22 April 1907 Simon to Gruenwald, SR/FA A9.0–32/yellow file folder (correspondence mainly Cologne Re 10/1906–8/1907), 2 *et seq.*

[562] 24 April 1907 Gruenwald to Simon, SR/FA 1907, 5 *et seq.*

[563] 23 July 1906 Gruenwald to Simon, SR/FA A9.0–29/folder III/S.F. 18 April 1906/Diverse Corresp. (mainly reinsurance 6/1906–6/1907), 85 *et seq.*

[564] Phoenix carried about 25% of the reinsurance risks and Cologne Re apparently 40%. 23 May 1907 Royal to Gruenwald (copy Gruenwald to Simon), SR/FA A9.0–32/yellow file folder (correspondence mainly Cologne Re 10/1906–8/1907), 89 *et seq.*

[565] SR/FA A9.0–32/yellow file folder (correspondence mainly Cologne Re 10/1906–8/1907), 5 *et seq.*

received similar communications from the Royal.[566] The smaller reinsurance companies were especially affected. Olsen (*Nordisk Gjen*, 'Norwegian Re') expressed his 'shock' to his friend Simon over the demands of the English company.[567] Herlitz wrote that for his company, the question relating to the Royal was of utmost significance 'since we get almost all of our business outside of Scandinavia from the Royal'.[568] Even Director Behre from the Rossija, which had no contractual connections to the Royal, expressed 'alarm' and encouraged a 'demonstration' of the part of the reinsurers.[569]

Through McLaren, Simon had the Royal know that their undertaking was 'reasonable' from the point of view of such a large and powerful company, but raised the question for the reinsurers whether they would be able to survive a second 'San Francisco'.[570] The directors attempted to learn the particulars on the planned risk from the Royal.[571] They pointed out that they had to include their board of directors and their retrocessionaires in the decision-making process.[572] No one entertained any hope for an intervention of the F.O.C. any more.[573] The concern was all the greater that the other British companies could follow the 'earthquake policy' embarked

---

[566] SR/FA A9.0–32/yellow file folder (correspondence mainly Cologne Re 10/1906–8/1907), 5 *et seq.*

[567] End of April 1907, [probably Olsen] (*Nordisk Gjenforsikrings-Selskab*) to Simon, SR/FA 1907, 4.

[568] 27 April 1907 Herlitz (Skandia) to Simon, SR/FA 1907, 15 *et seq.*

[569] 24 April 1907 Gruenwald to Simon, SR/FA 1907, 5 *et seq.*

[570] 24 April 1907 Simon to McLaren, SR/FA A9.0–32/yellow file folder (correspondence Royal Ins., Liverpool), 6 *et seq.* Similar: 27 April 1907 Herlitz (Skandia) to Simon, SR/FA A9.0–32/yellow file folder (correspondence mainly Cologne Re 10/1906–8/1907), 15 *et seq.*

[571] 23 April 1907 Gruenwald to Royal (Liverpool), SR/FA A9.0–32/yellow file folder (correspondence mainly Cologne Re 10/1906–8/1907), 8 *et seq.*: questions on contract limits; 24 April 1907 Simon to McLaren, SR/FA A9.0–32/yellow file folder (correspondence Royal Ins., Liverpool), 6 *et seq.*: question as to the possibility of developing a 'reasonable fund' for earthquake disasters; 27 April 1907 Herlitz to Royal, copy Herlitz to Simon, SR/FA A9.0–32/yellow file folder (correspondence mainly Cologne Re 10/1906–8/1907), 18: question as to what districts are what contracts intended.

[572] 29 April 1907 Herlitz to Simon, SR/FA A9.0–32/yellow file folder (correspondence mainly Cologne Re 10/1906–8/1907), 30; 27 April 1907 Simon to Olsen, SR/FA 1907, 19 *et seq.*; 24 April 1907 Simon to McLaren, SR/FA A9.0–32/yellow file folder (correspondence Royal Ins., Liverpool), 6 *et seq.*; 22 April 1907 Simon to Gruenwald, SR/FA A9.0–32/yellow file folder (correspondence mainly Cologne Re 10/1906–8/1907), 2 *et seq.*

[573] 23 April 1907 Herlitz to Royal, copy to Gruenwald, from there to Simon, SR/FA A9.0–32/yellow file folder (correspondence mainly Cologne Re 10/1906–8/1907), 26; 23 April 1907 Herlitz to Royal, copy to Simon, SR/FA 1907, 17; 27 April 1907 McLaren to Simon, SR/FA A9.0–32/yellow file folder (correspondence Royal Insurance Co., Liverpool), 9; 2 May 1907 Simon to Gruenwald, SR/FA A9.0–32/yellow file folder (correspondence mainly Cologne Re 10/1906–8/1907), 31 *et seq.*

upon by the Royal.[574] But the Royal was not willing to make any concessions. Only one week after Alcock had drafted the letters to the European
reinsurance companies, their resistance to the adoption of the earthquake
fire risk collapsed.[575] On May 2, Simon decided to maintain the contractual relationship with the Royal.[576] Only in the event of a demand for the
lowest possible maximums for individual cities did the directors wish 'to
stand shoulder-to-shoulder'.[577] But the Royal also took a tough stand on
this point. On one occasion, it was alleged that the demand was so great
that they could no longer postpone their answer;[578] on another occasion,
it was said that the demand was so small that it was 'almost absurd' to
discuss areas' maximums.[579] On May 25, the reinsurers attempted to find
a common denominator at a Berlin conference.[580] Most of the Royal's reinsurers attended.[581] Thieme and Lindner from the Earthquake Commission
as well as the director of the Bavarian Insurance Bank, Ernst Drumm, were
also included. The insurers met knowing that in the meantime, other English fire insurance companies intended to follow the Royal—among them

---

[574] 23 April 1907 Gruenwald to Royal (Liverpool), SR/FA A9.0–32/yellow file folder (correspondence mainly Cologne Re 10/1906–8/1907), 8 *et seq.*; 24 April1907 Simon to McLaren,
24 April 1907 Simon to McLaren, SR/FA A9.0–32/yellow file folder (correspondence Royal
Insurance Co., Liverpool), 6 *et seq.*

[575] Lindner, who had no business connections to the Royal, recommended a prudent
middle course: 'where the exclusion of the earthquake danger is legally permissible', its
adoption should 'be decidedly contested'. 'In contrast, I would regard the insurability of
earthquake fire damages in such areas as possible and even as desirable, where through
legal prescription of the wording of the policy conditions the exclusion of such damages
cannot be achieved at present […]' (26 April 1907, Lindner to Simon, SR/FA A9.0–32/
yellow file folder [correspondence mainly Cologne Re 10/1906–8/1907], 13 *et seq.*). Herlitz in
the meantime had gone to England and returned with new convictions, believing 'that the
policy of the Royal [was] the proper, perhaps the only possible one' (27 April 1907 Herlitz
to Gruenwald; same letter to Simon, SR/FA 1907, 24 *et seq.*).

[576] 2 May 1907 Simon to Gruenwald, SR/FA 1907, 31 *et seq.*

[577] 29 April 1907 Gruenwald to Herlitz, SR/FA 1907, 28 *et seq.*; compare 27 April 1907
Herlitz to Gruenwald (same letter to Simon), SR/FA 1907, 24 *et seq.*

[578] 7 May 1907 Lindner to Gruenwald, SR/FA 1907, 52 *et seq.*

[579] Enquiry with full cover: at Royal 23, at Commercial Union twelve, at Guardian among
others, 'first class Companies' also approx. twelve; 13 May 1907 McLaren to Simon, SR/FA
A9.0–32/yellow file folder (correspondence Royal Ins., Liverpool), 15 *et seq.*

[580] 3 May 1907 Gruenwald to Simon, SR/FA A9.0–32/yellow file folder (correspondence
mainly Cologne Re 10/1906–8/1907).

[581] Present were Gruenwald, Simon, Olsen, Mutzenbecher and von Hollitscher. The
Hartford Phoenix had not been informed. Herlitz and Spycket excused their absences on
grounds of prior commitments. Only Engels of Lloyd Belgium refused the invitation to
attend; he saw no reason to further resist the Royal; 28 May 1907 communication from
Engels (Lloyd Belge), SR/FA 1907, 97 *et seq.*

the mighty Commercial Union[582] and the Guardian.[583] Once again, the resistance to the assumption of earthquake risks flared up.[584] Most of the reinsurers, however, argued for a 'dilatory treatment' of the question. They wanted to wait for the responses of the other English companies and that of the F.O.C., which was scheduled to meet on June 11, 1907.[585]

During the meeting, Gruenwald received a written communication from the Royal that urged a decision.[586] Two days later, the news spread that a reinsurer was going to follow the Royal.[587] This was probably the American company Phoenix of Hartford,[588] with whom the European reinsurers had no contact. This fact undermined the hope that the Royal could be forced to make at least some minor concessions.[589]

The managers of the Royal used the opportunity to increase the pressure on their reinsurers. They announced that for them, loyalty in the earthquake question was the precondition for the continuation of contracts.[590] The first to give in, at the command of its Petersburg Director, Belozwetow, was the *Salamandra* Company.[591] The others reduced their demands for the limits on the maximums, the identification of the earthquake risks in their own reporting bordereaux and a legally effective earthquake clause for the other contracts.[592]

---

[582] 26 April 1907 Lindner to Simon, SR/FA 1907, 13 *et seq.*; 4 May 1907 Gruenwald to Simon, SR/FA 1907, 42 *et seq.*; 8 May 1907 Morant (Commercial Union) to Simon, SR/FA 1907, 58 *et seq.*

[583] *The Times* reported on the General Manager of the Guardian on the 25th of May 1907: 'His own view, which was represented to the other fire offices, was that the earthquake fire risk would best be dealt with by making it subject of a distinct and separated policy, carrying a separate and special premium'. Copy of the article through KR, SR/FA 1907, 91 *et seq.* An enquiry on assuming earthquake fire risks was also received by the Gladbach Re, 25 July 1907. Gladbach Fire Insurance Co, Ltd., to KR, SR/FA 1907, 99 *et seq.*

[584] Hollitscher argued against it the most. But Olsen, Drumm and Thieme tended towards this view. 25 May 1907 Minutes of the meeting of the Royal conference, SR/FA A9.0–32/yellow file folder (correspondence mainly Cologne Re 10/1906–8/1907), 87 *et seq.*

[585] 25 May 1907 Minutes of the meeting of the Royal conference, SR/FA 1907, 87 *et seq.*

[586] Ibid.

[587] 27 May 1907 Gruenwald probably to Lloyd Belge, copy Gruenwald to Simon, SR/FA 1907, 94 *et seq.*

[588] Since it was apparently not Lloyd Belge, compare 28 May 1907 communication from Engels (Lloyd Belge), SR/FA 1907, 97 *et seq.*

[589] 27 May 1907 Gruenwald presumably to Lloyd Belge, copy Gruenwald to Simon, SR/ FA 1907, 94 *et seq.*

[590] 29 May 1907 Simon to Gruenwald, SR/FA 1907, 122 *et seq.*; 1 June 1907 Mutzenbecher jr. (Salamandra) to Gruenwald, SR/FA 1907, 103.; 3 June 1907 Gruenwald to Simon, SR/FA 1907, 107 *et seq.*

[591] 1 June 1907 Mutzenbecher, Jr., (Salamandra) to Gruenwald, 1907, 103.

[592] 29 May 1907 Gruenwald to v. Hollitscher (Rossija, St. Petersburg), SR/FA 1907, 99 *et seq.*; 3 July 1907; SR to McLaren, SR/FA A9.0–32/yellow file folder (correspondence Royal

In the middle of June, the son of the director of Lloyd Belgium, Engels, went to England to conduct negotiations. Here the reinsurers learned for the first time that the Royal desired to assume the earthquake fire insurance risk as a means of competing with Lloyds of London.[593] In fact, the offices comprising the F.O.C. experienced great competitive pressure from external insurance companies at this time.[594]

A little later, the director of the Parisian *Société Anonyme de Réassurance*, Spycket, went to London and Liverpool and learned that two tendencies were predominant in the offices comprising the F.O.C. One faction, he wrote to Simon, rejected the earthquake fire risk as unnecessary and too dangerous; the other was not interested in the discussion and expressed no particular opinion. If, however, the F.O.C. introduced the new policy, he continued, all of the companies would be forced to offer it to their customers.[595] Spycket reported further that the directors of the Royal had impressed him as thoroughly prudent and explained that they would possibly introduce city limitations if the insurers were to accept the offer in unexpectedly large amounts.[596] The liability was to be limited at £20,000 per country. All of the respective risks were to be disclosed to the reinsurers,[597] albeit not in separate reporting bordereaux.[598] At present, the Managers of the Royal wrote to Simon, they were considering accepting the 'strongest possible clause' wherever this was possible.[599]

Ins., Liverpool), 24.; 7 June 1907 Simon to Gruenwald, SR/FA A9.0–32/yellow file folder (correspondence mainly Cologne Re 10/1906–8/1907), 112 *et seq.*; 11 June 1907 Stahl (Salamandra) to Gruenwald, SR/FA 1907, 113; 3 June 1907 Herlitz to Gruenwald, SR/FA 1907, 104 *et seq.*

[593] 15 June 1907 Engels, Sen., to Gruenwald, SR/FA 1907, 116; 24 June 1907 Spycket to Simon, SR/FA 1907, 118 *et seq.*

[594] In Westall's study (1984, 140 *et seq.*) of the British domestic market, 1907 appears to be especially problematic. Important reinsurance negotiations between the F.O.C. and Lloyds stalled and were finally discontinued at the end of the year. At the same time, external companies increased their shares in the market, so that the cartel businesses were forced to lower their premiums.

[595] 24 June 1907 Spycket to Simon, 1907, 118 *et seq.* Gruenwald sent Simon a report on the general meeting of Scottish Union, 'where the necessity of sufficient protection through earthquake clauses was mentioned', 29 May 1907 Gruenwald to Simon, SR/FA 1907, 101.

[596] 24 June 1907 Spycket to Simon, SR/FA 1907, 118 *et seq.*

[597] 3 July 1907 McLaren to SR, SR/FA A9.0–32/yellow file folder (correspondence Royal Ins., Liverpool), 27.

[598] 15 July 1907 McLaren to Simon, SR/FA 1907, 28.

[599] 17 July 1907 Royal to SR, SR/FA 1907, 30.

At the end of June 1907, after the court cases in Valparaiso and Jamaica had been concluded,[600] the members of the F.O.C. decided to permit the assumption of the earthquake fire risk in exchange for extra premiums.[601] The Royal began to offer the risk, although in a very restrained manner, as McLaren reported to Zurich. Its Manager Alcock had repeatedly assured him that he desired not to engage in 'big business' in this field.

By the end of July, all of the reinsurers had given up their resistance. Gruenwald and Simon were the last to notify the Royal that they accepted the assumption of the new risks.[602]

2.3.3. *Adherence to the Concept of the Earthquake Clause*

Royal's policy threatened the project of the reinsurers who wanted to exclude the earthquake danger across the globe. On March 7, 1907—prior to the escalation of the conflict with the Liverpool company—the four directors had met in Berlin for the purpose of advancing their own concept. Besides Gruenwald, Thieme, Simon and Lindner, Director Behre of the St. Petersburg reinsurance company Rossija took part as a guest at the meeting. The strategy of the Earthquake Commission can be inferred from the resolution recorded in the minutes of the meeting. The directors wanted to mount a comprehensive investigation including short résumés of the situation in each of the individual countries.[603] This investigation was to be sent to all the reinsurance and insurance companies with whom the four were in touch, 'so that they could improve their clauses' (trans.).[604] The reasons for this was the perception that the introduction of the earthquake clauses into the individual business districts could best be implemented by the insurers locally.[605]

Gruenwald shouldered the main burden of the additional work. On April 9, 1907, he sent the first draft of the brochure to the press in order to

---

[600] 24 June 1907 Spycket to Simon, SR/FA A9.0–32/yellow file folder (correspondence mainly Cologne Re 10/1906–8/1907), 118 *et seq.*

[601] Gruenwald strictly confidentially sent the resolution of the F.O.C. to the participants of the Berlin conference. 1 July 1907 Gruenwald to all conference participants (SR/FA 1907, 127 *et seq.*).

[602] 15 July 1907 Gruenwald to Simon, SR/FA A9.0–32/yellow file folder (correspondence mainly Cologne Re 10/1906–8/1907), 136 *et seq.*; 27 July 1907 SR to Royal über McLaren, SR/ FA A9.0–32/yellow file folder (correspondence Royal Ins., Liverpool), 34 *et seq.*

[603] 7 March 1907 Minutes of the meeting of the Earthquake commission, SR/FA A9.0– 32/yellow file folder (correspondence Swiss Insurance companies), loose material.

[604] Mid-April 1907 Simon to Drumm, SR/FA A9.0–32/file folder/corresspondence relating to the earthquake clause 1906/1907/Bavarian Insurance Bank, 10.

[605] Gruenwald et al. 1907, 4.

have test copies be prepared.[606] However, before these copies were ready, the reinsurers received the Royal's demand to assume parts of the earthquake fire risks in the future. Despite the advanced stage of the commission's work, fundamental questions immediately arose. Under the pressure of the "Royal crisis", Simon wrote in letters to McLaren and Herlitz at the beginning of May that the existence of parallel 'policies including earthquake insurance and policies without earthquake insurance' only guaranteed protection 'if the earthquake clause was formulated in a manner that the policy is suspended for a certain time in the case of an earthquake shock' (trans.).[607] Herlitz agreed with him; the head of his company and 'perhaps the most prominent jurist in Sweden' (trans.) had also called for a suspension of the policies.[608] Gruenwald and Lindner also agreed that this model was the 'only thoroughly satisfactory', 'rock-solid earthquake clause' (trans.).[609]

Nevertheless, the reinsurers did not deviate from their previous course. They probably feared the loss of time that would have resulted from a correction of their investigation. The pressure to respond to the offensive action on the part of Lloyds Underwriters, the Royal, the Commercial Union and the Guardian was enormous. Moreover, an all too radical break with the existing exclusionary clause may have seemed too difficult to convey to them. Perhaps they feared that courts could dismiss the temporary suspension of insurance protection as unlawful. Be that as it may, the concept of the earthquake clause continued to exist even if it was no longer considered perfect.

On April 27, 1907, Gruenwald sent his three colleagues the first copy of the investigation[610] and drafts of covering letters[611] for corrections. A few days later, Gruenwald and Simon arranged for the French version to be produced in Zurich and the English version in Cologne.[612]

Thieme unexpectedly raised an objection. He did not so much call into question the concept of the earthquake clause but rather the entire strategy of the Earthquake Commission. The Munich director was concerned

---

[606] 9 April 1907 Gruenwald to the members of the Earthquake Commission, SR/FA A9.0–32/yellow file folder (correspondence, mainly Cologne Re 1907), 3 et seq.

[607] 3 May 1907 Simon to Herlitz, SR/FA 1907, 33 et seq.

[608] 7 May 1907 Herlitz to Simon, SR/FA 1907, 57.

[609] 7 May 1907 Lindner to Gruenwald, SR/FA 1907, 52 et seq.

[610] 27 April 1907 Gruenwald to Thieme, Lindner, Simon, SR/FA 1907, 8 et seq.

[611] One each for the fire insurers and the reinsurers. 2 May 1907 Gruenwald to Simon, SR/FA 1907, 17 et seq.

[612] 1 May 1907 Gruenwald to Simon, SR/FA 1907, 15 et seq.

because the strategy seemed to 'argue for or against the individual exception clauses' (trans.). He did not merely consider the fire insurer's reactions, but also the court cases involving the damages in San Francisco,
Valparaiso and Kingston: '[…] if our appraisal is relatively positive, it
would reduce the possibly existing tendency to replace the old clause with
a stricter version, and if it is relatively negative, it would make it easier for
a judge to decide against the insurers' (trans.).[613] Thieme suggested removing the résumés and the names of the companies that did not include
earthquake clauses in their policies from the study.[614] Thus, the committee's proposal would acquire a 'thoroughly uncontroversial character as a
generally valuable collection of materials' and could be used as 'an attach-
ment to the letters to the direct insurers' (trans.).[615] Obviously, Thieme
wanted to avoid that the fire insurance companies regarded the study as
a binding demand to adapt their clauses. In his alternate draft of an introduction, he thus went on to state:

> Whether and when the earthquake clauses can be completed in the indi-
> vidual countries in the sense intended depends not only on the will of the
> insurers but also on a large number of extraneous factors of a political, legal
> and economic nature. The material assembled here, however, gives the
> insurer the chance to compare the clauses used all over the world and the
> opportunity to become acquainted with those clauses currently in specific
> and *effective* use in the respective area of business and to adapt them to his
> protection (trans.).[616]

Thus, Thieme, himself the chairman of the committee, questioned the
wisdom of the Earthquake Commission's project. His arguments could
not simply be dismissed. Although it was correct that many an insurer
was right to believe that the study put him on ground, these insurers were
less important than those who carried no, or an inadequate, exclusionary
clause. And could it be seriously imagined that a judge in the area where
the damages had occurred would get his or her hands on the study? Thieme's motives ultimately remained unclear, but caution may have been
one of them. He presumably considered the danger of further earthquake
disasters lower than his colleagues did.

---

[613] 1 May 1907 Thieme to Gruenwald, copy Gruenwald to Simon, SR/FA A9.0–32/yellow
file folder (correspondence, mainly Cologne Re 1907), 22 *et seq.*
[614] Ibid.
[615] Ibid.
[616] Ibid.

The other three directors knew that they could not do without the weight of the Munich Re. Only through protracted negotiations did they succeed in maintaining Thieme's cooperation.[617] Above all, they energetically protested against watering down the responsibility of the fire insurers as Thieme's draft proposed to do. Gruenwald wrote:

> In my opinion, our demonstrations to date, all of our efforts to date, and everything that the world of the reinsurers expects from us, culminate in exactly the opposite point of view. Without wishing to somehow raise the question whether [the introduction of a clause depends upon extraneous circumstances] or not, I believe it cannot be the purpose of a work like ours to prioritise this point of view. In addition, the further point of view [...] that each exception possesses a flexible character and is susceptible to differing interpretation is not, I submit, our business to emphasise. We expect that the earthquake clause from which we expect protection in Valparaiso will also protect us in Kingston, and we are of the opinion that a clause must be created that guarantees similar protection in the entire insurance world, irrespective of where this is. Thus, I believe, it cannot be our job to point to the various interpretations in the individual countries (trans.).[618]

Here was the firm intention to persistently adhere to the concept of a standardisation. Whereas Thieme would have been satisfied with gradual, variously far-reaching improvements, Gruenwald was committed to the enforcement of the earthquake clause as an invariable standard. Gruenwald placed a high degree of importance precisely on the uniformity of the future regulation.

Finally, the reinsurers agreed to publish the study, the introduction and the cover letter in the originally planned form. In the cover letter, they recalled the historical earthquake fires in Basel (1356) and Lisbon (1755) in order to demonstrate to the European public as well the uncontrollable seismic hazard lurking on their own continent.[619]

On June 14, the Cologne Re sent the German printed version of the publication to the three other companies.[620] The reinsurers decided after consultation with other directors[621] to send the study to approximately six hundred fire insurance companies worldwide,[622] numerous public

---

[617] 3 May 1907 Gruenwald to Thieme, copy to Simon, SR/FA 1907, 27 *et seq.*
[618] Ibid.
[619] 8 April 1907 Simon to Gruenwald, SR/FA 1907, 1 *et seq.*; 10 April 1907 text excerpt, SR/FA 1907, 6.
[620] 17 June 1907 Simon to KR, SR/FA 1907, 49 *et seq.*
[621] 26 June 1907 Gruenwald to Thieme, Lindner, Simon, SR/FA 1907, 53 *et seq.*
[622] Ibid. See also the country table of 1907 in chapter 3.3.1.4.

insurance institutions,[623] reinsurance companies[624] and the German regulatory agency.[625] An additional meeting at the beginning of July brought the Earthquake Commission together in the headquarters of *Helvetia* in St. Gallen, who had invited its reinsurers to a conference because of the San Francisco court cases.[626] Two weeks later, everything was ready, and on June 18, 1907, Gruenwald telegraphed to Thieme, Lindner and Simon: 'The earthquake paper can be sent out today' (trans.).[627]

One of the first reactions originated from the pen of George C. Morant, Managing Director of the English Commercial Union.[628] In a diplomatic but pungent language, he declared that in view of the cases being conducted overseas, it was not an opportune moment to discuss the matter. The earthquake question would be dealt with by the British offices, but no action was foreseeable in the coming months. Morant did not mention that his own company was already planning to accept the earthquake fire risk.[629]

Acting upon Morant's suggestion, the four directors of the reinsurance companies were willing to postpone sending the study to the companies oversees.[630] They also refrained from officially distributing it in the United States and Canada.[631] They agreed, however, to provide, as each saw fit,

---

[623] Dispatch after consultation with the insurance directors Thiele (Colonia), Altvater, v. Rasp and Vatke. 17 July 1907 Gruenwald to Thieme, Lindner, Simon, SR/FA 1907, 81 *et seq.*

[624] All signatories of the resolution of 30 April 1907 as well as the *Süddeutsche Rück*, the *Wiener Rück* and the *Internationale Rück* (Vienna) received the study. 18 July 1907 Gruenwald to Thieme, Lindner, Simon, SR/FA 1907, 83.

[625] 28 June 1907 Simon to Gruenwald, SR/FA 1907, 58 *et seq.*

[626] 19 June 1907 Gruenwald to Simon, SR/FA A9.0–29/folder III/S.F. 18 April 1906/ (diverse correspondence mainly reinsurers 6/1906–6/1907), 218 *et seq.*; 4 July 1907 Gruenwald to Thieme, Lindner, Simon, SR/FA A9.0–32/yellow file folder (correspondence, mainly Cologne Re 1907), 65 *et seq.*

[627] Telegram certification, 18 July 1907 Gruenwald to Thieme, Lindner, Simon, SR/FA 1907, 83.

[628] Morant had apparently received a copy in advance. The British Offices were officially written to in October 1907. Communication KR to English insurers, SR/FA A9.0–32/folders and booklets/England.

[629] 29 July 1907 C. Morant (Commercial Union) to Gruenwald, SR/FA A9.0–32/yellow file folder (correspondence, mainly Cologne Re 1907), 92; 7 August 1907 Gruenwald to Thieme, Lindner, Simon, SR/FA 1907, 104.

[630] 7 August 1907 Gruenwald to Thieme, Lindner, Simon, SR/FA 1907, 104; 5 August 1907 Gruenwald to Thieme, Lindner, Simon, SR/FA 1907, 101 *et seq.*

[631] 30 July 1907 Gruenwald to Thieme, Lindner, Simon, SR/FA 1907, 93 *et seq.*

private copies to their American business friends.[632] In addition, they resolved to keep each other up to date on incoming reactions. [633]

2.4. A New Standard for the World: Results of the Second Part

The concept for the change in the earthquake regulations that the four reinsurance directors had developed in one year shows all the characteristics of a standardisation process. The Earthquake Commission had, with the greatest legal precision, developed a new exclusionary clause[634] that was designed to achieve worldwide application.

The reinsurers pursued definite goals typical of standardisation in the uniformity of this clause. The first was that the earthquake clause was to render the limits of liability clear to the insured, the judges and the regulatory boards in a case of disaster. The four directors had recognised that the confusion reigning up to then in the differing and manifoldly inadequate regulations was unfavourable to them. Therefore, the unambiguous definition of the liability exclusion was the most important goal of their work. In their opinion, it was not sufficient for the individual companies to improve their insurance conditions according to their own lights. The reinsurers considered that substance and wording had to correspond exactly, the latter at least within the individual business areas.

Moreover, they hoped that an internationally uniform contractual regulation would have normative effects. This hope founded itself upon the notion that the internationally uniform use of certain business practices would establish customary law. This notion, a natural one for the practitioners, was the result of their experiences in the development of modern insurance law. Since the nineteenth century, numerous new regulations had widely spread in the form of standard contract terms and had consolidated to legal norms in the course of time. This evolution was visible above all in the treatment of the regulations in the judiciary and the scholarly literature. In part, they even became established in insurance contract law.

---

[632] 7 August 1907 Gruenwald to Thieme, Lindner, Simon, SR/FA 1907, 104.

[633] Gruenwald urged them once again to meet on the sidelines of the transport conference on 12–14 of September. 7 August 1907 Gruenwald to Thieme, Lindner, Simon, SR/FA 1907, 104.

[634] See 3.3.1.5 above.

Finally, the reinsurers were interested in creating stable, controllable and, above all, calculable conditions. This is also characteristic of the process of standardisation. The California disaster had shown the reinsurers that the possible obligations in the case of an earthquake could only be calculated on the basis of uniform earthquake regulations in the fire insurance contracts. This also applied to future events. Since the reinsurers regarded earthquake damages as uninsurable, a uniform exclusion of liability was the only possible solution they would consider.

It is remarkable how deftly the reinsurers proceeded in the development of the earthquake clause. To begin with, they overcame the lack of institutions that could have guided an international process of standardisation by means of their own organisation. The involvement of the Munich Re was important, as its enormous economic weight proved indispensible in a later implementation of the earthquake clause. The same holds true for the early inclusion of the fire insurance companies through the activation of a common worldwide network, for the future success of standardisation lay primarily in the hands of the local insurers. Likewise, the abstention to formulate a 'perfect' earthquake clause assigned the fire insurers an active role in its future implementation that added support to the project. Whether the reinsurers were conscious of this role is a matter on which the historical record is silent.

CHAPTER THREE

THE EARTHQUAKE CLAUSE IN FIRE INSURANCE CONTRACTS:
THE LIMITS OF INTERNATIONAL STANDARDISATION (1907–1912)

In the era of nation States, international standardisation of law meant that regulations that were designed to apply uniformly across State boundaries had to be incorporated into every national legal system. This did not only hold true for rules that were designed to be put into effect on the basis of international treaties—an example is the uniform freight law on the basis of the Berne Convention of 1890—but, as a matter of principle, for all private standard form contracts and contract clauses. However, the business stakeholders could act all the more freely the less their branches were subject to State control and the less State legislation affected their law. The law of overseas trade and the law of reinsurance, for example, developed more or less independently from State influences.[1]

The earthquake clause was a part of fire insurance law, which in all important business areas had been regulated by the State. Thus, the clause's introduction was not simply a matter of its acceptance by the fire insurers as future users, but required its incorporation into every individual legal system. The respective effort, success and failure of the process depended upon very different legal and financial circumstances. The description of the efforts to achieve the implementation of the earthquake clause, therefore, simultaneously outlines the limits of this standardisation.

The following three sections will trace the developments in the reinsurance industry's fourteen most important European and North American business districts. The division into fourteen business districts corresponds to the organisation of the material found in the Earthquake Commission's files, although, in fact, more than fourteen legal systems regulated the districts. This discrepancy results from the fact that the reinsurers classified more than one State or federal state under one system of insurance law, for example, in the cases of Scandinavia and the United States. In addition, the reinsurers also dealt with the earthquake regulations in some countries' colonies or in other overseas territories.

The dispatch of the earthquake clause study to the fire insurers corresponded to the reinsurers' request to alter insurance policies in

---

[1] See chapters 5.1 and 5.2.

conformance to the set standard. The directors in Cologne and Stuttgart and in Munich and Zurich first waited for the reactions of the companies they had written to and then notified each other of the results.[2] Towards the end of 1907, they began to exert their influence upon the most important stakeholders in the business areas.[3]

The reinsurers assumed that the decision on the changes in the contractual conditions primarily lay with the private fire insurance companies and their pressure groups. Only in a few countries did they also take into consideration mutual associations and the State insurance institutions; this was necessary, for example, in Switzerland, where almost no private insurance companies existed.

As a matter of principle, the reinsurers left lobbying local legislators and regulatory agencies to the fire insurers. Only at home did the reinsurers exert their influence upon State institutions.

3.1. The Introduction of Unitary Earthquake Clauses

3.1.1. *Basic Features of National Developments*

3.1.1.1. *Spain and Portugal*

In Spain and Portugal, the exertions of the Earthquake Commission led to overwhelming success. Standard clauses were introduced under very similar circumstances in both countries that precisely corresponded to the reinsurers' preconceptions. On the entire Iberian Peninsula, local public limited companies dominated the fire insurance business. The interest of these companies in excluding their liability for earthquake damages was consistently intense—if for no other reason than the memory of the destructive earthquake of Lisbon in 1755 that had also been accompanied by a large tidal wave.[4] In addition, they had enjoyed business relations with central European reinsurance companies for decades and most likely desired to avoid clashing with them. Finally, neither in Spain nor in

---

[2] For example, 25 February 1908 Simon to Gruenwald (excerpt), SR/FA A9.0–32/yellow file folder (correspondence Swiss insurance companies)/loose material; 27 February 1908 Simon to Gruenwald (excerpt), SR/FA/loose material; 28 February 1908 Gruenwald to Simon (excerpt), SR/FA/loose material.

[3] 27 December 1907 Simon to Cerise, SR/FA/loose material.

[4] Hardly any disaster had etched such scars in the historical memory as this one. On the effects of this history, see Eifert, 'Das Erdbeben von Lissabon 1755. Zur Historizität einer Naturkatastrophe', *HZ* 274 (2002), 633 *et seq.*, as well as the essays in *NZZ-Beilage*, 29 October 2005.

Portugal did State institutions have an influence in the substantive shaping of insurance policies.

The week after the study had been sent out, the director of the Swiss Re, Simon, received a letter from the Spanish company *El Día* (Cartagena). This company had added to its old and less complex exclusionary clause the words '... [causados] directa ó indirectamente...' in February 1907.[5] In the letter to Simon, the directors expressed complete agreement in that 'l'adoption générale d'une clause dégageant les Compagnies d'une façon complète'[6] was necessary. The communication continued:

Nous sommes d'accord, également, avec les appréciations émises dans l'étude en question, et nous pensons que les Compagnies de notre pays sont disposées à procéder aux réformes nécessaires des conditions de leurs polices, car, nous mêmes, nous en avons déjà donné l'exemple.

En outre, à la première occasion, nous réformerons les conditions de notre police dans le sens des observations 2 et 3 de votre étude résumé sur les Compagnies espagnoles, ces réformes nous paraissent très opportunes. De même, nous ferons tout notre possible pour amener toutes les Compagnies espagnoles à adopter des conditions uniformes, d'après lesquelles toutes les conséquences, soit directes, soit indirectes, des tremblements des terre ou d'autres phénomènes seront exclues.[7]

We agree with the estimates in the study [of the earthquake clause] and believe that the companies in our country tend towards moving in the direction of the necessary reforms of their policy terms because we have already provided an example ourselves.

Moreover, we will be changing our terms at the next opportunity in the sense expressed in the observations that your study summarises with respect to the Spanish companies in Nos. 2 and 3; these changes appear very practical. Likewise, we will be doing everything in our power to persuade every Spanish company to accept the uniform terms that exclude all direct and indirect consequences of earthquakes and other natural phenomena (trans.).

---

[5] 23 February 1907 *El Día* to SR, SR/FA A9.0–32/yellow file folder (correspondence Spanish and Portuguese insurance companies), 31. The old clause read: 'Article 2. *La Compañía no garantiza los daños de incendio, de explosion ú otros, causados por volcanes, temblores de tierra, huracanes ó por todo fenómeno meteorológico que non sea el fuego del cielo*' ('The company is not liable for damages from fires, explosions or other sources caused by volcanoes, earthquakes, tornadoes or from all meteorological phenomena except lightning'), cited, SR/FA A9.0–32/folders and booklet/Spain, 1.

[6] Trans.: 'the general introduction of a clause that releases the company in a comprehensive manner', 24 July 1907 *El Día* to SR, SR/FA A9.0–32/yellow file folder (correspondence Spain, Portuguese insurance companies), 34.

[7] 24 July 1907 *El Día* to SR, SR/FA, 34.

The Board of Directors of *El Día* were thus prepared for a second change in their earthquake regulation within six months, even one concerning the burden of proof and a clear definition of the excluded damages as fire damages.

Numerous other insurance providers expressed a similar willingness towards reform, among them *La Alborada*,[8] *Le Polar*,[9] *El Norte*—who had changed its *Condiciones Generales* in the way *El Día* had done[10]—*La Vasconia*,[11] *Hispania*[12] und *La Catalana*.[13] Only *La Unión y el Fénix Español* expressed opposition to a change in the business conditions. The Directors declared that they saw no reason to change policies, since the earthquake danger was completely excluded[14]—although their clause by no means complied with the standards set by the reinsurers.[15]

Meanwhile, *El Día* had taken the initiative and called upon every Spanish fire insurance company to introduce not only a uniform earthquake clause but also common *Condiciones Generales*. The Directors specifically referred to the reinsurers' study. They recommended a meeting in October in Madrid when Parliament would be dealing with the project of a *Ley para regular el foncionamiento de las Compañias de Seguros*.[16] *La Vasconia* wrote to Zurich that results that agreed with the ideas expressed in the study were expected.[17]

Simon took note of these reactions with the greatest interest.[18] He attempted to persuade the reluctant companies to take part,[19] pointed out in clear language the importance of the exact uniformity of the earthquake clauses[20] and warned *La Unión y El Fénix Español* about their unsatisfactory

---

[8] 24 July 1907 *La Alborada* to SR, SR/FA, 35.

[9] 6 August 1907 *Le Polar* to SR., SR/FA, 41 *et seq.*

[10] 3 September 1907 *El Norte* to SR, SR/FA, 45.

[11] 5 September 1907 *La Vasconia* to SR, SR/FA, 49.

[12] 11 September 1907 *Hispania, Compañia General de Seguros* (Barcelona) to SR, SR/FA, 53.

[13] 18 September 1907 *La Catalana* to SR, SR/FA, 55 *et seq.*

[14] 4 September 1907 *La Unión y el Fénix Español*, SR/FA, 46.

[15] Compare SR/FA A9.0–32/folders and booklets, Spain, 3.

[16] 1 August 1907 *El Día* to all Spanish fire insurance companies (apparently a copy to SR), SR/FA A9.0–32/yellow file folder (correspondence Spanish and Portuguese insurance companies), 37 *et seq.*

[17] '[…] *algo que esté en armonia con el estudio por Usd. remitido*'. 5 September 1907 *La Vasconia* to SR, SR/FA, 49.

[18] 9 August 1907 SR to *El Día*, SR/FA, 43.

[19] 25 September 1907 SR to *Alborada, El Norte, La Vasconia, La Estrella, La Catalana, El Día* and probably additional companies, SR/FA, 61.

[20] 23 September 1907 Simon to *Hispania*, SR/FA, 57 *et seq.*

clause.[21] The self-organisation on the domestic level that was necessary for the introduction of the standard proceeded only slowly.

Then an extraordinary turn of events occurred. *La Unión y El Fénix Español* surprisingly corrected their policies. The new earthquake clause perfectly corresponded to the reinsurers' perceptions:

La Compañia no garantiza los daños de incendio, de explosion ú otros causados por volcanes, temblores de tierra, [...] sino quando el asegurado pruebe que aquellos no provienen directa ni indirectamente de algunas de las causas antes indicadas.[22]	The company is not liable for damages caused by fire, explosion or others caused by volcanoes, earthquakes ..., except if the insured proves that these [damages] do not originate from one of the causes just mentioned either directly or indirectly (trans.).

The company also followed Simon's recommendation to take part at the conference in Madrid[23] and wrote him on November 8, 1907 that they were honoured to be able to inform him that their clause had been adopted by the majority of the other companies at the conference.[24] Thus, *La Unión y El Fénix Español* became the 'central address'[25] for the reform of the Spanish earthquake clause and played a role that in other countries was exercised by syndicates or associations.[26]

In December, Simon learned from *El Día* that the number of the fire insurance companies that had not reformed their earthquake regulations was still considerable.

At the end of February 1908, Simon wrote Gruenwald that he wanted to induce the remaining companies to adopt the Madrid earthquake clause.[27] Once again, he engaged in intensive correspondence in which he advocated a uniform clause.[28] He succeeded, and on April 29 he was able to report to the Copenhagen insurance company director Lars Iversen:

---

[21] 25 September 1907 Simon to *La Unión y el Fénix Español*, SR/FA, 59 *et seq.*
[22] 30 September 1907 *La Unión y el Fénix Español* to SR, SR/FA, 64.
[23] 5 October 1907 SR to *La Unión y el Fénix Español*, SR/FA, 66.
[24] 8 November 1907 *La Unión y el Fénix Español* to SR, SR/FA, 67.
[25] Approximately 29 November 1908 document, SR/FA, 92.
[26] Ibid.
[27] 27 February 1908 Simon to Gruenwald (excerpt), SR/FA A9.0–32/yellow file folder (correspondence Swiss insurance companies)/loose material.
[28] For example, to the *Hispania*, which had introduced another effective clause. Compare 19 March 1908 SR to *Hispania*, SR/FA A9.0–32/yellow file folder (correspondence Spanish and Portuguese insurance companies), 90 *et seq.*

Table 12.   State of the Clause Reform in Spain (November/December 1907).
Source see footnotes 29, 30 and 31.

Companies with new earthquake clauses: La Catalana, La Unión y El Fénix Español, El Norte, La Aseguradora Española, La Vasconia, La Estrella, Aurora, New Fenix, Credito Nacional, Seguros y Rentas, Realidad, El Día.[29]

Spanish companies without new clauses: La Prevision Española, La Polar, Patria, Hispania, La Alianza de Santander, La Prevision Nacional, La Alborada, La Esperanza, La Positiva, El Credito Nacional, La Actividad.

Foreign companies without new clauses: L'Urbaine, La Paternelle, L'Union, Le Phénix, La Foncière, L'Aigle, Western, Phoenix Assurance Comp., Liverpool, London & Globe, General Accident, Fire & Life, Sun Fire Office, Commercial Union, London & Lancashire, Palatine, Royal Exchange,[30] North British & Mercantile, La Prévoyante, Hanseatische.[31]

The majority of the Spanish companies resolved to introduce a comprehensive earthquake clause at a conference in Madrid last year, and the other Spanish companies as well as the foreign companies working in Spain have been persuaded to adopt the identical earthquake clause for the sake of uniformity (trans).[32]

The Spanish fire insurers were the first in the world to adopt the standardized earthquake clause.[33]

In Portugal, the introduction of the earthquake clause seems to have taken a similar course, even if the process was not quite as rapid as in Spain. At first, Simon achieved thoroughly positive reactions to the study.[34] For example, the *Companhia Tagus* in Lisbon thanked him for the initiation, because their native city had many times been decimated by earthquakes. They send a draft of uniform clauses to Zurich.[35]

---

[29]   25 November 1907 *El Día* to SR, SR/FA, 71.

[30]   16 December 1907 *El Día* to SR, SR/FA, 80 *et seq.*

[31]   Undated document, most likely from SR, SR/FA, 82.

[32]   29 March 1908, Simon to Iversen (*Københavns Brandforsikring*), SR/FA A9.0–32/ folder/ correspondence regarding earthquake clause 1906/1907/ *Bayerische Versicherungsbank*, 39 *et seq.*

[33]   The last announcement on the matter arrived at the beginning of 1909; New Fenix to SR, SR/FA A9.0–32/yellow file folder (correspondence Spanish and Portuguese insurance companies), 94.

[34]   23 July 1907 *Companhia de Seguros Indemnisadora* (Porto) to SR, SR/FA, 32; 26 July 1907 *Previdencia, Companhia General de Seguros* (Lisbon) to SR, SR/FA 36; 3 September 1907 *Garantia, Companhia de de Seguros* to SR, SR/FA, 44.

[35]   '*La Compagnie n'est responsable ni des dommages provenant de tremblements des terre ou irruptions vulcaniques, ni de ceux causés par l'incendie determinés par ces catastrophe*' [sic] ('The company is liable neither for damages that result from earthquakes or volcanic

The introduction of a new insurance contract law was also planned in Portugal. The *Sociedade Portugueza de Seguros* wrote that it would be desirable to discuss the question in view of this law's impending adoption.[36] But nothing happened at first. In December, the Swiss Re reminded those interested in the project to determine a uniform earthquake regulation for the country. The reinsurers encouraged a meeting of the Portuguese companies and, between the lines, urged them to adopt the new clause of the Spanish companies.[37] Simon received a list of all the fire insurance companies active in Portugal from the Tagus company.[38] This included many more than the eight companies known up to this point:

Table 13. Fire Insurance Companies Active in Portugal (December 1907).
7 December 1907 SR to Tagus, SR/FA, 77.

Portuguese Companies

In Lisbon: Companhia Bonança, Companhia Equidade, Companhia Fidelidade, Companhia Internacional, Companhia Previdencia, Companhia Probidade, Companhia Portugal, Companhia Reformadora, Companhia Tagus, Companhia Universal, Sociedade Portugueza de Seguros, Lloyd Portuguez.

In Porto: Companhia Confiança Portuense, Companhia a Commercial, Companhia Douro, Companhia Indemnisadora, Companhia a Portuense, Companhia Segurança, Companhia Tranquillidade Portuense, Companhia Urbana Portugueza.

Other places: Companhia Fraternidade (Braga), Companhia Alliança Maderiense (Funchal/Ilha da Madeira), Companhia Açoriana (Ponte Delgada/Ilha de S. Miguel)

Foreign Companies, all in Porto: La Unión y El Fénix Español (Agent Lima Mayer & Co.), Norwich Union (James Rawes & Co.) Royal (Basto & Piombino), Commercial Union (A. Marinho da Cruz), Queen, Alliance[39]

Not much happened in Portugal up to the beginning of 1908, although Simon forcefully urged them to act.[40] It proved especially detrimental for

---

eruptions nor for such damages that are caused by disaster-related fires'.) Cited in 6 September 1907 *Tagus* to SR, SR/FA, 49 *et seq.*

[36] 4 September 1907 *Sociedade Portugueza de Seguros* to SR, SR/FA, 47.

[37] 5 December 1907 SR to *Sociedade Portugueza de Seguros, Previdencia, Companhia de Seguros Indemnisadora, Garantia und Companhia de Seguros Tagus*, SR/FA, 72 *et seq.*

[38] 7 December 1907 SR to *Tagus*, SR/FA, 77.

[39] 14 December 1907 *Tagus* to SR, SR/FA, 78 *et seq.*

[40] 27 February 1908 SR to some Portuguese companies, SR/FA, 84 *et seq.*; compare 27 February 1908 Simon to Gruenwald (excerpt), SR/FA A9.0–32/yellow file folder (correspondence Swiss insurance companies)/loose material.

the project that 'possible head offices for the reform of the earthquake clause' or 'any companies to be viewed as such' did not exist (trans.).[41]

It is not know when and how the Portuguese finally reached an agreement.[42] It is certain, however, that a new earthquake regulation that satisfied the reinsurers was introduced. On January 26, 1911, the Swiss Re thanked the *Tagus* company and the *Sociedade Portugueza de Seguros* for its cooperation during the past few years in the reform of the earthquake clause: 'Cette question a été heureusement résolue'.[43]

3.1.1.2. *France and Belgium*

The French and the Belgian fire insurers' reaction to the urgent request of the reinsurers was not unlike that of their counterparts on the Iberian Peninsula. Although other circumstances existed, these proved similarly favourable. The differences were that the fire insurers in France and Belgium were organised in interest groups, a fact that simplified the communication and coordination of a unitary reform of the policies.

As in Portugal and Spain, public limited companies dominated the insurance business in France and Belgium, and they also were dependent upon the cooperation of the reinsurers. In France, the introduction of a law on insurance contracts was imminent. For this reason, a general reform of the policies seemed necessary, or at least reasonable, to the insurers. As in Spain, earthquakes were considered to be a latent rather than an imminent danger. French and Belgian insurers were not especially active on the world market, but the destruction of the city of St. Pierre by a volcanic eruption on the island of Martinique in 1902 had shown them that they could be confronted with disaster damages on a large scale as well.[44]

In the period in which the San Francisco disaster occurred, four domestic and two foreign companies in France had been using clauses that were in conformity with the principles advocated by the reinsurers.[45] After

---

[41] 29 November 1908 (?) document, SR/FA A9.0–32/yellow file folder (correspondence Spanish and Portuguese insurance companies), 92.

[42] Presumably after the introduction of the new law governing insurance contracts.

[43] ('This question has fortunately been resolved') 26 January 1911 SR to *Tagus* and to *Sociedade Portugueza de Seguros*, SR/FA, 98 *et seq.*

[44] French journals, for example, *L'Argus* (2 August 1906), had reported extensively on the matter.

[45] '*La Compagnie ne répond pas des incendies occasionnés par volcans, tremblements de terre,* [...]. *Dans chacun de ces cas l'assuré, pour avoir droit à une indemnité, doit faire la preuve que l'incendie ne provient ni directement ni indirectement de l'une de ces cause*' ('The company is not liable for fires that were caused by volcanoes, earthquakes [...] In each of

receiving the Earthquake Commission study, many other fire insurance companies added such clauses to their policies. Simon learned from the President of the *Syndicat des Compagnies Françaises d'Assurances contre l'Incendie* ('Syndicate of French Fire Insurance Companies') that a revision of the earthquake clause contracts was intended in the course of a general reform of insurance conditions that would occur after the law on insurance contracts had come into effect. The matter was to be put on the agenda of the Syndicat's coming meeting in October. Simon immediately began to promote an agreement on a unitary formulation among the members of the association 'dans l'intérêt de l'efficacité de la clause'.[46] He recommended the same to Guillaume Baron Cerise, the President of one of the other French insurance associations.[47] Simon struck an admonitory tone in recalling the experiences made in San Francisco. According to him, Europe was in danger as well:

Les récents tremblements de terre en Italie et les dégâts causés par eux ont de nouveau prouvé la réalité du danger; s'il n'y a pas eu feu c'est qu'il n'y avait ni gaz ni électricité dans les localités ravagés.[48]	The most recent earthquakes in Italy and the devastations caused by them have demonstrated anew the reality of the danger; if no fires broke out, it is only because neither gas nor electricity was present in the destroyed villages (trans.).

Reacting promptly, Cerise designed an exclusionary clause for the French policies. Simon regarded the clause as 'excellent' and supported Cerise in his determination to have the introduction of this condition accepted in

---

these cases, the insured must provide proof that the fire was not the result, either directly or indirectly, of one of these causes in order to have a claim for indemnity for losses') Cited in Gruenwald et al., '*La clause d'exclusion des tremblements de terre* [...]', 11 *et seq.*

[46] That is, 'in the interests of the effectiveness of the clause' (26 September 1907) SR, respectively, to *Unión y Fénix Español, Assurances Réunies, La Flandre, Cie française du Phénix, Le Nord, L'Abeille, La Paternelle, Le Siècle, Assurances Rémoises (Reims), Afrique française, La Métropôle*, SR/FA A9.0–32/yellow file folder (correspondence Swiss insurance companies)/loose material.

[47] Cerise was the *Président du Comité de Défense du Syndicat Général des Compagnies d'Assurances à primes fixes contre l'Incendie à Paris.*

[48] 30 November 1907 Simon to Cerise. SR/FA A9.0–32/yellow file folder (correspondence Swiss insurance companies)/loose material. Simon advised Cerise in addition to revise the clauses in his own company, the Urbaine. Heavy earthquakes had occurred on the 7th to the 9th of September, 1905, in Calabria and Sicily (Baratta 1906, 22).

his association.[49] Simon sent the wording of the Spanish clause of October, 1907, to another company as a model.[50]

In March 1908, it was clear that the majority of the French fire insurance companies would participate in a general reform of their insurance conditions.[51] In April 1908, Simon expressed his pleasure at the success obtained in France to the Director in Copenhagen, Iversen: some of the companies had already adopted a convincing clause; the draft of a law on insurance contracts allowed for the exclusion of earthquake risks; and, most importantly, it was certain that a definitive reform of the general conditions of insurance including the earthquake clause would occur following the introduction of the law.[52]

The reform of the earthquake clause had at the same time reached a similar point in Belgium. Simon reported that the *Comité des Assureurs Belges* (Belgian Insurers' Committee) was engaged in the editing of a 'new completed clause and [that] the matter is still pending' (trans.).[53] This committee consisted of eight Belgian companies. In addition, foreign, especially French, companies offered their support.

The reinsurers' study noted that the members of the comité had included a new clause in their policies in November of 1906. It excluded the following damages from liability:

[...] des incendies ou dommages quelle que soit leur nature, occasionnés soit directement soit indirectement par [...] tremblements de terre ou autres convulsions de nature, effondrements du sol et feux souterrains.[54]	[...] fire or other damages irrespective of their form that are caused directly or indirectly by [...] earthquakes or other convulsions of nature, irruptions of the earth or subterranean fires (trans.).

This clause fulfilled two of the reinsurers' demands: the excluded damages expressly encompassed the fire damages as well as indirectly caused damages. Four additional Belgian and a number of foreign companies made

---

[49]   27 December 1907 Simon to Cerise, SR/FA A9.0–32/yellow file folder (correspondence Swiss insurance companies)/loose material.

[50]   This can be seen in a later communication (14 March 1908 Simon to l'Union, SR/FA)/loose material.

[51]   14 March 1908 Simon to l'Union SR/FA/loose material.

[52]   29 April 1908 Simon to Iversen (*Københavns Brandforsikring*), SR/FA A9.0–32/file folder/ correspondence regarding earthquake clause 1906/1907/ *Bayerische Versicherungsbank*, 39 *et seq.*

[53]   Ibid.

[54]   Gruenwald et al., 'La clause d'exclusion des tremblements de terre [...]', 5 *et seq.*

use of similar formulations.[55] During the new reform on which Simon reported in April 1908, the main issue was to shift the burden of proof, which in Belgium had already been shifted in the context of war-induced damages.

3.1.1.3. *Germany and Austria-Hungary*

The reinsurers' project also proved successful in Germany and Austria-Hungary. The introduction of the uniform earthquake clause in Germany will be discussed in a separate chapter (4.3.1 and 4.3.2). On the other hand, the information on Austria-Hungary is scarce, as the Swiss Re had not attended to the companies active in that country concerning the earthquake matter. Nevertheless, it can be assumed that the efforts of the reinsurers were also successful in Austria-Hungary.

The great diversity in the forms of organisation was an anomaly both countries shared in their insurance industry. In the course of the nineteenth century, public limited companies had taken over a large portion of the fire insurance market. Mutual societies had developed similarly, if somewhat less, successfully. Both groups were organised in large associations. The many local, regional and State insurance companies lost out on this development. After the turn of the nineteenth century, however, they played a more significant role.

For the reinsurers, the limited and mutual companies that handed over fire risks on a large scale were the groups most relevant in reforming the earthquake clause. Changes in the conditions governing the public insurance institutions could also prove beneficial, as the reinsurers ascribed great importance to the uniformity of the regulations irrespective of the form of organisation of the company involved.[56]

As in other countries, the introduction of laws governing insurance contracts was pending in Germany and Austria-Hungary. That is why the fire insurance conditions were to become more stringent, which increased the readiness to change the earthquake regulations.

---

[55] Ibid.

[56] In the fire insurance business, the public limited companies allocated the following percentages of their gross premiums to reinsurance: in Germany 45.2%, in Austria-Hungary 46%; the mutual companies: 8.6% (Germany), 43.5% (Austria-Hungary); public institutions: 10.8% (Germany), 42.5% (Austria-Hungary). On the average, 31.9% of the fire risks were reinsured in Germany, in Austria-Hungary 45.4%; in both countries, the majority at home (all statistics apply to 1909; Jahn 1912, 53, 90 *et seq.*, 118 *et seq.*).

The Austrian fire insurance companies, who were organised in a so-called *Konkordat*, maintained a simple exclusionary clause in their general insurance conditions.[57] The Hungarian insurers had followed suit.[58] Differing conditions were mainly employed by German and Italian companies that were guided by the conditions set by the umbrella organisations in their native countries.[59]

In May 1907, that is, two months before the distribution of the reinsurers' study, the *Konkordat* companies initiated the introduction of an effective earthquake clause at the instigation of the Director of the Pest insurance institution, M. Ribári. The directors appointed a committee to devise a draft. Ribári, himself a member of this committee, suggested an exchange of the collected material to Simon.[60] In response, Simon announced that he would send him the study and requested that no changes be made until then.[61]

A year later, the Austrian law on the insurance contracts had still not come into force. The draft envisaged a non-mandatory condition that excluded the liability of the insurer for earthquake fire damages.[62] The Austrian and Hungarian companies wanted to await the publication of the law, but stuck to their decision to introduce new earthquake clauses.[63]

How closely the earthquake clauses adopted by the Austrian and Hungarian companies corresponded to the reinsurers' demands is not known. The earthquake clauses of the German limited liability and mutual companies corresponded to the Earthquake Commission's suggestions in every detail.[64]

3.1.1.4. *First Results*

A comparison of the developments in the business areas and the legal systems just described allows for a first answer to the question as to the

---

[57] Gruenwald et al. 1907, 16. Only the Austrian *Elementar-Versicherungs-Gesellschaft* did not belong to the *Konkordat*.

[58] Gruenwald et al. 1907, 23.

[59] Ibid., 16.

[60] 22 May 1907 M. Ribári (*Pester Versicherungs-Anstalt*) to Simon, SR/FA A9.0–32/folder/ correspondence regarding earthquake clause 1906/1907/ *Bayerische Versicherungsbank*, 31 *et seq.*

[61] 27 May 1907 Simon to Ribári (*Pester Versicherungs-Anstalt*), SR/FA, 33.

[62] 14 March 1908 Simon to l'Union SR/FA A9.0–32/yellow file folder (correspondence Swiss insurance companies)/loose material.

[63] 29 April 1908 Simon to Iversen (*Københavns Brandforsikring*), SR/FA A9.0–32/folder/ correspondence regarding earthquake clause 1906/1907/ *Bayerische Versicherungsbank*, 39 *et seq.* The law was enacted, however, on the 23rd of December 1917 (Coing 1989, 565).

[64] See 4.1.2.7.

circumstances under which the implementation of the earthquake clause was accomplished. Three factors that apparently facilitated the Earthquake Commission's success in promoting the standard can be isolated. Firstly, it was beneficial if the fire insurance business was primarily conducted by public limited companies and if these were constrained to share parts of the risks with reinsurance companies. This finding can be verified using the example of Germany, where insurance organised under public law was equally common, and in comparison to Scandinavia, Russia and Switzerland. Secondly, the decision to introduce an earthquake clause was made considerably easier if the insurance business was preparing to reform the general insurance conditions anyway. This was the case in all European countries in which the introduction of laws governing insurance contracts was imminent at the time. Thirdly, it is apparent that in several business areas, individual companies or entire associations had discussed or carried out changes in the rules of liability for disaster scenarios even before the distribution of the reinsurers' study. The reinsurers' suggestions fell upon fertile ground here.

To what extent the individual economic affliction experienced in the disasters of the past or the degree of domestic seismic danger influenced the readiness to reform the clause must be examined in light of additional examples. The domestic authorities who bore a responsibility for the supervision of the insurance industry appear to have exercised little influence. This was possibly different in Germany. In addition, the degree of organisation in any given domestic insurance industry was of little importance. Individual companies stepped in where no interest associations existed.

3.1.2. *Germany: A Broad Consensus on the Earthquake Question*

Germany was part of the business areas in which an earthquake clause that corresponded to the reinsurers' preconceptions was introduced. The following individual study will present the circumstances leading to this result. Aspects already mentioned in the previous reports on various countries such as the importance of the insurers' forms of organisation and their participation in the disasters of 1906 and 1907 are relevant here as well. The impression that State institutions played no role in the question of earthquake fire damages will also be reviewed.

Moreover, the examination will shed light on the means and methods by which the reinsurers exercised their influence upon the stakeholders in the earthquake question, the form of the exploitation of consensus within the insurance industry, the importance of legislation governing insurance contracts that came into being at the same time for the decisions made in the earthquake problem and the treatment of this question in foreign business involving German companies.

3.1.2.1. The Fire Insurance Industry at the Beginning of the Twentieth Century

Around 1900, fire insurance was very common among private and commercial or industrial property owners in Germany. The industry had developed more rapidly than in other European countries in the course of the nineteenth century and had in many respects given up its original orientation on England in favour of its own developments.[65] The well-developed reinsurance industry that had been created after the great fire in Hamburg in 1842 was an especially strong element in this evolution.[66]

In 1906, Germany had a population of about 60 million people. Property of about \$33.6 billion was insured against fire. Every year, the fire insurance companies earned more than \$58.5 million in annual premiums for this coverage.[67] These numbers already proved the immense importance of the insurance industry to its contemporaries.[68]

Private-sector companies dominated in the German insurance industry. At the time of the San Francisco disaster, thirty-two domestic and thirty-four foreign public limited companies as well as seventeen mutual companies did business in Germany. In contrast, there were fifty-five public sector fire insurance institutions,[69] whose number, however, did not correspond to their economic importance. Although property owners were

---

[65] On the example set by the English insurance industry, compare Neugebauer 1990, 23 et seq.; Lammel 1993, 98 et seq.; Hax, 'Die Bedeutung des Versicherungswesens im Industrialisierungsprozeß', Zeitschrift für die gesamte Versicherungswirtschaft 1963, 22 et seq.

[66] The first reinsurance company, the Kölnische Rück ('Cologne Re'), was established in 1846. In 1908, thirty-two reinsurance companies were active in the German Reich and collected the gross sum of \$76 million (319.7 million marks) in premiums and paid \$28.8 million in damages (Emminghaus, 'Rückversicherung', Handwörterbuch der Staatswissenschaften, 3rd ed. [1911], vol. 7, 167). In other business areas, especially in England and the United States, risks were spread among co-insurers (Wandel 1998, 126 et seq.).

[67] In German currency, 174.6 billion and 304 million marks (Emminghaus, 'Feuerversicherung', Handwörterbuch der Staatswissenschaften, 3rd ed. [1911], Vol 4, 94). As a comparison: the total amount of direct tax in Prussia in 1904 was about 220 million marks and the national debt arround 7.25 billion marks (Speech made by the Secretary of State in Reichsjustizamt Nieberding at the German Lower Chamber on the 22nd of January, 1906, Stenographische Berichte über die Verhandlungen des Reichstags, XI. Legislaturperiode, II. Session (1905–1906), 725 et seq.

[68] Speech by the Secretary of State in the Reichsjustizamt Nieberding (1905–1906), 726.

[69] Gruenwald et al. 1907, 8. Slightly different numbers are named by Liebig 1911, 29.

still required to join compulsory fire insurance systems in many cities and regions and even though there were numerous regional insurance institutions based upon public law,[70] the criticism of these institutions that had lasted for decades had begun to make itself felt and the private companies had benefited from the growth of the insurance business.[71]

The German insurance industry had compact organisational structures and easily fits into the picture of the *Reich* as a 'State of federations'.[72] The non-Prussian public institutions had been the first to unite in the *Vereinigung öffentlicher Feuerversicherungs-Anstalten* ('Association of Public Fire Insurance Institutions') in 1867.[73] In 1872, this association became the *Verband deutscher öffentlicher Feuerversicherungs-Anstalten* ('Federation of German Public Fire Insurance Institutions') and was dominated by the Prussian companies. The public companies together attempted to engage in a 'skirmish'[74] against the private companies, who had also created interest groups.[75] The public limited companies had already established the influential *Verband deutscher Privat-Feuerversicherungs-Gesellschaften* ('Federation of German Private Fire Insurance Companies') in November of 1871. The *Verband deutscher Feuerversicherungs-Gesellschaften auf Gegenseitigkeit* ('Federation of German Mutual Fire Insurance Companies') joined it in 1896.[76]

Although the three large associations had no public tariff policy, the association of German private fire insurance companies can at least be referred to as a cartel. At their regular closed-session conference of directors, the member companies agreed upon principles for the course of business and measures for the suppression of unwanted competition. More importantly, they made use of uniform *Allgemeine Versicherungsbedingungen* (*AVB*, 'general insurance conditions') as of 1874. Given the lack of compulsory legal regulations, the *AVB* formed the bedrock of

---

[70] In Prussia, municipal institutions were at issue; in most other areas of Germany, State institutions (Gerhard et al. 1909, 27).

[71] At the end of 1906, 48.6% of all property insured against fire damage was insured with German stock companies, 6.7% with foreign stock companies, 7.6% with (German) mutual companies and 37.3% with public institutions (Liebig 1911, 65).

[72] The term is taken from Blaich (1979).

[73] In the 1850's, the first attempts to form an association on the part of the private insurance companies failed (Arps 1965, 557).

[74] Manes, 'Feuerversicherungs-Vereinigungen', *Masius' Rundschau* 1906, 81.

[75] Liebig 1911, 28 *et seq.*

[76] Besides the three large associations, a number of regional cartels and special tariff associations that handled specific fire insurance objects existed (Fischer, *Zeitschrift für die gesamte Staatswissenschaft / Ergänzungsheft XXXVIII* [1911], 114 *et seq.*).

insurance law and every individual insurance contract. Moreover, they were much more important for the insurance business than general business conditions were for other branches, as only the insurance conditions gave shape to the object of the contract.[77] The use of unitary *AVB* thus had effects similar to price-fixing.[78]

The activity of the associations had ambivalent consequences for the relationship between the insurers and their contract partners. On the one hand, the influence that the insured party could exercise on the contract's contents remained illusory.[79] The companies that participated in the associations tended to exploit their factual law-making power and to force unilaterally unfavourable conditions upon the insured.[80] On the other hand, the policyholders also profited from the activity of the association. Uniform *AVB* permitted them to obtain an overview of an insurance market that was at best difficult to assess. The *AVB* also facilitated the organisation of the co- and reinsurance of large industrial risks. Moreover, individual interest groups succeeded in influencing the definition of *AVB*.[81]

In 1895, the federation directors' conferences of German private fire insurance companies suggested to expand the cartel. On November 15, 1900, the 'Federation of Private Fire Insurance Companies in Germany' was formally established with forty founding members whose number soon increased.[82] Despite close institutional connections,[83] the Union differed from the federation of joint stock companies in three respects. Firstly, the Union accepted a number of mutual insurance companies as

---

[77] Arps 1965, 558.
[78] Meschke (1935, 29 *et seq.*) also advanced this view.
[79] Ehrenberg 1893, 79.
[80] Coing 1989, 565 *et seq.*
[81] Duvinage names the Elders of the *Berliner Kaufmannschaft* ('Berlin mercantile community'), the German Agricultural Council and the Boards of Trade in the context of the revised version of the 1874 *AVB* in 1886 (Duvinage 1987, 54).
[82] In 1906, there were forty-two members, and four years later fifty-two. Undated list of members of the *Vereinigung der in Deutschland arbeitenden Privat-Feuerversicherungs-Gesellschaften*, probably from 1910, BA B 280–644.
[83] According to statute no. 2 of the bylaws of the Union, the executive organ (the 'committee') consisted of four representatives chosen from the members of the federation of the joint stock companies, three from the non-federation members, and two additional members to be chosen by the general meeting of the Union. The Union and the Federation shared an office in Berlin in accordance with no. 9, g3, of the statutes, but in separate administration of their respective business matters (Bylaws of the *Vereinigung der in Deutschland arbeitenden Privat-Feuerversicherungs-Gesellschaften*, ed. November, 1910, BA B 280–644).

members and thus established a bridge to their federation;[84] the readiness of the private companies to cooperate with the public institutions was also new.[85] Secondly, it admitted foreign companies who offered insurance services in Germany. Thirdly, the Union engaged in the price war in the industrial insurance market which suffered heavy losses and into which the earlier federations had not dared to venture.[86] The bylaws of the new cartel allowed for enough leeway by charging the Union 'to shape a fruitful basis upon which the private insurance business can flourish and to regulate, in the light thereof, the competition among the companies'.[87]

The minimal tariffs with fixed premium rates calibrated to the degree of risk established by the Union and the change in specific insurance conditions met with great opposition within the industry. Although the *Centralverband Deutscher Industrieller* (*CVDI*, 'Central Federation of German Industrialists') explicitly recognised the authority of the fire insurers to form a syndicate—the idea was by no means foreign to large industrial companies—, it discussed the establishment of a protective federation in order to avoid being cheated.[88] Several organisations of this kind came into existence.[89] The strongest and most lasting was the *Deutscher Feuerversicherungs-Schutzverband*,[90] which in 1901 was launched as a reaction

---

[84] The Union had been co-founded by six mutual companies (Meschke 1935, 36, fn. 48).

[85] E.g. in 1909 in the struggle against the estate agent industry (Anonymus, 'Vereinigung der in Deutschland arbeitenden Privat-Feuerversicherungs-Gesellschaften', *Hamburgischer Correspondent*, 24 November 1909).

[86] Meschke 1935, 34 *et seq.*

[87] Bylaws of the *Vereinigung der in Deutschland arbeitenden Privat-Feuerversicherungs-Gesellschaften* (*no.2*), ed. November 1910, BA B 280–644.

[88] Delegates' meeting of the CVDI on the 2nd of October, 1901 ('Versicherungschronik', *ZVersWiss* 2 [1901], 205–207).

[89] Worth mentioning are the *Haftpflicht-Schutzverband Deutscher Industrieller* ('Liability Protection Federation of German Industrialists') founded in 1892 (in 1902: *Deutscher Haftpflicht- und Versicherungsschutz-Verband*; in 1911: *Allgemeiner Versicherten-Verband* ['General Policyholders-Protection Federation']), the *Deutscher Versicherten-Verband* ('German Policyholders Federation') as well as the *Mulhusienne*, the *Deutsche Feuerversicherungs-Genossenschaft* ('German Fire Insurance Cooperative'), the *Feuerversicherungs-Verband deutscher Fabriken* ('Fire Insurance Federation of German Factories'), the *Österreichische Elementar-Versicherungs-Aktiengesellschaft* ('Austrian Basic Insurance Company Limited') and the *Feuerversicherungs-Genossenschaft deutscher Buchdrucker* ('Fire Insurance Cooperative for German Book Printers') (Manes, *Masius' Rundschau* 1906, 82; Duvinage 1987, 55).

[90] The federation was founded by 151 members that comprised a total wealth of 150 million marks in insurance sums (*ZVersWiss* 2 [1901], 205–207). According to its own figures, it represented some 4,000 members around 1910, among them fifty-one trade and

to the Union of the Private Fire Insurers.[91] Even the medium-sized Coalition of Manufacturers welcomed its foundation.[92] Under the management of Otto Prange, the 'Protection Federation' aspired to form its own cooperative insurance company.[93] This plan failed,[94] in part because representatives of the industry and the insurance business succeeded in defusing the strongest conflicts.[95] The activity of the insurance cartel remained, however, controversial.[96]

Two other fundamental changes were to be expected around the turn of the century. The formation of a central authority for the supervision of the insurance business[97] and the adoption of laws regulating insurance contracts were being planned.[98] Both projects had been discussed since the unification of the German territorial states in 1871. The constitution of the German Reich of January 1, 1871 assigned to the Reich the

---

agricultural chambers and magistrates as well as 134 business associations with a total of 180,000 members (Meschke 1935, 51, fn. 81).

[91] Duvinage 1987.

[92] Declaration of the general meeting of the 22nd of Oktober, 1901 (*ZVersWiss* 2 (1901), 205–207. According to Meschke (1935) the BdI was a co-founder of the 'Protection Federation'.

[93] Manes, *Masius' Rundschau* 1906, 82.

[94] The *Deutsche Reform-Versicherungsbank* ('German Reform Insurance Bank') was founded in 1910, but adjusted very soon to the tariff policy of the *Vereinigung*. It was converted into another company in 1915 after large losses (Meschke 1935, 73 *et seq.*).

[95] In a closed session on May 29 and 30, 1902, delegates from the *Vereinigung der in Deutschland arbeitenden Privat-Feuerversicherungs-Gesellschaften* met with the Fire Insurance commission of the CVDI in which all of the industries subject to a tariff were represented. The link between the federations was H. A. Bueck as General Secretary to the CVDI and Chairperson of the committee of the *Vereinigung*. Without very much help from the protection federation, a clarification of the tariff policy and other points of contention was achieved.

[96] Besides the protection federation, almost all of the parties represented in the *Reichstag* (German Parliament) expressed criticism of the organisations of the insurance business. Positive statements originate from different publicists and the Imperial Supervisory Agency for Private Insurance ('Debatte über das VVG', *Stenographische Berichte über die Verhandlungen des Reichstags, XII. Legislaturperiode, I. Session (1907/1908)*, 1821 *et seq.*; Rüdiger, 'Das Versicherungswesen, sein Zustand und seine Stellung in Wirthschaft, Gesetzgebung und Wissenschaft', *ZVersWiss* 1 (1901), 16; Manes, *Masius' Rundschau* 1906, 81; Schramm-Macdonald, 'Das Feuerversicherungskartell' *Der Tag*, 5 October 1910 (BA B 280–644); *Gutachten des Kaiserlichen Aufsichtsamtes für Privatversicherung an die königlich bayerische Regierung bezüglich der Verstaatlichung der Mobiliar-Feuerversicherung (1910)*, cited in Meschke 1935, 62.

[97] A systematic supervision had existed up to then only in Prussia (Maurer 1911); Ehrenberg 1923, 2.

[98] Up to this time, only maritime law was codified in the *ADHGB* and was used in the other branches in part analogously (Duvinage 1987, 58; Ehrenberg 1923, 2).

legislative competence for the area of the insurance industry.[99] Neverthe-less, the existing structures remained untouched at first. The legal science was also largely uninterested in the insurance industry, with the excep-tion of maritime insurance.[100] The judiciary was more active. The High Commercial Court cautiously began to place the contents of *AVB* under scrutiny in order to protect the insured as the weaker party to the con-tract. The *Reichsgericht* continued on this course.[101]

As of 1878, the national policy concerning insurances tended towards intervention, thus contrasting with the radical free trade demands of the 1870's.[102] It did not go so far, however, as to fulfil the demands for nation-alisation of the insurance industry.[103]

On November 26, 1898, the draft of a nationally uniform *Versicherungs-aufsichtsgesetz* (*VAG*, 'law on the supervision of insurance') was presented to the public and, scarcely altered, as a government draft to the *Reichstag* ('German Imperial Parliament') on November 14, 1900.[104] Its guiding prin-ciple was substantive State supervision; Sect. 64, paragraph 2 of the later *VAG* prescribed:

> [The supervisory body] is authorised to make those arrangements that are appropriate to accommodating business activities to the legal regulations and the business plan or to resolve grievances that endanger the interests of the insured party or that bring the business activities into conflict with the conventions of good practice (trans.).[105]

A strict system of regulation including both the insurers' general obliga-tion to seek a licence and 'preventive monitoring' was planned. The lat-ter meant that the individual insurance contracts would require official authorisation. A central governmental supervisory agency with expansive authority and wide discretionary powers was to implement this concept. The public institutions were to be excluded from supervision.

---

[99] The Reich's competency for the law of supervision resulted from Article 4, para. 1 and the competency to regulate insurance contracts from Article 4, para. 13 of the Constitution of the German Reich, the Reich's Law Gazette 1871 (Seydel 1897, 67).

[100] Emminghaus,' Versicherungswesen', *Handwörterbuch der Staatswissenschaften*, 1rd ed. (1894), Vol 6, 451. The *Zeitschrift für Versicherungs-Recht und Wissenschaft* (*ŽVersRW*) was established in 1895. Previously, only a few commercial law historians had dealt with the legal area, especially Konrad Malß and Levin Goldschmidt.

[101] Neugebauer 1990, 150; Ogorek, *ZHR* 150 (1986), S.103 *et seq.*

[102] Arps 1965, 37 *et seq.*

[103] Wandel 1998, 126 *et seq.*

[104] Büchner in Rohrbeck, *50 Jahre materielle Versicherungsaufsicht I* (1951), 13 *et seq.*

[105] Cited in Deybeck 1902, 105.

These principles were intensely debated in the parliamentary plenary session and committees. The monitoring was eliminated, but its later inclusion was left to the discretion of the individual federal states.[106] The members of parliament, however, did not undertake any other important changes. In May of 1901, the *VAG* was adopted and came into force on January 1, 1902. The Imperial Supervisory Agency for Private Insurance began to operate on the same day.

In its early years, the agency concentrated on the companies' accounting practices and their introduction of the so-called principle of specialisation, that is, the operational division between property and life insurance.[107] Moreover, the standardisation of *AVB* constituted another main area of activity.[108] It aimed to render the insurance protection more transparent for the policyholders. Since the adoption of a *Versicherungsvertragsgesetz* (*VVG*, 'Insurance Contract Law') and thus a basic revision of all *AVB* was pending, only the conditions of those branches in which up to then no uniform federation conditions had been in practice were revised. Where such conditions had been introduced—as in the fire insurance business—, the supervisory agency only dealt with individual, especially controversial clauses.[109] The fire insurance federation vigorously rejected additional revision of the federation conditions.[110]

The efforts of the supervisory agency to achieve uniformity led to the development of the legal institute of *Normativbedingungen* ('normative conditions'). The agency published so-called 'model conditions' that satisfied the minimum requirements that appeared necessary for the protection of the policyholders' interests. For the most part, all the organised interest groups had elaborated these conditions in a cooperative effort. An insurance company that applied to have its business establishment approved and in the process included the normative conditions could thus anticipate that permission would be granted. From the very beginning, the supervisory agency rejected any and all deviations.[111] The reactions from insurance circles were at first extremely negative. Paternalism,

---

[106] Marck, 'Geltung von Landesrecht neben der reichsgesetzlichen Aufhebung der Präventivkontrolle', *ZVersWiss* 3 (1903), 371.

[107] Blanck, 'Die Feuerversicherung', in Rohrbeck, *50 Jahre materielle Versicherungsaufsicht II* (1951), 161.

[108] Arps 1965, 560.

[109] Examples in 1951, 162.

[110] *Veröffentlichungen des Kaiserlichen Aufsichtsamts für Privatversicherung* 1903, 110; Gerhard et al. 1909, 376.

[111] Hagen, 'Die neuen Versicherungsbedingungen', *ZVersWiss* 10 (1910), 204 *et seq.*

police-state mistrust and a 'volcanic flow of bureaucracy' (trans.)[112] were some of the terms of complaint. However, with increasing practice, the principle of normative conditions was accepted as 'one of the most important means of supervision' (trans).[113]

A legal regulation of substantive insurance law was not achieved before the San Francisco disaster. The *AVB* formed the 'important legal sources' (trans.)[114] of private insurance law in every branch:

> That private insurance law is not lacking where it is not codified goes without saying. Not just in the area of maritime insurance—in all areas of the insurance industry, autonomy has always been active and competition has also provided for a certain regularity in the autonomous development. Jurisprudence and judicial work have taken care of the rest [...] The insurance conditions, *leges contractus* for the individual insurance contract, are the chief areas of autonomous formation of law; they are invalid only if they contravene absolute [i.e. statutory] laws (trans.).[115]

In the fire insurance business, the 1886 *AVB* of the Federation of German Private Fire Insurance Companies, a revision of the 1874 conditions, predominated.[116] All thirty-two of the German public limited companies in the fire insurance branch made use of these so-called federation conditions.[117] Many of the other common stock and mutual companies looked to them as well.

The legal conditions that existed in the federal states no longer corresponded to the needs of business.[118] In 1878, a parliamentary commission in the German Parliament counted approximately one hundred different legal regulations for fire insurance.[119] In Prussia, for example, a scarcely discernible network of conditions from the Prussian Civil Code of 1794, the first German codification of insurance law, and earlier conditions was still existent.[120] For this reason, the insurance companies and the policyholders

---

[112] *Zeitschrift für Versicherungswesen* 1910, 1 *et seq.*; Hagen 1907, 207.

[113] Tigges 1985, 93.

[114] Raiser 1930, 42. Lewis writes (1889, 3) that insurance law 'has retained up until recently the character of customary law'.

[115] Emminghaus, 'Versicherungswesen', *Handwörterbuch der Staatswissenschaften* 1rd ed. (1894), vol. 6, 458.

[116] Sammlung der Versicherungsbedingungen (...), I, 75*ff* (75).

[117] Gruenwald et al. 1907, 8.

[118] Rüdiger, *ZVersWiss* 1 (1901), 15; König in Endemann, *Handbuch des Handelsrechts* (1885), vol. 3, 743.

[119] Rüdiger, *ZVersWiss* 1 (1901), 15, fn. 1.

[120] Gerhard et al. 1908, VII.

had campaigned for a creation of a uniform *VVG* since the 1870's.[121] Despite the explicit willingness of Parliament to seize the initiative,[122] the government under Chancellor Otto von Bismarck rejected a national legal regulation of substantive insurance law.[123]

For two decades, little happened to create a legal basis for the insurance contract.[124] It was only on January 15, 1899 that the Imperial Legal Office presented a partial bill that contained general conditions for all insurance branches. Additional drafts and intensive discussions involving various interest groups followed.[125]

Finally, the Imperial Legal Office completed a *VVG* draft that, on November 17, 1904, was presented to the upper house of Parliament as a bill in the form of a 'governmental draft'.[126] On November 28, 1905, the upper house sent the draft to the lower house of Parliament with minor changes. From this point on, it was referred to as the third draft or 'the Parliamentary Bill'.[127] After two readings on January 22 and 23, 1906,[128] the Parliament's plenary session sent the draft to the VIIIth Commission, which was required to provide the plenary session with a statement on the proposal. This was the state of legislative process in April 1906.

---

[121] The third German Trade Association in Frankfurt in 1865 categorically opposed the legal regulation of insurance contract law. A decade later, in 1875, the 16th Congress of German Economists advocated a nationally uniform *VVG*, just as, in the following year, the *Verband Deutscher Privat-Feuerversicherungs-Gesellschaften* ('Federation of German Private Fire Insurance Companies'), the *Verein deutscher Lebensversicherungs-gesellschaften* ('Union of German Life Insurance Companies') and the *Internationale Transport-Versicherungsverband* ('International Transport Insurance Federation'). In 1878 and 1879, the insurance industry once again sent petitions to the relevant commissions in the Prussian House of Parliament and in the *Reichstag* (Gerhard et al. 1908, X *et seq.*; Arps 1965, 35 *et seq.*).

[122] Resolution of the *Reichstag* of 14 May 1879 (Gerhard et al. 1908, X *et seq.*

[123] Gerhard et al. 1908, XII; Prange, 'Einiges aus der Brandschaden-Regulirungspraxis', *ZVersWiss 1* (1901), 178.

[124] The *Reichsgericht* Official Otto Baehr drafted 'by proxy' a *VVG* draft in 1883, which he made public in 1892, apparently because there was no interest in the law in the responsible ministry. The adoption of the material in the Civil Code (German: BGB) was considered, but not carried out (Gerhard et al. 1908, XII *et seq.*).

[125] Draft of *VVG*, published by the legal department of the *Reich* (1903); 'Denkschrift der Vereinigung der in Deutschland arbeitenden Privat-Feuerversicherungs-Gesellschaften vom 15. Dezember 1901', *ZVersWiss 2* (1902), 253–315; Prange 1904; Ehrenberg, 'Entwurf eines Gesetzes über den Versicherungsvertrag. Einleitende Besprechung', *ZVersWiss 3* (1903), 316; Manes, *Veröffentlichungen des Deutschen Vereins für Versicherungswissenschaft II*, 5 *et seq.*; 'Einleitung' in Gerhard et al. 1908, XVII.

[126] Compare Gerhard, 'Der Gesetzentwurf über den Versicherungsvertrag als Bundesratsvorlage', *ZVersWiss 5* (1905), 171 *et seq.*

[127] Ibid., 34 *et seq.*

[128] Gerhard et al. 1908, XX.

Finally, the strong international engagement of the German fire insurance industry must be emphasised in view of the San Francisco catastrophe.[129] While the foundation of the Empire had stimulated the reforms described above,[130] business had taken the end of the Franco-Prussian War (1871) as a signal for internationalisation. Many German companies, especially retailers, established branches abroad, insured by German companies. Starting from here, many insurance companies established their actual foreign business until the turn of the century.[131] The professional insurance journals[132] and the insurers' frequent congressional meetings reflect this awakening.[133] The reinsurance companies also became very active abroad. The Munich Re, founded in 1880, quickly became the world's largest company of its kind.[134] Reinsurers 'balanced dangers internationally'[135] and facilitated the entrance of German public limited companies into other business areas.

In the direct foreign insurance business, the branch of the fire insurers was the most active. It earned about \$14.4 million and paid out about \$8.6 million in claims in 1905.[136]

3.1.2.2. 'San Francisco' Reaches Germany

In view of the strong presence of German fire insurers in overseas business, the news of the San Francisco disaster was received with great anxiety in Germany.

---

[129] Borscheid, *VSWG* 88 (2001), 311 *et seq.*

[130] Cf. Stolleis in Starck 1992, 15 *et seq.*

[131] Manes, 'Auslandsgeschäft', *Versicherungslexikon*, 1st ed. (1909), col. 166 *et seq.*; Wandel 1998, 61; Borscheid 1990, 440.

[132] As of the 1870's, *Elsner's Repertorischer Assekuranz-Almanach* increasingly reports on business in foreign countries. This tendency is also apparent in the advertisement section. In 1885, the Assecuranz JB transforms itself from an Austro-German to a European publication with an eye on the developments overseas. The same holds true for other professional journals.

[133] The life insurers were especially active; they held meetings in 1895 in Brussels, in 1898 in London—where insurers of all branches came togethers—, in 1900 in Paris, in 1903 in New York and in 1906 in Berlin. Arps 1965, 449 *et seq.*

[134] That is why the historian Eckhard Wandel sees the actual "beginning of business abroad for German insurers" in the establishment of the Münchener Rück. In 1970, 70 percent of the company's premium revenue came from foreign country. Wandel 1998, 61 *et seq.*

[135] Moldenhauer, *Versicherungslexikon*, 1st ed. (1909), col. 1044.

[136] 60,643 million and 36,367 million Deutsche Mark in German currency. Manes, *Versicherungslexikon*, 1st ed. (1909), col. 167. Cf. the statistics in *Elsner's Repertorischer Assekuranz-Almanach* 1907, 158 *et seq.*

The German insurance business was forced to assume the third-largest part of the claims. Fire insurers as well as reinsurers in part suffered painful losses. The Aachen-Munich Insurance Company, the Prussian National Insurance Company and the Hamburg-Bremen Insurance Company had been working with a standard policy, that is, without an earthquake clause, and had to pay damages of $7.4 million.[137] The Rhine & Moselle Company and the *Norddeutsche Feuer* Insurance Company opposed all damage claims on the basis of their earthquake clause. The *Transatlantische* Insurance Company was likewise not prepared to satisfy claims. These three companies withdrew from California in 1906.[138] The *Transatlantische* and the *Norddeutsche Feuer* were unable to withstand the losses and were liquidated.[139] Among the companies indirectly involved in California, the Aachen Fire Company, the Cologne Re and Munich Re were severely affected. Many German companies were unable to pay planned dividends and had to increase their capital stock, give up their independence through mergers or strike similar compromises.[140]

Not only experts, but also the broad public learned of the economic consequences of the distant earthquake disaster and was able to follow the court cases against German insurance companies in Germany and abroad. Calls from California urged politicians, the supervisory agency, the chamber of commerce and even the emperor to intervene.[141] The insurers attempted to launch competing accounts.[142]

---

[137] 31 million Deutsche Mark in German currency. 'Geschäftsbericht des Kaiserlichen Aufsichtsamts für Privatversicherung für das Jahr 1906', *Stenographische Berichte über die Verhandlungen des Reichstags, XII. Legislaturperiode, I. Session, Anlagen*, no. 503, 2666. On the behavior of German corporations, notably the *Hamburg-Bremer*, cf. Chinatown Pan, The Impact of the 1906 Earthquake on San Francisco's Chinatown (1995), 101–105.

[138] The *Allianz* also considers this. *ÖVZ* 1906, 309.

[139] The *Transatlantische* had debts of over 4 million US$. The contracts were transferred to the *Albingia* after the liquidation. The *Rhein & Mosel* was able to cope with the losses. 'Geschäftsbericht des Kaiserlichen Aufsichtsamts für Privatversicherung für das Jahr 1906', *Stenographische Berichte über die Verhandlungen des Reichstags, XII. Legislaturperiode, I. Session, Anlagen*, no. 503, 2666 *et seq.*

[140] The following corporations participated indirectly in paying damages: *Aachener Rück, Badische Rück- und Mitversicherungsgesellschaft, Berlinische Feuer, Globus, Hamburg, Kölnische Rück, Minerva, Münchener Rück, Süddeutsche Rück*. The participation of *Allianz, Badische Bank, Preussische, Süddeutsche Bank, Thuringia, Westdeutsche Versicherungsbank* remains uncertain. For full particulars, cf. the table of companies involved in damages in San Francisco attached in the annexe.

[141] Cf. for instance the statement of the German-American Association of California of October 1st, published in 'San Francisco und die Feuerversicherungs-Gesellschaften', *Der Versicherungsfreund*, 1 December 1906, 5 *et seq.*

[142] Simon congratulated his Cologne colleague Gruenwald on an article in the Kölnische Zeitung whose description of the San Francisco liquidations shed a favorable light on

Altogether, it can be assumed that the San Francisco disaster and its consequences were more clearly perceived in Germany than in other European countries. The intensive discourse involving the future earthquake regulations and the different reactions that followed within the legal system support this assessment.

3.1.2.3. Contemporary Estimates of the Earthquake-Fire Danger in Germany

In 1906, contemporaries considered the actual threat of disasters such as those experienced in San Francisco to be marginal.[143] It is striking how seldom they were mentioned in German publications on the earthquake-fire problem.

This feeling of security was not based on systematically derived information, but rather on diffuse perceptions. It is important that the population of the German Reich did not remember any noteworthy earthquakes from memory or tradition and that this situation continued into the future.[144] Contemporary empirical studies supported this notion, but only for the preceding decades.[145] There were, of course, no scientific guarantees; the German-speaking scientific literature demonstrated great uncertainty as to the causes of earthquakes.[146] Only since the turn of the century was seismological research supported.[147] The memory of the greater central European earthquakes could also have led to uncertainty—for example, the one in Basel in the fourteenth century[148] and that in Stuttgart in the

---

them: 18 December 1906 Simon to Gruenwald, SR/FA A9.0–29/ folder III/ F. 18 April 1906/ diverse corresp. (mainly Rückv. 6/1906–6/1907), 200.

[143] For example, Gröppler (1910, 59) writes that earthquakes—if not serious ones—were conceivable. Similar estimates: written communications of the Gothaer Company to SR, cited in 3 December 1906 Simon to *Bayerische Versicherungsbank*, SR/FA A9.0–32/ folder/ correspondence regarding earthquake clause 1906/1907/ *Bayerische Versicherungsbank*, 15 et seq.; *Berliner Börsen-Courier* 92, 24 February 1915, supplement, 1–2.

[144] Hurtig and Kowalle 1988, 51 *et seq.*

[145] Germany is not listed in Montessus de Ballore's earthquake catalogue, which includes twenty-four countries and regions of the world (*La Semaine*, 23 December 1906, 8).

[146] See the discussion in chapter 3.2.2.

[147] The Centre for Earthquake Research in Strasbourg was established in 1900, where the first international earthquake conference took place in 1901. In 1904, the International Association of Seismology was founded. Additional research centres were founded in Göttingen, Jena und Potsdam ('Die erste internationale Erdbebenkonferenz zu Straßburg', *Petermanns Geographische Mitteilungen* 47 (1901), 115–119; Hecker 1924.

[148] The earthquake occurred on October 18, 1356 (Drumm, 'Die Beweislast bei der Erdbebenklausel in den deutschen Feuerversicherungsverträgen', *ZVersWiss* 7 [1907], 374); cover letters for the brochures of the Earthquake Commission, SR/FA FA 9.0–32/yellow file folder (correspondence, mainly Cologne Re 1907), 6. 17 *et seq.*

eighteenth century.[149] Therefore, some voices warned that earthquakes could also wreak havoc in Germany.[150]

This latent imponderability of the earthquake risk must be seen in opposition to the very vivid memory of the devastating urban conflagrations, whatever their causes. The contemporaries remembered above all the Hamburg firestorm of 1842. The risk of conflagrations, however, had been reduced through improvements in construction and technology in the past fifty years.[151] This contributed to the sentiment that earthquake-fire catastrophes were unlikely in Germany.

3.1.2.4. *The Earthquake Regulations at the Time of the San Francisco Disaster*

Legal regulations of the insurer's liability for earthquake-fire damages did not exist. The decisive regulations were to be found in the general insurance conditions. At the time of the San Francisco disaster, the *AVB* of the Federation of German Private Fire Insurance Companies, an 1886 amendment of the 1874 conditions, predominated. They stipulated the following:

> Sect. 1 [...] para. 3. Excluded from the insurance are such damages that originate during a war through military measures ordered by a commander or are the consequence of an insurgence, breach of the peace or an earthquake (trans.).[152]

This formulation was used by all thirty-two German public limited fire insurance companies.[153] Of the thirty-four foreign public limited companies, thirty-one had adopted or introduced similar clauses. The distribution

---

[149] The often mentioned earthquakes could not be identified, but were apparently known to contemporaries. Speech by the Parlimentarian Kaempf, *Stenographische Berichte über die Verhandlungen des Reichstags, XII. Legislaturperiode, I. Session (1907/1908)*, 1824 *et seq.*; Ruttke, *Mitteilungen für die öffentlichen Feuerversicherungs-Anstalten* 1909, 237 *et seq.*; Liebig 1911, 87.

[150] *Der Versicherungsfreund*, 1 March 1909, 4 *et seq.* This estimate has been substantiated by recent seismological research. The danger of earthquakes in Germany was the subject of an annual meeting of the German Geophysical Society in 2001 in Frankfurt (Rademacher, 'Schwere Beben in Deutschland nicht unmöglich', *Frankfurter Allgemeine Zeitung*, 4 April 2001, N1). Compare the earthquake statistics and maps in Leydecker 2000.

[151] Urban historical research has produced numerous examples. The most prominent of many: Jung-Köhler 1991, 43, 54 *et seq.*, 148; Scholz 1999, 13 *et seq.* Additional references in Ranft and Selzer 2004, 22.

[152] Printed in *Sammlung der Versicherungsbedingungen* [...], I, 75 *et seq.* (75).

[153] Gruenwald et al. 1907, 8.

of the burden of proof was not specifically regulated; [154] this means that the insurer would have had to prove the causality between the earthquake and the fire damages.[155]

Only three foreign companies used the so-called *Hamburger Börsen-police* as a basis for their contracts. This is remarkable because it combined a temporary linkage of earthquakes and damages with a reversal of the burden of proof:

> Excluded from insurance liability are such damages as those that occur as a result of a wartime situation... or an earthquake....
>
> In the case of all damages that occur during the events just mentioned, it will be assumed that they are a consequence of those events, except if the insured can unquestionably prove the opposite.
>
> In no case is the insurer liable for damages that can be traced back to official measures, with the exception of such fire-fighting measures that were taken during the fire.[156]

Most of the seventeen German mutual insurance companies looked to the federation conditions of the public limited companies. Ten of them excluded the earthquake risk, four of them by adopting the wording in the 'federation conditions'. The fifty-five public fire institutions, on the other hand, adopted almost without exception the liability for earthquake damages, ten even expressly. Only six public institutions excluded their liability by contract.[157]

There was a need for action from the viewpoint of the reinsurers' Earthquake Commission. Therefore, the public limited companies had to be persuaded to revise the earthquake clause, which up until 1906 had gone unnoticed in their federation conditions. As many as possible mutual fire insurance companies and public institutions had to follow suit.[158]

---

[154] According to the federation conditions, the insurer was authorised to investigate 'the value of the damages as well as their origin and amount and to require the insured to present records supporting their statements and other evidence that they can provide' (§8). Both parties enjoyed the right to make use of expert testimony (§9) (*Sammlung der Versicherungsbedingungen* [...], I, 75 *et seq.*).

[155] Domizlaff, 'Der Feuerversicherungsvertrag nach künftigem deutschem, schweizerischem und österreichischem Recht', *ZVersWiss* 9 (1909), 56; Drumm, *ZVersWiss* 7 (1907), 375.

[156] Gruenwald et al. 1907, 8.

[157] Ibid., 8 *et seq.*

[158] Ibid.

3.1.2.5. *The German Discourse on the Earthquake Regulations in the AVB and Law*

Directly after the San Francisco earthquake, discussions on the liability of the fire insurance companies in disasters of this kind began in Germany. At first, the statements were limited to the interpretations of the existing *AVB* and generally regarded demands for an earthquake clause. Only by the middle of 1907, however, did different models for legislation and a revision of the existing *AVB* enter the discussion.

Only seldom was the exclusion of liability for any damages caused by earthquakes regarded as self-evident.[159] This view was supported by three arguments. Firstly, *Elsner's Repertorischer Assekuranz-Almanach* argued that earthquake-fire damages need not be indemnified 'because their scope *a priori* completely lacks any commercial justification and reasonable calculation' (trans.).[160] In the case of larger disasters, the fire departments would fail, and the population would not save their property, but rather their own lives. Secondly, the exclusion of earthquake dangers followed from the system of German policy conditions, which treated earthquake dangers along with other uninsurable events such as war, insurgence and breaches of the peace.[161] Thirdly, as the director of the *Bayerische Versicherungsbank* ('Bavarian Insurance Bank'), Ernst Drumm, argued at a different occasion, if contract law centred upon the will of the parties, this will demonstrated that the parties undoubtedly did not wish to include indemnity for damages resulting from earthquakes.[162]

This position was defended in view of the threatening indemnity obligations in California. Their arguments resembled the public statement of the European reinsurance companies of April 30, 1906.[163] However, they had to yield to the argument that collateral earthquake damages were—despite all the circumstances—customarily not excluded. The cause of a fire was basically irrelevant.[164] This discussion disappeared after 1907.

The statement in the *Assekuranz-Almanach* and Drumm's essay are remarkable because they expressly referred to the legal situation in the German Reich. They jointly concluded that in substantive law, earthquake-related damages were comprehensively excluded from coverage pursuant

---

[159] For example, an anonymous author in *Zeitschrift für Versicherungswesen* 1906, 280.
[160] 'Brandfolge infolge eines Erdbebens', *Elsner's Repertorischer Assekuranz-Almanach* 1907, 154 *et seq.*
[161] Ibid., 155.
[162] Drumm, *ZVersWiss* 7 (1907), 375.
[163] *Masius' Rundschau* 1906, 226.
[164] Hagen, *DJZ* 1906, col. 741; Knebel-Doeberitz in Gerhard et al. 1909, 390.

to the 'federation conditions of 1886'. Drumm concentrated on the problem of the burden of proof in relation to the fire causality of an earthquake. In view of the difficult Californian trials, he demanded that the judge need

> not necessarily insist that the defendant prove beyond the shadow of any doubt the facts that are capable of outweighing the claim of the plaintiff. Here also, the judge must be satisfied with a high degree of probability, unless he wishes to deprive the defendant *a priori* of any chance of providing contrary evidence (trans.).[165]

The Munich Director argued in favour of leaving room for 'factual conjectures' that 'in accordance with recognised legal principles must not be proven because everyone is aware of them' (trans.). Applied to San Francisco, this principle would mean that the factual assumption of causality between earthquake, conflagration and the destruction of individual houses in the fire was valid for the destroyed houses within the fire zone. Outside of this 'conflagration area,' it would be a 'matter for the insurance company [...] to prove the alleged relationship between earthquake and fire' (trans.).[166]

Drumm went no further than the interpretation of the existing earthquake clause. However, if one believed, as he did, that an earthquake-fire disaster was possible in Germany, it was risky to rely upon a judge's favourable interpretation of the existing exclusionary clause. Nevertheless, the German companies seldom demanded the introduction of improved clauses.[167]

The Imperial Supervisory Agency for Private Insurance provided the prelude for this clause at the end of August 1906. In a written communication to every domestic and foreign company working in Germany, the agency wrote that the disaster just experienced was an

> urgent reminder to subject the insurance conditions in use in foreign business operations to a careful review as to whether the non-liability for earthquake damages is expressed sufficiently clearly in the respective insurance conditions, and to eliminate possible ambiguities therein (trans.).[168]

---

[165] Drumm, *ZVersWiss* 7 (1907), 376 *et seq.*

[166] Ibid., 377.

[167] An exception is the resolution of the twenty reinsurance companies on April 30, 1906, *ÖVZ* 1906, 234.

[168] 'Geschäftsbericht des Kaiserlichen Aufsichtsamts für Privatversicherung für das Jahr 1906', *Stenographische Berichte über die Verhandlungen des Reichstags, XII. Legislaturperiode, I. Session, Anlagen*, no. 503, 2670.

The Berlin civil servants did not mention the business in Germany. They
were evidently concerned with preventing additional disaster-related capital outflow abroad.

The professional press loyal to the insurance business was pleased to
note this demand for earthquake clauses and wrote that the supervisory
agency was

> completely justified in maintaining that the earthquake clauses cannot be
> expressed clearly enough in the policies. The opportune publication of this
> decree has in our opinion facilitated the situation of many a German com-
> pany (trans.).[169]

The agency additionally requested the companies to provide information
on their direct or indirect participation in earthquake-fire risk insurance.[170]
The insurers had to send two copies of all the policies in use to Berlin
as well as in the case of forms drafted in foreign languages—with the
exception of English and French—, the translations. The agency was to
be informed about intended changes as well.[171]

This polite communication exposed an unexpected weakness of the
agency. It was not informed about the legal basis on which the companies
that were under their control operated, which obligations they were about
to face in California, and how they were going to react.[172] The agency's
archives disclose that up to 1908, the regulatory authorities had considerable difficulties in gaining access to information on the international
activities.[173] This was mainly because of the civil servants' lack of direct
contact with the well-informed reinsurance industry, as this branch was
not subject to supervision. There was also a lack of connection to the foreign supervisory agencies, companies and interest organisations. There
was even a partial lack of information in respect to the activities within
the German insurance business.[174] In order to be able to discharge their

---

[169] 'Das deutsche Aufsichtsamt über die Erdbebenklausel', *ÖRev* 1906, 202. Wach ('Die
Erdbebenklausel bei Feuerversicherungsverträgen', *LZ* 1907, col. 478 and *Feuerversicherung
und Feuerschutz* 1907, 164) also reported on this communication.

[170] 'Geschäftsbericht des Kaiserlichen Aufsichtsamts' 1906, 2664 *et seq.*

[171] Ibid., 2670.

[172] The fire insurers addressed were summoned insofar as they were present abroad as
reinsurers of retrocessionaires to inform the agency on any planned steps contemplated
vis à vis the direct insurers ('Geschäftsbericht des Kaiserlichen Aufsichtsamts für das Jahr
1906', 2670).

[173] Records pertaining to the earthquake clause from 1906–1908 are not extant in the
national archives.

[174] In a meeting of the insurance advisory board of the supervisory agency, it turned out,
for example, that the president of the agency had not been informed of the plans of the

duties, the civil servants had to have more information than was obtainable from daily newspapers and the insurance trade press.[175] Sporadically, they received information from German fire insurance companies.[176] However, many insurance companies did not recognise the authority of the agency to control their activities outside of the *Reich* and obstructed its work.[177] Only slowly did the agency succeed in enforcing its demand for information.

In this context, the board's call for clear exclusionary clauses for foreign business should not be overrated. It benefitted those groups that also recommended a reform, but did not put pressure on the companies.

At this point, the federations of the German fire insurance companies apparently did not see the need to look into the question of earthquake-fire damages. While uniform reforms of the regulations for business in foreign countries were discussed in England and the Netherlands at the end of 1906,[178] nothing happened in Germany.[179] The insurers had in any event rejected changes in the *AVB* for the domestic business by pointing to the impending *VVG*.[180]

The Earthquake Commission provided the decisive stimulus for the reform of the earthquake clause. In the middle of 1906, the reinsurers had begun corresponding with German fire insurance companies on the matter.[181] In response to an 'interpellation' by the Swiss Re, for example, the *Gothaer Versicherungsbank* ('Gotha Insurance Bank') had expressed its readiness to incorporate the earthquake clause into its policies. Its

---

insurers to revise the insurance conditions ('minutes of the entire meeting of the insurance advisory body of the Imperial Supervisory Agency on January 31, 1908', BA B 280–546, 3.).

[175] The archives of the supervisory agency include collections of articles from such diverse publications as the *Frankfurter Zeitung* and *Vorwärts*.

[176] For example, on developments in Holland, Dutch-India, the USA and England (BA B 280–25309, 3–5 R).

[177] On the earthquake question, especially the *Aachen-München* and the *Hamburg-Bremer* companies opposed the agency's directives. The Director of the *Hamburg-Bremen* Company, Buchenberger, was ordered to come to Berlin to clarify the matter in 1910 (BA B 280–25309, 3–5 R).

[178] See also chapter 4.2.1.

[179] However, the *Münchener Allgemeine Zeitung* demanded: 'It is therefore completely necessary that fire insurance companies exclude their liability for direct and indirect earthquake damages in the interest of all their policyholders [...]' (trans.) (cited in *Feuerversicherung und Feuerschutz* 1907, 164).

[180] *Veröffentlichungen des Kaiserlichen Aufsichtsamts für Privatversicherung* 1903, 110.

[181] 23 July 1906 Drumm to Simon, SR/FA A9.0–32/file folder/correspondence regarding earthquake clause 1906/1907/ *Bayerische Versicherungsbank*, 28.

justification shows how ready for reform the *Gothaer* directors were—and certainly not just them:

> Finally, with regard to the implementations of the earthquake risk, our present bylaws contain no clauses excluding the fire damages resulting from earthquakes, whereas a regulation of this matter was included in our previous bank conditions. The omission of this proviso from our new bylaws is in any case due to the consideration that earthquake damages are not to be feared in the business area of our bank, which merely includes Germany and German Switzerland. We by no means fail to recognise that this last assumption can be justifiably called into question and decided some time ago that in the revision of our bylaws, which will be undertaken immediately following Parliament's passing of the insurance bill that is currently under discussion, we will include an explicit proviso that excludes our liability for fire damages that result from earthquakes (trans.).[182]

On July 18, 1907, the four reinsurance companies sent their study to a total of eighty-three public limited companies and mutual companies active in Germany. The public institutions were to be included when 'the contract law was passed by Parliament' (trans.).[183] The recommendations of the reinsurers contained the familiar three points: 'detailed definition of the non-liability... for indirect damages'; 'assignment of the burden of proof to the insured' (trans.); and the precise identification of the excluded damages as fire damages.[184] These points were applicable to fire insurance companies of all stripes, since with the exception of the Hamburg stock exchange policy, none of the formulations corresponded to this benchmark.[185]

The fire insurance companies reacted positively. The position of the *Gladbacher Feuerversicherungs-Aktien-Gesellschaft* ('Gladbach Limited Fire Insurance Company') that the improvement had to be 'aspired to in the pending revision of the insurance conditions' is characteristic.[186] The implementation of the suggestions was only a matter of time.

---

[182] Written communication from *Gothaer* to SR, cited in 3 December 1906 Simon to *Bayerische Versicherungsbank*, SR/FA A9.0–32/file folder/correspondence regarding earthquake clause 1906/1907/ *Bayerische Versicherungsbank*, 15 *et seq.*

[183] 25 February 1908 Simon to Gruenwald (excerpt), SR/FA A9.0–32/yellow file folder (correspondence Swiss insurance companies)/loose material.

[184] Gruenwald et al. 1907, 9.

[185] Ibid., 8.

[186] 25 July 1907 *Gladbacher Feuerversicherungs-Aktien-Gesellschaft* ('Gladbeck Fire Insurance Limited Company') to KR, SR/FA A9.0–32/yellow file folder (correspondence, mainly with Cologne Re 1907), 99 *et seq.*

The *Deutscher Feuerversicherungs-Schutzverband* also supported the reform efforts. Apparently, the head of the company, Prange, recognised that his emotional demand that German fire insurers withdraw from business abroad was unpromising.[187] Lacking cognizance of the reinsurers' concept, he and others nevertheless advocated that liability for direct or indirect disaster damages be excluded by contract in the association journal *Feuerversicherung und Feuerschutz*.[188]

Finally, two proposals for the reform of the earthquake regulations that appeared in the insurance trade press in 1907 are worth mentioning. The first was an essay published before the distribution of the study by the Earthquake Commission in the prestigious *Zeitschrift für die gesamte Versicherungswissenschaft* and written by a Munich insurance company employee named J. D. von Witzleben. It turned out that von Witzleben was an employee of the Munich Re and had included the materials developed by the Earthquake Commission in his essay. The Director of the Munich Re, Thieme, had personally arranged for the publication of the article.[189]

Von Witzleben attempted 'to arrive at a theory of a more effective and less flexible earthquake clause' by comparing internationally used clauses and their weaknesses.[190] He succeeded in producing a draft that in substance, scope and style surpassed the most stringent stipulations in use across the globe.[191] The author's performance itself, however, undermined

---

[187] Prange, *Feuerversicherung und Feuerschutz* 1906, 106.

[188] Compare *Feuerversicherung und Feuerschutz* 1907, 161 *et seq.*

[189] It is likely that Thieme was related to the author of the article through his wife Else—a von Witzleben by birth. This publication earned him the displeasure of the Earthquake Commission. Gruenwald feared that, on the whole, it endangered their project; compare the postscript to Simon, 4 July, 1907, in Gruenwald to Lindner, Simon, Thieme (SR/FA A9.0–32/yellow file folder (correspondence mainly to Cologne Re 1907, 65 *et seq.*).

[190] Witzleben, *ZVersWiss* 7 (1907), 378.

[191] The insurance does not cover fire and other damages that during an earthquake or within a week after an earthquake or that directly or indirectly, immediately or subsequently, were caused or that were somehow or other the consequence of an earthquake or that were caused by arson or destruction that directly or indirectly were linked to the earthquake or were occasioned by one; when on the basis of this policy the insured party lodges any damage claims because of fire or other damages following an earthquake, he shall deliver to the company at its request the proof that the damages were occasioned independently of the earthquake and in no way were caused by same or were the consequence of same or of any related act of arson or destruction, and if this proof can not be brought, the company shall thus not be liable for these fire damages, neither in toto nor in part.

An 'earthquake' in the sense of the preceding remarks is understood as the visual or measureable damages or changes in the surface of the earth or to constructed buildings, pipelines and so forth, and, to be precise, that were generated or caused temporally within

his proposed aim of achieving the 'most precise clarity in the stylistic and editorial relationship',[192] for his draft demonstrated a great deal of redundancy and disorganisation. In his elaborations, he proposed even greater distinctions in the clause.[193]

This essay showed a clear, but too one-sided reliance upon the experiences of the insurance companies in San Francisco and Valparaiso. The proposed clause might well have solved all the legal problems that arose in the adjustment of damages and in the courts of California. However, it was so incoherent at the same time that its adoption had to appear completely unlikely. It is to be assumed that no company would have given the earthquake question so much room in their policy conditions—be it because of its own conviction or out of pity for its customers. Von Witzleben overlooked this aspect. His essay may well have served as a stimulus; his clause draft, however, was not adopted.

The second remarkable proposal originated from the pen of the Mainz insurance lawyer Ludwig Fuld.[194] He argued in October of 1907 that an improved collapse clause would satisfy the necessary conditions for the insurance industry:

> In any case, the disaster in San Francisco and most recently that in Chile ought to provide the occasion for the insurance companies to undertake an appropriate revision of the obsolete fallen building clause and, more to the point, in a united manner. It is not apparent from the existing differences among countries, be they of a natural, political, social or legal nature, that a more or less extensive modification would seem necessary. If the intended fallen building clause is properly formulated, then it appears that the special adoption of an earthquake clause, even given a prudential approach, is scarcely necessary (trans.).[195]

---

a period of one week before the outbreak of fire and spatially within the area of ten km from the risk.'

This clause was designed to appear separately from the stipulation of the basic liability in the fire insurance conditions, so that a systematic interpretation would not treat it as an exception to the liability that would have to be proven by the insurer. Moreover, the earthquake risk was to be dealt with separately from non-related dangers (Witzleben, *ZVersWiss* 7 [1907], 384).

[192] Witzleben, *ZVersWiss* 7 (1907), 380 et seq.

[193] For example, with the proposal to add a list of typical situations (defects in the water supply lines, emergency detonations, etc.) to the exclusion of indirectly caused earthquake-fire damages (Witzleben, *ZVersWiss* 7 [1907], 382 et seq.).

[194] On the influence of Fuld, see Schubert, 'Gesetzgebung und Sozialpolitik im ausgehenden 19. Jahrhundert-Zur Erinnerung an die rechtspolitischen Schriften von Ludwig Fuld' in Stolleis 1991, 421 et seq.

[195] Fuld, *ÖVZ* 1907, 307 et seq.

Fuld's demand for international uniformity of the regulation was clearly expressed. But he was alone in preferring a fallen building clause. His proposal also does not appear to have fallen on fertile ground. This failure presumably also depended upon the fact that the relevant fire insurers had already formed a preference for the proposals of the reinsurers. Moreover, the insurers' attention was directed towards Berlin, where in 1907, Parliament was once again involved in the drafting of a VVG. There was still time to find an answer to the question of the earthquake regulation in the insurance industry's policy forms.

3.1.2.6. *International Standardisation through Legislation* (*November 1907–May 1908*)

The draft of a VVG, which had been under consideration since January 1906 in the Parliament's VIIIth Commission under inclusion of the German governments, had not mentioned the earthquake question.[196] On the evening of April 18, 1906, the news of the San Francisco earthquake had reached Germany. Although the news of the disaster and its consequences for the German insurance industry had been registered with general alarm, the members of the Commission were nevertheless still satisfied with the exclusion of other risks that were judged to be uninsurable. The exclusionary regulations of the §§84 and 85 were adopted 'unchanged and without debate'.[197]

An unexpected incident had prevented the discussion of the VVG draft in the third reading, which had been planned for the last few days of 1906. On the 13th of December, the Chancellor Bernhard von Bülow had dissolved Parliament.[198] The adoption of a VVG for the German Reich, just within reach so recently, was once again beyond grasp. In the meantime, the earthquake question was brought repeatedly into the focus of public interest because of the disasters in Valparaiso (16 August 1906) and Jamaica (19 January 1907), the court cases against the German companies on the basis of their obligations in California, and the collapse of the three domestic companies.

---

[196] Prange 1906, 24.

[197] Report of the VIIIth Commission on the drafts of a law on insurance contract, a related introductory law and a law related to the change in the provisions of the trade law book on maritime insurance, *Stenographische Berichte über die Verhandlungen des Reichstags, XII. Legislaturperiode, I. Session (1907), Anlagen*, no. 242, 2029.

[198] The goal was a weakening of the centre and the SPD through new elections, since both had criticised the colonial policy of the government (Tormein, 'Der Reichstag im Kaiserreich' in Schwarz, *Biographisches Handbuch der Reichstage* 1965).

In this situation, the upper house of Parliament once again seized the initiative for the creation of nationally uniform *VVG*. On April 20, 1907, it adopted the *VVG* draft in the version prepared by the VIIIth Parliamentary Commission; the Chancellor presented the draft as a bill to Parliament.[199] And there it remained for months.

At that point, the reinsurers in the Earthquake Commission saw an opportunity to influence the earthquake regulation in the future *Versicherungsvertragsgesetz*. Their concepts envisaged not only the chance 'to induce *all* the companies active in an area of business to adopt a *standard* clause', but also

> to induce the legislative factors in each country to formulate the legal exclusion of earthquake damages from fire insurance as a means of establishing dispositive legal norms and to thus create a fixed legal point of view for the evaluation of these questions by the policyholders (trans.).[200]

Many of the advocates of the implementation of earthquake clauses shared this objective. The virtues and defects of a non-mandatory legal exclusion of the earthquake danger were debated at great length in *Der Versicherungsfreund*. The journalists rejected, in principle, legal exclusionary conditions in favour of entrepreneurial freedom of choice. However, they recognised the advantages of an earthquake exclusion by law, that is, because of the international 'moral effect'[201] of such a regulation:

> In Germany, the fact that earthquake damages are not covered by insurance would easily be accepted, especially since the danger of earthquakes danger is, if not exactly beyond the realm of possibility, at least rather unlikely in the German Reich. Abroad, however, especially in the notorious earthquake areas, such a regulation of the question would not ... be without influence,[202] and in the future, such an exploitation of fire insurance companies as has occurred in recent years in California through harmonious cooperation in disregard of law and statutes on the part of insurance companies, public authorities and the courts, would be quite impossible (trans.).

The authors thus expressed their most important motive governing a comprehensive revision of the German earthquake regulations. In the

---

[199] *Stenographische Berichte über die Verhandlungen des Reichstags, XII. Legislaturperiode, I. Session (1907)*, *Anlagen*, no. 364, 1992 [reprint].

[200] Gruenwald et al. 1907, 4. The words in italics are printed with spaces between the letters in the original.

[201] 'Die Erdbebenschädenversicherung', *Der Versicherungsfreund*, 1 January 1908, 3. In the original, the word 'moral' is printed with spaces between the letters.

[202] Ibid. The original reads 'would not *have been* without influence', since the author assumed that the earthquake clause had not been adopted.

foreground was not the concern with earthquake disasters in their own country, but rather with the anticipated long-term effect on the legal situation in the earthquake-endangered business areas abroad. The optimism was based upon the experience that insurance law regulations had always been developed through a comparative approach. The German reforms could, on the international level, strengthen the idea of the exclusion of earthquake dangers after all and contribute to the formation of a general principle of law. The authors also interpreted similar paragraphs in French, Austrian and Swiss drafts in this sense.[203]

The Earthquake Commission became active between April and November 1907. The Director of the Munich Re, Thieme, had the best contacts in Parliament.[204] It can be regarded as certain that he exerted the most significant influence on the consideration of the earthquake question in the *Versicherungsvertragsgesetz*.[205] The parliamentarian of the *Freisinnige Volkspartei* ('Liberal People's Party'), Johannes Kaempf, who sat on the board of directors of the Munich Re, paved the way for this.[206]

Parliament discussed the revised draft on November 27, 1907 in the first plenary reading. The sufficiently well-known draft found general acceptance in the discussion.[207] The only one to reject it in principle was the social democrat Stadthagen, who favoured the nationalisation of the insurance industry or at least an increase of the mandatory provisos.[208]

The representatives of the five parties[209] scarcely deviated from their statements they had already given on the 22nd and 23rd of January, 1906. None of the conservative parties was fundamentally opposed to the

---

[203] Ibid.

[204] Thieme informed the members of the Earthquake Commission on the development. The following documents are located in the archives of the SR: 4 December 1907 (date of entry stamp, SR) excerpt from the speech of MP Kaempf (27 November 1907 in RT); excerpt from the speech of the MP v. Damm (27 November 1907 im RT); *Kommission zur Berathung des Gesetzentwurfes über den Versicherungsvertrag* (Liste der MdR). SR/FA A9.0–32/yellow file folder (correspondence Swiss insurance companies)/loose material.

[205] This emerges from the following letter: 6 March 1908 Simon to Thieme, SR/FA A9.0–32/yellow file folder (correspondence Swiss insurance companies)/loose material.

[206] 10 July 1908, Minutes of the 140th Meeting of the Board of Directors (present v. Finck, Kaempf, v. Maffei, Dr. Pemsel; Director Thieme; absent v. Cramer-Klett), MR/A E-25 Lfd. Nr. 50 (damages/San Francisco).

[207] Speeches of the MP Wellstein (*Zentrumspartei*), Heinze (*Nationalliberale Partei*), Schultz (*Deutsche Reichspartei*), Kaempf (*Freisinnige Volkspartei*), v. Damm (*Wirtschaftliche Vereinigung*), Dove (*Freisinnige Vereinigung*), Ricklin (*b.k.F/ Elsaß-Lothringen*). *Stenographische Berichte über die Verhandlungen des Reichstags, XII. Legislaturperiode, I. Session (1907/1908)*, 1821 *et seq.*

[208] Ibid., 1826 *et seq.*

[209] The major parties were National Liberals, Left Liberals, Conservatives, Centre MPs and Social Democrats. Some of the national or special interest groups formed independent

private insurance industry. The social democrats also succeeded in exercising plausible criticism in the framework of the draft law.[210] The lawyer Wolfgang Heine, a pupil of the socialist economist Adolph Wagner,[211] judged that the draft's recognition could not be denied since numerous provisions attempted to protect the population that had a less favourable standing and was less experienced.[212] Here, the social democratic opinion agreed with that of all the conservative parties.

Two issues were much disputed in the plenary: the exemption of the public fire societies from law and the question of freedom of contract including the role of the federations in the insurance business. The *VVG* draft remained, however, unchanged in this respect. Following these controversies, various speakers offered individual proposals on November 27, 1907. The left-wing Liberal Kaempf addressed the issue of the earthquake problem. As President of the Elders of the Mercantile Community of Berlin and a member of the Committee of the German Chamber of

---

minorities: Poles, Danes, Alsace-Lorrainers, Guelphs, as well as the Bavarian Agricultural Alliance.

The proportions of the parties in the 1903 and 1907 Parliaments:

	National Liberals	Left Liberals	Conservatives	Centre	Social Democrats
1903:					
Votes in %	13,8	9,3	13,5	19,7	31,7
Seats in %	12,8	9,1	18,9	25,2	20,4
No. of Seats	50	30	75	100	81
1907:					
Votes in %	14,5	10,9	13,4	19,4	29,0
Seats in %	13,6	12,4	21,1	26,4	10,8
Seats	56	42	84	105	43

Voter Participation 1903: 76%; 1907: 85%. Sources: Hofmann 1993, 23, 72, 74; Frank 1911, 5, 46 *et seq.*

[210] The MP W. Heine explained that the challenge to his party was 'to protect the rights of the policyholder in private insurance contracts and thereby to make the insurance industry a social asset'. He went on to say that this could only benefit a future official insurance industry. 'Speech of the MP Heine in the Lower Chamber of the Imperial Parliament' 22 January 1906, *Stenographische Berichte über die Verhandlungen des Reichstags, XI. Legislaturperiode, II. Session (1905–1906)*, 728 *et seq.*

[211] In 1887, Heine had taken part as an intern in the Berlin political science seminar conducted by the political economist Wagner, who in 1881 had attracted the public spotlight with his demand that the insurance industry be nationalised.

[212] Speech by the MP Heine in the German Lower House, 22 January 1906 (*Stenographische Berichte über die Verhandlungen des Reichstags, XI. Legislaturperiode, II. Session* [1905–1906], 728 *et seq.*).

Commerce (*Deutscher Handelstag*), he possessed 'a high degree of expertise'[213] in the field of insurance. Kaempf demanded to incorporate the exclusion of the earthquake risk into the non-mandatory provision of §84 *VVG*. The justification of his position shows that he had thoroughly considered the matter. First he referred to the disaster of the last few months, and then to the earthquake danger in Germany. As an example of the latter he recalled a devastating tremor that had occurred in Stuttgart in the middle of the eighteenth century. He then went on:

> Such a clause, however, would be important for another reason. It would put Germany into agreement with the draft bills that presently contain the so-called earthquake clause in France and, as far as I know, in Austria. It would be highly desirable if in this context, an international standardisation of the conditions would be initiated through a similar piece of legislation in the different States, and it would also have a beneficial influence upon the American circumstances, since it would morally urge that policies and clauses such those that I have mentioned also be adopted in America (trans.).[214]

Kaempf's arguments were identical to those of the reinsurers and parts of the insurance trade press. This consensus supports the conjecture that Thieme had advanced this matter in Parliament with Kaempf's help. The notion of an international standardisation of law by means of harmonious legislation was characteristic of the time in which comparative law was celebrated as the most recent achievement of jurisprudence.[215] The European reinsurers and the lawyer Ludwig Fuld[216] had, in their Frankfurt statement of April 30, 1906, expressed themselves in a similar manner regarding the earthquake clause.[217]

---

[213] Gerhard et al. 1908, XX.

[214] *Stenographische Berichte über die Verhandlungen des Reichstags, XII. Legislaturperiode, I. Session (1907/1908)*, 1824 *et seq.*

[215] On the occasion of the *Exposition Universelle* of 1900 in Paris, the French legal scholar Raymond Saleilles organised the first International Congress of Comparative Law. Saleilles's idea on the exploitation of 'droit idéal relatif' in the process of comparative law practice proved especially popular (Berger, 'The New Law Merchant and the Global Marketplace', Berger 2001, 5).

[216] Uniform standard clause as contribution to the international 'Rechtsausgleichung auf dem Gebiete des Versicherungsrechtes': Fuld, *ÖVZ* 1906, 307.

[217] The issue was Article 46 of the draft of a French insurance contract law and Article 76 of the corresponding Austrian draft. The reinsurers cited the reasoning behind the French draft: '*Les primes sont généralement fixées d'après des statistiques qui servent de base à des calculs de probabilité*' ('the premiums are in general established according to the statistics that serve as a basis for the calculations of probability'); therefore, '*incendies causés par des cataclysmes au sujet desquels aucune prévention ne peut être faite, aucun calcul ne peut être*

In the Lower House, the Member of Parliament for the *Wirtschaftliche Vereinigung* ('Economic Union'), the lawyer Kurd von Damm, took up Kaempf's proposal. He also advocated the discussion of the earthquake question in the new Commission.[218] Von Damm explained to the Parliamentarians that the previous Commission had not recognised 'that the damages from earthquakes required special provisos', for 'the San Francisco earthquake was the first bring attention to this point' (trans.).[219]

The Members of Parliament referred the *VVG* draft to the appropriate committee one last time. The XIIth Commission constituted for this work discussed the last changes in the draft from November 28, 1907 until January 30, 1908. Once again, representatives of the allied German governments participated in these meetings. The privy senior counsel Heinrich W. Dove, Counsel of the Berlin Chamber of Commerce and city counsellor and representative of the *Freisinnige Vereinigung*, proposed to include the damages caused by earthquakes in the exclusionary conditions in §84 of the *VVG* draft.[220] The Commission's report reproduces the comprehensive statement of the grounds of the proposal with the well-known arguments.[221]

A representative of the government explained that there were no objections to the proposal in this form. At the same time, he warned against the adoption of a compulsory provision that would give the German companies abroad a competitive disadvantage in relation to the English and other companies. It appeared to him more advisable to leave the decision to the supervisory agency whether and under which safety precautions the individual companies were allowed to adopt the earthquake danger.[222]

The opponents of the proposal pointed out that the provision was totally unnecessary for Germany. Abroad, the companies could protect

---

établi' ('fires caused by the catastrophes against which no prevention is possible cannot be subject to calculation') (*Masius' Rundschau* 1906, 226). This article represents an explanation offered by twenty European reinsurers.

[218] *Stenographische Berichte über die Verhandlungen des Reichstags, XII. Legislaturperiode, I. Session (1907/1908)*, 1828.

[219] Ibid.

[220] *Der Versicherungsfreund*, 1 January 1908, 3, in reference to the journal *Handel und Industrie*.

[221] *Bericht der XII. Kommission zur Vorberatung der Entwürfe eines Gesetzes über den Versicherungsvertrag, eines zugehörigen Einführungsgesetzes und eines Gesetzes, betreffend Änderung der Vorschriften des Handelsgesetzbuchs über die Seeversicherung, Verhandlungen des Reichstags, XII. Legislaturperiode, I. Session (1907–1908), Anlagen, Nr.* 626, 4237 *et seq.*

[222] The representative feared, in addition, difficulties in obtaining reinsurance through foreign companies (*Bericht der XII. Kommission* [...] 1907/08, 4237 *et seq.*).

themselves by means of their conditions. They saw trouble coming from the supervisory agency: should it insist upon a rigorous enforcement of an earthquake clause, the international competitiveness of the German insurance business would surely suffer as a result.[223] This suspicion was not unfounded: the supervisory agency itself had explained to Parliament in a report that it must consider objecting to the activity of the insurance companies without an earthquake clause.[224]

Dove's proposal was defeated by a small majority.[225] Only in the second reading did the Members of Parliament consent to the proposal after a State secretary from the Ministry of Justice had explained that none of the government federation members had any misgivings toward the change and that the supervisory agency's scepticism toward the practice was not shared by the Ministry.[226]

All the Members of Parliament could read the newly formulated §84 in the final report of the XIIth Commission of February 6, 1908.[227] The statutory exclusionary clause now contained the following earthquake regulation: 'The insurer is not liable if the fire or the explosion was caused by an earthquake or by measures that were ordered in a period of war by a military commander' (trans.).[228]

According to §287 of the Code of Civil Procedure, the burden of proof for the causal relationship between earthquake and damage still lay with the insurer.[229] §§83 and 84 of the VVG applied to damages induced by collapsed buildings and stipulated that they were not to be indemnified as long as they were separable from fires that occurred later. In the case of doubt as to the relation between the causes of the damage, the proportion of the given damages was to be assessed ad hoc pursuant to §287 of the

---

[223] Ibid., 4238.

[224] 'Geschäftsbericht des Kaiserlichen Aufsichtsamts für Privatversicherung für das Jahr 1906', *Stenographische Berichte über die Verhandlungen des Reichstags, XII. Legislaturperiode, I. Session (1907–1908), Anlagen*, no. 503, 2670.

[225] 'Bericht der XII. Kommission […]', *Stenographische Berichte über die Verhandlungen des Reichstags, XII. Legislaturperiode, I. Session (1907–1908), Anlagen*, no. 626, 4238; *Der Versicherungsfreund*, 1 January 1908, 3 with reference to *Handel und Industrie*.

[226] Knebel-Doeberitz in Gerhard et al. 1909, 389.

[227] 'Bericht der XII. Kommission […]', *Stenographische Berichte über die Verhandlungen des Reichstags, XII. Legislaturperiode, I. Session (1907–1908), Anlagen*, no. 626, 4287 *et seq.*

[228] Cf. the 'Bericht der XII. Kommission, BA B 280–577', 12–14. The wording of the law has been maintained to this day.

[229] Hagen in Gerhard et al. 1909, 256, with reference to the corresponding legal jurisprudence in Gaupp and Stein, 'Die Civilprozessordnung für das Deutsche Reich (1906–1908)', *§287 II 3 Anmerkung* 16.

Code.[230] Following the last reading in the Parliament's plenary session on the 1st and 2nd of May, this insurance contract bill was introduced into law on May 7, 1908.[231]

The reinsurers had achieved an important goal. In a letter to Thieme, Simon expressed his 'great satisfaction' with the earthquake regulation and thanked the Munich director: '[…] it is thanks to your efforts and those of the honourable Member of Parliament Kaempf […]' (trans.).[232]

3.1.2.7. A New Earthquake Clause in the New AVB (1908–1909)

The federations of the various insurance branches already started tackling the drafting of the new insurance conditions in 1907. The future AVB had to be brought into agreement with the *Versicherungsvertragsgesetz* and were scheduled to take effect together with the law on January 1, 1910.[233]

The fire insurance companies set the goal of implementing uniform conditions for all public limited and mutual companies. The standardisation was designed to facilitate the development of a uniform case law on the one and the participation of several companies in greater risks on the other hand.[234] A joint commission of the *Vereinigung der in Deutschland arbeitenden Privat-Feuerversicherungs-Gesellschaften* and the *Verband Deutscher Privat-Feuerversicherungs-Gesellschaften auf Gegenseitigkeit* ('Federation of German Private Mutual Fire Insurance Companies') chaired by the General Secretary of the coalition, H. A. Bueck, and benefitting from the participation of the General Secretary of the federation of the mutual companies, Otto Ziegler, began to work on the drafts for the general insurance conditions.[235] Two drafts formed the foundation of the

---

[230] Hagen in Gerhard et al. 1909, 258 *et seq.*

[231] 147th meeting of the parliament on May 1, 1908, *Stenographische Berichte über die Verhandlungen des Reichstags, XII. Legislaturperiode, I. Session (1908)*, 4995.

[232] This is clear from a letter from Simon; 6 March 1908, Simon to Thieme, SR/FA A9.0–32/yellow file folder (correspondence Swiss insurance companies)/loose material.

[233] Hagen, *ZVersWiss* 10 (1910), 204 *et seq.*

[234] Domizlaff 1914, V.

[235] Hagen, *ZVersWiss* 10 (1910), 204. The members of the commission were Altvater (*Leipziger Feuer*, 'Leipzig Fire Insurance Company'), Dietzsch (*Gothaer Feuerversicherungsbank*, 'Gothaer Fire Insurance Bank'), Domizlaff (Concordia/Hannover), von Geyer (*Württembergische Privatfeuer/Stuttgart*, 'Württemberg Private Fire Company/Stuttgart'), Harbers (Providentia/Frankfurt), Kahle (*Lübecker Feuer*, 'Lübeck Fire Insurance Company'), Ludewig (Thuringia), von Marck (*Hagel & Feuer*, 'Hail & Fire', Greifswald), Müller (Viktoria/Berlin), v.d. Nahmer (Allianz/Berlin), Reichel (*Berlinische*), Schumann (*Landwirtsch. Feuer, Dresden*, 'Agricultural Fire Insurance Company'), Vatke (*Magdeburger Feuer*, 'Magdeburg Fire Insurance Company'). Sir Carl Rasp and Drumm (both of the *Bayerische Versicherungsbank*, 'Bavarian Insurance Bank, Munich) were present at a few sessions. Domizlaff 1914, V *et seq.*

discussion, one originating from the Director of the Frankfurt *Providentia*, Harbers, the other from the mutual insurance companies.[236]

In reshaping the conditions, the insurers did not merely restrict themselves to an alignment with the new legal basis of the *Versicherungsvertragsgesetz*, but rather undertook such changes that 'had proven necessary or desirable, advisable or required' in the course of time in addition to the *Versicherungsvertragsgesetz*.[237] This included the development of a new earthquake clause. The future regulations were to correspond to the standards of the study conducted by the four reinsurers. These possibly directly interfered in the development by proposing the wording of a future earthquake clause in June of 1907.[238] This is not actually supported by primary sources, but the influence of the reinsurers in this question had become known in the meantime.[239]

At first, an agreement between the private fire insurance companies on a suitable formulation was required. Pursuant to the principle of having to obtain a license (§4 *VAG*), this clause afterwards had to be approved by the supervisory agency as part of a complete draft. Only then were business operations using the new normative conditions admissible. This elaborate procedure shows how firmly the German State had gained control of the contractual bases of the insurance industry. In this context, it could only be spoken of autonomously created legal structures of business in a severely limited sense. The exigency of an official and institutional authorisation brought technical standardisation close to a standardisation through the State. This sanction could also, on the other hand, increase the claim to validity of the future contractual bases.

A phase of close and objectively limited cooperation between the agency and the federations began. The commission of the public limited and the mutual companies presented drafts for general insurance conditions besides additional conditions for agriculture and security provisions for factories and commercial facilities. These drafts first underwent a preliminary discussion in the supervisory agency. Then, under the agency's supervision, the representatives of the insurance companies negotiated

---

[236] Domizlaff 1914, V *et seq.*

[237] Hagen, *ZVersWiss 10* (1910), 204 *et seq.*

[238] Domizlaff (1908, 18) believes that in June, 1907, the reinsurers had proposed the following wording: 'The company is not liable when damages from a fire or an explosion are directly or indirectly caused by an earthquake or a volcanic eruptions or by an uprising or measures ordered in war or by the declaration of war by a military commander'.

[239] Manes ('Erdbebenversicherung', *Versicherungslexikon*, 1st ed. (1909), col. 341 *et seq.*) mentions this explicitly.

with experts from the various insured parties, that is, from industry, trade and agriculture, on the prospective basic principles of their contracts.[240] In November 1908, a first *AVB* draft was completed.

A comparison of the old, still valid earthquake clause with the results of the first round of negotiations demonstrates that the authors had taken their cue from the guidelines of the reinsurers' study:[241]

> §1 (4) The insurer is not liable for *damages from fire or explosion* that occur *during* an earthquake, a volcanic eruption [...] *or as a result* of these events, [...] unless the origin of the fire or the explosion or its spread have neither any direct nor indirect connection whatsoever with the effects or the consequences of the named events (trans.).[242]

Nevertheless, this draft was universally judged insufficient. The burden of proof remained with the insurers. In addition, there were numerous details that would require improvement. The interest groups continued to discuss matters through the winter of 1908–1909.[243] The reinsurers also asked the advice of their legal advisors and produced their own draft.[244]

---

[240] *Geschäftsbericht des Kaiserlichen Aufsichtsamts* 1908, 37; Hagen, *ZVersWiss 10* (1910), 204.

[241] Gruenwald et al. 1907, 9.

[242] *Entwürfe der neuen Allgemeinen Versicherungs-Bedingungen für Feuerversicherungen* (Drafts of the new general insurance conditions for fire insurance), November 1908, SR/FA A9.0–29/file/loose material (emphasis added).

[243] *Geschäftsbericht des Kaiserlichen Aufsichtsamts für Privatversicherung für das Jahr 1908*, BA B 280–543, 37.

[244] The legal advisor of the Swiss Re, Professor Roelli, preferred his own formulation in §2 of the new fire insurance law of July 2, 1908, to the German draft: 'If damages occur during (*bei*) the events of war or insurgency or during the resulting military or police measures, as well as during earthquakes, the company is only liable for compensation if the damage is demonstrably neither the direct nor the indirect consequence of these events'. He criticised the combination of the elements *bei* ('in/during') and *infolge* ('as a result of') as confusing: 'If damages that occur during (*bei*) an earthquake are excluded, this exclusion *a forteriori* ['for a stronger reason'] also applies to damages that originate as a result of an earthquake; in the first case, only a spatial or temporal coincidence is required, whereas the relationship between cause and effect (causal nexus) is necessary in the second case'. He suggested for the German *AVB*: 'For damages that occur during an earthquake, during a volcanic event, during insurgency, during a breach of the peace or through explosion, the insurer is liable only if the damage demonstrably is neither a direct nor an indirect consequence of these events with respect to origin, scale and spread'. Another advisor of the Swiss Re, Justizrat Schniewind, apparently advocated the suspension of the insurance contract for a longer period. Simon criticised the relation between rule and exception in Roelli's draft and formulated the following: "The insurer is not liable for damages through fire or explosion that occur during (*bei*) earthquakes, during volcanic eruption, during insurgency, during a breach of the peace, during war events or military events, unless the damages occur directly in some relationship to the named events with respect to origin, scale and spread'. This clause, Simon writes, agrees with Harbers' draft, the Director of

In March of 1909, the result of the second Berlin round of negotiations was presented.[245] However, the earthquake clause proved yet again to be disappointing. The authors had intended to provide systematic improvements,[246] but the formulation was even more unclear than its predecessor. The question of the burden of proof also remained open.

It was presumably for these reasons that the fourth paragraph was revised one last time and the following wording was agreed upon:

> §1 (4) In the case of domestic turbulence or events of war of any kind as well as in the case of earthquakes, the insurer is liable only when the policyholder proves that the damage neither directly nor indirectly bears a relationship to these events (trans.).[247]

Prudentia (Frankfurt) (5 December 1908 Simon to Gruenwald, SR/FA A9.0–32/yellow file folder; [correspondence Swiss insurance companies]/loose material).

[245] '§1 (1.–4.) [Basic principle of limitation, definition of fire event and explosion, exclusion of war damages] (5) In the event of an earthquake or a volcanic eruption, the insurer is only liable if the incidents of damage or damages [*that is, the event of fire and explosion*] specified in paragraphs 1 to 3 have, in respect to their origin, scope or spread, neither directly nor indirectly and neither totally or in part any connection to the earthquake or the volcanic eruption or to the effects of these events or to the condition of destruction or lack of order that results' ('Entwurf der neuen Allgemeinen Versicherungs-Bedingungen für Feuerversicherungen (March 1909)', SR/FA A9.0–29/ file/loose material).

[246] Among others, they had left out the treatment of warlike states of emergency and natural disasters and attempted to add a temporal connection between earthquakes and subsequent damage.

[247] According to Raiser's commentary on the general fire insurance conditions (1930, 1 *et seq.*, 18, 42), the complete exclusionary regulation in the *AVB* of the *Vereinigung der in Deutschland arbeitenden Privat-Feuerversicherungsgesellschaften* and the *Verband Deutscher Privat-Feuerversicherungsgesellschaften* of 1909, in force as of the January 1, 1910 following the authorisation by the Imperial Supervisory Agency [resolution of the Senate of the 26th of August, 1909, VA 1909, 266, compare 155], read:

> §1 1. The insurer is liable according to the stipulations in the following conditions for the damage that occurs to the insured items through fire or lightning or through explosion of city gas of all kinds, even if its purpose was other than lighting, or through explosion of household heating devices and light fixtures. The liability of the insurer for damage from explosions of other kinds requires a special agreement.
>
> 2. In the case of fire, the insurer must pay compensation for damage through destruction or partial damage insofar as the damage applies to the insured property that was destroyed or damaged and insofar as the destruction or the damage results from the effects of the fire or during the fire through extinguishing, demolition or clearing or is the unavoidable consequence of a fire that occurred on the property or the adjacent property on which the insured objects are found. The insurer must also compensate for the value of the insured property that was lost in the fire. The insurance only covers additional damage, especially additional indirect damage, as well as loss resulting from the occurrence of the claim, insofar as these matters have been specially agreed upon.
>
> 3. [Scope of liability for lightning and explosion]

Thus, the authors acceded to the recommendations of the reinsurers in all points. At the same time, they clearly went beyond the conditions in §84 of the *Versicherungsvertragsgesetz* that neither placed the burden of proof on the policyholder nor clarified the exclusion of liability with respect to the indirectly caused damages.[248]

This clause was authorised by the Senate resolution of August 26, 1909 together with the remaining drafts of the new *AVB* for fire insurance companies elaborated by the *Vereinigung der in Deutschland arbeitenden Privat-Feuerversicherungs-Gesellschaften*.[249] They went into effect with the *Versicherungsvertragsgesetz* on January 1, 1910. Immediately, all of the insurance companies adopted the new standard conditions.[250] The supervisory agency had succeeded in its quest to confront avoidable variations of even the non-mandatory provisions of the law and to require special reasons and unique circumstances for an elimination of the legal regulatory provisions.[251] A new uniform legal situation had been created for the entire private fire insurance industry in Germany.

The new regulation of the private fire insurance companies' liability for earthquake-induced damages was accepted on a positive note, but was little discussed.[252] In 1908, Hugo von Knebel-Doeberitz wrote rather sceptically in the large commentary on the *Versicherungsvertragsgesetz* edited by Alfred Manes that one would

> not be able to achieve an absolute non-liability for all damages relating to an earthquake even in the face of the most optimistic extension of a contractual exclusion of this kind, especially when the fire damage has been influenced by other causes not related to the earthquake, for example, insufficient extinguishing facilities, inappropriate measures taken in the fighting of the fire and so forth (trans.).[253]

---

4. In the case of domestic insurgency or events of war of any kind as well as in the case of earthquakes, the insurer is only liable if the policyholder proves that the damage occurred neither in direct nor indirect relationship to these events.

5. [Liability only in the event of fire] (trans.).

[248] Domizlaff 1914, 13.

[249] *Geschäftsbericht des Kaiserlichen Aufsichtsamts für Privatversicherung für das Jahr 1909*, 37.

[250] Partially with minor changes that corresponded to the idiosyncrasies of the individual companies. Hagen, *ZVersWiss 10* (1910), 204 *et seq.*

[251] Ibid., 205.

[252] No mention is found in the insurance contract law commentaries of Hager and Bruck 1908 and Lindner and Fell 1909. The decision of the Hamburg regional court on an American earthquake clause is mentioned in the later commentary in Hager and Bruck 1913, 244, and 1926, 273.

[253] Knebel-Doeberitz (comment on §84 *VVG*) in Gerhard et al. 1908, 390. Hagen (1908, 256) discusses the burden of proof.

After the new *AVB* were authorised, the Berlin jurist Otto Hagen commented that the earthquake clause was

> remarkably stringent [...], which seems understandable following the San Francisco experiences. The question is of a lesser importance for Germany; with respect to business abroad, the emphasis lies on the approach of the reinsurers; in the Parliamentary Commission, members warned against a rigorous policy of the supervisory agency towards the companies active in the earthquake areas during the discussion of §84 of the *VVG* [...] (trans.).[254]

In this question, clashes between some of the companies operating abroad and the supervisory agency already loomed on the horizon.

3.1.2.8. *No Business Abroad without an Earthquake Clause?*

The argument concerning the obligation of the German insurance companies to exclude their liability for earthquake-induced damages even in foreign business dealings broke out shortly after the new *AVB* for Germany came into force.

The civil servants in the supervisory agency considered extending the supervision of the insurance companies to include business abroad since 1908. At issue was the exclusion of the earthquake danger abroad as well as an extension of the regulatory activity to include the reinsurance branch.[255] Both closely connected considerations were justified with the experience of the collapse of German fire insurance companies in the wake of the San Francisco earthquake in the agency's annual report for 1908. That is, the agency opined that the German fire insurance companies had punched above their weight in their transatlantic business dealings because of their connections to the reinsurance companies.[256]

The planned regulations could, however, create problems for the fire insurance companies in international competition. As a result, two companies petitioned that they be 'allowed to include the earthquake fire risks

---

[254] Hagen, *ZVersWiss 10* (1910), 226, with reference to Knebel-Doeberitz in Gerhard et al. 1909, note 4 on §84 (389).

[255] In 1908, the *Bundesrat* ('Federal Council') made use of its competence to extend the State regulation to the reinsurance branch and subjected it chiefly to the accounting regulations of the law on insurance supervision (*Verordnung vom 12. Mai 1908, RGBl. 37 (1908)*, 409; Emminghaus, *Handwörterbuch der Staatswissenschaften*, 3rd ed. (1911), vol. 7, 167 and 'Die staatliche Beaufsichtigung der deutschen Rückversicherung', *ÖRev* 1908, 146.

[256] *Geschäftsbericht des Kaiserlichen Aufsichtsamts für Privatversicherung für das Jahr 1908*, 69 *et seq.* Manes (*Versicherungslexikon*, 1st ed. (1909), col. 341 *et seq.*) reports the same.

in the overseas areas' (trans.) at the beginning of 1910.[257] They feared disadvantages in business abroad because British insurance companies offered the acceptance of the earthquake risk worldwide after the affirmative resolution of the Fire Offices Committee of June 1907.[258] In their application, the two German companies explained that they would tread very carefully and accept the risk only 'where it was demanded in the interests of business' (trans.).[259]

In order to convert these pledges into verifiable commitments, the supervisory agency recommended limiting future accepted earthquake-fire risks through maximum amounts or special reinsurance contracts.[260] However, the petitioners rejected limitations as 'impractical'.[261] In response, the supervisory agency placed the question on the agenda of the next meeting of the insurance subcommittee. On March 14, 1910, the members convened from all over Germany.[262] The responsible division head of the agency reported on the state of the matter. Then he indicated the readiness of the Board for further cooperation. The minutes of the meeting documented:

> The agency members are finally considering the idea whether the desired authorisation could not be granted for a defined period, say for two or three years. In the meantime, experiences could be gathered as to whether insurance policies of this kind would actually be concluded to a degree worth mentioning (trans.).

An intense discussion immediately erupted. However, the application of the two companies did not constitute the focal point. The first to speak was the Director of the Cologne Re:

> Director Gruenwald enquired how the agency arrogates to itself the right to entertain the notion of drafting resolutions on the permission to accept the risk of earthquakes, since this is only a possibility for business abroad. After the Chairperson [the President of the supervisory agency, Ernst Gruner] had

---

[257] Explanation of the head of division in the supervisory agency, in excerpt of the minutes of the *Sitzung der Gruppe IV Feuerversicherung des Versicherungsbeirat beim Kaiserlichen Aufsichtsamt für Privatversicherung am*, in BA B 280–25309. The company names were not mentioned.

[258] See chapter 3.3.2.2.

[259] Explanation of the head of division in the Regulatory Board, in excerpt of the minutes of the *Sitzung der Gruppe IV Feuerversicherung des Versicherungsbeirat beim Kaiserlichen Aufsichtsamt für Privatversicherung am*, in BA B 280–25309.

[260] *Ausführung des Referenten des Aufsichtsamtes, Ausschnitt aus dem Protokoll* [...].

[261] *Ausschnitt aus dem Protokoll* [...].

[262] Ibid.

explained the jurisdiction of the agency in this matter, General Secretary Schröder stated the following:

> The agency was not in any way authorised to grant permission for insurance conditions that were to be applied abroad, since the companies doing business in foreign States were required to adapt their conditions to the local legislation. In addition, the agency has never raised any objections against the foreign conditions of any companies representing it (trans.).[263]

The insurers' statements demonstrate that they emphasised only having an obligation to inform the agency. A clear answer to these questions was not forthcoming. However, the President of the supervisory agency maintained his standpoint. He responded to the directors

> that the insurance companies are subject to the regulation of the agency with respect to their entire business activities outside of Germany, but that the agency nevertheless did not object to business activities outside of Germany as long as the relevant foreign regulations were duly observed. The adoption of the earthquake-fire risk, however, is an important question and of such wide-ranging significance that the agency is obligated to pay the greatest attention to it and in examining this question cannot merely be satisfied if foreign regulations are observed (trans.).

Here was a collision between economic and business positions. The insurance directors had obligations towards their companies and were fighting for their freedom in the foreign business market in order to earn the highest possible profits. The agency's civil servants, on the other hand, recognised the danger that the economic disaster of San Francisco could repeat itself; they associated this danger with damages to innumerable policyholders and shareholders.

The insurers ceased contradicting President Gruner. Instead, they concentrated on persuading the agency to at the very least refrain from imposing sanctions in this specific case. Gruenwald argued that in view of the relation between the total business volume and the proportion of the earthquake risks including fire insurance, the question had 'only a minor importance'.[264] The General Director of another company, Vatke, objected that a temporary limitation of the authorisation made the jobs of the business leaders unnecessarily difficult and advocated an authorisation 'pending further notice'.

---

[263] Ibid.
[264] Ibid.

However, the united efforts of the insurers did not yield any positive results. The President of the supervisory agency declared that Vatke's proposal was unacceptable 'because [...] in that case, the agency could only intervene on the basis of §67 of the *VAG*' (trans.).[265] Finally, his proposal was accepted and the authorisation was granted for two or three years at first.[266]

In the aftermath, German fire insurance companies were active without an earthquake clause in the United States and a few other business areas in which they were forced to cover the risk of earthquake in exchange for additional premiums 'with regard to the competition'. However, the volume of this business remained small due to the premiums' amount.[267]

3.1.2.9. *Adoption of the Earthquake Clause by Public Institutions*
The introduction of the earthquake clauses was also discussed among the public institutions.

The *Versicherungsvertragsgesetz*—and thus its §84—did not apply in the rare cases of insurance mandated by law. One of these cases was the purchase of a house. It was up to the legislative of the respective federal state, not the central government, to determine the conditions of insurance.[268]

The applicability of the *Versicherungsvertragsgesetz* was disputed in the cases of voluntary membership in one of the many regional insurance institutions operating under public law.[269] The supreme courts opined that by their nature, these legal relations belonged to private law.[270] Nevertheless, they were also excluded from the *VVG*.[271] A corresponding reform was planned.[272]

---

[265] Ibid.

[266] Ibid.

[267] Liebig 1911, 87.

[268] Knebel-Doeberitz in Gerhard et al. 1909, 377; Speech by the State Secretary in the Imperial Department of Justice, Nieberding, in the German Parliament on 22 January 1906, *Stenographische Berichte über die Verhandlungen des Reichstags, XI. Legislaturperiode, II. Session (1905–1906)*, 727.

[269] Called 'fire partnerships', 'fire societies' etc.

[270] *Entscheidungen des Reichsoberhandelsgerichts*, vol. 9, 132; *Entscheidungen des Reichsgerichts in Zivilsachen*, vol. 48, 332 *et seq.*; additionally Gruchot 1877, vol. 25, 1119; vol. 30, 1142.

[271] Speech by the State Secretary in the Justice Department Nieberding in the *Reichstag*, 22 January 1906, *Stenographische Berichte über die Verhandlungen des Reichstags, XI. Legislaturperiode, II. Session (1905–1906)*, 727.

[272] Speech by the State Secretary in the Justice Department Nieberding, 22 January 1906, cited in Gerhard et al. 1909, 32.

In 1907, the members of the *Vereinigung öffentlicher Feuerversicherungs-anstalten in Deutschland* ('Union of Public Fire Insurance Institutions in Germany') received a newsletter from their board of directors. On the occasion of the planned introduction of an earthquake clause in the policies of the private companies, the members were requested to declare whether they regarded this step as desirable for the public insurance companies.[273] At that time, only seven of the fifty-five institutions had excluded the risk,[274] one more than at the time of the San Francisco disaster.[275]

Two years later, the Prussian law governing the public fire insurance institutions provided an occasion to discuss the matter together. The law's earthquake regulation read as follows:

> The association is not liable if the fire or an explosion [...] [was] caused by an earthquake or a volcanic eruption. For all damages that occurred during an earthquake or directly afterwards, it will be assumed that they were caused by the earthquake, unless the policyholder proves that they would have occurred without the earthquake (trans.).[276]

At the 41st annual meeting of the *Vereinigung* in Constance on June 23, 1909, Dr. Ruttke, the Director of the Prussian *Provinzial-Feuersozietät* ('Provincial Fire Association') in Posen, spoke 'about insurance coverage against earthquake damages and other incalculable dangers',[277] a lecture that was received 'with a great deal of applause'.[278] Ruttke, to whose association the Prussian law applied, energetically opposed following the private insurance companies in the earthquake question. He distributed a number of proposed resolutions as a basis for discussion, the first of which read as follows:

> The public fire insurance associations will only fulfil their obligation to protect the economic interests of their policyholders (...) if they guarantee

---

[273] *Berliner Börsen-Courier* 92, 24 February 1915, supplement, 1–2.

[274] *Berliner Börsen-Courier* 92, 24 February 1915, supplement, 1–2; with reference to the report by Dr. Ruttke, Director of the *preußische Provinzial-Feuersozietät* ('Prussian Provincial Fire Society') in Posen, delivered on the 23rd of June, 1909 in Konstanz. Compare *Mitteilungen für die öffentlichen Feuerversicherungs-Anstalten* 1909, 184 *et seq.*, 237 *et seq.*

[275] Gruenwald et al. 1907, 8; *Berliner Börsen-Courier* 92, 24 February 1915, supplement, 1–2.

[276] *Berliner Börsen-Courier* 92, 24 February 1915, supplement, 1–2.

[277] The 41st annual meeting of the *Vereinigung öffentlicher Feuerversicherungs-Anstalten in Deutschland* on the 23rd and 24th of June, 1909 in Konstanz, *Mitteilungen für die öffentlichen Feuerversicherungs-Anstalten* 1909, 184 *et seq.*, 237 *et seq.* as well as BA 280-25309, 39–41.

[278] Ibid.

coverage even for earthquake damages in contrast to the private companies and save the individual from financial ruin at the cost of many (trans.).

The following points dealt with limiting the assumed risk to pure fire damages. Ruttke thus had in mind a regulation that resembled the North American collapse clause. The policyholder was responsible for proving the proportion of damages arising from fire and the collapse of the building. Those companies 'that are by principle opposed to covering earthquake damages' should suggest to the assembly '*eventualissime*' a uniform wording that corresponded to that of the private companies.[279]

A member of the Prussian law commission, Wenneker, immediately contradicted Ruttke and warned those present against adopting his proposal 'without further ado'. Some of the representatives of public insurance associations agreed with Wenneker;[280] others sided with Ruttke.[281] They emphasised the difference between private and public insurance institutions, the latter of which 'ought to go further in the coverage of damages than the private companies' (trans.).[282]

The assembled directors refrained from making a decision. The Prussian law went into effect with its exclusionary regulation.[283] Outside of Prussia, the earthquake regulations of some additional institutions were changed by law, but the majority of the regulations remained in effect.[284]

---

[279] Ibid.

[280] The Directors Vorster, von Roth, and Sommer, 41st annual meeting of the *Vereinigung öffentlicher Feuerversicherungs-Anstalten* [...] 1909.

[281] The Directors Hermes, Schoch, Bonitz (*Sächsische Brandversicherungskammer* ['Saxon Fire Insurance Chamber'], 41st annual meeting of the *Vereinigung öffentlicher Feuerversicherungs-Anstalten* [...] 1909.

[282] This is how Director Schoch expressed himself, 41st annual meeting of the *Vereinigung öffentlicher Feuerversicherungs-Anstalten* [...] 1909.

[283] The exclusionary conditions in §1, paragraph 4, of the *Allgemeine Versicherungsbedingungen der öffentlichen Feuerversicherungsanstalten für Feuerversicherung* ('General insurance terms and conditions of the public fire insurance institutions'), passed on occasion of the Prussian law on May 9, 1911, corresponded to the new earthquake clause of the private fire insurers (*Mitteilungen für die öffentlichen Feuerversicherungs-Anstalten* 1911, 589 et seq.).

[284] The following institutions and places expressly remained liable for fire damages caused by earthquake in the years immediately following: *Hzgt. Sachsen-Altenburg* (*Landesbrandkassen-Gesetz* ['law on regional fire societies'] of December 18, 1909), Hamburg (*neues Feuerkassen-Gesetz* ['new fire society law'] of February 28, 1910), *Württemberg* (*Entwurf eines Gebäude-Brandversicherungsgesetzes* ['Draft of a law on fire insurance relating to buildings'], still in negotiation in 1915). No mention of damage cause, i.e. liability: *Kgr. Sachsen* (Law of 1 July 1910), *GHzgt Sachsen-Weimar* (*Gesetz über die Gebäude-Brandversicherungsanstalt* of 13 March 1909 ['law on the fire institution for buildings']), Mecklenburg (*Gesetz der Dominial-Brandversicherungsanstalt* of 29 October 1909 ['law on the Dominial fire insurance institution']). Baden (*Gebäudeversicherungs-Gesetz* of 7/27

3.1.3. *Preliminary Results*

The study of the change in the earthquake regulations in Germany supports some presumptions as to the reasons for the partial success of the reinsurers. As in Spain, Portugal, France, Belgium and Austria, private companies that worked closely with the reinsurance industry dominated the German fire insurance market and thus were especially receptive to their suggestions. As in other countries, there was an increased willingness for reform in Germany because a new version of the general insurance conditions was pending in any case.

A few particular circumstances facilitated the introduction of the earthquake clause in Germany. The disaster in San Francisco had hit the German insurance industry more severely than others. As of then, at least the internationally active companies worked in the awareness of being economically endangered. The situation of the insurers abroad shaped the discussion in Germany stronger than all other aspects did. It was the defining argument with which the Members of Parliament and the lobbyist Kaempf were able to persuade the XIIth Parliamentary Commission to reinforce the *Versicherungsvertragsgesetz* with an exclusionary clause. In this context, the—in retrospect naive—notion that uniform provisions in Europe could persuade the legislators of actually endangered countries to likewise support the exclusion of the earthquake danger is interesting. An effect of this kind has not been apparent anywhere. At the same time, the dependence of the provision in §84 of the *VVG* on French, Austrian and Swiss drafts aimed at reducing the economically deterrent differences in the substantive legal norms. Here, the idea of the creation of a 'world business law' found its way into legislation.

The roles of the legislative and the supervisory agency in the development of the earthquake clause should, however, not be overrated. The often mentioned §84 of the *VVG* did not include a mandatory regulation. The insurers' shaping of the policies remained decisive. The posture of the insurance industry towards the supervisory agency varied between solicitous reticence and downright obstruction. It only improved in the course of the cooperative creation of 'prototypical conditions'. The agency's support for the implementation of more stringent exclusionary clauses may well have facilitated the decision of the *Vereinigung der in Deutschland*

October 1912 ['building insurance law']). Oldenburg excluded damages caused by earthquakes (*Gesetz über die Oldenburgische Brandkasse* of 28 April 1910 ['law on the Oldenburg fire society']). *Berliner Börsen-Courier* 92, 24 February 1915, supplement, 1–2; Rieber 1913, 23.

arbeitenden Privat-Feuerversicherungs-Gesellschaften to adopt this course. The insurers would presumably not have acted otherwise without the assistance of the authorities.

Finally, an additional result can be recorded. The introduction in six European countries of exclusionary clauses in keeping with the concept of the Earthquake Commission already constitutes a standardisation. Other insurance companies perhaps decided on the same regulations in countries on which no records exist.

3.2. Rejection of the Earthquake Clause and its Alternatives

3.2.1. *The Outlines of National Developments*

3.2.1.1. *Great Britain and the Netherlands*
From the point of view of the reinsurers, the most pressing need for action in Europe was to be found in Great Britain and the Netherlands. In neither of the two countries did the fire insurance companies exclude their liability for earthquake-caused damages. This was made worse by the fact that the British and Dutch insurers were very active on the international level and even in their business abroad did not provide for liability limitations that corresponded to the concepts of the reinsurers.[285]

Private insurance companies dominated the markets in both countries. Many of the British public limited companies had unusually large reserve funds at their disposal.[286] And they competed against private individuals that acted for associations such as Lloyds of London. These associations regularly assumed risks that other insurance companies had rejected and could thus indirectly exercise a great influence on the business. The Dutch insurance market, on the other hand, was one of the most highly competitive in the world. Domestically, a vast number of companies provided a large supply of insurance services. However, the lucrative overseas business had for a long time no longer been the exclusive province of the Dutch alone. Many other European fire insurance companies had penetrated into this market.[287]

---

[285] Gruenwald et al. 1907, '*La clause d'exclusion des tremblements de terre* [...]', 14.
[286] These derived from business abroad that the Britons had developed earlier than others (Liebig 1911).
[287] Gruenwald et al. 1907, '*La clause d'exclusion des tremblements de terre* [...]', 14.

Despite their large financial losses suffered in San Francisco, Valparaiso and Kingston at the end of June 1907, British insurance companies united under the aegis of the Fire Offices Committee had resolved to authorise the adoption of the risk of earthquake fires. Various factors had contributed to this decision—especially the decision of Lloyds Underwriters to cover the risk in their policies, and the calculation of the Royal, the Commercial Union and other companies to increase their business abroad through the aggressive adoption of the earthquake fire risk.[288] Moreover, in contrast to the reinsurers, presumably the majority of British insurance companies considered seismicity to be a calculable risk.[289] The decision concerning the inclusion or exclusion of the earthquake danger, however, depended upon the individual market. The same applied to the Netherlands.

The Dutch fire insurance industry was made up of three markets that differed in their legal features. The domestic market was characterised by a tangle of smaller and larger mutual and public limited companies that used different policies. The situation of the insurance business in the colonies was similar. The remaining part of the overseas business was traded at the stock markets in Amsterdam and Rotterdam and included mandatory policies.[290]

The Dutch insurance companies perceived the lack of earthquake regulations to be threatening for the first time after the disasters in San Francisco, Valparaiso and Kingston. At the beginning of 1907, 120 companies set up a commission to bring about an agreement on the earthquake clauses, chaired by a representative of the Imperial Insurance Company, M. P. de Clercq. The Commission first resolved to wait for the introduction of an earthquake clause by the British companies 'in order to create a corresponding and technically advanced clause for the Netherlands' (trans.).[291] Here, the notion of legal standardisation appeared once again.

At the end of June, it became known that the British companies had resolved not to adopt a uniform earthquake clause. In response, the Dutch

---

[288] Moreover, it was a feature of the British Offices' amour propre to be a worldwide spearhead in the insurance branch. This position was, among other things, manifested by the British in their principle of regarding nothing as uninsurable. In the US, the British Offices were in fact successful in balancing their losses within four years by means of the growth in business volume (Liebig 1911, 80).

[289] See in addition chapter 3.2.2.

[290] Gruenwald et al. 1907, 'La clause d'exclusion des tremblements de terre [...]', 14.

[291] 29 April 1908 Simon to Iversen (Københavns Brandforsikring), SR/FA A9.0–32/ file folder/ correspondence regarding the earthquake clause 1906/1907/ Bayerische Versicherungsbank, 39.

Commission began to develop its own earthquake clause. Its secretary F. C. J. Scheurleer optimistically stated: 'Informed opinion indicates that the vast majority of the companies operating with the stock exchange policy will adopt a uniform earthquake clause' (trans.).[292] The members of the Commission formulated drafts to supplement the regular domestic insurance terms as well as the comprehensive policies for the business areas of the Netherlands and the Dutch East Indies. Then they invited the companies involved to a general assembly for March 27, 1908.

The number of participants was smaller than in the previous year, with a third of the companies not attending. The Earthquake Clause Commission chose a cunning means of beginning the conference. It had the attending insurance companies at first discuss a joint regulation for the business in India,[293] where the Dutch insurance companies by now almost never concluded any contracts without earthquake clauses.[294] The sole issue was to accept a uniform clause. A proposal aimed at this end was adopted per acclamation and the Commission then authorised to circulate the agreement for signing. The change in the clause was only intended to come into force if a sufficient number of signatories had agreed to the proposal.

The participants could not agree on earthquake clauses for the Netherlands. The discussion had been too contentious. Among other things, the representatives from German and English companies had made amendment motions that required elaborate discussion. For this reason, the resolution declared that the Commission should examine the clause more closely in consideration of the motions.[295] This happened. However, Scheurleer reported that the members of the Commission did not desire to commit themselves to any fixed formulation of the clause 'until the German and English companies achieve a universal clause that we might be able to follow. A universal clause will, of course, be easier to realise' (trans.). In the meantime, the Dutch Commission intensely tried to arrive at the broadest possible agreement on the supplement to the Dutch-East Indian policies.[296] The expectations were very optimistic.

---

[292] 27 July 1907. C. J. Scheurleer (Secretary of the Dutch Commission for the Earthquake Clause) to Simon, SR/FA A9.0–32/file folder/ correspondence regarding earthquake clause 1906/1907/ *Bayerische Versicherungsbank*, 52.

[293] 9 April 1908 M. P. de Clercq to the German fire insurance companies listed on the Amsterdam and/or the Rotterdam stock markets, SR/FA, 42 *et seq.*

[294] With the exception of plantation insurance policies (20 August 1908 van Ommen to SR, SR/FA, 60 *et seq.*).

[295] 9 April 1908 M. P. de Clercq to German fire insurance companies represented on the Amsterdam and/or to the Rotterdam stock market, SR/FA, 42 *et seq.*

[296] Ibid.

Thus, it was all the more surprising that the attempt at standardisation failed. On July 18, 1908, the Earthquake Clause Commission addressed a circular containing the news that cooperation in reaching an agreement had not fulfilled the expectations to all the fire insurance companies listed on the Amsterdam or Rotterdam stock market. While it was true that 106 parties had signed the agreement, the Commission had refrained from allowing the agreements to go into effect[297] in view of the numerous opponents.[298]

Later, Scheurleer expressed his opinion on the motives of the opponents of the agreement:

> Most of them are reluctant to participate in an improvement; moreover, a number of the named underwriters decidedly argued to the effect that they no longer desired to sign such agreements that in their opinion simply serve the interests of the opposition. In addition, for others it was also the covert notion that by abstaining they would be in a position to acquire many insurance contracts in the event that an earthquake clause was introduced. Fishing in muddy waters is a very popular sport here. Finally, four of the named companies accept no risks whatever in the Indies and for this reason believed it to be a worthless formality to be forced to sign the agreement (trans.).[299]

The blockade in the Netherlands resulted in part from the situation that had developed a year previously in the British Fire Offices Committee. At that time, the Royal and some other companies had refused to exclude their liability for earthquake-induced fire damages for economic reasons. On the one hand, they had feared the disadvantages in relation to Lloyds Underwriters, who were accepting the earthquake risk worldwide. On the other hand, they had anticipated a market advantage if they did not limit the risk in contrast to the practices of other companies. The development of business in California had proven them to be right in this respect.[300]

Now, this situation recurred in the Netherlands. A part of the Dutch insurance companies feared disadvantages on the world market in relation to British competition and hoped for a competitive edge over companies that aimed at introducing the earthquake clause. In response, the reform-minded majority of Dutch insurers decided against the adoption

---

[297] 18 July 1908. Dutch Earthquake Clause Commission to the German fire insurance companies listed on the Amsterdam and/or the Rotterdam stock markets, SR/FA, 46 *et seq.*

[298] Nineteen Dutch agents were named and the agents from fifteen foreign companies, among them seven British firms.

[299] 8 August 1908 F. C. J. Scheurleer to Frankona, SR/FA, 58.

[300] See chapter 3.1.8.

of the earthquake clause—exactly as the reform-minded British managers had done the year previously. 'It was feared that too much business would be lost unless *all* of the companies went along without any reservations' (trans.),[301] reported the representative of the Swiss Re in Amsterdam, van Ommen.[302]

The consequences of this failure reached beyond the colonial business region. Some underwriters had already announced their decision to vote against an earthquake clause even in the mother country. The members of the Commission recognised that an agreement for the Netherlands was even less likely to succeed than that for the East Indies.[303] For this reason, they unanimously resigned their positions on the Commission. They declared their willingness to take part in a new assembly with the delegates if a standard clause was adopted abroad. Then, they went on, a 'new committee yet to be constituted and promising to be more success-ful' (trans.) could take up the activities anew.[304]

Simon and Dumcke, an associate of Lindner,[305] attempted to learn whether any likelihood of an agreement remained.[306] They received thor-oughly pessimistic answers. The Dutch insurance business was far too dependent upon British companies,[307] for whom a turnabout concerning the earthquake question seemed unthinkable. In addition, all the compa-nies were suffering under an immense economic pressure: 'In this small country of ours, there are far too many companies and agencies, which means that the competition is downright cutthroat, and improvements of business are very difficult to achieve' (trans.).[308]

---

[301] 20 August 1908 van Ommen to SR, SR/FA, 60 *et seq.* Underlined as in the original.

[302] Van Ommen wrote that paradoxically, precisely those English companies that domi-nated the transatlantic business had been prepared to adopt a standard exclusion of the earthquake risk; later, the German and Swiss companies too. The agreement failed with insurance companies who were not active overseas (24 August 1908 van Ommen to SR, SR/FA, 64).

[303] 18 July 1908 Dutch Earthquake Clause Commission to the German fire fnsurance companies listed on the Amsterdam and/or Rotterdam stock exchange, SR/FA, 46 *et seq.*

[304] The signers: De Clercq and twelve other Commission members. 18 July 1908 Dutch Earthquake Clause Commission to the German fire insurance companies listed on the Amsterdam and/or Rotterdam stock exchange, SR/FA, 46 *et seq.*

[305] Dumcke was an employee of the Frankona Company (Frankfurt), which in the meantime had merged with the *Badische Mit- und Rückversicherungsgesellschaft* ('The Badense Coinsurance and Reinsurance Company').

[306] 4 August 1908 SR to van Ommen, SR/FA, 54; 6 August 1908 Dumcke (Frankona) to J. ter Meulen, Amsterdam (member of the Dutch Commission), SR/FA, 56; 6 August 1908 Dumcke (Frankona) to F. C. J. Scheurleer, Amsterdam, SR/FA, 57.

[307] 20 August 1908 van Ommen to SR, SR/FA, 60 *et seq.*

[308] 17 August 1908 J. ter Meulen to Frankona, SR/FA, 59.

Simon dispiritedly wrote to Lindner that 'given these peculiar conditions' (trans.), it was not to be imagined that the earthquake matter be changed for the better in the Netherlands. He suggested waiting for a more favourable time in which to once again confront the Dutch with this question.[309]

3.2.1.2. *The United States of America and Canada*
The reinsurers did not learn much about the developments in the earthquake question in the United States and Canada. They had only sent their study to a selected few of their North American business friends in order not to disturb the pending San Francisco court cases. In 1907, some committees dealt with the question of the exclusion of the earthquake danger,[310] but the general tendency developed in another direction.[311] Standard policies were being prepared by law that threatened to make the exclusion of the disliked liability impossible. This movement will be investigated in a special chapter based upon the example of California.

In his report sent to Iversen, Simon simply noted: 'The United States: nothing is happening here in the matter' (trans.).[312] The same applied to Canada where the British companies had accepted the earthquake-fire risk since March 1907.[313] The reinsurers began to come to terms with this situation. Since the earthquake risk had to be assumed in the future in any case, they at least hoped to receive an additional premium in exchange for the coverage.[314]

---

[309] 29 August 1908 Simon to Lindner, SR/FA A9.0–32/yellow file folder (correspondence Swiss insurance companies)/loose material.

[310] Spycket reports on a Canandian and an American committee, 24 June 1907 Spycket to Simon, SR/FA A9.0–32/yellow file folder (correspondence mainly Cologne Re 10/1906–8/1907), 118 *et seq.* Gruenwald too was aware of a committee in the USA that was set up by the fire insurance companies united in the Eastern Union (30 July 1907 Gruenwald to Thieme, Lindner, Simon, SR/FA, 93 *et seq.*).

[311] Gruenwald reports that on the Pacific coast, only six companies still carried an earthquake clause (8 July 1907 Gruenwald to Simon, SR/FA, 68.)

[312] 29 April 1908 Simon to Iversen (Københavns Brandforsikring), SR/FA A9.0–32/file folder/ correspondence regarding earthquake clause 1906/1907/ *Bayerische Versicherungsbank*, 39 *et seq.*

[313] The British companies there accepted the earthquake clause risk in accordance with a decision of the Foreign Fire Offices' Committee (*The Journal of Commerce* 25 March 1907, 13).

[314] 24 June 1907 Spycket to Simon, SR/FA A9.0–32/yellow file folder (correspondence mainly Cologne Re 10/1906–8/1907), 118 *et seq.*

3.2.1.3. *Preliminary Results*
The developments in Great Britain and the Netherlands including the
respective foreign business territories show clear parallels. In both
cases did the standardisation of the earthquake clause fail under similar
circumstances.

The powers of competition, intensified through a high degree of competitive pressure, proved highly decisive. In both countries, a strong
minority of insurance companies rejected to cooperate in the reform of
the earthquake regulations. The events look like a chain reaction from outside. The aggressive policy favoured by Lloyds Underwriters of assuming
earthquake-fire risks should not be accorded a too large degree of importance in economic terms. However, the policy gave the Royal Insurance
Company a welcomed argument to demand the same from the reinsurers and the other British Offices members, whereupon individual companies and finally the entire British fire insurance cartel followed suit. Thus,
the Dutch insurance industry, for which foreign business was similarly
important, apparently came under pressure. The British Offices, which in
London had decided to deregulate the liability for earthquake-fire damages, advocated the exclusion of the same risk from these policies in the
Netherlands. The reason can only be that they speculated that following a
voluntary agreement of the Dutch insurance industry to adopt the earthquake clause, the Dutch competition overseas would be weakened. Given
this consideration, the Dutch decision to reject the earthquake clause is
understandable. Finally, a rejection of the proposal by a minority of the
companies sufficed for standardisation to fail here too.

In the case of Great Britain, a few circumstances additionally contributed to facilitating the decision against the implementation of the earthquake clause. Reinsuring parts of their portfolios was not a matter of life
and death for British insurance companies. This was mainly due to the
Offices' large reserves and the well-developed system of coinsurance.
The Dutch were less independent.[315] In addition, seismicity tended to be
regarded as a calculable risk rather than an unpredictable danger in Great
Britain. Here was another difference to the Netherlands, where 120 companies had met for the reform of the earthquake regulations even before
the initiative of the reinsurance directors.

---

[315] The only English reinsurance company went bankrupt in 1908/1909. The business
was run by Lloyds and foreign reinsurance companies (Jahn 1912, 88).

Factors that facilitated the reform of the earthquake clause in other countries were lacking in both Great Britain and the Netherlands; in neither country was a general overhaul of the standard insurance terms pending. No State institutions supported the introduction of earthquake clauses. The Dutch insurance industry had suffered minimal, if any, losses in the catastrophes of 1906 and 1907; the British Offices had been able to meet the greatest demands with their existing cash reserves.

3.2.2. California: Standard Policies as the Threshold for International Standardisation?

California offered a picture that departs from the conclusions reached for Great Britain and the Netherlands. In 1909, the California legislature introduced a standard policy into law that prescribed in detail which risks insurance companies were obligated to accept. It is to be assumed that the immediate experience of the San Francisco disaster decisively contributed to the fact that the insurance companies were not permitted to introduce an earthquake clause.

At first glance, the State-mandated standardisation of the terms of contract appears to have established a threshold for the international standardisation of earthquake regulations. But the reality was more complex, and the question whether the decision against earthquake clauses did not rather depend on the market plays an important role in the investigation of the developments in California.

3.2.2.1. The Insurance Industry at the Turn of the Twentieth Century

Although California had a population of hardly two million at the beginning of the twentieth century,[316] the fire insurance market—as stated above[317]—was as one of the most lucrative in the world. The young state promised a fantastic potential for profit with its high premiums and small damage quotas and was popular with American and foreign insurance companies. San Francisco, the trade and financial centre of the West Coast, was the headquarters of the larger insurance companies and at the same time California's most important fire insurance market.[318] The city had for the most part been destroyed during the disaster of April 1906.

---

[316] US census 1900: 1.48 million residents; 1910: 2.38 million residents (Forstall 1996).
[317] See chapter 3.1.2.
[318] In the 1880s, half of the insurance premiums paid in California derived from San Francisco (McIntosh 1954, 3 *et seq.*)

Tens of thousands of insurance contracts were settled. The city's recon-struction heralded a redistribution of the entire San Francisco fire insur-ance market.

As in all states of the United States of America, public limited com-panies dominated the Californian insurance business.[319] Public insurance institutions did not exist, mutual companies only in a few cases.[320] Many of the large insurance companies were members of the National Board of Fire Underwriters.[321] This federation, which operated throughout the country, had withdrawn from collective bargaining policies in 1877 and as of then mainly devoted itself to insurance science such as the education of insurance businessmen as well as technical, architectural and city plan-ning measures for fire prevention.[322] National Fire Protection Federation[323] and local unions also worked in this field.[324]

Regional associations behaved like cartels. The Board of Fire Under-writers of the Pacific dominated the West Coast.[325] The Fire Underwriters' Association of the Pacific, which included 100 members, acted in a scien-tific capacity[326] and cannot be regarded as a cartel.

The insurance contract law that applied in California formed a part of the common law. Accordingly, jurisprudence from the legal sphere of the common law assumed a pre-eminent importance. It was applicable along-side the Civil Code's provisions on the insurance contract and the public limited insurance company.[327] The Civil Code had originated in 1871–72 in the framework of statutory codifications. The Californian legislature had reformed and codified the entire body of civil and public law at the time. However, the Civil Code had lost its law-like primacy among the different sources of law in the course of the re-establishment of the common law in 1888.[328]

---

[319] Ibid., 2.

[320] 'Historische Entwicklung der Feuerversicherung in den Vereinigten Staaten', *Elsner's Repertorischer Assecuranz-Almanach* 1907, 177 *et seq.*; McIntosh 1954, 8 *et seq.*

[321] In 1906, 111 companies belonged to the Board (*Proceedings of the 40th Annual Meet-ing*, New York, May 10, 1906, 8).

[322] National Board of Fire Underwriters (ed.) 1941, 118.

[323] *Elsner's Repertorischer Assecuranz-Almanach* 1907, 184.

[324] Ibid., 187.

[325] McIntosh 1954, 25. In 1906, the Board consisted of forty-seven members; compare the table of the companies involved in the San Francisco catastrophe.

[326] Manes (*Masius' Rundschau* 1906, 79), however, regarded it as the most important organisation of fire insurers in the States.

[327] Civil Code, sec. 331–332, sec. 414–451 and sec. 2527–2766.

[328] See chapter 3.1.5.

The courts and the provisions of the Civil Code only limited the private autonomy in insurance law to a small degree. The most important source of substantive insurance law in California were the contracts.[329] A large complexity of insurance conditions and standard contract forms had developed. The most widely used was the New York Standard Form of Fire Insurance Policy.[330]

The New York state legislature had introduced these standard contract forms into law in 1887.[331] All the insurance companies that carried fire insurance contracts were obligated to use the same wording. The Standard Policy Law also prescribed the physical appearance of the policy in detail.[332] Deviations were punished with fines.[333] However, the New York insurance supervisory agency later received authorisation to approve additions to the policies in the form of inserted riders.[334] These clauses were announced publicly. In 1906, the Standard Policy Law was valid in nineteen states:

> Connecticut, Iowa, Louisiana, Maine, Massachusetts,[335] Michigan, Minnesota, New Hampshire, New Jersey, New York, North Carolina, North Dakota, Oklahoma, Oregon, Rhode Island, South Dakota, Washington, West Virginia, Wisconsin.[336]

Thus, the standardisation of contract forms did not originate in the business world, but in the activity of the State. All the earlier attempts of the insurers to introduce standard policy forms had failed.[337] Contemporary professional literature unanimously pointed to the deficiencies in the insurance industry in order to explain the legislative interference: shady insurance companies had used the contract forms as part of their

---

[329] Hardy 1913, 1.

[330] See chapter 3.1.5.2 and *Elsner's Repertorischer Assecuranz-Almanach* 1907, 184.

[331] Annual Report of the Superintendent of Insurance of the State New York (for 1887), cited in: Hardy 1913, 21.

[332] Ibid.

[333] Ibid.

[334] For example, New York. Kennedy 1922, 40.

[335] In 1873, Massachusetts was the first state to introduce a standard policy, whose use was obligatory as of 1881 (Hardy 1913, 21).

[336] Ibid., 25.

[337] The National Board of Fire Underwriters had unsuccessfully attempted to introduce a standard policy (*Elsner's Repertorischer Assecuranz-Almanach* 1907, 184). In the 1880's, a similar attempt on the part of the New York Board of Fire Underwriters had also been unsuccessful (Kennedy 1922, 22).

fraudulent intentions to camouflage disadvantageous contract terms.[338] In addition, the multiplicity of policy forms had impeded the regulation of the insurance business[339] and obstructed the development of a coherent case law, as the same factual circumstances repeatedly led to contradictory decisions due to the variety of contract terms.[340]

Although the introduction of standard policies meant a considerable reduction of contractual freedom, there had always been some insurance companies who supported these State regulations.[341] The first reason for this was that uniform contract terms facilitated the companies' control of the accepted risks.[342] The second was that the equivalence of the contract terms simplified the distribution of the large risks among several companies.[343]

At the beginning of the twentieth century, the language and the style of the New York standard policy was regarded as old-fashioned among the insurers. The reason why many companies nevertheless used it in California was that in the meantime, each of its clauses was embedded in a thick mesh of court decisions: 'There is a tendency, as there was in England, to feel like though the language may not seem to state what courts have ruled it to state, there is at least a solid foundation given to the transaction by the expressed opinion of the courts as to what the document means'.[344] In fact, the number of legal disputes in the fire insurance business was exceedingly small measured by the number of damage claims.[345] The insurance scholar Edward R. Hardy regarded this number as evidence

---

[338] The scathing criticism of an insurance form in the case of Delancy vs. Rockingham Farmers' Mutual Fire-Insurance Co., 52 N.H., 581, June 1873, is famous; cited in Hardy 1913, 18 *et seq.*; Deitch 1905, 3 *et seq.*; *Elsner's Repertorischer Assecuranz-Almanach* 1907, 184; Weinstock and Maloney 1955, chapter 9; Kennedy 1922, 20.

[339] Kennedy 1922, 20.

[340] Annual Report of the Superintendent of Insurance of the State New York (for 1887), cited in Hardy 1913, 22.

[341] Weinstock and Maloney 1955, chapter 9.

[342] They simplified the control of the activities of the widely scattered agents who often made their own unauthorised decisions (Weinstock and Maloney 1955, chapter 9).

[343] Kennedy (1922, 20 *et seq.*) writes that two cases in which the variety of policy forms led to problems for the co-insurers had provided the inititative for the introduction of the New York Standard policy.

[344] Hardy 1913, 6.

[345] '[...] it is a fact that ninety-five per cent of all the losses in fire insurance are settled with a very little, if any friction. Only the remaining five per cent form the subject of extended negotiations and a still smaller number that find their way into the court [...] Certainly a document which is the evolution of two hundred and twenty-five years of experience, may richly deserve and invite an acquaintance with its principles for itself alone'. Hardy, 1913, 2.

of the high legal quality of the traditional forms. New policies, he wrote in 1913, would require judicial interpretations over numerous years until the most glaring legal ambiguities were eliminated.[346]

In California as well, various leaders within and external to the insurance business had campaigned for the introduction of a standard policy even before the turn of the century.[347] However, the only initiative had failed on constitutional grounds in 1899. The senator Samuel Braunhart had proposed requiring the insurance commissioner to openly display in his office a 'California Standard Fire Insurance Policy' that corresponded to the New York standard policy. The insurance companies were then to be legally urged to use this form.[348] While this matter was being discussed in a senate committee, however, the insurance cartel of the time, the Pacific Insurance Union, objected that the legal prescription of standard forms had been declared unconstitutional in other states of the union. The basis of this decision was that the supervisory agencies had received quasi legislative authorisation that not even the legislature could delegate to them. The Californian senate committee was unable to reach a decision and the matter was postponed. In the years thereafter, the topic was repeatedly raised, especially among San Francisco insurers,[349] but there were no further initiatives.[350]

The law on the supervision of insurance in the state of California was regulated by the statutes in the Political Code.[351] The system was personalised; i.e., many of the provisions were centred on the Insurance Commissioner as executive officer of the state of California.[352] In order to practice their business, all insurance companies and agents required the authorisation of the Insurance Commissioner.[353] Pursuant to Californian law, the most important prerequisite for the incorporation of a company was proof of a capital stock of at least $200,000; the same was required

---

[346] Ibid., 6.

[347] Weinstock and Maloney 1955, 121.

[348] Senate Bills Nos. 177, 178.

[349] Coogan, 'History of the California Standard Form of Fire Insurance Policy', *Proceedings of the annual meeting of the Fire Underwriters' Association of the Pacific* 1910, 121.

[350] Ibid., 122.

[351] Political Code, sec. 368–369 and sec. 594–634. Weinstock and Maloney 1955, chapter 2.

[352] Political Code, sec. 368–369. *Insurance Laws of the State of California* 1904, 5 *et seq.* In 1906, the Insurance Commissioner Wolf had only six associates working for him: 1 Deputy, 2 Examiners, 2 Clerks, 1 Clerk-Stenographer, 1 Stenographer (California Blue Book or State Roster 1907, 68).

[353] Political Code, sec. 596; amended, statutes 1873–74, 9, 61; 1877–78, 13; 1880, 89 (*Insurance Laws of the State of California* 1904, 8 *et seq.*).

of non-Californian companies desiring authorisation to begin business transactions in the state.[354] In the past, these companies had been occasionally required to make deposits with the Insurance Commission,[355] but not at the time previous to the earthquake.[356] Instead, all companies had to establish funds from the accumulated premiums surpluses over which the Insurance Commissioner had control.[357]

The insurance supervision was carried out for the most part by means of annual financial statements.[358] In the case of suspicion of bankruptcy, the Insurance Commissioner was allowed to check the finances of any company or appeal to the state attorney to institute bankruptcy proceedings.[359] Remarkable in this context is the legal provision stating that owners of insurance company shares were personally liable to indemnify damages. For a long time already before the San Francisco catastrophe, this regulation had not been enforced,[360] but it was theoretically still in force.[361] Additional and more stringent provisions concerning insurance served to impede shady and deceptive practices of insurers or policyholders.[362]

All in all, the Californian insurance supervisory agency constituted a complex licensing and control system that went beyond the purely formal monitoring of the implementation of conditions and regulations to which insurance companies were subject. That the sole function of the Insurance Commissioner was the 'enforcement of insurance legislation'[363] does not really correspond to the reality of supervision. The officers' opportunities for guiding interventions into the insurance business and the large degree of their administrative discretion became clear, at the very latest,

---

[354] Civil Code sec. 419; amended, statutes 1873–73, 269; 1877–78, 80 (*Insurance Laws of the State of California* 1904, 39).

[355] McIntosh 1954, 16.

[356] Political Code, Sec. 618–620; amended, statutes 1877–78, 18–19 (*Insurance Laws of the State of California* 1904, 25 *et seq.*).

[357] Civil Code §427, amended statutes 1886–7, c. 27, 22; C.C. 432, added Stat 1886–7, c. 27, 22 (Weinstock and Maloney 1955, chapter 2).

[358] Political Code, Sec. 611–612; amended, statutes 1873–74, 10; 1877–78, 15; 1887, 9 (*Insurance Laws of the State of California* 1904, 17 *et seq.*).

[359] Political Code, Sec. 597–602; amended, statutes 1880 19; 1887, 7 (*Insurance Laws of the State of California* 1904, 9 *et seq.*).

[360] They were interpreted narrowly (McIntosh 1954, 5).

[361] Whitney 1906, 52.

[362] Tarbell (1927, 10 *et seq.*) provides a comprehensive list.

[363] Patterson (1927, 536) represents this notion in broad application to the institution of Insurance Commissioners in the United States.

in crisis situations.[364] For this reason, one can speak of a substantive State supervision.

Two additional aspects characterised the relationship between the state institutions and the insurance business. The first was the coordination of the regulatory measures among the forty-eight states. For this purpose, the regulatory officers had met in the National Convention of Insurance Commissioners since 1871 to discuss current problems and to provide uniform solutions.[365] Attempts to set up federal regulation failed in 1868, 1892 and 1897 due to the lack of federal legislative competence.[366] Secondly, the impression had developed among insurance companies that the real function of insurance supervision was to collect taxes, given that tax legislation had been tightened so often.[367] However, California did not belong to the numerous states that had introduced 'anti-compact laws' directed against cartels and monopolies since the 1880's.[368]

3.2.2.2. Contemporary Estimates of the Earthquake-Fire Danger in California

The likelihood of violent earthquakes in California was in principle judged to be high. San Francisco had been hit hard in 1868,[369] and since the catastrophe of 1906, American seismologists developed new hypotheses that anticipated later scientific results and were used as the basis for predictions. Several scientists now held the view that a period of calm lasting several decades was to be expected.[370]

Nevertheless, a feeling of calmness and security was not widespread among branches of business that had just experienced the catastrophic

---

[364] Among others, after the California catastrophe of 18–21 April 1906.

[365] Tarbell 1927, 13.

[366] The reason was the United States Supreme Court's view 'that Insurance is not Commerce' and that therefore, there was no federal competence for supervision. Decisions relating to this matter were made in 1858 (Paul vs. Virginia) and 1895 (Hooper vs. California) (Tarbell 1927, 14).

[367] La Semaine (4 November 1906, 8) also reported that the American insurance press regarded many of the insurance commissioners as incompetent. The Adjuster (33, July 1906, 1) wrote about the California Insurance Commissioner: 'The absence of technical knowledge on the part of Insurance Commissioner Hon. E. Myron Wolf has prevented him from being a real value during the last two months, either to policyholders or to insurance companies'.

[368] Schneiberg 1999, 14 (Fig. 2) and additional references.

[369] Bronson 1959, 17 et seq.

[370] For example, Omori, in Jordan 1907 and Ransome, The National Geographic Magazine, May 1906, vol. 17, no. 5.

results of an earthquake.[371] This was due to the well-known danger of fire in the larger cities of North America.[372] In the previous few decades, disastrous fires had struck Chicago, Boston and Baltimore. There had been many fires in San Francisco too. For this reason, many considered that the solution to the earthquake-fire problem was to be sought in a general increase in fire safety.[373]

3.2.2.3. *The Earthquake Regulations at the Time of the San Francisco Catastrophe*

At the time of the catastrophe, the companies active in the insurance business in California were using different earthquake regulations.[374] Pure collapse damages were in principle not to be indemnified. If an insured building collapsed in part, the New York standard policy stipulated that the liability for later fire damages ceased to exist (fallen building clause). The insurers with earthquake clauses were not liable for all fire damages that were caused directly or indirectly by earthquakes. In this context, there were numerous different formulations.

The exclusionary clauses collided neither with the rules of common law nor with the provisions of the Civil Code. Nevertheless, insurance companies that refused to indemnify the insured for certain damages were regularly required to pay after all. This was mainly due to the distribution of the burden of proof. In the absence of contractual agreements that stated something different, the insurers had to prove that the exceptional facts upon which they relied were fulfilled. They almost always failed to do so.[375]

3.2.2.4. *'Drastic Insurance Legislation expected'* (1906)

In California too, the discussion on the future inclusion and exclusion of earthquake-fire damages constituted a part of the reaction to the earthquake catastrophe.

---

[371] *The Journal of Commerce*, 23 January 1907, 12. The *Coast Review* held a different opinion: 'Only the destruction or dispension of the water supply makes the latter a serious danger—a "suspension" not likely to ever occur again [...] Pacific Coast—where the existence of shallow-rooted trees 3,000 years old proves that this is not truly an "earthquake country"', 'Marked Discrimination Against Quake-Clause Policies', *Coast Review*, April 1909, 204.

[372] *The Adjuster* 33, October 1906, 189 *et seq.*

[373] Henry Evans, the President of the New York company Continental, held this view (*The Journal of Commerce*, 25 January 1907, 13).

[374] See chapter 3.1.5.

[375] See chapter 3.1.7.1.

Some insurance companies inserted earthquake clauses into their policies that they held to be valid:[376] 'Old policy blanks have the clause attached as a rider. New policy blanks have the objectionable clause printed among the "not liable for" clauses, and the policy must be read carefully in order to detect the joker'.[377] But why the hurry, the insurance journal *Coast Review* asked in August 1906, if the legislature would be intervening anyway in five months' time? 'It is not doubted that the Coast Legislature will provide for a standard form of policy, similar to or more liberal than that of New York'. [378] In addition, it was already apparent that the policyholders preferred companies that remained willing to indemnify for earthquake-fire damages.[379]

In the weeks and months after the earthquake catastrophe, the California media repeatedly called attention to the question of the standard policy and urged the legislature to act. A basic reform of the insurance law was expected.[380] There was a rumour that the Insurance Commissioner E. Myron Wolf had put the finishing touches on the introduction of a 'standard policy' and a 'deposit law'.[381] The California insurance business started looking unnerved. Wolf was requested to make his legislative plans known to the public in order to permit a public discussion. The local monthly newspaper of the insurance branch, *The Adjuster*, argued that even if Wolf was incompetent professionally, he could still adequately serve as a 'first-class arbitrator' at a hearing with insurers and policyholders.[382]

In the middle of July 1906, the *Journal of Commerce* confirmed the rumours.[383] The Insurance Commissioner described his idea of a new policy to a California newspaper: 'It will be shorter and simpler than the New York Standard Form; it will be more like the policy in use by the State of Massachusetts. The New York Form is too cumbersome, too ambiguous; no policyholder can read it or understand it, while it is of too decided

[376] *ÖVZ* 1906, 265. Among them were also the British Offices (Trebilcock 1998, vol. II, 279).

[377] 'New Earthquake Clauses', *The Coast Review*, August 1906, 298.

[378] Ibid.

[379] *ÖVZ* 1906, 265.

[380] Coogan in *Proceedings of the annual meeting of the Fire Underwriters' Association of the Pacific* 1910, 122.

[381] 'Insurance Situation in San Francisco', *The Journal of Commerce*, 17 July 1906, 13.

[382] 'The Insurance Commisioner', *The Adjuster* 33, July 1906, 1.

[383] *The Journal of Commerce*, 17 July 1906, 13.

assistance to the insurance companies'.[384] He received support from the powerful Policyholders' League. At its inaugural meeting, the members had not been able to pass a resolution equivalent to that of the legislature, but in August they included the demand for a standard policy in the bylaws of their organisation. Their economic and legal programme for the design of the future framework of the fire insurance industry envisioned comprehensive reforms:

> [...] 6. To make efforts to induce all solvent and fair-dealing insurance companies now in existence or hereafter organized to do business in California, so that reasonable rates of insurance may prevail.
>
> 7. To co-operate with the municipal authorities, the fire department, the representatives of the fire insurance companies and policyholders to secure and maintain the best possible protection against fire.
>
> 8. To suggest and watch insurance legislation that will benefit the community and that will be fair both to the insurance companies and to the policyholders.
>
> 9. To endeavour to secure the adoption of a uniform form of fire insurance policy that will be clear and fair both to the insurance companies and to the policyholders, and to keep policyholders advised of any changes in forms of policies that may be made by insurance companies from time to time.
>
> 10. That this association co-operate with all efforts by other organizations here or elsewhere to improve and perfect protection against fire and to secure reliable insurance against loss'.[385]

Late in the summer of 1906—at the height of the settlement of damages and at the beginning of the court disputes on the complexity of the policy terms—, an intense debate on the future basic principles of the insurance contracts began. Just as the Insurance Commissioner had done, the California press rejected the New York standard policy with which numerous unfavourable terms, including the collapse and earthquake clauses, were associated.[386] The *San Francisco Examiner* described the posture of the insurance industry:

---

[384] Coogan in *Proceedings of the annual meeting of the Fire Underwriters' Association of the Pacific* 1910, 123.

[385] *The Adjuster* 33, August 1906, 65; 'Policyholders' Protective League; Board of trustees; statement of purposes', *The Journal of Commerce*, 4 August 1906, 13.

[386] Examples and quoted statements in Coogan in *Proceedings of the annual meeting of the Fire Underwriters' Association of the Pacific* 1910, 122 *et seq.*

The entire business community of San Francisco is eagerly awaiting the coming session of the State Legislature at Sacramento [...]. [...] The insurance men are full of anxiety, for they fear drastic legislation that may curtail their emoluments, if it does not drive them out of business altogether. The merchants and others of the business community are in a state of uncertainty. [...] The insurance companies, separately and collectively, will have their own men up at the Capital City; and, so far, they are agreed upon just one thing—that there must be a standard form of fire policy for universal adoption. There is no solid agreement as to what shape this standard form shall take; many of the old insurance men, most, in fact, want the New York Standard Form. 'It has stood the test of thirty years', they say. This old, complicated and lengthy form of policy appears to be regarded with a sort of reverence even by many property owners who take out insurance, but there are wise men who say that the day has come when another and simpler form should be adopted—one that can be understood by the insured as well as by the insurer. It sounds like heresy, but in quarters where the question has really been studied it is emphatically declared that the old New York Standard Form must go, must give way to one that gives fewer loopholes to the insurance companies relying upon technicalities to evade obligation'.[387]

This description renders the nervousness among the San Francisco companies almost tangible. How rigorously would the legislature in the 'capital city' of Sacramento regulate substantive insurance law? The introduction of a standard policy was considered certain. The editors of the *Examiner* made no bones about their objections to the New York standard form. But what would arrive in its stead? How much room for the autonomous design of individual contract contents would remain in the hands of the insurance business? It was not only in relation to earthquake clauses that the insurance companies' private autonomy could be restricted.

Hidden from the scrutiny of the public, the interested circles began to draft policies and build alliances. A central position was occupied by the Policyholders' League.[388] They established their own committee that under the chairmanship of the businessman Andrew Carrigan intended to produce a policy draft.[389] A second commission was designed to coordinate this activity with part of the insurance business. The place and membership of these secret meetings are very revealing: they took place

---

[387] According to Coogan (*Proceedings of the annual meeting of the Fire Underwriters' Association of the Pacific* 1910, 122), this quotation adequately characterised the mood within the insurance industry.

[388] Statement by the Chairman H. Weinstock ('Uniform policy', *The Journal of Commerce*, 16 August 1906, 13) on the legal work of the league.

[389] Coogan in *Proceedings of the annual meeting of the Fire Underwriters' Association of the Pacific* 1910, 123.

in the Ferry Building where following the earthquake, the Chamber of
Commerce as well as the Committee of Five of the 'dollar for dollar companies' had set themselves up. This latter group consisted of the thirty-two
companies that in the absence of earthquake clauses and thanks to large
amounts of financial capital provided almost complete damage compensation and for this reason enjoyed enormous popularity among business
circles.

In fact, it was precisely these interest groups that met. Joseph D. Grant,
Andrew Carrigan and L. M. King represented the Policyholders' League;
George W. Spencer (Aetna) and Charles D. Haven (London, Liverpool &
Globe) spoke for the interests of the underwriters. The local insurance
managers were represented by Rolla V. Watt (Royal and Queen), who as
one of the most vehement opponents of the earthquake clause was known
even to the Earthquake Commission of the European reinsurance companies.[390] The common discussion of the future basic principles of the insurance contracts strengthened the participating insurance companies and
deepened mutual trust.

There were heated discussions in the committee on the drafting of a
standard policy. Insurers such as Edward F. Bedall (Royal and Queen)
advocated an introduction by law of the New York standard policy. Policyholders such as the Merchants' Association favoured the form used in
Massachusetts. The underwriter George W. Spencer kept the Board of Fire
Underwriters of the Pacific aware of the plans. The insurers allied in the
cartel used the opportunity to enter into the discourse. Spencer conveyed
a statement to Carrigan, the Chairman of the Standard Policy Committee,
under the auspices of the Board. He argued in favour of the New York
form, but demonstrated his readiness to negotiate:

> I understand from this communication and the information you have given
> me, that the Policyholders' League [...] and the board of directors of the
> Merchants' Association of San Francisco have considered with favour a form
> based on the one in use in Massachusetts, with certain modifications. With
> your permission, I would make the following suggestions with reference to
> the form of policy proposed by you.

Specific proposals for changes to the Massachusetts standard policy
followed.[391] In situations such as these, it became clear that it was the

---

[390] 3 October 1906 Simon to Gruenwald, SR/FA A9.0–32/yellow file folder (correspondence mainly Cologne Re 10/1906–8/1907), 1.
[391] Coogan in *Proceedings of the annual meeting of the Fire Underwriters' Association of
the Pacific* 1910, 124.

policyholders, and not the insurers, who had the power to determine future contract terms.

At the same time, the President of the New York company Continental, Henry Evans, was working on the most ambitious plan for reform of insurance contract law. In August of 1906, he demanded in the *Journal of Commerce* that a simplified standard policy be introduced uniformly in all states. Evans' argument was based upon the experiences gained following the catastrophe from San Francisco in which the complexity of regulations had created problems and permitted some companies to 'haggle'. He desired the elimination of earthquake clauses: 'The exclusion clause and the provisions covering the voiding of the policy should be bold down and be made as simple and clear as possible'.[392] The nationwide standardisation of policies was to begin in California. For this reason, Evans personally worked on a draft that he intended to present to the legislature in Sacramento.

The New York manager's reform programme was in conformity with the spirit of the times in two respects. First of all, following the California catastrophe, numerous existing terms of insurance law were regarded as obsolete everywhere in the United States. The *Journal of Commerce* reported in the fall of 1906 under the title 'Drastic Insurance Legislation expected' that in the coming winter, the legislative branches would meet in forty-four states in the universal expectation that new regulations would be drafted.[393] Second of all, there was a growing willingness towards legal standardisation in economic questions in the United States.[394]

In California, numerous public institutions issued statements on the question of insurance law legislation. All of them—from the Republican Party, which stood for election for the Senate, the Assembly and the office of governor,[395] to the California Attorney General, General Ulysses S.

---

[392] 'Simplifying the Policy', *The Journal of Commerce*, 28 August 1906, 13.

[393] 'Drastic Insurance Legislation expected', *The Journal of Commerce*, 7 November 1906, 13.

[394] The legal unification was, however, more effectively accomplished on the federal level than through uniform legislation of the individual states (Gray, *RabelsZ 50* [1986], 117, 122 *et seq.*).

[395] At the Republican State Convention on October 5, 1906, the Republicans advocated a 'deposit and standard policy'-legislation and called upon their candidates to campaign for this and other laws that protected the insured; quotes of the resolutions: 'California Republican State Convention [...]', *The Coast Review*, August 1906, 295; 'Insurance in Platform/ Republicans in California adopt Commissioner Wolf's Resolution', *The Journal of Commerce*, 12 September 1906, 12; 'Back Talk', *The Adjuster* 33, September 1906, 121. *The Adjuster* made Insurance Commissioner Wolf responsible for the adoption of the cited passages.

Webb, who was involved in the trials and bankruptcy proceedings against the insurance companies—demanded the introduction of stricter standard policies.[396]

The insurance scholar Albert W. Whitney also subscribed to this demand. However, in his report on the settlement of the damages resulting from the catastrophe that was sent to the San Francisco Chamber of Commerce on November 13, 1906,[397] he emphasised other matters. On the one hand, he gave a good grade to the overall regulation practices of the insurance companies in the wake of the catastrophe. On the other hand, he was aware of the crucial necessity to maintain the attractiveness of the California insurance market for the insurance companies in order to guarantee appropriate protection for the large cities. That is why he admonished and warned:

> There is no more inexorable economic fact than that unwise legislation will do one of two things, either raise the rates or drive the companies out of business. The best thing that could possibly be done for the insured is to remove all unnecessary restrictions from the companies and to encourage the formation of organizations for the properly adjusting rates and preserving stable conditions.[398]

This liberal appeal to allow the insurers to regulate their business themselves and even to support the activity of the associations was unusual given the animosity in the entire US towards cartels and monopolies. By way of explanation, Whitney described the mode of operation of the insurance cartels called *Boards*:

> [...] there is nothing in the fundamental nature of a Board as a rate-maker that tends to restrict competition; quite the opposite; for this information regarding rates must of necessity become largely public property, and it is to that extent generally available for whoever will to use. There will always be non-Board companies and rates will always be kept down by competition.[399]

---

[396] On the occasion of the delivery of his two-year report to Governor G. C. Pardee, Webb ('To amend Insurance Laws in California/ Recommendations of State Attorney General', *The Journal of Commerce*, 13 October 1906, 13) criticised the insurance law as ineffective and recommended, among other things, the implementation of a standard form policy as an improvement.

[397] A Chamber of Commerce committee consisting of Charles H. Bentley (1st Vice-President), George H. Butler und George D. Gray (Trustees) was responsible for the report. Butler was familiar with the insurance business from his earlier activity. However, Whitney was chiefly responsible for the contents of the report, which for this reason was later also called the 'Whitney-Report' (1906/1972).

[398] Ibid., 50.

[399] Ibid.

This understanding that the danger of restricting competition could be balanced by the positive influence of the disclosure of the economic principles of business is supported by more recent historical research in economics.[400]

Commensurate with these maxims, Whitney's recommendations for legislation aimed at founding business on reliable principles and abstaining from deterrent regulations. He recommended the New York form as future contractual basis—including some remarkable modifications:

> 1st, it is the best existing form. It was made carefully by a committee from the insurance companies and the state superintendent of insurance.
>
> 2nd, the creation of a new form would be a work that should require far more time and thought than could possibly be given to it now.
>
> 3rd, the New York standard form has been adopted by a number of states and, in the twenty years it has been in use, has received a number of legal interpretations. This is unquestionably the point of greatest importance, since a policy has no surely ascertained meaning till it has received the interpretation of the courts.
>
> The policy, to be sure, does not impress one with its simplicity nor its fairness to the insured; it is not an ideal policy; but its faults are lessened by the interpretations of the courts. At any rate this is no time to experiment. San Francisco needs now more than ever all the insurance that in can get and it is not expedient, to say the least, to run the chance of driving companies away that are already not over sure that they wish to stay.
>
> If a standard form of policy is adopted there should be some prescribed method of adding qualifying clauses, as for instance in red ink. There are some companies that will not do business at the coast without an earthquake clause. They should be allowed to offer their goods for sale, provided the goods are properly marked.[401]

Whitney had recognised that not only the pending introduction of a standard policy, but also precisely the possible prohibition of excluding earthquake-caused damages made insurance companies uncertain.

He also resolutely rejected a drastic deposit law: it would be sufficient for the protection of the policyholder if non-Californian companies deposited money for the insured in all of the United States in one

---

[400] Schneiberg and Bartley, 'Regulating American Industries: Markets, Politics and the Institutional Determinants of Fire Insurance Regulation', *American Journal of Sociology 107* (July 2001), 101 *et seq.*

[401] Whitney 1906, 51.

state.[402] Capital-related commitments that went beyond this point would drive the insurers out of the country. Whitney demanded to abolish the individual liability of shareholders in insurance companies with the same arguments.[403] Some additional proposals for the improvement of the basic principles governing the insurance business followed.

It is important that Whitney and the Commission demonstrated that the standardisation of the policy forms and the use of earthquake clauses were not mutually exclusive.

Insurance Commissioner Wolf appears to also have seen this possibility. After meeting with representatives of the policyholders and members of the legislature in December of 1906, he explained that deviations from the future standard policy should be allowed but made clear by means of large lettering and red ink.[404] In the meantime, however, the policyholders were aligned against the exclusion of the earthquake danger to an extent that individual companies voluntarily began to remove earthquake clauses from their contracts.[405]

The newspaper *The Adjuster* remained one of the last bastions of the advocates for using the earthquake clause in California.[406] In an emotional appeal at the end of 1906, its editors attacked those companies who since the catastrophe sought to gain an advantage by rejecting the earthquake clause and endangered an agreement in the Board of Underwriters of the Pacific. They offered their pessimistic prognosis of the coming developments in a few paragraphs. They concluded that the possibility of such occurrences represented an incalculable risk:

> [...] the correct policy of the future as toward the Coast cities lies in limiting the acceptance of liability within certain areas to that figure which is reasonable, inclusive the earthquake hazard. In other words, if the earthquake exemption clause cannot by agreement be introduced, then the liability maximum must be that figure only, which could be paid for without unduly weakening the company, whether the cause be earthquake or not, exceptional or normal.

---

[402] Whitney (1906, 51 *et seq.*) explicitly criticised the plans of 'one of the political parties', by which he meant the Republicans.

[403] Ibid., 52.

[404] 'Commissioner Wolf on Insurance Legislation', *The Journal of Commerce*, 21 December 1906, 13.

[405] For example the Phoenix (Hartford). *The Adjuster* 33, September 1906, 84.

[406] 'Couple of Cast Iron Earthquake Clauses', *The Adjuster* 33, October 1906, 147; *The Adjuster* 33, September 1906, 84, 121.

It is safe to say that the next Legislature will introduce a standard form of policy; and (because of the companies themselves) will successfully ward off the inclusion of any clause formally exempting liability for loss or damage caused by or through earthquake, proximately or remotely.

The next step must then be a discriminatory rate […]

In either event, a new element of competition has been introduced among us; and we do not hesitate to predict that the day will soon come when the 'we'll-charge-you-no-more-for-earthquake-hazard' inducement will, to save the Board itself, have to be laid aside as a competitive element, and a uniform policy of agreed exemption adopted.

In the meantime those companies whom the recent earthquake has hit the hardest and who now block the exclusion clause, will have had the opportunity to rake in sufficient premium to satisfy them—and we will all begin again to travel around some new circle. But the best course by far would be the immediate bold adoption through the Board of the full exemption clause; the Legislature would very quickly shrink from an unprofitable attack on an unassailable, impregnable fortress.[407]

The interest in the question of the earthquake regulations slacked off at the beginning of 1907. A few contrary statements from insurance circles were published here and there,[408] but the overall design of the coming standard policy seemed more important now than this particular aspect. Interested parties could read how imperative a comprehensive reform was in the *Journal of Commerce* on the very morning in which the Californian legislative session was opened.[409]

3.2.2.5. *The Development and Failure of the First Standard Policy Draft (1907)*

On January 7, 1907, the members of the two legislative chambers, the Senate and the Assembly, met in Sacramento.[410] The governor George C. Pardee, whose tenure in office ended shortly thereafter, spoke at the opening of the session. Two days later his successor, James N. Gillett, also spoke. The two politicians advocated standard policies. Both appealed against giving insurance companies the chance to exclude earthquake damages. But they emphasised matters differently. While Pardee decidedly

---

[407] 'The Earthquake Clause', *The Adjuster* 33, October 1906, 189 *et seq.*

[408] *The Journal of Commerce*, 23 January 1907, 12; 25 January 1907, 13; 'Earthquake clause', *The Coast Review*, February 1907, 63.

[409] 'Wolf on Legislation', *The Journal of Commerce*, 7 January 1907, 13.

[410] Coogan in *Proceedings of the annual meeting of the Fire Underwriters' Association of the Pacific* 1910, 125.

demanded regulations for the protection of the insured,[411] Gillett took a more cautious approach:

> [...] we should act with calm deliberation, proceed cautiously and be only actuated by a desire to enact such laws as will amply protect the insured in his contract, which must be fair and just, and afford protection to the company as well. Insurance is a legitimate business and a very important one, and should be so considered. In legislating, care should be taken not to enact laws containing provisions that will be so onerous to the companies that they will be forced to withdraw from the State, or that will entail upon our people more expensive insurance than they pay to-day.[412]

Not only was this excerpt from Gillett's address reminiscent of the opinion expressed by Albert Whitney. His concept of a moderate deposit law was also identical with the recommendations offered by the insurance expert. Similar admonitions urging caution emerged from the camp of the Policyholders' League.[413] Obviously, the exchange of opinions between the policyholders and the insurance companies had effected a relaxation in their contentious relations.

Both legislative houses established Committees on Insurance and Insurance Law that occasionally met jointly.[414] On January 14 and 15, 1907, Senator Frank W. Leavitt and Assemblyman Alexander M. Drew introduced the Insurance Commissioner's draft, named 'Wolf Bills' after their author,[415] into their respective chambers.[416] Wolf had taken his cue from the New York standard policy because it had been used by numerous companies,[417] but his draft differed from his model in many points. The main point was that the policy had to specify the obligations of the insurer clearly and

---

[411] Pardee, *Journal of the Senate of the State of California*, 7 January 1909, *37th Session of the Legislature*, 16–52 (quotation, 39).

[412] Gillett, Appendix to the *Journals of the Senate and the Assembly*, 9 January 1907, *37th Session of the Legislature of the State of California*.

[413] Statement by the insurance lawyers L. A. Redman ('Coast Notes', *The Adjuster* 34, January 1907, 37).

[414] In the senate commission, the discussion included F. W. Leavitt (Chairman; Rep.); J. C. Bates (Rep.), C. M. Belshaw (Rep.), H. A. Broughton (Rep.), J. B. Curtin (Dem.), H. H. Lynch (Rep.), H. B. McCartney (Rep.), W. F. Price (Rep.), E. I. Wolfe (Rep.); and in the Assembly commission the members included A. M. Drew (Chairman; Rep.); J. O. Davis (Dem.), C. M. Fisher (Rep.), G. J. Hans (Rep. and U.L.), T. Kohlman (Rep. and U.L.), H. C. Lucas (Rep.), W. F. Ludington (Rep.), P. A. Stanton (Rep. and Dem.) und J. W. Stetson (Rep.). (*Journal of the Assembly of the State of California*, 37th Session of the Legislature, 95).

[415] Coogan in *Proceedings of the annual meeting of the Fire Underwriters' Association of the Pacific* 1910, 125.

[416] Senate Bill no. 21, *Journal of the Senate of the State of California*, 37th Session of the Legislature, 21; Bill no. 224, *Journal of the Assembly of the State of California*, 37th Session of the Legislature, 122.

[417] 'Commissioner Wolf's Report', *The Journal of Commerce*, 15 January 1907, 14.

simply: 'It is a standard form of policy providing for loss by fire, explosion or collapse due to earthquake'.[418] Exclusionary clauses were to be permitted in the form of riders as long as it was certain that the policyholder did not overlook terms such as 'earthquake clause'.[419] Wolf explained in interviews that he considered his proposals to be largely in agreement with the recommendation of the legislative committee of the National Convention of Insurance Commissioners.[420] The insurance industry rejected Wolf's draft.[421]

The legislative committees dealt with four additional concepts next to the 'Wolf Bills'.[422] Senator Leavitt brought up for discussion a standard policy that O. G. Jones, an expert in insurance law, had drafted.[423] Jones was influenced by the New Hampshire form that had in turn been developed from the Massachusetts form. The *Journal of Commerce* noted positively that the 'Jones Bill'[424] was shorter than Wolf's draft. Leavitt emphasised that the decisions of the highest United States courts of the last three decades had been taken into consideration.[425] The Senate designated Jones himself to advise the Committee on Insurance and Insurance Laws.[426] The additional three drafts were presented by Senator Curtin, an adversary of Leavitt and Jones, by Henry Evans, the President of Continental (New York), who was aiming at a nationwide standardisation of the policies,[427] and by the underwriters of San Francisco.[428]

---

[418] 'New Insurance Law for California', *The Journal of Commerce*, 11 January 1907, 13.

[419] *The Journal of Commerce*, 15 January 1907, 14.

[420] At issue were presumably the proposals of the Committee of Fifteen of the Conference of Governors, Attorneys Generals and Insurance Commissioners of Februar, 1906. ('Wolf on Legislation', *The Journal of Commerce*, 7 January 1907, 13).

[421] Coogan in *Proceedings of the annual meeting of the Fire Underwriters' Association of the Pacific* 1910, 126.

[422] All cases dealt with the issue of the independent drafts of laws. The provisos of the Civil Code on fire insurance (sec. 2753–2759) were not changed in 1907 (*Insurance Laws of the State of California* 1912, 84 *et seq.*).

[423] Senate session of the 23rd Januar 1907/Bill no. 394, *Journal of the Senate of the State of California, 37th Session of the Legislature*, 167.

[424] Coogan in *Proceedings of the annual meeting of the Fire Underwriters' Association of the Pacific* 1910, 126.

[425] In detail: 'California Legislation', *The Journal of Commerce*, 30 January 1907, 12.

[426] Ibid. Because of Jones's previous employment in the insurance business, his nomination attracted the opposition of the congressman John Curtin, which was greeted with amusement in California (quoted from the *San Francisco Chronicle* by Coogan in *Proceedings of the annual meeting of the Fire Underwriters' Association of the Pacific* 1910, 126).

[427] Printed in the *Coast Review*, April 1907, 160–162. The draft did not include an earthquake clause.

[428] The draft was written by W. J. Dutton (Fireman's Fund, Home Fire & Marine), W. H. Lowden (Norwich Union) and G. H. Spencer (probably Aetna). Copies were distributed to the respective offices and discussed. The criticism and additional proposals of the

The deliberations showed that there were objections to all concepts. The lawyer T. C. Coogan voiced the misgivings of the insurance industry in the Assembly.[429] He criticised Wolf's draft and advocated to adopt the New York form as precisely as possible in order to promote legal uniformity with other states.[430] In fact, the 'Wolf Bills' were the first to be rejected by the legislative committees of the Senate and the Assembly.[431]

The other drafts met with resistance in insurance circles because of certain clauses that increased the risk of the insurers.[432] After exhaustive discussions with the Attorney General, the Insurance Commissioner and representatives of the insurance business[433] had not brought about positive results, the legislative commissions rejected all of the drafts in a joint session and replaced them with a 'Committee Substitute for Senate Bills 21 and 394'.[434] They made this action publicly known by means of a flyer that was reprinted in the *Journal of Commerce*. According to this flyer, the members of the legislature were willing to radically change the terms of insurance in favour of the policyholders. Limitations of the accepted risks through earthquake, collapse or explosion clauses were not planned. In addition, there was a lack of regulations for the prevention of insurance fraud.[435] In the future, the fire insurers would no longer be able to influence the structure of risk:

---

insurers—among others by C. M. Kinne (Liverpool, London & Globe), R. W. Osborn (Pennsylvania Fire), C. D. Haven (Liverpool, London & Globe; President, Board of Fire Underwriters of the Pacific), R. V. Watt (Royal, Queen) and W. H. Sexton (General Adjuster, Fireman's Fund)—were passed on to Sacramento (Coogan in *Proceedings of the annual meeting of the Fire Underwriters' Association of the Pacific* 1910, 127).

[429] Hearing, Committee on Insurance and Insurance Laws of the California Assembly. 'Favors New York Form/ Opposition to Commissioner Wolf's Standard Policy for California', *The Journal of Commerce*, 9 February 1907, 13. Coogan was intimately connected to the Board of Fire Underwriters of the Pacific as an adviser and presumably represented them. He was considered to be the author of the standard policy draft of the Board of Fire Underwriters ('California Standard Policy/ Senate Committee Adopts Form Drawn by O. G. Jones', *The Journal of Commerce*, 20 February 1907, 13).

[430] Coogan was silent on the weak fallen building clause, 'which seems to favour the companies' (*The Journal of Commerce*, 9 February 1907, 13).

[431] Coogan in *Proceedings of the annual meeting of the Fire Underwriters' Association of the Pacific* 1910, 127.

[432] *The Journal of Commerce*, 20 February 1907, 13.

[433] Coogan in *Proceedings of the annual meeting of the Fire Underwriters' Association of the Pacific* 1910, 127.

[434] Printed in the *Journal of the Senate of the State of California, 37th Session of the Legislature*, 1032–1034. The name makes it clear that the new draft replaced that of Wolf's (Bill no. 221) and Leavitt/Jones's (Bill no. 394).

[435] Printed in the *Journal of the Senate of the State of California, 37th Session of the Legislature*, 1032–1034. The 'Proposed California Standard Fire Policy/Contains Many Dangerous

Section 5. No rider may be attached to any policy and no contract may be made between the insured and the insurer under and by virtue of which the liability of the insurer shall be diminished, suspended, or avoided, except as provided in the foregoing form of policy. All that portion of any such rider or contract as is in violation of the provisions of this section is null and void.[436]

The representatives of the insurance industry immediately protested against these and other prescriptions. They declared that they would be unable to continue their business activities in California under these circumstances.[437] Senator Leavitt attempted to mollify them and to limit the prohibition of riders to the question of earthquake and collapse damages. His proposal, however, met with resistance in the Senate,[438] as there was little or no willingness to negotiate with the insurers in Sacramento.[439] The Senate accepted the policy draft and forwarded it to the Assembly.[440] In addition, the regulation constraining all foreign companies to make a deposit of $200,000 began to take shape.[441]

In the meantime, public criticism of the planned law was increasing.[442] The opposition did not only originate locally, but also in the insurance centres on the East Coast. Several managers threatened the governor with the withdrawal of their companies from California.[443] Premiums had

---

Provisions not in N.Y. Form' was critical of this point, *The Journal of Commerce*, 5 March 1907, 13.

[436] Committee Substitute for Senate Bills 21 and 394, section. According to sec. 6, additions to the adopted risks were permitted (*Journal of the Senate of the State of California, 37th Session of the Legislature*, 1034).

[437] A committee of underwriters protested to the Assembly. Members of the committee were Wm. Dutton, Whitney Palache (Hartford Fire) and C. D. Haven (Coogan, *Proceedings of the annual meeting of the Fire Underwriters' Association of the Pacific* 1910, 127).

[438] For example, Senator Wolfe (San Francisco) argued that if the riders were allowed to remain in this form, the standard form would be worthless ('California Legislation/ Plan to excinde Earthquake and Falling Wall Clause From Policy', *The Journal of Commerce*, 26 February 1907, 13).

[439] The insurers had proposed that a committee comprised of the chairmen of the Committee and five 'gentlemen' to be named by the governor should draft a new standard form. But the senate members who were consulted rejected additional discussion (Coogan in *Proceedings of the annual meeting of the Fire Underwriters' Association of the Pacific* 1910, 128). The adoption of the 'Committee Substitute for Senats Bills 21 and 394' by the Committee on Insurance and Insurance Laws was announced in the *Journal of the Senate of the State of California, 37th Session of the Legislature*, 1010.

[440] *Journal of the Senate of the State of California, 37th Session of the Legislature*, 1110 et seq.

[441] 'Oppose to harsh Laws', *The Journal of Commerce*, 6 March 1907, 13.

[442] 'Proposed California Standard Fire Policy/ Contains Many Dangerous Provisions not in N.Y. Form', *The Journal of Commerce*, 5 March 1907, 13.

[443] Coogan in *Proceedings of the annual meeting of the Fire Underwriters' Association of the Pacific* 1910, 128.

already risen drastically. It became difficult to acquire any insurance coverage in San Francisco.[444] That is why the Merchants' Association of San Francisco joined in the insurers' protests. They wrote to all the members of the Senate and the Assembly that the legislation had exceeded rational boundaries and threatened to drive welcome members of the business community out of California.[445]

The protests seemed to be heard. The Assembly enacted a few changes in the standard policy draft, especially permitting the use of riders. At a closer look, however, this cooperation proved to be deceptive: not only did the insurance companies have to clearly highlight changes in contract terms, but the policyholder was, in the future, required to sign every clause that deviated from the standard form individually.[446] Officially, this reading was intended to provide clarification for the insured party, but it bordered on a stigmatisation of those insurance companies who wished to provide their own concept of risk.

One day prior to the vote on the law, the President of the Firemen's Fund (San Francisco), William J. Dutton, warned of an additional rise in the premiums and the withdrawal of many companies from California.[447] San Francisco would be endangered as the insurance centre of the west.[448] Nevertheless, the Senate still voted for the 'Committee Substitute for Senate Bills 21 and 394' on March 9.[449] Shortly thereafter, Governor Gillett received the bill in order to sign it into law.[450]

---

[444] 'Hard to get Insurance', *The Journal of Commerce*, 4 March 1907, 15; 'California Standard Form', *The Journal of Commerce*, 8 March 1907, 13; Mackenzie 1907.

[445] *The Journal of Commerce*, 6 March 1907, 13.

[446] 'Section 5. No rider may be attached to any policy and no contract may be made between the insured and the insurer under and by virtue of which the liability of the insurer shall be diminished, suspended, or avoided, except the same shall be printed in red ink and attached thereto, and the printing thereon shall be in type larger than that used for printing the other conditions of the policy; and in case of any such addition or additions being made, there shall be printed in red ink and large bold-faced type at the head of the policy whereon such riders are attached the words 'This policy contains provisions not found in the California standard form'. Any rider restricting, reducing, or limiting the liability of the insurer shall be accepted and signed by the insured or his authorized agent before the same shall take effect' (*Journal of the Senate of the State of California, 37th Session of the Legislature*, 1668 et seq.; 'California Policy Law', *The Journal of Commerce*, 8 March 1907, 13).

[447] *The Journal of Commerce*, 8 March 1907, 13.

[448] Ibid.; a similar statement from another manager: 'California Standard Form', *The Journal of Commerce*, 12 March 1907, 13.

[449] *Journal of the Senate of the State of California, 37th Session of the Legislature*, 1665, 1669.

[450] 'Standard Fire Insurance Policies/California Assembly Passes Committee Report', *The Journal of Commerce*, 11 March 1907, 13; Coogan in *Proceedings of the annual meeting of the Fire Underwriters' Association of the Pacific* 1910, 128.

Now, the opponents of the law pulled out all the stops to persuade Governor Gillet to veto the bill. The most important signs of protest were telegrams from prominent New York companies and the British Fire Offices Committee addressed to the California governor[451] as well as the public statement of the San Francisco Chamber of Commerce criticising the standard policy. Three members of the Chamber informed the governor of their position.[452] In addition, a committee from the insurance industry— W. Palache, W. Dutton, George H. Tyson und C. D. Haven—paid a visit to the governor.[453]

At the end of March, Gillett made use of his veto and refused to sign the Standard Policy Bill.[454] He defended his rejection in interviews: he too regarded the rider clause as unacceptable. Moreover, he took the general lack of sympathy for the bill seriously.[455] The governor proposed the establishment of a new commission composed of underwriters, businessmen, bankers and the Insurance Commission that would be able to draft a new standard policy.[456] However, no moves in this direction were made until December of 1907.

---

[451] In the New York telegram, the companies Home (New York), Aetna, German American, Royal Exchange, Phoenix of London, Continental, Fidelity, Phoenix (Hartford), In Co. of North America, Hartford, Sun Fire, National (Hartford), Fire Association, Hanover, Caledonian, Norwich Union, North British and Mercantile announced their withdrawal from California. The precise wording: copies of telegrams sent to to Governor Gillett 'About the Standard Form', *The Cost Review*, March 1907, 140; also in this paper, a report on an additional telegram from Springfield Fire & Marine; report of the New York telegram: 'California Policy', *The Journal of Commerce*, 15 March 1907, 13; on the British telegram: Trebilcock 1998, 279.

[452] In addition, all California Chambers of Commerce were admonished to prevent the adoption of the 'Leavitt insurance standard policy bill' (*The Journal of Commerce*, 21 March 1907, 13).

[453] The committee consisted of W. Palache, W. Dutton, George H. Tyson (German Alliance, Phoenix/Hartford, New Hampshire Fire) and C. D. Haven. Also present were O. G. Jones, whose presence Governor Gillett requested as his most important adviser. Jones's scepticism moved Gillett to exercise his veto (Gillett, Appendix to the *Journals of the Senate and the Assembly*, 9 January 1907, *38th Session of the Legislature of the State of California*, vol. I, 3–26 (citation 25 *et seq.*); Coogan in *Proceedings of the annual meeting of the Fire Underwriters' Association of the Pacific* 1910, 128.

[454] 'California Governor Vetoes the Standard Policy Bill', *The Coast Review*, March 1907, 138.

[455] Coogan in *Proceedings of the annual meeting of the Fire Underwriters' Association of the Pacific* 1910, 129.

[456] 'California Bill Not Signed', *The Journal of Commerce*, 26 March 1907, 13.

3.2.2.6. *Reform of the Law of Civil Procedure and of the Law of Supervision (1907)*

In the same session of 1907, the California legislature enacted some additional reforms that were accepted by Governor Gillett. The senators and the assemblymen had recognised the importance of the burden of proof in the cases against the insurance companies following the San Francisco catastrophe. In order to prevent the insurers from shifting this burden to the insured in the future, they inserted a proviso into the Code of Civil Procedure to make exactly this transformation impossible.[457] After a short period, however, a California court declared this proviso to be unconstitutional because it discriminated against the insurance companies with respect to procedural law.[458]

On March 8, 1907, the entire part of the Political Code that affected the Insurance Commission and the regulation of the insurance industry was revised.[459] The members of the legislature settled on a moderate deposit law. Companies without headquarters in the United States were allowed to pursue their business interests in California only after they had made special financial deposits in one of the states of the union.[460] Moreover, the holder of insurance policies obtained the right to ask questions about his terms of insurance to the Insurance Commissioner which the latter had to answer or forward for a mandatory answer on the part of the given company.[461]

---

[457] Code of Civil Procedure, sec. 437a.: 'In an action to recover upon a contract of insurance wherein the defendant claims exemption from liability upon the ground that, although the proximate cause of the loss was a peril insured against, the loss was remotely caused by or would not have been occurred but for a peril excepted in the contract of insurance, the defendant shall in his answer set forth and specify the peril excepted contributed to the loss or itself caused the peril insured against, he shall in his answer set forth and specify upon what premises or at what place the peril excepted caused the peril insured against'. Code of Civil Procedure, enacted statutes 1907, 836.

[458] Board of Education v Alliance Assurance Co. (C.C.), Fed. Rep. 994. *Insurance Laws of the State of California* 1912, 86.

[459] *Partial recodification of the insurance laws of the State of California* 1907, chapter 119; 39th Annual Report of the Insurance Commissioner of the State of California for the year 1906, 25.

[460] Political Code, sec. 594a, enacted statutes 1907, 143; amended, statutes 1909, 910. *Insurance Laws of the State of California* 1912, 10 et seq.; *Partial recodification of the insurance laws of the State of California* 1907, chapter 119.

[461] Political Code, sec. 598, repealed and enacted statutes 1907, 148. *Insurance Laws of the State of California* 1912, 16 et seq.; *Partial recodification of the insurance laws of the State of California* 1907, chapter 119.

3.2.2.7. *The Market Decides it All: The Insurers' Discussion and Removal of the Earthquake Clauses (1907)*

In the months following the governor's veto, the question concerning the earthquake regulation was decided for California and the entire North American continent. In May of 1907, it was known that the introduction of an earthquake clause was discussed by the Board of Fire Underwriters of the Pacific[462]—at least for the mountainous territories on which the *Coast Review* had any information. The journal cited a remarkably strict draft: 'This company is not liable for loss caused directly or indirectly by earthquake or other convulsion of Nature, nor for any loss occurring at the time of or within sixty days after the occurrence, unless the assured can establish to the satisfaction of the company that such loss was not occasioned either directly or indirectly thereby'.[463] However, in view of the opposition of several large American companies, it was improbable that the companies active in California would be able to agree upon the introduction of such an earthquake clause. While it was true that legal necessity to accept the earthquake risk had become unlikely in the wake of the governor's intervention, this necessity could nevertheless develop on the Californian fire insurance market without State assistance: 'If two or three leading American companies, which now oppose the clause, refuse to write with it, that will end the controversy. The foreign companies now writing the clause will then, we believe, write the standard form'.[464] This prediction made by the *Coast Review* proved to be correct. The efforts of the Board of Fire Underwriters ran aground. At the same time, the group of companies that voluntarily accepted the risk of earthquakes in exchange for additional premiums was growing. Among them were many of the 'dollar for dollar companies' that had recognised an opportunity to increase their market position by waiving the earthquake clause. The pressure they exercised upon the competitors increased at the end of June 1907 following the decision of the British Fire Offices Committee that allowed members to accept liability for earthquake damages throughout the world.

There were no initiatives to introduce earthquake clauses. The reinsurers from the Earthquake Commission, whose proposals had in the meantime set the standard for future exclusionary clauses on the European continent, still refrained from sending their study to North America.

---

[462] *Der Versicherungsfreund*, 20 May 1907, 1 *et seq.*; 24 June 1907 Spycket to Simon, SR/FA A9.0–32/yellow file folder (correspondence mainly Cologne Re 10/1906–8/1907), 118 *et seq.*
[463] *The Coast Review*, June 1907, 297.
[464] Ibid.

As of October of 1907,[465] many insurance companies active in California removed the earthquake clauses from their policies. The *Coast Review* counted only eleven British, German and American companies whose policies includes earthquake clauses.[466] There may have been more, but by no means over thirty, the previous year's number.[467] Many companies used the opportunity to call attention to themselves and publicly announced their waiver of the exclusionary clauses: among these were Northern Union,[468] Glens Falls and Security,[469] Hanover,[470] Phoenix Association (London) and Pelican (New York),[471] Commercial Union and Palatine.[472]

The insurance press accurately identified the companies' motivation as stemming from the fear of losing their share in the Californian insurance market.[473] Other companies—among them the London Royal Exchange—decided not to forgo earthquake clauses and withdrew from California.[474]

3.2.2.8. *The Development and Success of the Second Standard Policy Draft (1907–1909)*

In view of this self-regulation within the fire insurance industry—whose dynamic influence no company could escape—, legislation played a merely secondary role in the question of earthquake regulations. In December of 1907, Governor Gillett convened an interim commission that discussed the introduction of a standard policy anew.[475] Once again, the larger California business organisations and the fire insurers cartel were represented:

---

[465] Previously: Phoenix (Hartford); *The Adjuster* 33, September 1906, 84.

[466] 'Taken out', *The Coast Review*, October 1907, 531.

[467] See the table in the annexe listing the companies involved in the San Francisco catastrophe.

[468] 'Northern Union Removes the Word Earthquake From Its Policies', *The Coast Review*, November 1907, 642.

[469] 'Glens Falls and Security Also Take Out Earthquake Clause', *The Coast Review*, November 1907, 642.

[470] 'The Hanover in California', *The Coast Review*, November 1907, 642.

[471] 'Phoenix and Pelican Take Out Earthquake Clause', *The Coast Review*, November 1907, 642. The Phoenix company had introduced the earthquake clause only one year previously (Trebilcock 1998, 278).

[472] 'Drop Earthquake Clause', *The Journal of Commerce*, 12 October 1907, 9.

[473] *The Coast Review*, October 1907, 531.

[474] Supple 1970, 250.

[475] Weinstock and Maloney 1955, chapters 2 and 9.

Table 14. Members of the interim commission for the creation of a standard policy. Coogan in *Proceedings of the annual meeting of the Fire Underwriters' Association of the Pacific* 1910, 129.[476]

Organisation/Institution	Representatives
Insurance Commissioner	E. Myron Wolf (Chair of the Commission)
San Francisco Clearing House	Percy T. Morgan (Pres. der California Wine Association)
San Francisco Chamber of Commerce	F. W. Van Sicklen (Dodge, Sweeney & Co.)
San Francisco Merchants' Association	Allen W. Wright (Attorney)
Merchants' Exchange	Ernest Reuben Lilienthal (President of the Lilienthal Co.)
Board of Fire Underwriters of the Pacific	Wm. J. Dutton (President of the Fireman's Fund Insurance Co.)
San Francisco Board of Trade	Joseph Kirk (Attorney)
Representing the governor	Fletcher A. Cutler (Attorney, Judge)

In addition, the deliberations of the Commission were subject to the influence of external developments. Occupying pride of place was the effort to originate a nationwide standardisation of the standard policy form. In 1907, Evans had failed to push through his draft of a standard policy in California and New York.[477] However, the National Association of Credit Men picked up his idea concerning a comprehensive standardisation of the policy.[478] Several speakers at the National Convention of Insurance Commissioners of 1908 demanded the same,[479] especially its Chairman Charles C. Lemert.[480] The California Insurance Commissioner Wolf did

---

[476] Coogan in *Proceedings of the annual meeting of the Fire Underwriters' Association of the Pacific* 1910, 129. The 41st Annual Report of the Insurance Commissioner of the State of California for the year 1908, 19, names the Attorneys at law T. Coogan and Lester H. Jacobs, the General adjuster of the Fireman's Fund, W. Sexton, and R. Gray from the Department of the Insurance Commissioner in addition.

[477] On Evans' first draft, see [note] in *Insurance Monitor*, 5 January 1907, 5; on his second and improved draft, 'New Standard Policy Form', *Insurance Monitor*, 6 May 1907, 174.

[478] At its annual meeting in Denver, 25 June 1908 (Judge Lemert, 'Desirability of a Simplified Form of Standard Fire Insurance Policy', *National Convention of Insurance Commissioners, Proceedings* 1908, 255).

[479] Carefully formulated: Hon. Reau E. Folk (Tennessee), President's Annual Address, *National Convention of Insurance Commissioners, Proceedings* 1908, 20 *et seq.*; Statement Young, *National Convention of Insurance Commissioners, Proceedings* 1908, 256.

[480] Judge Lemert, 'Desirability of a Simplified Form of Standard Fire Insurance Policy', *National Convention of Insurance Commissioners, Proceedings* 1908, 256.

not attend every session of the Convention,[481] but remained in constant contact with Lemert during the development of the new standard policy draft.[482]

After more than one year, the Commission presented the results of their work to the governor.[483] The New York standard policy had obviously been the model for the new draft, and the committee had simply brought it up to date in specific respects.[484] Gillett was impressed and recommended that the California legislature adopt the draft.[485] At the end of January of 1909, Senator J. Clem Bates and Assemblyman Harry W. Pulcifer introduced the draft into their respective legislative bodies as a bill.[486] Both houses forwarded it to the appropriate committees for discussion.[487]

The public observers interested in the matter received the new version with great acclaim. The *Journal of Commerce* praised it as a compromise between the insurance companies and the economic associations.[488] An anonymous author called an 'expert' declared, 'On the whole [...] it is probably the best form of policy, from the companies' standpoint, that has been adopted for a standard in any State where the New York form is not used'.[489] Special attention was paid to the degree of liability and

---

[481] *National Convention of Insurance Commissioners, Proceedings* 1908, 23.

[482] *The Journal of Commerce*, 16 December 1908, 13.

[483] Coogan in *Proceedings of the annual meeting of the Fire Underwriters' Association of the Pacific* 1910, 130. The article 'California Laws', *The Journal of Commerce* (16 November 1908, 13) reports on the high expectations on the legislation.

[484] In greater detail: 'Standard Fire Policy Before California Legislature is Modeled on New York Form', *The Journal of Commerce*, 5 February 1909, 13.

[485] Gillett, 'Biennial Message to the Legislature, Jan. 9, 1909', *Appendix to the Journals of the Senate and the Assembly, 38th Session of the Legislature of the State of California*, vol. 1, 3–26 (quotation 25 *et seq.*). Cited by *The Weekly Underwriter*, 16 January 1909, 45 *et seq.* The importance of the occasion can be shown by the fact that the seriously ill Gillett raised only this one point at the opening of the session.

[486] 'Senate Bill no. 706' (28 January 1908), *Journal of the Senate of the State of California, 38th Session of the Legislature*, 322. 'Assembly Bill no. 913', *Journal of the Assembly of the State of California, 38th Session of the Legislature*, 314.

[487] In the Committee on Corporations of the Senat were J. C. Bates (Chairman, Rep.), C. B. Bills (Rep.), C. Brownell (Rep.), L. G. Burnett (Rep.), T. F. Finn (Rep. and U.L.), T. J. Kennedy (Dem. and I. L.), E. O. Miller (Dem.), L. H. Roseberry (Rep.), G. Walker (Rep.), R. J. Welch (Rep. and U.L.), L. A. Wright (Rep.), H. B. McCartney (Rep.) and in der Commission on insurance and insurance law of the Assembly H. W. Pulcifer (Rep.), A. M. Dean (Rep.), J. N. O. Rech (Rep.), R. Melrose (Rep.), E. L. Hawk (Rep.), E. J. Callan (Rep.), H. N. Beatty (Rep.), K. C. Gillis (Dem.), J. L. Mendenhall (Rep.). *Journal of the Senate of the State of California, 38th Session of the Legislature*, 50; *Journal of the Assembly of the State of California, 38th Session of the Legislature*, 92.

[488] *The Journal of Commerce*, 5 February 1909, 13.

[489] Comprehensive statement: 'New California Policy Proposed Standard Form Reviewed By an Expert', *The Journal of Commerce*, 6 March 1909, 13. Similarly positive was Coogan's estimation (1910, 131).

to the regulations for departures from the policy.[490] Additions or altera-
tions to the policy were to be permitted; although they had to be made
clearly recognisable,[491] not every limitation on liability had to be separately signed by the policyholder, in contrast to the failed policy of 1907.
The condition had lost its stigmatising character, thus facilitating the use
of the earthquake clauses.[492] Nevertheless, all limitations of liability, i.e.,
earthquake clauses as well, required acceptance by the Insurance Commission. Wolf warned early in the proceedings that infringements of this
condition would be treated as offences.[493]

Following minor changes by the Commissions,[494] the draft bill was
adopted in both houses of the legislature[495] and signed by the governor.[496]
On the 1st of August, the California Standard Form of Fire Insurance[497]
entered into effect.[498]

3.2.2.9. Reactions from the Insurance Industry and the Public

The insurers immediately adjusted to the new situation. The Board of
Fire Underwriters of the Pacific established a committee[499] that clarified

---

[490] *The Journal of Commerce*, 5 February 1909, 13.

[491] 'Section 8. No clause shall be inserted or rider attached affecting the standard form
liability of the insurer for loss or damage by fire occasioned either directly or indirectly by
earthquake, hurricane, volcanic eruption or other disturbance of nature, unless the same
shall be printed in red ink in type larger than small pica and at the head of the policy there
shall be printed in red ink and in large bold-faced type the words: 'This policy contains
limitations of liability not permitted in the California standard form'. An act to establish
a standard form of fire insurance policy and to prevent variations therefrom, excepting
under certain stated conditions and restrictions, *Appendix to the Journals of the Senate and
the Assembly, 37th Session of the Legislature of the State of California*, vol. I, 411.

[492] 'Insurance Legislation/California', *The Weekly Underwriter*, 3 April 1909, 246.

[493] 41st Annual Report of the Insurance Commissioner of the State of California for the
year 1908, 20.

[494] The word 'direct' was excised from the passage 'against all direct loss or damage by
fire'. The insurers regarded this change as unimportant, since they corresponded to the
court's interpretation ('Standard Fire Policy Bill in California Legislature Favorably Reported',
The Journal of Commerce, 20 February 1909, 13; Weinstock and Maloney, chapter 9).

[495] Unanimously in the Senate on the 26th of February, 1909, and in the Assembly on
the 11th of March 1909, *Journal of the Senate of the State of California, 38th Session of the
Legislature*, 1076, 1596.

[496] On the 23rd of March, 1909, *Journal of the Senate of the State of California, 38th Session
of the Legislature*, 2084.

[497] Printed in the 41st Annual Report of the Insurance Commissioner of the State of
California for the year 1908, 21–26 and in *Insurance Laws of the State of California* 1912,
125–131.

[498] Coogan, *Proceedings of the annual meeting of the Fire Underwriters' Association of the
Pacific* 1910, 130.

[499] The members were R. W. Osborn (Pennsylvania Fire), H. Folger (German-American,
Hartford Fire), E. T. Niebling (Commercial Union), F. B. Kellam (Royal) and W. Speyer

the necessary measures on the part of the insurance industry and made reports to the companies.[500] The question of the liability for earthquake damages remained in the discretion of the individual insurance companies; they did not establish a common policy. But the introduction of the standard policy once again gave one group of companies the impulse to abandon their earthquake clauses: Phoenix (London),[501] Caledonian, Caledonian-American, Scotch Underwriters[502] and Svea were among these companies.[503]

The additional use of earthquake clauses became impossible as a matter of business policy. The *Coast Review* reported in April of 1909:

> The few companies *inserting* earthquake clauses in their policies [...] are suffering from 'discrimination', or 'selection against' [...] on the Pacific Coast. [...] if a company in its policy asserts that there is danger and that it will assume no liability therefor, the property-owner sits up and takes notice, and of course gives to more liberal companies his best business surely and all in fact that they will readily write. The new standard policy form will make this discrimination still more marked than at present, when many are not aware of the existence of the clause in their policies. We advise these companies to accept the standard form without addition of a quake clause rider, and allow their agents to share of the good and profitable business of the Pacific Coast [...].[504]

The last of the earthquake clauses disappeared very quickly. They were no longer included in E. R. Hardy's collection of more than one hundred pages of standard clauses from 1913—that is, the approved additions to the standard policies.[505]

3.2.3. *Preliminary Results*

The investigation of the developments in California leads to the at first surprising result that the introduction of earthquake clauses did not fail at all because of the introduction of the obligatory standard policy. The

---

(New Zealand). Coogan in *Proceedings of the annual meeting of the Fire Underwriters' Association of the Pacific* 1910, 130.

[500] Ibid., 131.

[501] *The Journal of Commerce*, 24 December 1908, 9.

[502] 'Caledonia Takes Out Earthquake Clause', *The Coast Review*, April 1909, 214.

[503] 'Svea Takes Earthquake Clause Out of All Policies', *The Coast Review*, June 1909, 311.

[504] 'Marked Discrimination Against Quake-Clause Policies', *The Coast Review*, April 1909, 204; emphasis in the original.

[505] Cf. Hardy 1913, 89–98 (New York), 93 (Massachusetts), 98–101 (California) and the entries on the individual companies in the annexe.

decision resulted from developments on the market. In this respect, the reinsurers' project of the reinsurers remained unsuccessful in Great Britain, the Netherlands and California for similar reasons.

This result is remarkable because very different circumstances prevailed in these three countries. The British Offices and some companies on the American East Coast commanded large cash reserves and were able to make business policy decisions independently of the influences exercised by the reinsurance industry. Other American and all Dutch companies were facing severe financial pressures; they were the ones upon whom the Earthquake Commission could have most likely exerted pressure. However, the reinsurers officially declined to send their study overseas in order not to disturb the ongoing damage settlements and court cases. Thus, their concept received little attention in the United States.

An additional difference lies in the perception of the chance of future earthquakes as a risk or—in the Netherlands—as a present danger. However, there was a lack of additional impulses in all three business areas that would have intensified an interest in the introduction of earthquake clauses. As soon as individual companies began to aggressively accept liability for earthquake damages in these insurance markets, dynamics that no insurance provider could ignore developed. In the Netherlands, it was only the agreement on standard earthquake clauses that failed; the individual fire insurers could continue to decide whether they would accept the risk or not. In California, the exclusion of the earthquake danger would have meant the end of their business activities for each company.

The fact that the San Francisco catastrophe generated processes of standardisation in California and other states in the country that differed from those in Europe—namely the additional spread of the standard policies—is thus only a phenomenon on the periphery of the history of the standardisation of the earthquake clause. However, it is nevertheless interesting, for it underscores that a tendency towards standardisation of the basic principles governing contracts also prevailed in the United States.

3.3. No Consensus on the Earthquake Clause

In some States, there were no clear developments in favour of or against the introduction of the earthquake clause.

3.3.1. *Character of National Developments*

3.3.1.1. Switzerland

In Switzerland, the organisation of many fire insurance institutions according to the rules and principles of public law constituted the chief impediment to the implementation of earthquake clauses. Cantonal and urban insurance institutions dominated the Swiss insurance industry. In addition, there were a few public limited companies from neighbouring countries. The most important domestic fire insurance companies were *Helvetia* (St. Gallen), Basel Fire Insurance Company (*Bâloise* or *Baseler Feuer*) and the *Schweizerische Mobiliar-Feuerversicherung* ('Movables Fire Insurance Company') from Berne.[506]

None of the public insurance institutions excluded earthquake-related fire damages. Consequently, most of the directors cordially acknowledged the receipt of the study, but rejected changes in the contract terms.[507] Many of them justified their positions in detail. The *Staatskasse* ('state bank') in Solothurn wrote:

> [...] our establishment is a State mutual institution whose task is to protect its members against fire damages at the risk of suffering large losses. Since our establishment, as just mentioned, is State-supported, changes in the legal terms can only be made by legislation, and it would be questionable whether in the face of the current atmosphere further conditions could be implemented by means of a public referendum (trans.).[508]

To the fire insurance institutions in the cantons of Berne and Zurich, the implementation of comprehensive earthquake clauses seemed possible

---

[506] Realty insurance was obligatory almost everywhere. Emminghaus, *Handwörterbuch der Staatswissenschaften* 1st ed. (1909), vol. 4, 94 *et seq.*

[507] 20 July 1907 *Staatskasse* ('State Bank') Solothurn to SR, SR/FA A9.0–32/yellow folder (correspondence Swiss insurance companies), 36*ff*; 24 July 1907 finance department of the canton of Lucerne to SR, SR/FA 1907, 40; 25 July 1907 *Eidgenössisches Versicherungsamt Bern* to SR, SR/FA 1907, 42; 26 July 1907 finance directors of the *Kanton* Basel-region to SR, SR/FA 1907, 41; 19 August 1907 *Assekuranz-Kommission* of the *Kanton* Appenzell ti SR, SR/FA 1907 43; 30 August 1907 *Département militaire et des assurances du Canton de Vaud* to SR, SR/FA 1907, 44; 6 September 1907 *Brandversicherungs-Anstalt* of the *Kanton* Zurich to SR, SR/FA 1907, 50; 7 September 1907 *Brandversicherungs-Anstalt* of the *Kanton* Bern (Schwab) to SR, SR/FA 1907, 52; 9 September 1907 finance department of the city of Basel to SR, SR/FA 1907, 54; 12 September 1907 finance department of the *Kanton* St. Gallen to SR, SR/FA 1907, 55 *et seq.*; 17 September 1907 *Kantonale Brandversicherungsanstalt* Niewalden to SR, SR/FA 1907, 57; 26 September 1907 *Aarg. Versicherungsamt* to SR, SR/FA 1907, 62; 26 November 1907 *Kanton* tax commission Schaffhausen to SR, SR/FA 1907, 72 *et seq.*

[508] 20 July 1907 *Staatskasse* Solothurn to SR, SR/FA, 36 *et seq.* Similarly: 26 November 1907 *Kantonales Steuerkommissariat* Schaffhausen to SR, SR/FA, 72 *et seq.*

only if the gap in the protection of the insured would be closed again through earthquake insurances.[509] The finance department of the canton of St. Gallen put it more succinctly: exclusionary terms did not exist. Fire damages for which the ordinary premiums for the coverage of the annual expenditures proved insufficient would 'be paid for by the *State* according to the principle of equity' (trans.). [510] In Neuchâtel, the position was that changes in the law were 'very time-consuming' (trans.).[511] In Aargau, moreover, the burden of proof could not be transferred to the insured as the cause of fire was established by a public investigation.[512]

Many insurance personnel arrived at the pre-emptive and astonishing conclusion that since they did not live in an earthquake region,[513] earthquake clauses were utterly unnecessary.[514] After all, the reinsurers had explicitly pointed to the historical earthquake-fire in Basel. Nevertheless, some insurers had advocated for the exclusion of the earthquake danger. Schwab, the Director of the Fire Insurance Institution of the canton of Berne, wrote to Simon: '[The] public (State-run) establishments [...] will scarcely wish to completely ignore the movement that is currently developing [...]' (trans.).[515] But even he considered it unlikely that revisions in the law would be undertaken solely for the purpose of adopting an earthquake clause.[516] On October 7, 1907, Schwab once again wrote to the Swiss Re, this time in his function as President of the *Vereinigung kantonaler Feuerversicherungs-Anstalten* ('Union of Cantonal Fire Insurance Institutions'). He cautiously indicated that the question of the earthquake clause could be discussed at the next meeting of the members and thus

---

[509] 7 September 1907 *Brandversicherungs-Anstalt* of the *Kanton* Bern to SR, SR/FA, 52. Similarly: 6 September 1907 *Brandversicherungs-Anstalt* of the *Kanton* Zürich to SR, SR/FA, 50.

[510] 12 September 1907 finance department of the *Kanton* St. Gallen to SR, SR/FA, 55 *et seq.* 'State' spaced out in the original.

[511] 25 September 1907 *République & Canton de Neuchâtel* to SR, SR/FA, 60.

[512] 26 September 1907 *Aarg. Versicherungsamt* to SR, SR/FA A9.0–32/ yellow file folder (correspondence Swiss insurance companies), 62.

[513] 19 August 1907 *Assekuranz-Kommission* of the *Kanton* Appenzell to SR, SR/FA, 43; 12 September 1907 finance departement of the *Kanton* St. Gallen to SR, SR/FA, 55 *et seq.*

[514] 30 August 1907 *Département militaire et des assurances du Canton de Vaud* to SR, SR/FA, 44; 17 September 1907 *Kantonale Brandversicherungsanstalt* Niewalden to SR, SR/FA, 57.

[515] 7 September 1907 *Brandversicherungs-Anstalt* of the *Kanton* Bern to SR, SR/FA, 52; similarly: 26 September 1907 *Aarg. Versicherungsamt* to SR, SR/FA, 62; 26 November 1907 *Kantonales Steuerkommissariat* Schaffhausen to SR, SR/FA, 72 *et seq.*; 25 September 1907 *République & Canton de Neuchâtel* to SR, SR/FA, 60.

[516] 7 September 1907 *Brandversicherungs-Anstalt* of the *Kanton* Bern to SR, SR/FA, 52.

indirectly exercise some influence upon legislators. He proved unable to inspire unlimited confidence in the reinsurers.[517]

Along with the sobriety induced by the attitudes towards reform in the State-run insurance institutions, the probability that the private insurance companies would adopt the earthquake clause had also decreased. In May of 1907, the directors of the *Helvetia*,[518] which had been involved in the San Francisco catastrophe, had responded to an according question from Simon[519] that a revision of the general insurance terms and conditions 'in which, of course, the earthquake clause would be included in the clearest and most precise form' (trans.) was being worked on.[520] The Directors suggested that the *Verband konzessionierter schweizerischer Versicherungs-gesellschaften* ('Federation of Licensed Swiss Insurance Companies') take the matter under advisement and authorise Professor Hans Roelli as 'the most qualified expert' (trans.) to head the discussion. The President of the Federation, Dr. Schärtlin, had expressed his willingness to raise the matter at its next meeting. The Directors of *Helvetia* also promised that they would try to introduce standard terms together with other insurance companies should the Federation not do so.[521]

In September, *Helvetia* sounded a sceptical note. Only the Bâloise was apparently prepared to go along; the other insurers dragged their feet because the Swiss legislative organs were drafting a law on insurance contracts at this time. For *Helvetia* and *Bâloise* to exercise any influence on the legislative process appeared impossible, '[...] but if the draft assumed the definitive force of law, the Swiss companies and those foreign companies active in Switzerland might well agree upon a new clause that would then be forwarded to the Parliament for approval' (trans.).[522] In November, this hope was dashed as well. Rather dispiritedly, the Directors at *Helvetia* concluded that the chances of the private insurers' introducing an earthquake clause into Switzerland were 'very low' (trans.). Apparently,

---

[517] 7 October 1907 *Vereinigung kantonaler Feuerversicherungs-Anstalten* Bern (Schwab) to SR, SR/FA, 70.

[518] The *Helvetia* presumably indemnified a damage of a million dollars and retreated from California in 1907. Cf. the table of companies involved in indemnifying fire damages in San Francisco attached in the annexe.

[519] 19 May 1907 Simon to Helvetia, SR/FA A9.0–32/ yellow file folder (correspondence Swiss insurance companies), 74.

[520] Letter of 22 May 1907 from Helvetia to SR, SR/FA 1907, 75.

[521] Ibid.

[522] 24 September 1907 Helvetia to SR, SR/FA 1907, 59.

the other companies took their cue from the negative stance adopted by the State-run fire insurance institutions.[523]

Simon remained carefully optimistic. In 1908, he corresponded with the lawyer Roelli on the matter of the wording of a possible earthquake regulation.[524] A joint statement issued by the Swiss private insurers on the earthquake clause appeared possible to him after the national law on the insurance contract had gone into effect in 1909.[525] However, this statement does not seem to have materialised.

3.3.1.2. *Scandinavia, Russia, and Italy*

There are a few additional business areas in which the introduction of the earthquake clause remained an open question. The Scandinavian countries, Russia, and Italy belonged to this group, but the reasons for the failure to introduce the clause could hardly have been more different in these countries.

In November of 1907, the Directors of the Swiss Re learned from the pay scale agreement reached by the Danish fire insurance companies that the negotiations on the introduction of a moderate earthquake clause would probably be completed soon.[526] Five months later, the Director of the *Københavns Brandforsikring* ('Copenhagen Fire Insurance Company'), Lars Iversen, stated that his company had introduced the following regulation to the statutes as a rider:

> For losses sustained during martial actions or during an earthquake, the *Københavns Brandforsikring* will provide no indemnification when in consideration of all the circumstances it must be assumed that the fire or the explosion is the direct consequence of these events. The term "direct consequence" applies to all cases in which the origin, spread or unusual effect of the fire is generated by the causes named above and takes place at the same time or directly thereafter (trans.).[527]

---

[523] 16 November 1907 Helvetia to SR, SR/FA 1907, 71.

[524] 30 November/5 December/12 December 1908 written communications, probably Roelli to Simon, SR/FA A9.0–32/ loose material, document 13.

[525] 29 April 1908 Simon to Iversen (*Københavns Brandforsikring*), SR/FA A9.0–32/file/ correspondence regarding earthquake clause 1906/1907/ *Bayerische Versicherungsbank*, 39 *et seq.* The law was adopted on 2 April 1908 by the National Assembly and the Council of States (Brodtbeck 1908, 323).

[526] 29 April 1908 Simon to Iversen (*Københavns Brandforsikring*), SR/FA 1908, 39 *et seq.* In Denmark, there were four public limited companies and six mutual associations (Emminghaus, *Handwörterbuch der Staatswissenschaften* 3rd ed. [1909], vol. 4, 95).

[527] 27. April 1908 Iversen (*Københavns Brandforsikring*) to Simon, SR/FA A9.0–32/file/ correspondence regarding earthquake clause 1906/1907/ *Bayerische Versicherungsbank*, 37 *et seq.*

This condition was designed to apply only on an interim basis. Presumably, that is the reason why the *Københavns Brandforsikring* had not changed their policies. The Directors counted on the companies active in Denmark and abroad to introduce 'an as much as possible uniform, joint and international insurance condition with reference to damages resulting from earthquakes' (trans.).[528] The *Nye Danske* ('New Danish Insurance Company') and the *Skandinavia*, two companies substantially involved in damage indemnification in San Francisco, could also have been interested in such a condition.[529] However, Simon heard nothing new by the middle of April 1908.[530] Additional information from Denmark is not extant.

In Norway and Russia, the efforts to secure the introduction of earthquake clauses seem to have come to nothing as well. The Norwegian insurance industry largely consisted of mutual insurance companies. Public limited companies were active only in the industrial market. Foreign companies were as good as non-existent.[531] It was known only that the Norwegian insurers had formed a special committee for the treatment of the earthquake clause. Results of any negotiations have not come to light.

In Russia, a large variety of provincial and State insurance institutions, mutual and public limited companies dealt with the business of insurance.[532] Political unrest disturbed every form of economic activity. A Russian insurer described the constant threat to the companies with this drastic formulation: '[…] the fire insurance enterprises of Russia are, if one may use the expression, in a state of war'.[533] For this reason, it is almost astonishing that the Premium Federation of the Russian Fire Insurance Companies was concerned with the earthquake question and had directed it to its 'legal consultants' for additional discussion at the beginning

---

[528] Ibid.

[529] Cf. the table of companies involved in indemnifying fire damages in San Francisco attached in the annexe. DK was less significant for the reinsurance business; in 1906, only 20.8% of all fire risks were reinsured here, notably at two domestic companies. Jahn 1912, 124.

[530] 29.4.1908 Simon to Iversen (*Københavns Brandforsikring*), SR/FA A9.0–32/folder/ correspondence regarding earthquake clause 1906/1907/ *Bayerische Versicherungsbank*, 39 et seq.

[531] Hansson 1908, 444. A high quota of the fire risks was reinsured, but declined (1906: 65.6%; 1908: 49.6%); Jahn 1912, 88, 129.

[532] These reinsured 49.7 % and thus a high percentage of their fire risks in 1906, notably in foreign countries. Jahn 1912, 86 *et seq.*, 125.

[533] Sergowsky, 'Fire Insurance in Russia' in Who is Who in Insurance 1908, 455.

of November 1907. Simon noted in 1908: 'The results of this discussion remain to be seen' (trans.).[534]

In Sweden, it became certain that 'at this time there is little hope for the improvement of the clauses used there'.[535] The larger share of the market was dominated by domestic mutual insurance companies. The public limited companies, which had reached agreement on financial matters regarding insurance terms and conditions,[536] were more willing to reform, as three of them had been forced to transfer considerable compensation payments to California.[537]

In Italy, the fire insurers were also unable to reach any agreement on the earthquake regulations. The circumstances and the procedures will be treated separately in the following. Changes in the law only came about when an earthquake had rocked the southern provinces of the country in December of 1908 and the question of the liability for earthquake-related fire damages were handled in court.

3.3.1.3. *Preliminary Results*

The developments in Switzerland, Scandinavia and Russia fit into the picture that emerged from the above examination of the business regions in which the earthquake clause was introduced or rejected.

The case of Switzerland demonstrates how the dominance of the insurance institutions regulated by public law could negatively influence the reinsurers' project. Many mutual companies in the Scandinavian countries and Russia were apparently similarly aloof to the reinsurers' proposals. The reasons for their positions are complex; they do not simply lie in the non-commercial concepts of bearing risk. The business policies of public law institutions and the mutual companies in individual business areas differed more strongly among each other than they did among public limited companies. The former group tended to be less cooperative and willing to reform. Changes in the limitations of risk were more difficult to

---

[534] On 29 April 1908 Simon wrote to Iversen (*Københavns Brandforsikring*), SR/FA A9.0–32/folder/ correspondence regarding earthquake clause 1906/1907/ *Bayerische Versicherungsbank*, 39 *et seq.*

[535] Ibid. The interest of the reinsurers was not negligible, presumably because of the high quota of reinsured fire risks which reached a total of 45.9% in 1906, mainly abroad (Jahn 1912, 86, 122).

[536] Heijkenskjoeld, 'Fire Insurance in Sweden' in Who is Who in Insurance 1908, 486 *et seq.*

[537] These were the *Astræa*, the *Skandia* and the *Svea*. See the annexed table of the companies involved in the compensation of fire damages in San Francisco.

enforce in these organisations than in public limited companies. Moreover, neither the public insurance institutions nor the mutual companies
were stakeholders in international business and had made no contribution to damage indemnification in San Francisco; thus, they had no interest in the international developments of fire insurance.

For these reasons, the discussions of the earthquake clause did not
bring about any positive results in these countries. The indecisiveness
had an impact at least in part on the public limited companies, who—for
example, *Helvetia*—had to find their own ways. The reasons for the failure
to reach an agreement in the Danish insurance business, which was dominated by public limited companies and had participated in the reparation
of the damages in San Francisco, are more uncertain.

3.3.2. *Italy: Discourse Control instead of Clause Reform*

3.3.2.1. *The Fire Insurance Industry at the Beginning of the Twentieth Century*

Despite the Italian tradition of insurance stretching back over centuries,[538]
the Italian fire insurance industry had not developed into a strong economic power comparable to other countries of central and northern
Europe and North America in the nineteenth century.[539] Instead, a collective Italian fire insurance business had slowly come into being after the
territorial unification of the country in 1860.[540]

There were about two dozen important fire insurance companies at the
time of the San Francisco earthquake and in the years following. Almost
all of them had been established in northern Italy; nine of them had their
headquarters in Milan and four in Turin. Only one large company had
taken up residence south of the Arno River.[541] The economic imbalance

---

[538] Transport insurance originated in the High Middle Ages in the port cities in northern
Italy (Zedtwitz 1999, 84 *et seq.*; Nehlsen von Stryk 1986).

[539] Small regional insurance companies developed in the first quarter of the nineteenth
century. The first large companies were the *Compagnia di Milano* (1825) and the *Turin Società Reale mutua* (1829) (Virgilii, 'Storia delle assicurazioni in Italia', *Assicurazioni 3* (1936),
183 *et seq.*; Bolognesi 1939, 14; 'Origine e sviluppo delle Assicurazioni', *Annuario delle assicurazioni in Italia* 1907, 56).

[540] The *C.ia di Milano* was one of the first companies to operate nationwide. (...) *Le
Monde* (1865), *La Metropole* (1883), *La Paternelle* (1883) and *L'Union* (1884) opened branches
in quick succession. The *Fondiaria* (Firenze, 1879) and the *Società Anonima Cooperativa
Italiana* (1889), a mutual association owned by the Milan industrialist, were established for
nationwide business (Di Renzo 1932, 9; *Annuario delle assicurazioni in Italia* 1907, 54, 56).

[541] A global statistic on earthquake clause created by the Swiss Re listed five domestic
and ten foreign public limited companies as well as eight domestic mutual associations.

between the north and the south of Italy is reflected in this distribution of company headquarters. The northern regions were densely populated and economically—and industrially—highly developed, whereas the south was dominated by agriculture. Accordingly, the lucrative markets for fire insurance lay in the economic centres of the north. Here, their business volume grew significantly for decades.

In 1905, the Italian insurance industry provided material coverage for values of about $6.8 billion and earned some $8.5 million in premiums.[542] At this time, Italy had a population of about 35 million people.[543] As the spread of fire insurance increased, the amount of damages also went up alarmingly.[544] Nevertheless, the industry achieved 'rather pleasing results' in 1906.[545]

The corporate forms were limited to public limited companies and mutual associations in the fire insurance industry,[546] a State fire insurance institution not having been established. All of the foreign companies were limited companies, most of them French. The most powerful insurance company on the Italian market was, however, an Austrian company, the *Assicurazioni Generali di Trieste e Venezia*. The *Generali* and the *Adriatica di Sicurtà*, both of them based in Trieste and operating under the aegis of a Milan branch, divided a third of the Italian fire insurance market up among themselves.[547]

The intensive cooperation among the companies was a peculiarity of the Italian fire insurance business worth mentioning. No institution affected the development of the business more prominently than the fire insurance cartel, the *Concordato Italiano Incendio* (*CII*: 'Italian Concordat of Fire Insurance Companies'), established in 1883. Its success was based

---

It is conspicuous that the Venice branch, *Assicurazioni Generali*, does not appear in the list. Apparently, it was assigned to the Austrian-Hungarian sphere. In addition, some 160 smaller insurance companies, half of which were foreign, were included in the list. (SR/FA A9.0–32/ loose matter, doc. 2, 3 und doc. 1 (opinions); Pipia 1905, 469, fn. 1; Virgilii 1946, 44.

[542] In Italian currency: 35.1 thousand million liras and 44 million liras, respectively (Rocca 1911, 333).

[543] The number of residents was 33.57 million in 1901 and 36.18 million in 1911.

[544] The percentage of the compensation payments relative to the income went up from 50% to more than 70% (1905); Pipia 1905, 469 *et seq.*, fn. 1.

[545] *ÖRev* 1907, 304.

[546] That is, *Società anonime* and *mutue assicurative* or *società cooperative* (Vivante, *Trattato di diritto commerciale* 1893, vol. 1, 390 *et seq.*; vol. 2/1, 1894, 5 *et seq.*, 38 *et seq.*

[547] Of the insured value amounting to 32.075 thousand million liras in 1906, the Generali received 7.425 thousand million liras and the R.A. 4.035 thousand million liras (*ÖRev* 1907, 304).

upon a concept that originated in the 1840's[548] and was maintained well into the twentieth century. By means of combined market domination, the allied companies tended to exclude undesirable competition. However, their combined plotting clearly exceeded this goal, serving also to create mutual dependencies. This made the members of the *Concordato* trust that the agreements reached would be followed.[549]

The cooperation within the cartel was based upon a uniform system of risk analysis and common premiums. The companies established the risk classes[550] on the basis of a complex statistic that combined the data from the individual companies.[551] Rates defined by uniform business terms and premiums were linked to these risk classes.[552] In this respect, the activity of the cartel acted as a force of standardisation upon the entire actuarial practise of the allied companies. If a company wished to depart from the agreements made within the *CII*[553] in drawing up a specific policy, it was obligated to apply for authorisation from the cartel companies.[554]

In addition, the principle of obligatory mutual reinsurance and coinsurance ensured close linkage with each of the partners.[555] If a risk exceeded

---

[548] On the previous history, see Moretti, *Concordato italiano incendio rischi industriali. Celebrazione del 75° anniversario* (1958), 3; Sanzin, *Cent'anni di accordi fra le compagnie italiane nelle assicurazioni incendio* (1942), 3 *et seq.*, 20 *et seq.*, 25 *et seq.*, 55 *et seq.*

[549] Cavajoni (then secretary of the *CII*), *Il Concordato Intaliano Incendio nella 'sua' storia* (1962) and Sanzin, *Cent'anni di accordi fra le compagnie italiane nelle assicurazioni incendio* (1942), 10, 25 *et seq.* The *CII* itself regarded 1842 as its founding year. In contrast, Virgilii regarded 1883 as the beginning of *CII* (Virgilii 1946, 89).

[550] The risks were essentially classified in *Tariffe ordinari* (synonym *civili, semplici*) and *Tariffe industriali* (synonym *commerciali, mercantili*) (Di Renzo 1932, 30, 77 *et seq.*).

[551] Di Renzo 1932, 97 *et seq.*

[552] According to the definition in Article 1 of the cartel contract, the term *tariffa* included '*tanto la determinazione dei premi, quanto le clausole relative*' ('both the determination of the premiums and the relevant insurance conditions'); *Concordato di Bologna del 30 Ottobre 1883*, reprinted in Moretti, *Concordato italiano incendio rischi industriali. Celebrazione del 75° anniversario* (1958), 17–22. Each risk class had its own general and specific rates that, in part, differed territorially. The rates depended upon factors such as the frequency of damage claims, the manner of construction and the supply of water to fight fires (Pipia 1905, 472; Di Renzo 1932, 77–86).

[553] The most important agreements of the cartel ('*leggi*') were laid down in the so-called *Libro della Convenzione*. This book of rules included the cartel contract (*Concordato di Bologna del 30 Ottobre 1883*) and important additions. The version enacted in July of 1905 was in force until 1914. Additional agreements were found in the *Conferenze* (agenda and notes to the resolutions), in *libri delle Tariffe* and in the *Statistiche* (Di Renzo 1932, 70 *et seq.*, 94).

[554] Di Renzo 1932, 93 *et seq.*

[555] Industrial insurance originally represented the main activity of the cartel (Gr. U *et seq.* Giovanni Pavia, *Direttore Generale der Riunione Adriatica*, speech on the 16th of

the sum of 125,000 liras, the allied companies had to reinsure the surplus amount on a pro-rata basis.[556] Risks of more than 600,000 liras had to be assigned directly to coinsurance through the *CII* companies.[557] Finally, the work of the *Concordato* included the promotion of fire protection equipment.[558]

The activity of the *CII* had a great influence on the Italian insurance industry. Its rates prevailed; the non-cartel insurers adopted the standards of the cartel companies. Only the agricultural insurance business continued to operate on a completely different footing.[559] It is also likely that the cartel's activities are to blame for Italy's failure to develop an independent reinsurance branch. Umberto Pipia names only two internationally insignificant Italian companies in his *Trattato delle assicurazioni terrestri* of 1905.[560]

In the years following the San Francisco catastrophe, the *CII* counted a membership of at least seven public limited companies: *Anonima di Torino* (*CII* member from 1883), *Danubio* (Vienna; 1882–1894, again as of 1900), *Fondiaria Incendio* (as of 1883), *Assicurazioni Generali* (as of 1883), *Compagnia di Milano* (as of 1885), *Riunione Adriatica di Sicurtà* (as of 1883) and *L'Union* (Paris; as of 1894).[561]

Of the seven largest companies in the fire insurance market, only the Turin mutual association *Reale mutua*—who had the second largest share of the Italian fire insurance market[562]—was not a member.[563] But it, too,

---

October, 1926 at the 100. anniversary of *Compagnia di Milano*, cited in Di Renzo 1932, 67; Sanzin, *Cent'anni di accordi fra le compagnie italiane nelle assicurazioni incendio* (1942), 15, 17.

[556] *Concordato di Bologna del 30. Ottobre 1883*, Art. III–VII, Moretti, *Concordato italiano incendio rischi industriali. Celebrazione del 75° anniversario* (1958), 17 *et seq.* The amount is about $24,000.

[557] Agreement upon the initiative of the director of *Milano*, Poggi (1904). Di Renzo 1932, 106 *et seq.* The amount is about $115.400.

[558] Di Renzo1932, 87 *et seq.*

[559] Ibid., 30. Here, in part, a difference was made between rates for the *province settentrionali, p. centrali* and *p. meridionali, siciliani e sarde* (33).

[560] Pipia 1905, 469, fn. 1. In 1906, the reinsured quota of the gross premiums was relatively low at 25.9% (Jahn 1912, 53).

[561] Di Renzo 1932, 68.

[562] The *Reale mutua* had wanted to join, but was not permitted to do so because of its own statutes (Moretti, *Concordato italiano incendio rischi industriali. Celebrazione del 75° anniversario* [1958], 5).

[563] Compare the statistics in Pipia 1905, 470; all the concordat companies already concluded policies worth billions of liras in 1903, led by the Generali (6.537 billion liras). The Reale mutua underwrote for 4.553 billion liras in 1903.

was connected to the *CII*. In 1904, a number of non-cartel companies had declared their informal cooperation with the cartel: *Cooperativa Incendio, Métropole, Mondo, Paterna, Reale Mutuale, Urbaine* and—somewhat later—the *Nationale*. Two years later, the cooperation was placed on a solid footing. In 1906, the seven allied companies reached an agreement on common 'benchmarks' with the concordat companies in the *Condizioni generali di Polizza*.[564] In addition, they determined a policy on the treatment of certain risks, especially in the settlement of damages of co-insured properties. Additional measures such as the normalisation of common rates were discussed, but only adopted later.[565] In June of 1907, the concordat and the allied companies established the *Unione delle Compagnie d'Assicurazione* ('Union of Insurance Companies') in Rome. From then on, they met annually.

The State supervision of the insurance business was comparatively liberal in Italy,[566] and the activity of the insurance companies received explicit recognition.[567] The leading regulatory principles were publicity and legality of the business activities. A special supervisory agency did not exist, but the State authorities were counselled in their capacities as supervisors by an advisory board for provisional and social insurance.[568]

The *Codice di Commercio* of 1882 contained a few provisions on the insurance companies that were supplemented in an implementing regulation.[569] These regulations did not require an insurer to obtain a licence in order to start business. Simply registering with the commercial jurisdiction and with the *Ministero di Agricoltura, Industria e Commercio* was sufficient.[570] They had to submit their accounts to the department for *Credito e Previdenza* of the Ministry of Commerce every year for supervision.[571] These accounts were then checked for their compliance with legal

---

[564] That is, general terms and conditions of business.

[565] Di Renzo 1932, 108 *et seq.*

[566] For this reason, it corresponded to the politico-economic concept of the *Stato liberale*, which remained in place into the era Giolitti (Ghisalberti 1995, 184).

[567] Statement of the Ministers Boselli and Barrazuoli during the discussion on a reform of the government supervision ('Osservazioni generali sul progetto di legge', *Annuario delle assicurazioni in Italia* 1906, 67 *et seq.*).

[568] So-called *Commissione consultiva sulle istituzioni di previdenza e sul lavoro*. Formed in 1869, reorganised in 1905 (Rocca 1911, 230).

[569] Ordinance of 27 December 1882 (Manes, *Versicherungslexikon*, 1st ed. (1909), col. 1157).

[570] The documentation accompanying the business plan had to be presented at the same time (Rocca 1911, 224; Manes, *Versicherungslexikon*, 1st ed. [1909]).

[571] The provisions of Article 176, 177 *Codice di Commercio* as well as the Royal Decree of 9 January 1887 applied to limited companies and a number of ministerial orders

regulations.[572] The Ministry published the business plans, the accounts and the annual reports in a *Bolletino ufficiale* on the activity of public limited companies.[573]

Save for provisions on the depositing of security payments and on the use of the business assets, there were no other requirements that applied to fire insurance. In this respect, foreign companies were more heavily burdened than those based in Italy.[574] This also held true for the Trieste companies *Assicurazioni Generali* and *Riunione Adriatica di Sicurtà*, which were incorporated under Austrian law.

In light of the intensification of the insurance supervision in many European countries, the Commerce Ministry presented the draft of an insurance supervision law in 1905.[575] This recommendation envisaged the transition to substantive State supervision over the entire private insurance business and licensing requirements 'according to a modern model' (trans.).[576] In addition, an independent supervisory department was scheduled to be set up within the Ministry in continued cooperation with the advisory board for provisional and social insurance.[577]

Aroused from their complacency, the representatives of the private insurance companies immediately registered their opposition to this initiative.[578] In the 1906 edition of the *Annuario delle assicurazioni in Italia*, a statement that the Italian insurance companies had obviously authored in a joint meeting appeared. The insurers demanded a marked liberalisation instead of additional regulations.[579]

The legislative plans were discussed for half a year until the new Prime Minister Luzatti commissioned a panel to draft a supervisory law in

---

(especially the circular no. 9 of 6 March 1902 with regard to the *bilanci annuali*). Article 239 *et seq.* of the *Codice di Commercio* (Manes, *Versicherungslexikon*, 1st ed. [1909], col. 1158) applied to the mutual insurance associations.

[572] Rocca 1911, 224; Manes, *Versicherungslexikon*, 1st ed. (1909).

[573] According to Article 94, 95 of the *Codice di Commercio* as well as Article 55 of the implementing regulation of 27 December 1882 referred to by Manes 1909.

[574] *Annuario delle assicurazioni in Italia* 1906, 70, 74.

[575] The increase of comparable State interventions in business was increasingly demanded and discussed since the end of the nineteenth century (Ghisalberti 1995, 191 *et seq.*).

[576] Manes, *Versicherungslexikon*, 1st ed. (1909), col. 1158; ZVersWiss 5 (1905), 630 *et seq.*

[577] ZVersWiss 5 (1905), 630 *et seq.* Compare the draft in the *Zeitschrift für Versicherungswesen* 1905, no. 27/29.

[578] The insurance director Evan Mackenzie (*Alleanza Società di Assicurazioni*) mostly commented upon and criticised the legal plans. Mackenzie explicitly praised the existing Italian regulatory system (Mackenzie 1906, 6).

[579] *Annuario delle assicurazioni in Italia* 1906, 75.

1910.[580] A year later, the new draft, which very closely resembled its predecessor,[581] was presented to the parliament[582] and accepted.[583]

Since 1883, the general terms and conditions of business adopted by the *CII* determined Italian insurance contract law.[584] Cesare Vivante, one of the leading Italian jurists in the field of insurance law, cited these provisions only two years after their implementation.[585] As of the turn of the century at the latest, the joint clauses of the *Concordato* were recognised and used in the leading legal literature on insurance as the most important legal sources.[586] At that time, numerous non-cartel insurance companies already used the same or similar conditions.[587] An independent insurance contract law did not exist. The *Codice di Commercio* of 1882 contained provisions pertaining to insurance contracts, but allowed insurance companies considerable latitude to shape their own standardised contracts.[588]

Insurers and jurists considered the concordat policies to be actuarially modern and superior to older policies.[589] They were used for all kinds of private and industrial fire insurance. The *Condizioni Particolari* served to differentiate the handling of certain risk groups.[590] The last version prior to the catastrophe in San Francisco, designated the *Polizza Italiana Incendio*, dated from January, 1906.[591] This designation clearly demonstrates the dominance of this policy in Italy.

3.3.2.2. *Will 'San Francisco' Come to Italy?*

The San Francisco catastrophe had virtually no economic influence upon the Italian insurance business. As presumably the only company affected,

---

[580] Members of the *Consiglio della providenza e delle assicurazioni* were the insurance expert U. Gobbi, C. Vivante, Comm. V. Magaldi, Paretti und Rainaldi (*ZVersWiss* 10 [1910], 584).

[581] See *ZVersWiss* 12 (1912), 141.

[582] Manes, *Versicherungslexikon*, 1st ed./additional volume (1913), col. 672.

[583] The German insurance contract law of 1901 was regarded as a model. A noticeable feature was the assignment of the supervision's costs to the companies (compare *ZVersWiss* 12 [1912], 141).

[584] All the companies had used different contract texts previously. The use of *Atti di variazione*, that is, contract-changing additions, provided for some flexibility (Di Renzo 1932, 26, 30).

[585] Vivante, *Il contratto di assicurazione* 1885, vol. 1, 50, note 1.

[586] For example, in Pipia 1905.

[587] Di Renzo 1932, 26.

[588] 'Zum Feuerversicherungsvertrag in Libro I', *Titolo XIV*, Art. 417–453: *Del contratto di assicurazione*.

[589] Di Renzo (1932, 25) cites a policy in his study.

[590] The name remained at least until the end of the 1930's. Bolognesi 1939, 20.

[591] Ibid., 20. Di Renzo (1932, 73) documents the last change in 1903.

the *Riunione Adriatica di Sicurtà* compensated for damages of a few tens of thousands of dollars.[592] The Californian earthquake seems to have provoked very little interest in the insurance business.

3.3.2.3. *Contemporary Assessments of the Earthquake-Fire Danger in Italy*

Although Calabria and eastern Sicily were considered to be especially dangerous earthquake regions, the fact that southern Italy was repeatedly afflicted by serious earthquakes constituted a part of the permanent mindset of average Italians in 1906, regardless of their residence. This mental inclination was based less on scientific insights than upon the memory of historical earthquakes that even people far removed from the borders of Italy had heard of.

Probably the most famous earthquake had occurred in the Sicilian region on February 5, 1783, and claimed over 30,000 fatalities.[593] Besides Italian authors such as Michele Sarconi[594] und Giovanni Vivenzio,[595] Johann Wolfgang von Goethe contributed to the memory of the disaster in his report on his 'Italian Journey' in 1787.[596]

Further disastrous earthquakes occurred in the course of the nineteenth century.[597] The earthquake of December 16, 1857 that had cost the lives of some 12,300 people in the vicinity of Montemurro and Saponara (Basilicata) was especially present in the collective Italian memory.[598] Shortly before the San Francisco catastrophe, western Calabria was shaken on September 8, 1905,—2,500 deaths were registered[599]—and eastern Calabria suffered a similar fate in which hundreds of people died on October 23, 1907. August Sieberg, one of the leading German seismologists at the time, later lamented the 'irony of fate that this catastrophe had to occur on

---

[592] Cf. the table of companies involved in indemnifying fire damages in San Francisco attached in the annexe.

[593] Sieberg 1914, 83.

[594] Sarconi 1784.

[595] Vivenzio 1788.

[596] Goethe, *Italienische Reise I*, Report of 11 May 1787.

[597] Sofonea, 1908: *a Messina e Reggio Calabria la terra trema*, 7. A state broschure on the *Norme edilizie*—'building codes'—documents the followig catastrophes: Calabria 5 November 1660, *molti luoghi dello Stato Pontificio* 1781, Messina/Calabria 1783, Calabria 1832, Costa Toscana 14 August 1846, Basilicata 1851, Calabria 1857, Kingdom of Naples December 1857, Italy 12 March 1873, isola d'Ischia 28 June 1883, Italy 23 February 1887, Rome 23 February 1890, Calabria/Sicily 16 November 1894, Firenze [1895?], Calabria 8 September 1905. *Archivio Centrale dello Stato* (Rome), [file] *Presidenza del Consiglio dei Ministri* (PCM) 1909, 44/122/ [file]: PCM/Carte varie.

[598] Ibid., 84

[599] Ibid., 85.

the day on which the dedication of two newly renovated cities that had been destroyed in September 1905 was celebrated in the presence of two Ministers' (trans.).[600]

Up until the territorial unification of the small Italian states in the course of the nineteenth century, the earthquake danger, however, was regarded as a local problem of the south. The danger of earthquakes only seems to have become a topic that concerned northern Italians with the unexpected and highly destructive cataclysms in Liguria on February 23, 1887. This catastrophe provoked discussions on the implementation of a national earthquake insurance. The first to voice this demand was the Italian seismologist De Rossi,[601] whose recommendation at first had little effect, but ten years later was taken up in the Italian Parliament.[602] In 1899, the esteemed Italian earthquake researcher Mario Baratta worked out a concept for earthquake insurance on a mutual basis. The State was to support such a union and declare the membership obligatory. Baratta thought it would be even better if the large fire insurance companies decided to take on the risk in exchange for supplementary premiums.[603] On the 28th of January, 1906, Baratta repeated his recommendation for an obligatory insurance on buildings in the presence of the *Società Geografica Italiana*.[604]

The increase in the public interest in earthquakes at the turn of the century can also be seen from a number of publications on the seismology of Italy that in part appeared in very large print runs.[605] However, it must be doubted that the perception of an earthquake causing a fire catastrophe ever even existed. Italian cities were built out of stone and were thus regarded as less threatened by fire than by structural collapse. The

---

[600] Ibid., 85.

[601] De Rossi, *Bollettino del Vulcanismo italiano* XIV (1887), 113.

[602] The obligatory insuring of all buildings against earthquake damages was demanded (1897) (Hoffman 1928, 126). A collection of archives belonging to the Italian government documents that the Italian government dealt with the danger of earthquakes. Extant are historical earthquake statistics, conference materials, special studies on construction methods—cement, structural engineering, smokestacks, bricks, steel, railways, etc.;—on seismology—for example, on warning signals for the quake in San Francisco—; on construction methods in Japan, on fire danger, and so on (*Archivio Centrale dello Stato* (Rome), [file] *Presidenza del Consiglio dei Ministri* (PCM) 1909, 44/122/ [folder]: PCM/Carte varie).

[603] Baratta 1899.

[604] Baratta, 'I terremoti di Calabria', *Bollettino della Società Geografica Italiana, serie IV, vol. VII, no. 5* (1906), 454 *et seq.*

[605] For example, Gatta 1882; Negri et al. 1883; Reale Ufficio Geologico d'Italia, Carta geologica d'Italia (1889); Baratta 1901; in addition, *Bollettino della Società Sismologica Italiana* (from 1895).

experience gained in the preceding catastrophes proved this point. Only abroad was the earthquake danger for Italy mentioned with reference to the experiences in San Francisco.[606] Such deliberations are as rarely found in Italian newspapers as in the extant government documents.[607]

3.3.2.4. The Earthquake Regulations at the Time of the San Francisco Catastrophe

The impression that earthquakes were not perceived as potential catalysts of fires in Italy is confirmed in fire insurance law. The *Codice di Commercio* did not mention the problem of earthquakes—neither in Article 442, which extended the liability of the insurers to specific cases of damage,[608] nor in Article 441, which in connection with Article 434 placed limitations on the liability of the insurer.[609]

The problem was also scarcely considered in legal science. Apparently, none of the earlier commentators on the *Codice di Commercio* found it necessary to discuss the consequences of earthquakes with respect to the liability of fire insurance companies.[610] This lack is shown in the first

---

[606] The earthquake danger for this stretch of land was notorious ('Die Erdbebenkatastrophe in Süditalien', *ÖRev* 1909, 4).

[607] The archives of the Italian government on seismology only mention the problem of earthquake-fire in the context of San Francisco (*Archivio Centrale dello Stato* (Rome), [files] *Presidenza del Consiglio dei Ministri* (PCM) 1909, 44/122/ [files]: PCM/Carte varie).

[608] 'Article 442. *Sono parificati ai danni d'incendio se non vi è convenzione contraria: 1. I danni derivati alle cose assicurate dall'incendio avvenuto in altro prossimo edificio o dai mezzi impiegati per arrestare o per estinguere l'incendio; 2. Le perdite e i danni avvenuti per qualunque causa durante il trasporto delle cose assicurate eseguito allo scopo di sottrarle ai danni dell'incendio; 3. I danni derivati dalla demolizione dell'edificio assicurato eseguita allo scopo d'impedire o di arrestare l'incendio; 4. I danni prodotti dall'azione del fulmine, dalle esplosioni od altri simili accidenti, ancorchè non ne sia derivato incendio'.* As regards the history and interpretation of this norm see C. Vivante in *Bolaffio, Il Codice di Commercio. Commentato*, 1st ed. (1883), vol. V, 249.

[609] 'Article 441. *L'assicurazione contro i danni del fuoco comprende tutti i danni cagionati dall'incendio prodotto da qualsiasi causa, esclusa quella dipendente da colpa grave imputabile personalmente all'assicurato, ed esclusi i casi indicati nell'ultimo capoverso dell'art. 434. Comprende pure i danni derivati da vizio proprio dell'edificio assicurato, anchorchè non denunciato, se non si provi che l'assicurato ne avesse conoscenza al momento del contratto'.—'Art. 434. Sono a carico dell' assicuratore le perdite ed i danni che accadono alle cose assicurate, per cagione dei casi fortuiti o di forza maggiore dei quali ha assunto i rischi. L'assicuratore non risponde delle perdite e dei danni derivanti da solo vizio inerente alla cosa assicurata e non denunciato, nè di quelli cagionati da fatto o colpa dell'assicurato o dei suoi agenti committenti o commissionari. Egli non risponde dei rischi di guerra e dei danni derivanti da sollevazioni popolari, se non vi è convenzione contraria'.*

[610] For example, Vivante in *Bolaffio, Il Codice di Commercio. Commentato*, 1st ed. (1883), vol. V, 249 *et seq.*; Pagani Castagnola et al., *Nuovo Codice di Commercio* (1889), Vol V, 106.

textbooks that appeared under the application of the law.[611] The first Italian author to mention the question of earthquake fire was the Turin lawyer Francesco Cocito in his 1904 essay *'Le assicurazioni terrestri'*,[612] where he simply referred to the exclusion of the damages caused by earthquakes in the clauses of a contract.[613]

Nor did Umberto Pipia show more interest in the subject in his *'Trattato delle assicurazioni terrestri'* of 1905. Nevertheless, he declared that the insurer was not liable for damages that were caused by earthquakes or other specified causes. The legal sources on which Pipia based his opinion lead to a better understanding. Firstly, he named the *Codice di Commercio*—in which earthquake-caused damages are not mentioned—, secondly, the *Condizioni generali* of the *CII*, and thirdly, the conditions of a few non-cartel companies that he listed in the order of their importance for the Italian market: *'Cod. comm.*, art. 441, 434.—*Conc. ital. incendio*, art. 4; *Reale*, art. 11; *Providenza*, art. 4; *Coop. incendi*, art. 5; *Croce*, art. 2; *Suarazzese*, art. 4'.[614]

In the policy conditions of the concordat, the reader could find the following earthquake clause which at the time of the San Francisco catastrophe was in effect for the public limited companies:

La Compagnia non risarcisce i danni provenienti: da guerra, da tumulto popolare, da occupazione militare o da invasione, a meno che l'assicurato provi che il sinistro non ebbe origine dall'una o dall'altra di queste cause, da trombe, uragani, terremoti, eruzioni vulcaniche.[615]	The company will not cover any damages that result from war, national uprising, military occupation or invasion, unless the insured demonstrates that the damages do not originate in one of these causes, [or if they do result] from storm winds, tornadoes, earthquakes, volcanic eruptions (trans.).

The conditional clause in which the insurer transferred the burden of proof for specific damage causes that resulted in the exclusion of liability to the insured is significant. But in the case of earthquake fires, the burden

---

[611] For example, Vivante, *Il contratto di assicurazione* (1885), vol. 1.

[612] Cocito 1904, 80.

[613] Ibid., 80; Pipia 1905, 479.

[614] Pipia 1905, 479. Art. 441, 434 of the *Codice di Commercio* were irrelevant for earthquake fires.

[615] Gruenwald et al., *'La clause d'exclusion des tremblements de terre* [...]', 15; SR/FA A9.0–32/loose material document 2.

of proof clearly remained with the insurance company; the syntax does not permit any other interpretation.

A few foreign companies made use of more complex clauses that became known through the reinsurers' study of 1907. In view of the earthquake fire damages, these conditions did not differ from the concordat clause.[616] The Italian mutual associations also excluded the earthquake risk in a similar fashion.[617]

3.3.2.5. Recommendation of the Reinsurers on Clause Reform (July 1907)

After the earthquake in San Francisco, most Italian insurance companies were prepared to accede to the request of the Swiss Re to send in a copy of their policy forms.[618] The reinsurers analysed the conditions in force according to three criteria: exclusion of indirect damages, burden of proof of the insured and precise designation of the excluded damages as fire damages. Almost none of the policies fulfilled even one of these criteria.[619] It was only noted positively that all the insurance conditions mentioned the earthquake risk.[620]

---

[616] '1) *La Compagnia non risponde in nessun caso: dei danni causati da incendio, esplosione o scoppio, o dei guasti di qualsiasi natura quando sieno occasionati da guerra, invasione o tumulti popolari, dalla forza militare d'ogni specie, da terremoti od eruzione vulcaniche; dei danni cagionati da uragani, trombe o tempeste, a meno che questi danni sieno immediata conseguenza di incendio; dei danni di demolizione degli edifizi assicurati, eseguiti per impedire o arrestare l'incendio, a meno che la demolizione non sia stata ordinata dall'autorità'.*

2) *La Compagnia non risponde dei danni per incendio o per esplosione cagionati da guerra, invasione, sommosse popolari, forza militare qualunque, trombe, uragani, vulcani e terremoto. Queste esclusioni sono parmenti applicabili in tempo di pace, in caso di soldati presso l'abitato in seguito a mobilizzazione, manovre o semplice dislocamento di truppe, a meno però che, per una clausola manoscritta e mediante un premio di accettare questo aggravamento di rischio enventuale'.*

The wording of the whole clause is cited in Gruenwald et al., 'La clause d'exclusion des tremblements de terre [...]', 15; SR/FA A9.0–32/ loose material, document 2.

[617] 1) '*Non ostante l'assicuranzione la Società non è obbligata a risarcire i danni provenienti: da guerra, invasioni, sedizioni da tumulti popolari, da forza militare qualunque, da trombe, uragani, terremoti, eruzioni vulcaniche od altra forza maggiore'.*

2) '*La Sociatà non risponde dei danni provenienti da guerre, tumulti popolari, trombe, uragani, terremoti, eruzione vulcaniche'.* (Gruenwald et al., 'La clause d'exclusion des tremblements de terre [...]', 15; SR/FA A9.0–32/ loose material, document 2).

[618] Only the *Italiana* from Turin did not respond (SR/FA A9.0–32/ loose material, document 3 compared to 1 (explanations) (ca. 1907).

[619] Document from the first half of 1907 (SR/FA A9.0–32/ loose material, document 2. The clauses from individual French companies are emphasised as a positive exception.

[620] A catalogue from the *Gesellschaften (Anstalten) europäischer Länder, welche für ihr (in Europa belegenes) Arbeitsgebiet keine Erdbebenklausel anwenden* ('companies [institutions] from European countries for which no earthquake clause is used in their area of activity [i.e., located in Europe]'), from KR, SR/FA A9.0–32/ loose material, document 1.

The 'summary' of the reinsurers was worded accordingly:

Les conditions d'assurance de toutes les Compagnies opérant en Italie visent l'exclusion des dommages provenant directement ou indirectement de tremblement de terre; toutefois,
1. il est urgent de préciser avec plus de netteté la non-responsabilité de la Compagnie à l'égard des dommages indirects;
2. il est indispensible de mettre nettement la preuve à la charge de l'assuré (voir à la clause sous a), mettant à la charge de l'assuré la preuve à l'égard des sinistres causés par guerre etc.);
3. il est désirable de définir, par principe et d'une manière uniforme, comme dommages d'incendie, les dommages causés par un tremblement de terre qui doivent être exclus (voir clause b 1).[621]

The insurance conditions of all the companies active in Italy are aimed at excluding the damages that are directly or indirectly caused by an earthquake; nevertheless,
1. it is of the greatest necessity to precisely specify the non-liability of the company with respect to indirect damages;
2. it is essential to clearly transfer the burden of proof to the insured (see the clause relating to (a), in which the burden of proof in the event of war damages, etc., is incumbent upon the insured);
3. it is desirable to principally and uniformly designate those damages caused by earthquakes that are to be excluded as fire damages (see clause b 1) (trans.).

This result was sent to thirteen fire insurance companies active in Italy on July 18, 1907,[622] which included all Italian public limited companies and probably the larger of the foreign companies.

3.3.2.6. *No Reactions (1907–1908)*
After sending out the study, the Director of the Swiss Re, Simon, attempted to persuade the Italian fire insurance companies to implement the recommendations it contained. But the companies maintained an implacably reticent stance. Only the answer of the *Società di Assicurazione Danubio* from Austria is extant, whose director thanked Simon for the reinsurers' study and promised to examine it carefully.[623]

---

[621] Gruenwald et al., '*La clause d'exclusion des tremblements de terre* [...]', 15. Italics like in the original text.
[622] SR/FA A9.0–32/ yellow folder (correspondence, mainly the Cologne Re 1907), 83, 53 *et seq.*
[623] 3 September 1907 Danubio to SR, SR/FA A9.0–32/files/correspondence regarding earthquake clause, 1906/1907/ *Bayerische Versicherungsbank*, 34.

At the end of 1907, Simon mentioned to the President of the French Union, Baron Cerise, that the reforms in Italy had stalled.[624] In February of 1908, Simon wrote to his Cologne colleague, Gruenwald, that the Turin insurance director, Brocchi, had written him that the *Concordato Italiano Incendio* would not be discussing the earthquake clause until May or June.[625] He expressed his optimism in a letter: 'Italy: the reform of the earthquake clause will be achieved in the meeting of the concordat (tariff) companies scheduled for May or June. The other companies will likewise be incorporating the clause completed and introduced by the concordat into their policies' (trans.).[626]

However, this appointed day came and went without a resolution on the earthquake clause. Additional meetings of the *Concordato* failed to yield results.[627] The extant archives of the *Concordato* give the impression that the subject was utterly ignored. Neither was the earthquake danger excluded in a modified form nor were there opposing recommendations or initiatives to accept the liability for earthquake damages resembling those proposed in Great Britain.[628]

In 1909 and 1910, several newspapers cited the Italian earthquake clause that was current at the time. At issue was the same regulation as in 1906.[629] Vivante's commentary on the current concordat policy from 1922 shows as well that the earthquake clause continued to exist without change up to this time.[630] Neither did the Italian legislature become active. The

---

[624] 27 December 1907 Simon to Cerise, SR/FA A9.0–32/yellow folder (correspondence Swiss Insurance companies)/loose material.

[625] 27 February 1908 Simon to Grünwald (excerpt), SR/FA/loose material.

[626] 29 April 1908 Simon to Iversen (*Københavns Brandforsikring*), SR/FA A9.0–32/file/ correspondence regarding earthquake clause 1906/1907/ *Bayerische Versicherungsbank*, 39 *et seq.*

[627] 'Italienische Feuerkonkordatkonferenzen', *ÖRev* 1908, 205 with reference to *L'Assicurazione*. Various rates and conditions for industrial and agricultural risks were adopted or discussed, but the earthquake clause was not mentioned.

[628] Of the printed minutes to the conferences of the *CII*, called 'Concordato-Incendio per i rischi industriali. Convenzione' (as of 1912, 'Verbali'), only selected copies are still extant. They were possibly prepared as of 1883 by the respective presiding companies. The volumes between 1906 and 1911 are missing in the known insurance archives. The extant holdings in the archives of the *Assicurazioni Generali di Trieste*—including those from 1912 and 1913—document no references to discussions of the earthquake question.

[629] *ÖRev* 1909, 4; H. T. [Tarnke], 'Zum Erdbeben in Süd-Italien', *AnnVW* 2, 13 January 1909, 17 *et seq.*; Sraffa 1910, vol. I, 20. The *Kölnische Zeitung* (30 December 1908, BA-B 280–25309, 26) erred when it it wrote that the earthquake clauses were changed after 1906.

[630] Vivante, *Codice di Commercio/commentato* VII (1922), 289 *et seq.*

pertinent conditions of the *Codice di Commercio* remained unchanged.[631] For this reason, the exclusion statutes in the old *Condizioni Generali di Polizza* were the criteria for the question of liability in a damage case.[632]

What were the reasons for the lack of interest of the Italian insurance industry in a change in its clauses at a time when it stood eye to eye with the earthquake danger in its own country? Since nothing happened—not a trace of a discussion or any resolutions has survived—, the explanation must lie in the situation existing in the years between 1906 and 1908. It is to be assumed that in principle, the Italian insurance companies were aware of the advantage of excluding the risk of earthquakes from its policies. Only at the beginning of 1906 had the *Concordato Incendio* and the associated companies amended their *Condizioni Generali* and thereby retained the hitherto existing exclusion of the earthquake risk.[633]

The recent amendment of the terms and conditions of the insurance business can be counted among the reasons why the Italian insurers did not act. Any change in the insurance conditions entailed a considerable organisational, financial and actuarial investment; all the standard forms would have had to be reprinted and distributed, the insurance representatives briefed and the premiums calculated anew. Especially if changes gave the impression of a diminution of the accepted risk, they could create uncertainty among the insurance customers and frighten off potential new ones. These kinds of reactions could have been provoked by the explicit exclusion of damages caused indirectly by earthquakes and by the transfer of the burden of proof to the insured.

It would have been even more unpromising from the point of view of the insurers to provoke a counter-reaction from the government. The directors possibly feared a further increase in State regulation given the planned law on insurance supervision. Perhaps they did not want to provoke the legislature or the supervisory agencies into an unexpected

---

[631] Article 442 *Codice di commercio* did not change the liability of the insurance companies. The versions that Vivante in 1883 and 1922 commented upon agree in their wording. Reference to a discussion of the subject is to be found neither in the archives of the Italian government after 1906 nor in the parliamentary minutes (Vivante, *Codice di Commercio italiano* V (1883), 248; *Codice di Commercio/commentato* VII (1922), 284).

[632] Manfredi in Bensa et al., *Commentario al Codice di Commercio*, 1st ed., vol. V (did not appear before the end of 1909), 242.

[633] The *CII*'s liability for certain lightning damage, for damages in basements as well as the conditions on the use of gas lighting were substantially unchanged. Some external, mainly French companies, had followed the cartel in this matter (Di Renzo 1932, 73 *et seq.*).

reaction by excluding the earthquake risk, the worst case being an obligation to accept the earthquake-fire risk.

Moreover, the insurers knew that earthquake catastrophes in Italy occasioned reactions different from those experienced in California. Seismic catastrophes presumably seemed unlikely to them in the north of the country despite the experiences of 1894. In the south, large cities, especially Messina, could be hit. However, these localities differed from San Francisco, Valparaiso and Kingston in that they were for the most part stone-built. The *Österreichische Revue* thus speculated:

> That these insurers [...] never considered that in the southern Italian regions, which, as is generally well-known, are constantly exposed to the danger of earthquakes, their fire policies could entail disadvantages for them precisely because of this danger can already be seen in the fact that they retained very considerable sums for their own account in precise knowledge of the fact that the southern Italian stone edifices are very resistant to fire but not to earthquakes (trans.).[634]

Incidentally, only a relatively small percentage of the buildings was insured against fire in southern Italy. Despite the continuing growth in the fire insurance business in Italy, its acceptance in the agrarian south was sluggish in comparison to the prosperous, industrial north. What may have also played a role is that almost the entire insurance business was concentrated in Milan, Turin and a few additional cities in the north. From there, problems in the distant south possibly seemed less important than those on the local scene.

This would presumably have been different if the Italian insurance companies had lost anything approaching the sums German companies had lost in San Francisco. This experience had been an important impulse for the change in the earthquake regulations described above in Germany. The Italian insurance companies had survived the California catastrophe virtually unscathed; the same was true of the French companies operating in Italy at the time. Finally, it is conceivable that the Italian insurers had faith in that the existing, simplified earthquake clause would be recognised in damage cases that went to court. This faith was soon to be put to test.

---

[634] *ÖRev* 1909, 4.

3.3.2.7. *An Earthquake and its Consequences: 'Messina non c'era più'*
During the Christmas holidays of 1908, the residents of eastern Sicily and
Calabria experienced a few sporadic seismic shocks, but the tremors were
presumably so weak and similar phenomena so well-known that nobody
fled. However, on December 28, 1908 at 5:20 a.m., a shaking of the earth
announced an overwhelming earthquake. After a short pause, a violent
wavelike movement of the earth washed over the area. The entire phenomenon lasted for about half a minute. Smaller tremors followed.[635]

The destruction was immense. The earthquake's epicentre lay in the
middle of the straits between Messina and Reggio.[636] Everywhere, *palazzi*
and factories, apartment houses and churches collapsed.[637] Between 60,000
and 80,000 people died in Messina alone, up to 15,000 more in the region
of Reggio. Even more injured victims lay under the ruins, surprised in
their sleep by the disaster. No earthquake in history had claimed so many
victims in Italy. The numbers were so high also because the traditional
construction method had not been changed and safety standards had not
been improved despite earlier experiences with disasters. Pebbles held
together with weak limestone had been used even for modern *palazzi.*
Many buildings were too high for an earthquake zone and were erected
on weak foundations. Old buildings suffered the most damage.[638]

As in San Francisco, Valparaiso und Kingston, numerous fires broke
out immediately after the quake, caused by toppled lamps, ruined stoves
and gas escaping from ruptured mains. No one dared to enter buildings to
save those trapped inside or to put out fires since additional quakes were
feared. In addition, the broken water mains made extinguishing fires a
hopeless undertaking.[639]

Some ten minutes after the first destructive seismic shock, an additional
quake struck the seabed between Sicily and Calabria. Metre-high waves
formed and crashed into the ruins of the city, the dead and the living.[640]

---

[635] Sofonea 1908, 4.

[636] Sieberg 1914, 88.

[637] Sofonea 1908, 4.

[638] Ibid., 7; Mercadante 2009, 71. The same grievances had already enabled the extent of
the catastrophe of 1783, as Goethe (*Italienische Reise* I, 13 May 1787) reported.

[639] Sofonea 1908, 7.

[640] Eyewitnesses reported waves that were up to thirty-five feet high (Sofonea 1978, 7).
The respected seismologist August Sieberg (1914, 86) reported that water that had washed
up onto the land measured over three feet in depth.

The region had not been ready for the catastrophe. Citizens and government agencies were helpless. The Zurich psychologist Eduard Stierlin described their behaviour as follows:

> In southern Italy, just like in Valparaiso, the singular, stuporous, paralysed condition of the people conspicuous even in retrospect to both the uninvolved observer as well as those affected made every rational act and purposeful course of action, every calculated thought, virtually impossible. Crowds of people ran hither and thither in the streets in groups like a herd of headless sheep without being able to pull themselves together in order to make any reasonable decision or defend themselves against the dangers threatening their lives, and the government bodies—when and if they made their presence felt at all—gave the most contradictory, in part most ridiculous, commands possible (trans.).[641]

The shock also seized other, sometimes chance, witnesses of the events: Luigi Barzini wrote in a report for the *Corriere della Sera*:

Un grande piroscafo ignaro della catastrofe andò per sbarcare a Messina un carico di rimpatrianti, e soltanto quando fu entrato nel porto issando le bandiere, si accorse che Messina non c'era più.

Si sollevò improvvisamente dal ponte della nave un urlo alto di orrore, e la nave atterrita si gettò a machina indietro a tutta forza, uscì dal porto e fuggì.[642]

A large paddle-steamer that had not noticed the onset of the catastrophe was approaching Messina to unload some homecomers, and just as it was sailing into the harbour and had raised its flag, it noticed that Messina was no longer there. An appalled lament immediately arose on the bridge, and the 'horrified' ship threw its engines into full-speed astern, came about, left the harbour and fled (trans.).

The first helpers to arrive were soldiers from one Russian and two German war vessels.[643] The Italian government only received reports of the catastrophe after twelve hours because the earthquake had interrupted telegraph connections. Three days elapsed before the first assistance reached Messina.[644]

---

[641] Stierlin 1909, 81. He explained his observations as a psychogenic production of psycho-neuroses (135).

[642] Barzini (sen.), cited in Di Renzo 1932, 115.

[643] Sofonea 1908, 7.

[644] Ibid., 8.

Even days later, fire broke out in the ruins, as Barzini described:

In un luogo le macerie ancora fumano; tracce d'incendi sono ovunque. Al fetore della putrefazione si mescola l'odore speciale della roba bruciata. Chissà per quale tremenda complicità di sciagure, il fuoco segue quasi sempre il terremoto. Tutti gli elementi pare si si avventino. Anche molte rovine di Reggio si dice sieno bruciate. Le due rive dello stretto, nella spaventosa notte del 28 dicembre, illuminate dalle fiamme, dovevano presentare alle navi al largo un indescrivibile spettacolo d'orrore.[645]

At one place, the ruins are still burning; traces of the fire can be seen everywhere. The special smell of burned rubbish adds itself to the stench of putrefaction. Who knows what terrible complicity of unhappy circumstances dictates almost always that fire is a concomitant of earthquakes? All the elements appear to conspire in the destruction. Likewise, fires in many ruins are said to have begun to burn in Reggio. In the terrible night of the 28th of December, the light of the flames on both shores of the straits must have painted an indescribable picture of horror for the ships in the distance (trans.).

The directors and employees of the insurance houses working in the south were duly alarmed. In view of the reports made by Barzini and other journalists, they anticipated, in addition to a number of claims from the life insurance and accident insurance divisions,[646] claims for indemnification from holders of fire insurance policies.[647]

The international insurance industry was also worried at first when it received the news. There was general agreement that for the affected population, the disaster would surpass that of San Francisco and the other catastrophes.[648] However, the interest waned very quickly when it turned out that Italian firms were virtually the only insurance companies confronted with the question of damage indemnity. Only to a small degree did a few Austrian and French as well as one German fire insurance company expect claims for indemnity.[649] In addition, the reinsurance branch did not expect any special losses in the wake of the Italian earthquake. Fire insurers had ceded almost no risks in the south of the country.[650] In

---

[645] Barzini (sen.), cited in Di Renzo 1932, 115.
[646] Herzog n.d., 270 *et seq.*
[647] Di Renzo 1932, 115.
[648] *ÖRev* 1909, 4; Tarnke, *AnnVW* 2, 13 January 1909, 17.
[649] Ibid., 18 *et seq.*
[650] *ÖRev* 1909, 4.

these non-industrialised regions, there were only a few facilities whose value could not have been assumed by direct insurers on their own.[651]

In contrast to San Francisco, the fires in Messina and Reggio involved almost without exception stone structures that had already collapsed[652]— to the advantage of the insurers, as the *Kölnische Zeitung* remarked on December 30, 1908.[653] In response to queries by the insurance trade press, a few Italian insurance companies communicated their evaluations. None of the queried companies anticipated that the indemnity for the fire damages would endanger their stake in the market. Some pointed to the high percentage of collapsed buildings, others to their earthquake clauses.[654] The European insurance journals wrote in general agreement that there was nothing to fear from a legal perspective. The journalists regarded the Italian earthquake clauses as flawless[655] or at least believed that they would prevail in court, as they thought the connection between the earthquake and the fires to be obvious and undisputed.[656] The editor of the *Annalen des gesamten Versicherungswesens*, Tarnke, argued that since the earthquake in southern Italy belonged 'to the experiences of life', it would be clear for the public that 'a liability of the companies for earthquake-fire damages did not come into question'.[657] The journalists openly challenged the companies to resist possible claims 'in the most extreme form possible' (trans.).[658]

The local situation was not yet clear. Three days after the earthquake, Commissario Vencenzo Magaldi, the Italian government official responsible for the insurance industry, arranged measures for the clean-up of the disaster area.[659] In response, the insurance companies formed a

---

[651] Tarnke, *AnnVW* 2, 13 January 1909, 18 *et seq.*

[652] *Kölnische Zeitung*, 30 December 1908, BA-B 280–25309, 26; *ÖRev* 4 January 1909, 4; Comm. V. Magaldi, General Credit Director, *Fürsorgewesen und soziale Versicherung* ('Department of Public Welfare and Social Security'), to the Rome newspaper *Mercurio*, translation cited in *AnnVW*, 13 Januray 1909, 93 *et seq.*

[653] *Kölnische Zeitung*, 30 December 1908, BA-B 280–25309, 26.

[654] Statements by the *Unione Continentale*, the *Savoia* and the *Lloyd Sabaudo*, 'Über die Rückwirkungen der Erdbebenkatastrophe', *Der Versicherungfreund*, 10 February 1909, 6. Statements of the *Assicurazione Generali* and the *Riunione Adriatica di Sicurtá*, 'Das italienische Erdbeben und seine Bedeutung für die Versicherung', *ZVersWiss* 9 (1909), 414.

[655] *ÖRev* 1909, 4.

[656] Tarnke, *AnnVW* 2, 13 January 1909, 17; statement by a *'kompetenten Fachmannes'* ('responsible expert'), cited in *ÖRev* 1909, 4.

[657] Tarnke, *AnnVW* 2, 13 January 1909, 18.

[658] *AnnVW* 2, 13 January 1909, 94. Somewhat more reticent *ÖRev* 1909, 4.

[659] *Reale Decreto*, 1 January 1909. As far as can be ascertained from the archives of the *Archivio Centrale dello Stato* (Rome), the government paid scarcely any attention to the

Commissione consultiva under the administration of the director in Milan for the clarification of the matter of indemnity.[660] They presumably feared that evidence documenting the unfolding of the catastrophe could become lost. But Magaldi soon aligned himself with the legal position adopted by the insurers on the fire damages:

> The conflagration that completed the destruction of the buildings in Reggio and Messina developed only [...] after [...] the earthquake had already caused the terrible destruction. It can thus never be maintained that the fires in Reggio and Messina were the sole and exclusive cause of the damages suffered by the insured. For this reason I think that the fire insurers cannot be required to pay for any of the damages (trans.).[661]

In subsequent weeks, the fire insurance companies registered claims for indemnity. Apparently, there were more than just a few, for the members of the *Concordato Italiano Incendio* met together in order to devise a common position in response to the indemnity claims. The insurers were faced with a problem that was known from experience in America: the determination of the cause of the damages proved to be difficult in individual cases, especially when the damage report was received some considerable time after the event.[662] The cartel companies agreed not to reject the damage reports out of hand, but to emphasise to the insured that a legal obligation to indemnify the damages did not exist. As far as possible, out-of-court settlements on the extent of the damages should be sought with the injured party. Other non-cartel companies or those not associated with the *CII* adopted this policy as well.[663]

3.3.2.8. Reinterpretation of the Earthquake Clause in Court (1909–1910)

A few court cases in which the question of the liability of the fire insurance companies was dealt with from various points of view followed the earthquake and the fires in Messina. Three cases are of special importance

---

question of the liability of the fire insurance companies. This matter is isolated in [files] *Presidenza del Consiglio dei Ministri* 1909, 44/122/ [file] PCM/Carte varie).

[660] The committee was convened by a 'union of all insurance companies operating in Italy'; possibly by the *CII* or the *Unione delle Compagnie d'Assicurazione* (Di Renzo 1932, 116).

[661] Comm. V. Magaldi, General Credit Director, *Fürsorgewesen und soziale Versicherung*, to the Rome newspaper *Mercurio*, translation cited in *AnnVW* 2, 13 January 1909, 93 *et seq.*

[662] Di Renzo 1932, 116.

[663] Ibid.

because they document a change in judicature. They were taken note of internationally.[664]

In the first case, the owners of the *Palazzo Pennisi*, Riccardo and Eduardo Costarelli, sued the *Assicurazioni Generali di Venezia*. On January 18, 1909, their building on 33, via Teatro Vittorio Emanuele in Messina had burned to the ground—that is, three weeks after the earthquake. The Costarellis then demanded indemnity of 50,000 liras[665] in compensation for fire damages to the buildings and their contents.

The *Assicurazioni Generali* countered with several arguments. Firstly, they had excluded damages caused by earthquakes in Article 4c of their insurance policy.[666] Secondly, the earthquake had altered all the conditions on which the insurance contract had been based; the contract had been premised upon the principle of *rebus sic stantibus*.[667] The earthquake had increased the risk, for the municipality of Messina had become incapable of fighting the fire. For this reason, the contract had become invalid at the moment of the earthquake.[668] On this point, the insurance company was able to cite an additional decree passed by Commissario Magaldi; this had determined that the earthquake had created a much more serious situation in the affected region than would have occurred in the event of war. That is, the catastrophe had completely paralysed every function of civil life.[669] The third argument was only to apply in the event that the court should recognise the liability. According to the opinion of the *Assicurazioni Generali*, the insured had forfeited a possible entitlement to damages by not complying with two contractual obligations: they had not notified the company of the increase in risk after the earthquake and—allegedly—had not adequately fought the fire later.[670]

---

[664] In Europe, the German-language papers were the chief chroniclers of the developments in Italy.

[665] About $9,600.

[666] This was the earthquake clause of the *CII*.

[667] That is, 'things thus standing'; 'as matters now stand'. Article 432 paragraph 1 of the *Codice di Commercio* stated: 'L'assicuratore e liberato quando, per fatto dell'assicurato, i rischi vengano trasformati od aggravati col cambiamento di una circostanza essenziale in guisa che l'assicuratore non avrebbe dato il suo consenso alle medesime condizioni, se al tempo del contratto fosse esistito questo nuovo stato di cose'.

[668] *Il Foro Italiano* I (1910), 454 *et seq.*

[669] *Decreto Reale*, 3 January 1909. According to Article 434, paragraph 3 of the *Codice di Commercio*, war damages did not have to be indemnified (Visentini 1931, 41).

[670] *Il Foro Italiano* I (1910), 459 *et seq.*

The *Tribunale di Messina* decided in favour of the plaintiff on August 12, 1909. The Italian law journal *Il Foro Italiano* published the following guidelines:

La clausola contenuta nella polizza d'assicurazione, che esonera la società assicuratrice dall'indennizzo per incendi avvenuti in seguito a terremoto, è valida, ma deve intendersi limitata al caso d'incendio derivato direttamente dal terremoto come causa ad effetto, e non può quindi estendersi a quello d'incendio divampato qualche tempo dopo e del quale il fenomeno tellurico sia stata soltanto causa occasionale.	The policy clause that excludes the insurance company from indemnity for damages that were caused as a result of an earthquake is valid. It must, however, be understood to apply narrowly to the case of a fire that has directly resulted from the earthquake in the sense of an actual cause, and can thus not be expanded to the case of a fire that broke out some time after the earthquake and this only on the occasion of the telluric phenomenon.
La trasformazione o l'aggravamento del rischio determinato da caso fortuito o forza maggiore è a carico dell'assicuratore e non importa la risoluzione del contratto di assicurazione [...].[671]	The change or the increase in risk through contingency or an act of God shall be borne by the insurer and does not constitute the cancellation of the terms of the insurance policy [...] (trans.).

Some aspects of the decision's grounds are noteworthy. The *Tribunale di Messina* recognised the earthquake clause as valid and, specifically, consistent with the basic principle of liability in Article 434 of the *Codice di Commercio*.[672] This position would always be maintained in the future.

In interpreting the clause, the court made a distinction between damages whose *causa ad effetto* ('a direct cause') was the earthquake and later damages that had occurred *ad occasione del terremoto*, on the occasion of the earthquake. The result of this distinction corresponded to that between direct and indirect causality. In the case of a direct causality, the court accepted the exclusion of the liability through the earthquake clause. Indirectly caused damages occurring at the time of the earthquake

---

[671] A third guiding principle pertains to the impossibility of the contractual notification of the increase in risk and the fighting of the fire (*Il Foro Italiano* I (1910), 454 *et seq.* Likewise with a few guidelines, 'Tribunale di Messina (Pres. Collaca, Est. D'Amelio)—12 August 1909; Costarelli c. Assicurazioni generali di Venezia (Massima)', Giurisprudenza Italiana 1909, col. 955.

[672] *Il Foro Italiano* I (1910), 461 *et seq.* Article 434, paragraph 1 of the *Codice di Commercio* set out that in principle, the insurer was liable: 'Sono a carico dell'assicuratore le perdite ed i danni che accadono alle cose assicurate, per cagione die casi fortuiti o di forza maggiore, die quali ha assunto i rischi'.

were to be indemnified by the insurer. Thus was the situation in the case of Costarelli vs. *Assicurazioni Generali*, as the insurance company was unable to prove that the fire had smouldered from the moment of the earthquake to its outbreak in the ruins. The proof that the fire had originated from the quake was lacking. The court argued that the fires in the *Palazzo Pennisi* had broken out under unknown circumstances.[673]

The judges did not adopt the idea that the contract relationship had ended because of the discontinuation of the contractual basis. To be sure, they acknowledged the principle of actuarial equilibrium on the basis of which a contract termination was claimed. However, the enforcement of this principle appeared impossible to them because they believed the maintenance of the contractual relationships to be more important. They based this point of view on an inverse conclusion from Article 432 of the *Codice di Commercio*, according to which the contract could be dissolved if the insured had caused an increase in the risk.[674] Consequently, the judges concluded, the insured should not bear liability for other increases in risk such as contingency or acts of God. The French courts had decided in a similar fashion in the case of war-related fire damages from 1870.[675] Finally, the court declared, the Costarellis had not violated their obligations to register the increase in risk and to fight the fire. Since the entire fabric of civil life had totally broken apart in Messina, they would not have been able to fulfil these obligations.[676]

This was a welcome judgement from the perspective of the insured. However, whether it was actually 'of far-reaching significance' (trans.),[677] as the journal *Vorwärts* of December 17, 1909 had concluded, could not be foreseen in 1909. The *Tribunale di Messina* stood on the lowest level of the Italian courts, and it was to be expected that the insurance companies would attempt to contest this ruling in higher courts.

The interest in the *Palazzo Pennisi* case was large among judges and lawyers and in insurance companies and academic legal departments. Two Italian jurists, Pietro Manfredi and Angelo Sraffa, responded with scholarly publications on the decision in which both of them energetically attacked the arguments of the *Tribunale*. The Milan lawyer Manfredi analysed in some detail the question of the liability for earthquake-fire

---

[673] *Il Foro Italiano* I (1910), 462 *et seq.*
[674] Wording of Article 432, paragraph 1 of the *Codice di Commercio*, 288, note 667.
[675] *Il Foro Italiano* I (1910), 467.
[676] Ibid.
[677] *Vorwärts*, 17 February 1901, 45.

damages in a new large commentary to the *Codice di Commercio*[678] at the end of 1909.[679] Why he devoted so much space to the liability question[680] is unclear. In addition, it cannot be said with any certainty why he argued in favour of the insurer so decidedly. The fact that he worked as an insurance lawyer in Milan, where some of the most important Italian companies had their headquarters, allows us to conjecture that professionally, he closely represented their interests. In any event, Manfredi could not have failed to notice that additional court cases between the injured parties from Messina and the insurance companies in the north were being prepared in Milan. In one of these cases, Angelo Sraffa, a full professor at the University of Parma, represented the insurance company *Cooperativa Italiana* against a company that had suffered fire damages in Messina. His treatise on the interpretation of the earthquake clause was published at the beginning of March 1910 precisely in the time frame following the last oral argument[681] in which the judges would have to deliver their decision.

The argumentation of both texts showed close parallels. Sraffa presumably based his arguments on those of Manfredi.

Manfredi hinged his argumentation on the term *effetti* ('effects') in the *Decreto Reale* of January 3, 1909. He developed this term into an instrument that permitted the justification of the widest possible relationship between the relevant damages and the earthquake. In Manfredi's opinion, serious earthquakes such as that of December 28, 1908, continued to exert their influence days after they occur because earthquakes also shattered the social fabric of society. Like the *Decreto Reale*, Manfredi emphasised the parallels between war conditions and earthquakes. Both law and insurance policies excluded damages caused by war, Manfredi argued, because of their *effetti sociali*, the 'effects upon society'.[682] He regarded the legal

---

[678] The editors Enrico Bensa and Gustavo Bonell had engaged some leading Italian legal scholars to participate in the first edition: Luigi Franchi and Cesare Pagani (vol. 1), Umberto Navarrini and Gabriele Faggella (vol. 2), Gustavo Bonelli (vol. 3), Angelo Sraffa and Arnaldo Bruschettini (vol. 4), Pietro Manfredi (vol. 5), Antonio Brunetti (vol. 6) Gabriele Faggella (vol. 7), Gustavo Bonelli (vol. 8), C. F. Brusa und Antonio Grassi. The volumes were prepared between 1900 and 1924 and the work was published by the Milan *Biblioteca giuridica contemporanea*.

[679] Manfredi's commentary is undated. The dating is based upon the fact that Manfredi takes into consideration jurisprudence up to 1909, but no decisions thereafter (for example, *Tribunale di Milano*, decision of the 12th of March, 1910).

[680] Manfredi in Bensa et al., *Commentario al Codice di Commercio*, 1st ed., vol. V (did not appear before the end of 1909), 243 (note).

[681] It occurred on February 26 (*Tribunale di Milano*)—March 12, 1910. (Fatto), *Rivista di diritto commerciale* II (1910), 359.

[682] Manfredi in Bensa et al., *Commentario al Codice di Commercio*, 1st ed., vol. V (did not appear before the end of 1909), 242.

consequences of serious earthquakes as analogous. Here, the social effects mainly manifested themselves in the cessation of the protection of property and in the lack of means to fight fires. Risks were greatly increased under these conditions. Manfredi determined, based upon a Lloyds of London policy, the duration of this state of emergency to be seven days.[683]

The legal scholar Sraffa argued more theoretically than the more pragmatically oriented Manfredi. He firstly regarded the case from the perspective of the theory of the contractual basis that he celebrated as the resurrection of the 'old and triumphant principle of *rebus sic stantibus* in the *ius commune*' (trans.). Pointing to Article 432 of the *Codice di Commercio*, the insurance policies and the spirit of the insurance contract, Sraffa substantially tried to prove why this principle applied to insurance law.[684]

Sraffa then examined the actual question of the earthquake-fire damages and, like Manfredi, came to the conclusion that an earthquake could not only be the *cause efficiente* or *causa diretta* of fire damages, but also the *causa occasionale*.[685] Sraffa offered three reasons for this thesis. Firstly, he posited a uniform concept of causality in fire insurance law. Not only direct but also indirect damages that occurred on the occasion of the fire—for example, due to the water used to put out the fire—were recognised to be fire damages. Sraffa applied this principle to the problem of earthquakes and concluded that fire damages originating on the occasion of an earthquake were also caused by the earthquake and were therefore justifiably excluded from liability.[686] Secondly, Sraffa showed that the demand for a proof of the causality of an earthquake for fire damages led to absurdity: an earthquake itself was never the cause of fires because 'an earthquake does not burn' (trans.).[687] Between the two events—the earthquake and the fire—, there was always a third event, for example the escape and combustion of gas and other flammable materials.[688] Like whirlwinds and waterspouts,[689] earthquakes were only conceivable as a *causa occasionale* of damage. This was precisely what the exclusion of liability in insurance contracts meant. Sraffa examined the wording of the earthquake clause by means of a 'counter-experiment' and asserted that

---

[683] Ibid., 243.

[684] Sraffa, 'Le assicurazioni contro gli incendi e i danni provenienti da terremoto', *Rivista di diritto commerciale* I (1910), 203 *et seq.*

[685] On the differences between *causa efficiente/diretta* and *occasione/causa occasionale* see Sraffa 1910, 207, with reference to Carnelutti, *Rivista di diritto commerciale* I (1905), 21.

[686] Sraffa, *Rivista di diritto commerciale* I (1910), 205.

[687] Ibid., 206.

[688] Ibid., 206 *et seq.*

[689] Ibid., 207.

the term *proveniente da* could not only be understood causally but also in the sense of a temporal relationship, *precedente a conseguente*.[690] Manfredi's and Sraffa's conclusions agreed up to this point. Then, both posed the question as to the assignment of the burden of proof.

Manfredi first ascertained that the burden of proof of the causal link between quake and fire was incumbent upon the insurer.[691] However— and this was novel—a presumption (*presunzione*) suggested that fires following an earthquake were caused by it:

Tuttavia siccome l'esperienza ha stabilito che al terremoto le più volte segue l'incendio, cosi l'assicuratore è assistato dalla presunzione che gli incendii seguiti al terremoto sono provenienti dallo stesso.[692]	However, just as experience has demonstrated that an earthquake is followed by a fire most of the time, the presumption that the fires that follow an earthquake are caused by it helps the insurer (trans.).

Manfredi thus contradicted all the previous court decisions. In numerous cases from San Francisco, Valparaiso, Kingston and most recently from Messina, the courts had demanded more or less conclusive demonstrations of the causality between quake and fire from the insurers. No company had been able to provide this proof. Manfredi turned the tables in favour of the insurance companies. In his construction, a plausible demonstration of the earthquake situation on the part of the insurer was sufficient to permit the assumption of causality between the earthquake and certain fire damages. Then the insured had to attempt to rebut this assumption—a reversal of the burden of proof placed upon the insurer.[693] Sraffa followed Manfredi's opinion without citing him, and fleshed out some additional arguments.[694]

Manfredi was active as a legal architect in favour of the insurance companies in one additional point. The matter concerned the difficult

---

[690] Ibid.

[691] Manfredi refers to the cases in German courts on the San Francisco catastrophe (Manfredi in Bensa et al., *Commentario al Codice di Commercio*, 1st ed., vol. V (did not appear before the end of 1909), 243).

[692] Ibid., 243 *et seq.*

[693] Prior to Manfredi, the notion of refutable presumption of facts had been developed by the German insurance director Drumm. Even if Manfredi does not refer to Drumm, it is likely that he knew Drumm's essay, which had appeared in a prestigious German journal (Drumm, *ZVersWiss* 7 (1907), 374 *et seq.*).

[694] Manfredi in Bensa et al., *Commentario al Codice di Commercio*, 1st ed., vol. V (did not appear before the end of 1909), 244.

identification of the relationship between fallen building damages and fire damages. Manfredi wrote that the damage indemnity was reduced to the value of the ruins 'in all events'; for an additional refutable assumption signified that the earthquake had destroyed the building before the fire had wrought its destruction. The insured had the burden of proof that his house and his possessions had burned intact, 'a rather difficult matter to prove' (trans.).[695]

There is one other thing to say about the Messina judgement in the case of *Costarelli v. Assicurazioni Generali*. The case could hardly have been decided otherwise because the fire damages had originated three weeks after the earthquake. This decision served as a welcome opportunity for Manfredi and Sraffa to promulgate arguments that in the future could permit an exclusion of the insurance companies' liability.

The treatises did not fail to be noticed. Only on one further occasion did the *Tribunale di Messina* decide in favour of an insured party. Nothing is known about the specific case. But it can be conjectured from the head note of the *Rivista di diritto commerciale* that once again, the causality question was a central point in the decision. On March 11, 1910, the judges decided that the wording *danni provenienti da terremoto* ('damages that stem from the earthquake') in the earthquake clause of the *Assicurazioni Generali di Venezia*—that is, the concordat clause—only included damages directly caused by the earthquake. In obvious contradiction of the remarks made by Manfredi and Sraffa, the judges rejected an extension of the liability exclusion to damage cases that had originated on the occasion of the earthquake.[696]

On the following day, March 12, 1910, a decision in Milan initiated a reversal in the case law on the earthquake clause in line with the writings

---

[695] Ibid.

[696] Tribunale di Messina, the 11th of March, 1910: Barrera (avv. Barrera) c. Assicurazioni Generali di Venezia (avv. Ruggeri) [1. instance]. Headnote (*Massima*) of the *Rivista di diritto Commerciale*: '*La clausola del contratto di assicurazione che esonera l'assicuratore dal pagamento dell'indennizzo per i danni provenienti da terremoto è valida, ma deve intendersi limitata al caso d'incendio derivato direttamente dal terremoto come causa ad effetto e non può estendersi al caso d'incendio di cui il terremoto fu solo causa occasionale [...]. Gli assicuratori non decadono dal diritto al pagamento dell'indennizzo per mancata denuncia dall'avvenuto incendio nei termini e modi prescritti dalla polizza, se tale denuncia venne da essi fatta entro il termine di prorogo concesso dallo Stato*'. *Rivista di diritto commerciale* II (1910), 1091.

of Manfredi and Sraffa.[697] Legal journals and papers reported on the case to an extent commensurate with the importance of the decision.

The Messina company *Ferdinando Siracusano & figlio Giuseppe* had sued both of their insurance companies, *the Società Anonima Cooperativa Italiana* and the *Riunione Adriatica di Sicurtà*, in separate actions in the *Tribunale di Milano* for compensation for fire damages. Why the trial was held in Milan is not reported; the headquarters of the companies were probably stipulated as the place of jurisdiction in the insurance policies.[698]

The company *Siracusano* had insured all of their merchandise in their warehouse in Messina, 47 via Pozzoleone,[699] with the *Cooperativa Italiana*. On January 3, 1909, the flames of a fire that had allegedly leapfrogged from a nearby apartment building that the earthquake had reduced to rubble[700] destroyed the entire stock in the warehouse. The company had demanded indemnity for the damages that the *Cooperativa Italiana* rejected with the argument that the risk that had been the subject matter of the contract had become extinct with the earthquake on December 28, 1908. Consequently, Siracusano brought an action against the *Cooperativa Italiana* on March 22, 1909.

The insurance company defended itself with the usual argument that based on Article 5 of their *Condizioni generali*, it was not liable to replace *danni provenienti da terremoto* ('damages that stem from the earthquake').[701] In addition, the company was not liable for the indemnity because of the absolute abnormality of the risk, given the destruction of Messina.[702] On March 12, 1910, two weeks after the last court hearing,[703] the court decided against the Messina merchants. *Il Filangeri* summarised the legal contents of the head note:

---

[697] *Tribunale di Milano* (Pres. e Est. Granati)—*12 marzo 1910*—F. Siracusano (avv. Interdonato, Castagnone) c. Società Anonima Cooperativa Italiana per le assicurazioni contro l'incendio (avv. A. Pavia, Sraffa, Della Porta, Casrati), *Il Foro Italiano* I (1910), 454 et seq., 468 et seq.

[698] The *Tribunali Civili* were responsible for civil and commercial matters at first instance, the *Corti di Appello* at second instance and the *Corte di Cassazione* at the highest instance. The court of jurisdiction was determined by the place of residence of the defendant or by the place of the property in question—there was a special regulation for *società anonime*—, but could be otherwise determined by a contractual agreement (Mattirolo, *Trattato di diritto giudiziario civile italiano*, 5th ed. (1902), vol. I, 346, 355, 362 et seq., 620 et seq., 643).

[699] About $28,850.

[700] *Rivista di diritto commerciale* II (1910), 623.

[701] *Tribunale di Milano*, 12 March 1910. (Fatto), *Rivista di diritto commerciale* II (1910), 358.

[702] Ibid., 359.

[703] On the 26th of February, 1910.

La clausola del contratto di assicurazione che esonera l'assicuratore dal risarcimento dei danni provenienti da terremoto, trova applicazione anche nel caso di incendio divampato alcuni giorni dopo il movimento tellurico e di cui questo sia stato non la causa immediata e diretta, ma soltanto la causa occasionale.[704]

The contract clause that relieves the insurer from the liability to indemnify earthquake-caused damages also applies in the case where a fire breaks out a few days after the telluric occurrence that was not the direct cause of the fire, but by whose mere occurrence the fire originated (trans.).

In the decision's grounds, the court declared that the earthquake clause of the *CII* contained the solution to the case.[705] All parties were in agreement that the condition included the directly caused fire damages. In opposition to *Siracusano*, the *Cooperativa Italiana* believed that fire damages resulting from an earthquake were also excluded.[706] The court regarded this point of view as the 'most reasonable and just' (trans.).[707]

The judges adopted the position that the formulation *danni provenienti da guerra, tumulti popolari, trombe, uragani, terremoto, eruzioni vulcaniche*[708] could be broadly interpreted. The clause mentioned several events that undoubtedly could only cause fires indirectly. This principle also had to be sufficient in the case of earthquakes. The catastrophic events must be interpreted as situations that would facilitate the outbreak of fire.[709] This argument was originally Sraffa's, who personally took part in the lawsuit as an attorney.

The exclusion of earthquake clause damages was, in the view of the court, also due to actuarial practice. Insurance companies drafted the contract clauses on the premise that they served the essential creation of a certain relationship between risk and premium. For this reason, the court wished to accept the point of view argued by *Cooperativa Italiana* that the

---

[704] *Tribunale di Milano—12 marzo 1910—F. Siracusano (avv. Interdonato) c. Società Anonima Cooperativa Italiana per le assicurazioni contro l'incendio (avv. A. Pavia, Sraffa, Della Porta).* Headnote, *Il Filangieri* 1910, 631. Additional headnotes in the following journals: *Rivista di diritto commerciale* II (1910), 357; *Repertorio generale annuale della Giurisprudenza italiana* XII (1910), 38; *Il Foro Italiano* I (1910), 454; *Il Foro Siciliano* 1910, 196; *La Giurisprudenza di Torino* 1910, 453; *Il consulente commerciale e tributario* 1910, 258; *Diritto e Giurisprudenza* XXV (1910), 553; *Monitore die Tribunali* 1910, 596; *Tribuna giudiziaria* 1910, 277.

[705] The clause is cited in *Rivista di diritto commerciale* II (1910), 359.

[706] Ibid., 360.

[707] Ibid.

[708] 'Damages that were caused by war, insurrection, storm winds, tornadoes, earthquakes or volcanic eruptions'.

[709] *Rivista di diritto commerciale* II (1910), 360.

frequency of horrendous fire damages in earthquake catastrophes argued against regarding them as a part of the risk to be accepted. The insurer could only be judged to indemnify damages if the insured delivered the strict proof that no connection had existed between the earthquake and the fire.[710]

Interdonato, the attorney for *Siracusano*, was confronted with a legal catastrophe. He had proven the opposite of what would have convinced the court, namely that the fire had smouldered in the ruins of the warehouse for five days and then had developed its destructive power—thus demonstrating a case in which the fire had broken out on the occasion of the earthquake. Internonato's argument might have been successful in the *Tribunale di Messina*, but for the Milan judges, his demonstrations sufficed for a *presunzione grave e precisa* ('serious and precise assumption') of the causality of the earthquake in relation to the fire.[711] This formulation originated word-for-word from Manfredi's essay; the emphasis that the unusual severity of the earthquake spoke[712] for its causal relationship with the fire damages is also reminiscent of his commentary. The court finally followed him in detail when it included the social circumstances as part of the causal relationship between quake and fire.[713]

The publishing offensive and the efforts of Sraffa and two other lawyers on behalf of the *Riunione Adriatica di Sicurtà* had paid off. On March 12, 1910, the tables were turned in favour of the insurance companies. A stabilisation of the new legal perspective ensued in the following months thanks to a few Italian legal scholars and judges who, using arguments similar to those of Manfredi, Sraffa and the *Tribunale di Milano*, denied a liability of the insurers to indemnify damages.

The *Rivista di diritto commerciale* published an explanatory note of several pages by the Neapolitan Professor Arnaldo Bruschettini on the decision of the *Tribunale di Milano* of March 12, 1910. Bruschettini wholeheartedly agreed with the court: it had solved a question of unique interest in a manner that had never been seen before, the only valid one, *efficacissima nella sua argomentazione*.[714] He sang the praises of his colleague Sraffa, whose masterly course had been followed by the Milan civil court, right

---

[710] '[…] *mentre dovrà l'assicurato rigorosamente provare che l'incendio si sarebbe verificato anche senza l'avvenimento del terremoto'*. Rivista di diritto commerciale II (1910), 361.

[711] Ibid., 362.

[712] Ibid.

[713] Ibid.

[714] Freely translated: 'with a particularly effective argument'.

in the second sentence.[715] In his appraisal of the legal situation, Bruschettini even went one step further than Sraffa and the Milan court. On the question of causality, he thought that all the factors without which the damage would not have occurred were direct causes—i.e., the earthquake as well. Then he demonstrated why the principle of *rebus sic stantibus* had to apply precisely in the cases of severe earthquakes and why the contract had even become extinct with legal acuity and actuarial expertise.[716]

Two other legal scientists, the professors Giorgio Arcoleo and Carlo Fadda, drafted notes on the decisions from Messina and Milan for *Il Foro Italiano*. Arcoleo's contribution consisted of a comprehensive discussion of the extinction of an insurance policy in the event of a serious earthquake. On this question, he shared Sraffa's und Bruschettini's opinions that an earthquake such as that of December 28, 1908 cancelled the contracts *nunc et illic*.[717] Even if later fires occurred without any relationship to an earthquake, Arcoleo concluded, they were without any value in the absence of insurance. Thus, contrary to Manfredi's interpretations, the temporal distance between earthquake and damage event played no role.[718] Even a registration of the change in risk by the insured lost its significance.[719]

But even in the event of a continued applicability of the contracts after the earthquake, Arcoleo considered the liability for earthquake damages to be excluded. Like Manfredi, he inferred *a minore ad maius* from Article 432 of the *Codice di Commercio* that since the insurance company was exempt from liability in the event of war, this legal consequence definitely had to be valid in the event of earthquakes.[720]

Carlo Fadda examined the liability question from a completely different perspective than that of the other authors. He cleaved to a traditional understanding of the insurance contract as one depending upon chance.[721]

---

[715] Bruschettini, 'Le assicurazioni contro gli incendi e il terremoto', *Rivista di diritto commerciale* II (1910), 357.

[716] Ibid., 357 *et seq.*

[717] That is, 'at that time and at that place'. Arcoleo (Note to the Decision in *Trib. Messina*, 12 August 1909 and *Trib. Milano*, 12 March 1910), *Il Foro Italiano* I (1910), 456.

[718] Ibid.

[719] Arcoleo 1910, 457.

[720] Ibid.

[721] *Aleatoric contracts* are to be understood as those contracts that are characterised by chance or indeterminate elements, no matter whether the business deal results in advantages for one side or the other. This means that the bearing of risk as the subject-matter of the contract was not yet recognised. This point of view was still held by Vivante 1899, 335; Pipia 1905, 24 *et seq.* In opposition, Ehrenberg 1893, 72.

He failed to achieve an orientation on the actuarial practice of the early twentieth century. His references to Ulpian[722] possibly even struck the Romanist jurists as ignorant of reality.[723] Fadda contributed little to the solution of the liability question because he became bogged down[724] in general statements on the exceptional situation in Messina, the indeterminate contract, [725] the *clausula rebus sic stantibus* in fixed-term contracts and *bona fides*.[726]

All in all, legal science established a clear and innovative line of argumentation. Whereas the interest in a change of judicature still predominated for Manfredi and Sraffa, the theoretical discussion was the most important point for Bruschettini, Arcoleo and Fadda. Bruschettini and Arcoleo succeeded, as they strengthened Sraffa's doctrine of the extinction of the contract with additional argumentation.

Other court decisions that supported the decision of March 12, 1910 followed. In Milan, the company *Siracusano* continued the battle for the indemnity of its damages suffered in Messina. The scholarly legal literature reported on two of its cases in detail. The *Tribunale di Messina* dealt with one other case as well. On June 4, 1910, the *Tribunale di Milano* again decided against *Siracusano* in the court of first instance, this time in favour of the *Riunione Adriatica di Sicurtà*. Once again, the lawyer Interdonato had been unable to prevail against the lawyers Sraffa, Della Porta and Sacerdoti. The facts of this case were similar to those in the previous case *Siracusano v. Cooperativa Italiana*. The *Riunione Adriatica di Sicurtà* had insured merchandise in a warehouse that had burned down five days after the earthquake. This time, the fire had jumped from a nearby residential building that had collapsed. The company refused compensation on the grounds that the earthquake catastrophe that had destroyed Messina had terminated the coverage of the risk by the policy.[727] The lawyer representing *Siracusano* energetically opposed this interpretation. He picked up the legal debate of the past months and declared that the insurer's liability

---

[722] Fadda, note on the decision in *Trib. Messina*, 12 August 1909 and *Trib. Milano*, 12 March 1910, in *Il Foro Italiano* I (1910), 466.

[723] In Germany as well, the treatment of the insurance contract in the context of Roman law had long been rejected: the 'notion of insurance' was at best said to be the basis of the *foenus nauticum* (Lewis 1889, 1 *et seq.*, and Reatz 1870, 15 *et seq.*).

[724] He supported his statements with the views of jurists from Italy (Polacco, Vivante), France (Planiol) and Germany (Ehrenberg, Windscheid, Dernburg).

[725] Fadda 1910, 459.

[726] Ibid., 461.

[727] 'Eine gerichtliche Reminiszenz an das Erdbeben von Messina', *ÖRev* 1910, 177; *Rivista di diritto commerciale* II (1910), 623.

was neither excluded because of a change in the risk regardless of its origin, nor on the basis of a contractual stipulation.[728]

The judges went down the same path that the Milan justices had blazed in the preliminary decision of March 12, 1910.[729] The *Rivista di diritto commerciale* printed the entire seven-page justification in which the court had taken up all the basic questions.[730] Firstly, the *Tribunale* contradicted the view that the contract had been voided as a result of the earthquake. In this respect, the court agreed with the existing judicial decisions. With regard to Article 432 of the *Codice di Commercio*,[731] it was persuaded by the *argumentum e contrario* of the *Tribunale di Messina* that the contract did not become invalid when chance had caused an unforeseeable increase in risk.[732] The judges contradicted the opposing view of Sraffa and Arcoleo, who wished to infer the cessation of the validity of the contract by analogy from Article 432 or *a minore ad maius*, in detail. In that case, they explained, the recognised principles of *rebus sic stantibus* and the discontinuation of the contractual basis would not be applicable. The legislature had consciously anchored this possibility in Article 432 of the *Codice di Commercio:* only an increase in the risk caused by the insured could lead to an annulment of the contract. Exceeding this boundary was not permissible. At this point, the court dealt with Bruschettini's arguments in detail.[733]

The judges also followed the preliminary decision of the *Tribunale di Milano* by solely resolving the case on the basis of the contractually agreed earthquake clause. In their view, the term *provenienti da* in the earthquake clause meant

---

[728] *Rivista di diritto commerciale* II (1910), 623.

[729] The panel of judges consisted of different members than on the 12th of March, 1910. *Tribunale di Milano—4 giugno 1910—Siracusano (avv. Interdonato) c. Riunione Adriatica di Sicurtà (avv. Sraffa, Della Porta, Sacerdoti); President Raimondi, Est. Alberici.* Headnote of the *Rivista di diritto Commerciale:* '*Il patto inserito in una polizza di assicurazione contro i danni prodotti da incendio secondo cui la compagnia non deve rispondere dei danni provenienti da terremoto, fa sì che non occorre che questo sia causa diretta dell'incendio, ma basta che ne sia stato causa occasionale perchè la Compagnia non debba esser tenuta al risarcimento'*. Rivista di diritto commerciale* II (1910), 623.

[730] [Editorial note] *Rivista di diritto commerciale* II (1910) 623, note 1.

[731] Not Article 431, with which the lawyers of the *Riunione Adriatica* had argued (*Rivista di diritto commerciale* II [1910], 623).

[732] Ibid., 624.

[733] The court interpreted the almost identically worded Articles 29, 30 of the policy of the *Riunione Adriatica di Sicurtà* similarly to Article 432 of the *Codice di Commercio* (*Rivista di diritto commercial* II [1910], 624).

un collegamento da precedente a conseguente, un nesso occasionale per modo che il terremoto abbia contribuito a produrre o agevolato il manifestarsi dell'incendio.[734]	a connection between that which occurred previously and subsequently, an occasional connection in the sense that the earthquake has contributed to the creation or advancement of the outbreak of fire (trans.).

By using the words [...] *da precedente a conseguente* ('between that which [occurred] previously and subsequently'), the court adopted Sraffa's formulation from the *Rivista di diritto commerciale*, albeit without naming the author who was in court as the attorney of the *Riunione Adriatica di Sicurtà*. More clearly than in the earlier decisions, the restriction now read that the earthquake must have been at least an *occasione necessaria* ('a necessary occasion') or *concausa* ('contributive cause') of the damage.[735] In the explanatory statement, the judges once again took their cue from the decision of March 12, 1910, and made do with the assumption that a connection between earthquake and fire had existed. They followed both Sraffa and Manfredi in this respect. The justices finally based the specific assumption upon a number of official documents and statements.[736]

The decisions of the *Tribunale di Milano* manifest the intensive study of the scholarly publications on the problem of the earthquake-fire damages that the Italian judiciary conducted. They show a considerable readiness of the judges to set off on new paths. In two points they mainly followed Sraffa's concepts: firstly, in the creation of a very broad factual connection between earthquakes and fire damages and, secondly, in the reduction of the burden of proof on the part of the insurer to a presumption of facts. As for the perceptions of a cessation of the contractual basis, they were rejected by the Milan justices with convincing arguments in the decision of June 4, 1910. The publications of Bruschettini, Arcoleo and Fadda thus only made on impact insofar as they supported the grounds of the decision of March 12, 1910.

Both of the following judgements shall be briefly described:

On December 6, 1910, the *Tribunale di Messina* dismissed the action of a property owner, Enrico Calvi, who had demanded indemnity from the *Assicurazioni Generali* for fire damage that had originated after the

---

[734] Ibid., 627.

[735] Ibid., 627.

[736] Citation from the *Decreto Reale* of the 3rd of January 1909 and from the decisoin of the *Tribunale di Messina* of 12 August 1909 by Ing. Dragotti, *Rivista di diritto commerciale* II (1910), 628.

earthquake.[737] His house, which had stood beside the *Palazzo Pennisi* belonging to the Costarellis, had also burned down a few days after the earthquake.

In delivering this decision, the *Tribunale di Messina* retreated from its previous legal position and followed the *Tribunale di Milano* in all points.[738] In the grounds, the court went as far as to state that a fire could never be the direct cause of an earthquake, but only *causa remota, indiretta e mediate* ('a remote, indirect or mediate cause').[739] Even more remarkable are the statements on the law of evidence. The court wrote:

Ma qui l'onere della prova è invertito, giacchè a favore dell'ente convenuto sta forte presunzione che il fuoco ebbe a verificarsi per una delle predette cause eccettuate, e cioè pel terremoto; presunzione che è fondata sulla dolorosa esperienza, la quale ci fa apprendere che il crollo su vasta estensione di edifici contenuti in centri populati, attraversati da congegni o apparecchi destinati alla trasmissione di gas e di elettricità, suole essere accompagnato o susseguito a breve distanza da incendi.[740]	But here the burden of proof is the reverse, because the strong presumption prevails in favour of the defendant institution that the fire was caused by one of the aforesaid grounds of exclusion, and to wit, through the earthquake; a presumption that is based upon the painful experience that teaches us that the mass collapse of buildings in the centre of the city that are pervaded by appliances and instruments for the distribution of gas and electricity are habitually accompanied by fires or that these follow after a short time (trans.).

In all candour, the court demanded from the insured the proof that the fire damages had not been caused by the earthquake.[741] This proof was just as difficult to deliver as the proof of the opposite. The judges were not solely satisfied with the time interval between the earthquake and the fire because fires could smoulder in secret for a long time and then suddenly

---

[737] *Tribunale di Messina, sentenza 6 dicembre 1910 (Pres. Callore, Est. Scordia)—Calvi c. Assicurazioni Generali, Rivista di diritto commerciale* 1911 II, 443.

[738] *Tribunale di Messina, sentenza 6 dicembre 1910* (see above), 443. The headnote of the *Rivista di diritto commerciale* includes only a portion of the change: '*Il patto che una Compagnia di assicurazione contro i danni d'incendio non risponde dei danni provenienti da terremoto si estende anche ai danni indirettamente prodotti dal terremoto*' ('The agreement that a fire insurance company is liable for damages resulting from an earthquake also covers the damages that are indirectly caused by the earthquake').

[739] *Tribunale di Messina, sentenza* 6 December 1910 (see above), 445.

[740] Ibid., 444.

[741] Ibid., 445.

break out.[742] The burden of proof was thus not distributed to both parties of the contract but loaded onto the shoulders of the insured.

The plaintiff argued that the fire had leapfrogged from the Costarelli palace to his building. However, he could not prove this.[743] Thus, the court found that the earthquake was the *causa comune e presunta* ('common and presumed cause').

Finally, on February 24, 1911, the *Corte di appello di Milano* ruled on appeal on the dispute between *Siracusano* and the *Cooperativa Italiana*.[744] The court expressly followed the decision of the first court.[745] The new legal situation was stabilised with this decision at the very latest.

Eleven years later, Cesare Vivante commented on *Concordato Italiano Incendio*'s existing earthquake clause. The same clause that had been valid at the time of the San Francisco catastrophe was still at issue. From Vivante's commentary it is possible to infer that the new legal situation in Italy approached the standard that the reinsurers in the Earthquake Commission had developed. With respect to the manner of the excluded damages, the commentary concluded that the inexact description in the clause had not done any harm because it was clear from the context that the issue could only have involved fire damages.[746]

---

[742] Ibid.

[743] Ibid.

[744] *Corte di appello di Milano* (Pres. ed Est. Invera P. P.)—*24 febbraio 1911*—*Siracusano* (avv. Castagnone, Interdonato, Pozzi) c. *Cooperativa Assicuraz. Incendi* (avv. Sraffo, sacerdoti, Della Porta). Headnote of *Il Filangieri*: 'La clausola del contratto di assicurazione che esonera l'assicuratore dal risarcimento dei danni provenienti da terremoto, trova applicazione anche nel caso d'incendio divampato alcuni giorni dopo il movimento tellurico e di cui questo sia stato non la causa immediata e diretta, ma soltanto la causa occasionale'. *Il Filangieri* 1911, 289. Additional headnotes in the following periodicals: *Rivista di diritto commerciale* II (1911), 247; *Giurisprudenza italiana* 1911, col. 422 et seq.; *Repertorio generale annuale della Giurisprudenza italiana* XIII (1911); *Il Foro italiano* 1911, 451; *Il Monitore die Tribunali* 1911, 247; *Il Consulente commerciale e tributario* 1911, 248; *Nouva Temi* 1911, 287.

[745] *Rivista di diritto commerciale* II (1911), 248.

[746] At this point, Vivante cited in a footnote French court decisions that supported his position: 'La Cass. francese, con due sentenze 19 marzo 1907' (Dalloz, I, 184, e Assicuraz. nelle Giur., 1907, 155) ha deciso, conformemente al testo, che, quando una polizza incendio esclude i danni causati direttamente o indirettamente dal terremoto, dall'eruzione di un vulcano, ecc., l'assicurato non può pretendere che questa clausola esclude i danni diversi da quelli l'incendio, restando questi ultimi coperti dall'assicurazione. Interpretare in questo senso una clausola restrittiva della responsabilità dell'assicuratore introdotta in una polizza avente unicamente il rischio di incendio per l'oggetto, non avrebbe senso'. Analogamente aveva deciso l'App. di Parigi, 18 maggio 1905 (Dalloz, II, 1906, 396).—Vedi anche gli Annales de droit commercial, 1907, pag. 234.—Così pure: App. Milano, 24 febbraio 1911 (Rivista dir. comm., 1911, 247)'. Vivante in Bolaffio and Vivante, *Codice di Commercio/commentato* VII (1922), 289.

Vivante did not go as far as the courts in the Messina decisions in the question of the burden of proof. He presented his own, remarkably balanced, point of view according to which it was in principle the responsibility of the insurers to prove that by way of exception, they were not liable for fire damage because of its special cause. The proof would be much easier the more circumstances entailed the presumption that the destruction was caused by the earthquake. The judge could accept at his discretion specific indices for a presumption of facts such as the intensity of the earthquake or the direct temporal relation between quake and fire. In Italy, where the insurance industry had shown little inclination to reform their earthquake clause according to the agenda advocated by the reinsurers, an earthquake had precipitated almost precisely these changes in the law.

3.4. The Reasons for Success and Failure: Results of the Third Part

Under which circumstances could the international introduction of a uniform contractual element such as the earthquake clause succeed? Where were its boundaries to be established? As the result of this study, some factors that in part determined the success or failure of the projects launched by the Earthquake Commission can be defined. Some of these factors are transferable to other processes of standardisation, whereas others specifically relate to the problems associated with earthquakes.

A prerequisite for success was the meticulous preparation of the clause project by the reinsurance companies involved. In the development of the earthquake clause, the insurers attempted to draw the most effective consequences from the experiences in court following the earthquake catastrophes of 1906 and 1907. They succeeded by developing a standard clause that established the exclusion of the earthquake danger and was at the same time flexible enough to be included in all the relevant legal systems. The reinsurers limited their specifications to three of the most important features of an effective earthquake regulation. In addition, they integrated the future users, that is, the fire insurers in the various countries, into the process of standardisation right from the beginning. They did not attempt to bring about the introduction of the earthquake clauses by force, but rather to persuade the fire insurers of the efficacy of their concept.

Nevertheless, the introduction of the earthquake clause in the individual countries only succeeded if several favourable circumstances coalesced. The perception of danger to the existence of one's own insurance company domestically or abroad could have been one of the strong influences. This perception not only originated in view of the economic losses in San Francisco, but also as a consequence of the awareness that earthquakes were an incalculable force of nature. However, this awareness did not necessarily mean that the observers feared fire disasters. The southern Italian towns and hamlets were stone-built and considered less threatened by fire than by collapse.

Favourable situations arose when reforms in the conditions governing the insurance business were imminent independently of the earthquake problem. This was the case in many European countries. Conversely, the recently revised version of the *Condizioni Generali di Polizza* presumably reduced the readiness of the insurers to carry out additional changes in Italy.

The more companies depended upon insuring their portfolios with reinsures, the easier it was for the Earthquake Commission to influence these companies. The support of the national insurance unions, lawmakers and the supervisory agencies could facilitate the Commission's work.

On the other hand, two factors formed almost invincible barriers to the desired clause reform. The one factor was the momentum of the markets, which in Great Britain, the Netherlands and California made the introduction of a uniform exclusion clause impossible. In certain areas of business—especially where the powerful British firms were active—, no fire insurance company could afford any longer to exclude the liability for earthquake damages only two years after the San Francisco catastrophe. The second factor was the form of organisation of the given national insurance industry. No common reforms succeeded where public law insurance institutions or mutual societies predominated. The examples of Switzerland, Scandinavia and Russia amply demonstrate the variegated reasons upon which this tendency rested. They varied from the principle of accepting the largest possible guarantees of damage indemnity to the large expenditure of the processes of change—which was only limited in the case of the public limited companies—to a general lack of interest in processes outside of one's own narrow area of business activity.

The Earthquake Commission achieved its goal in some European countries. Where no earthquake clause was introduced, other complex processes that likewise led to changes in the law regulating fire insurance developed. In California and other states of the union, the San Francisco earthquake stimulated a new wave of harmonising fire insurance law in the form of standard policies. In Italy, the changes only occurred after the

Messina earthquake—and in an astonishingly different manner, namely through an interaction between the courts and legal scholars as to the liability of the insurance industry for earthquake-fire damages.

The efforts to introduce an internationally uniform earthquake clause began to ebb away in 1912. In the 1920's, the clause lost its importance when the danger of earthquake-induced fires in modern cities receded due to the improvements in urban planning and the infrastructure surrounding them. The last serious earthquake-fire disaster occurred on September 1, 1923, in Tokyo and Yokohama. Here too, a legal dispute broke out as to the legitimacy in Japanese commercial law of an earthquake clause invoked by insurance companies restricting the liability for damages directly and indirectly caused by earthquakes.[747]

---

[747] A look at the debate is offered, with references, in Noz, 'Die Gültigkeit der Erdbebenklausel, insbesondere nach japanischem Recht', *ZVersWiss* 27 (1927), 82 *et seq.*, a law professor at the University of Kyushu.

CHAPTER FOUR

SUMMARY: PARADIGMATIC CHANGES IN THE LAW

The development and introduction of the earthquake clause is merely one example of the international standardisation of contract terms and conditions. Paradigmatic changes of the law were associated with this phenomenon.

The internationalisation of business entailed novel requirements in the regulation of standards. In no branch were the existing national regulations alone sufficient for the development of the worldwide exchange of goods, services and capital.

Various stakeholders took pains to satisfy these needs. They created numerous new regulations of differing normative quality that only in part fit into national legal systems. The self-regulation of business played a prominent role in this context. Companies tried to introduce contract terms that reflected their own concepts and interests on their own. Here, the clear tendency towards replacing State law can be interpreted as a sign of the typical legal pluralism of the modern period.[1]

The history of the earthquake clause has been described as a phenomenon of standardisation. Numerous aspects that go beyond the analysis of the process of standardisation have been touched upon in the process. The question of the creation of law through the massive use of identical contractual terms and conditions is especially important. This question too will be dealt with in the following.

4.1. New Regulatory Requirements

The companies that were involved in international commercial transactions required—like all stakeholders in business transactions—clarity on the rules that formed the bases of their contracts. This necessity was especially important in the event of a failure of any given transaction.

---

[1] Gessner, 'Rechtspluralismus und globale soziale Bewegungen', *Zeitschrift für Rechtssoziologie 23* (2002), 277 *et seq.*; Griffith, 'What Is Legal Pluralism?', *Journal of Legal Pluralism 24* (1986), 1 *et seq.*

The problems frequently began with the question as to what legal system had jurisdiction for a specific contract. International private law, which had come into its own about 1900, offered no satisfactory solutions.[2] To be sure, the opinion of jurists such as the Italian statesman Pasquale Stanislao Mancini had received a certain amount of attention for the view that the States ought to introduce uniform norms to adjudicate the conflict of laws.[3] But only a few of the regulations that had been agreed upon in international treaties since 1893 dealt with commercial issues. Numerous individual questions remained controversial. In fact, universal consensus on the principles of international private law was lacking. In Central, Southern and Eastern Europe as well as in South America, the principle of nationality advocated by the Italian-French school had become established.[4] In the Anglo-American world, on the other hand, the 'conflict of laws' had been solved according to the principle of the domicile.[5]

In addition, many of the players in business were really only at home in their native countries' contract law. The applicability of another legal system forced them to come to terms with it in detail in order to avoid mistakes. At the very latest, they had to rely upon expensive legal counsel in the event of dispute.

Finally, many players avoided the State legal system because it included assessments that opposed their own interests. Many State regulations were considered antiquated or were unclear and necessitated interpretation. The cultural lag also embraced international trading.[6]

In view of this background, the use of contract terms and conditions in the international contractual practice can be considered as an attempt to limit legal risks.[7] Contractual terms and conditions had—once they were incorporated into individual contracts—priority over the provisions set by law and trading practices. Their use guaranteed legal clarity and certainty. In this sense, the jurist and humanist Eugen Rosenstock-Huessy

---

[2] Scherner 1992, 43; Ruck 1934, 331; Meyer 1992, 17, 35 et seq., 75.

[3] On the history of the international private law in the nineteenth century and Mancini's role, see Kegel 1995, 147 et seq.

[4] A lecture by Mancini in January of 1851 in Turin is regarded as the earliest expression of this doctrine (reprint 1994).

[5] The basic principles of the Anglo-American doctrine were established by Story 1834; Rauscher 2002, 10; on the problem of the non-uniform international private law, cf. Rabel 1936.

[6] On this point see the discussions in sections 2.2.2 and 2.2.3.

[7] Wanner (1938, 15) speaks about legal-economic risks in this context.

defined the function of the contract in the industrial age as 'the basis for the prevention of court cases' (trans.).[8]

These general requirements for regulation were not paramount in all contractual conditions that were used in international commerce. Many of them served in the first place as the solution to current problems specific to any given branch of business. The earthquake clause offers a graphic example in this respect. After the disaster in San Francisco, many fire insurers and reinsurers adopted the opinion that they could no longer take the financial responsibility for the acceptance of the earthquake-fire danger. By introducing the new regulation, they sought to achieve their changed interests in a manner that would prevail in court. Thus, in this case the change in the basic principles of contract did not come about for the mere sake of standardisation, but rather in order to achieve external—economic—goals.

4.2. NEW STRUCTURES OF THE FORMATION OF NORMS

The law applied between 1871 and 1914 in transnational economic relations offers a complex heterogeneous picture that differs from branch to branch. Contemporary jurists described it as a virtually impenetrable network of legal, customary and conventional international norms.[9] At the time, only a few recognised the importance of standardisation as the novel structure of creating norms.[10]

It was novel in many ways. For one thing, the decision on contractual contents was separated from the conclusion of specific agreements. Standard clauses and contracts were preformulated without relation to concrete business transactions as the uniform legal bases for large numbers of future contracts. In this respect, their origin is reminiscent more of the legislative process than of the usual business contract process. There were also strong parallels between legal and technical standardisation. In both systems of regulation, specific stakeholders defined standards or norms by which the user was to be guided. The aim was to achieve the greatest congruence possible. In the 1920's, the American engineer Harriman

---

[8] Rosenstock-Huessy 1926, 147.

[9] Gareis 1906, 94.

[10] Saleilles (1901), who in his essay on the declaration of will deals with the question of the normative quality of *contrats d'adhésion*, is one of the exceptions, as is Kohler, *Archiv für bürgerliches Recht* 31 (1908), 249, who introduced the term *Massenverabredung* ('mass agreement') in Germany.

recognised the structural parallels between technical standardisation and the practice of mass contracts and accordingly incorporated a group of contract forms—the 'state contracts'—into his large study of 'Standards and Standardisation'.[11] In a similar way, the legal scholar Johann Heinrich von Brunn later ascertained:

> For the commercial practice, the use of standard contract forms is the same as when economisation and automation are made use of in the field of technology. For the businessman, the whole thing is basically a comparable and very simple process [...] so that just as a standardised screw is still a screw, a standardised contract remains a contract (trans.).[12]

Brunn's notion that the standardised contract does not fundamentally differ from an individual contract does, however, go astray. Standardised contractual elements fulfilled other functions than the individual agreements between two parties to a contract did. They served the purpose of internal business economisation, the exercise of economic power and the elimination of State regulations, and created an arena for a permanent updating of the law. Only on the basis of standardised contracts could the increasingly more complex cooperation, investment measures and commercial relations developing in business practice be mastered.[13]

4.2.1. Scope, Conditions and Limits of the Standard Form Practice

The internationally standardised contractual elements affected the contractual reality to a differing degree in the individual branches. Their scope should not be overestimated for the period prior to World War I. The introduction of uniform contract bases only paid off for companies that were required to handle a large number of identical contracts.[14] For this reason, for example, general terms and conditions of contracts were uninteresting for reinsurance companies, who only concluded a few contracts of considerable financial importance and negotiated the conditions individually with the direct insurers. In this respect, however, the reinsurers represented an exception. Most branches involved in the global exchange of goods, services and capital operated with standardised contract elements.

---

[11] Harriman 1928, 225 *et seq.*
[12] Brunn 1956, VII.
[13] On the functions of standards, see chapter 2.2.2 and chapter 5.2.2 in this part.
[14] Rabel 1936, 38.

On the other hand, the contractual bases were seldom standardised on the international level. Companies generally used the same standardised pre-printed contract forms and clauses abroad as those employed at home or adopted the contractual bases common in the given business areas. This is demonstrated by the example of the foreign fire insurance companies active in California at the time of the earthquake. They all either used the American standardised forms—especially the standard policy of the state of New York—or had adapted the regulations they knew from home to the local conditions.

The emergence of special standard contracts, standard clauses or standard contract forms for international commerce depended upon several circumstances. In principle, the interest in a standardisation of the contractual bases was more intense the more the given branch was involved in world commerce. Just as on the level of individual States, the companies took pains to achieve an international standardisation of their contractual bases if State regulations were lacking or were deemed ineffective or outdated.[15] Between 1871 and 1914, legislatures of many States involved in world commerce became very active.[16] They put numerous types of contracts on a legislative basis. However, in the majority of the branches of law, they refrained from creating compulsory conditions, thus permitting businesses sufficient room to create their own contractual bases.[17] They especially abstained from regulation when they regarded intervention to protect the weaker party to the contract as unnecessary. For this reason, for example, overseas trade law and maritime law—which only affected businessmen—were subject to State regulation only to a minor degree.[18] The legislators also remained silent if they did not have the necessary expertise in the business practices and legal relationships in the given branch. The law of reinsurance serves well to document this point, since there was hardly any widespread knowledge of this activity among outsiders due to the discretion of the insurers involved.[19]

---

[15] In this respect, the same is true as for the national level. Papenheim (1915, 291 *et seq.*) describes and criticises the situation in business.

[16] Meili (1902) offers a list of the civil and commercial laws of the most important commercial nations.

[17] The European railway companies had to accept massive restrictions in private autonomy. In the United States, numerous states prescribed the permissible subject-matter of the fire insurers' contracts in the form of standard policies.

[18] See Pappenheim 1915, 295 *et seq.*

[19] Ehrenberg 1885, 2 *et seq.*

The less the State regulated the law of individual branches, the more did non-State regulations of commercial and legal transactions become widespread. Thus, the contract formulas *fob* and *cif*, which could be communicated easily by telegraph, dominated foreign trade.[20] Overseas merchants made use of the form contracts for more extensive financial arrangements. These were especially widespread in the trade with commodities such as grain, feed, rubber, coffee and sugar. The warehousing business at the trans-shipment centres of world trade was firmly based on the principle of the internationally recognised endorsable warehouse bonds.[21] The maritime transporters and inland waterway shippers used form contracts and bills of lading whose standardisation promoted their branch organisations and the large shipping companies.[22] This example includes some of the most important phenomena of standardisation on the level of international commerce.

But the example of the earthquake clause also foregrounds circumstances that prevented a more pronounced spread of the international standardisation of contract terms and conditions prior to World War I. In many branches of business, institutions that could have coordinated an international process of standardisation were entirely absent: the development of a new earthquake regulation presupposed that the interested reinsurers would organise themselves and include the fire insurance companies in the networks of their project. No less laborious in practice was the imposition of the clauses in the many different business areas. Here too, the lack of institutions had to be compensated for by spontaneous individual organising efforts of the players involved. These players took it upon themselves to master this labour despite the unknown odds of success because they perceived the danger of earthquakes as a very serious threat in light of San Francisco's destruction. They would presumably not have been prepared to make such a sacrifice of time and energy under less dramatic circumstances.

It proved to be less complex to develop and introduce standard clauses and form contracts in branches that were organised internationally. The

---

[20] Mittelstein 1918, 5.

[21] Gareis 1906, 109.

[22] Ibid. Maritime law as a sub-category of international law contained no regulations on the relationships between the contract parties. An exception was the contracts involving the York Antwerp Rules from 1864 in which numerous States promised each other the same legal treatment of large damages. *Einheitliche Feststellung von Regeln über den Zusammenstoß von Schiffen* ('Uniform Establishment of Rules pertaining to the collision of ships'), *RGBl.* 1913, 49; in addition, Bar and Manowski 2003, 39 *et seq.*

strong productivity of the International Transport Insurance Federation,[23] founded in 1874, impressively proves this assertion correct.

Finally, the introduction of new regulations could also fail because of conditions specific to a country. The reform of the earthquake regulations met its Waterloo where the fire insurance companies were too keenly in competition with each other. A rigid organisation of the insurance industry could also prevent changes in the contractual bases. This goes to show once again how every process of standardisation was dominated by external circumstances.

4.2.2. Standardisation of the Contractual Bases as a Novel Organisational Strategy

The importance of standardisation extends far beyond its more or less dominant influence on the contractual practices in the individual economic branches. It comprises as important an innovation for legal relations as it did for industrial production and other complex fields in the emerging mass culture. Standardisation has been described at the outset as a novel strategy for the development and maintenance of regulations. Precisely therein lay its large potential that business discovered in the nineteenth century and made use of in international business as well as of the 1870's.

Contract terms and conditions could be used by every stakeholder in legal relations. They left room for the deviation from existing regulations and for the creation of new contractual subject matters. Contract terms could be changed at any time. Their flexibility enabled permanent adaptations to the needs of business. They built economic bridges over the cultural lag precisely during a time of such great economic dynamics as in the period between 1871 and 1914, when a first world economy took shape. This phenomenon is also demonstrated in the history of the earthquake clause: after its introduction—which succeeded at least in part—, the legal situation was much more manageable and calculable than before.

The use of contract terms and similar elements gave the control of the contractual subject matter to those players who could enforce their use. In this sense, the stakeholders in business had already discovered standardisation as an instrument to exercise their economic power on the level of the individual States. They were able to deviate from the

---

[23] Compare the examples in the table on the international standardisation of contract terms and conditions in section 2.3.2.

judgements and assessments made by State legal regulations. They were able to shift the contractual risks to the prospective contractual partners. For instance, wholesalers and haulage contractors frequently excluded their liability for tardiness or spoilage during transportation. Contract terms, however, could also be negotiated bilaterally and represent a balance between the interests of different groups. An example for this is the creation of the German 'normative conditions' for insurance contracts that were agreed upon at the beginning of the twentieth century under State supervision between insurers and the insured.[24]

In the first part of this study, it was argued that the use of standard clauses and standard contracts in the course of transnational business entailed additional benefits as well. Through contractually agreed substantive regulations, the stakeholders from various countries, entrepreneurial and legal systems were able to determine themselves how possible cases of conflicts were to be resolved. Moreover, they were able to withdraw their conflicts from the State's sphere of influence through the establishment of arbitration courts and tribunals.

These considerations have been touched upon in many facets of the history of the earthquake clause. They cannot be easily demonstrated. Could the imponderables that arose in the collision of different legal systems really have been avoided by the use of the according contract terms? For example, such a collision of legal regulations was experienced by contemporaries after the San Francisco earthquake in the disputes between the Californian plaintiffs and the German insurances companies unwilling to pay compensation for damages. Legal problems of far-reaching consequences arose here: would German courts handle the lawsuits of the injured parties? According to which law were the German courts required to adjudicate the stipulated exclusion clauses? Would they interpret and apply the agreements differently—as the insurers hoped—than the California courts had done? Clarity would not be achieved before the cases were heard. The regional court in Hamburg declared that it would assume jurisdiction, applied California law and adjudged one of the German companies involved to pay damages. In other cases, the injured and the insurance companies fought their way through all of the courts on the question of the enforceability of Californian decisions in Germany.

---

[24] Hagen, *ZVersWiss 10* (1910), 204.

Finally, the *Reichsgericht* denied this enforceability pursuant to German international private law.[25]

These disputes would probably have turned out otherwise if the contract parties had submitted them to arbitration. Above all, this procedure certainly would have saved the participants huge legal costs. However, arbitration panels have always been unusual in fire insurance because the value of the claims was usually low. They were more frequent, on the other hand, in reinsurance contracts. Correspondingly, the reinsurers seldom sued their contractual partners.[26] It must be assumed that they made use of arbitrators or achieved out-of-court settlements.

The use of arbitrators entailed numerous tangible benefits. The players did not need to enter the quicksand of international private law. They could choose arbitrators that were acquainted with the difficult material of the law of reinsurance. They avoided a declaration of their business situation in court and, by necessity, in the presence of competitors. In addition, they saved themselves long-standing battles through the court instances.

However, international arbitration stood at the very beginning of its institutional development.[27] International intertwinements only developed as of the turn of the century. The same branches that had also sought an autonomous organisation of their substantive contractual bases apparently reverted to non-State mechanisms of conflict resolution. The focus of the new arbitration panel converged on shipping traffic, commodity trading, the stock market and the insurance industry.[28] In individual cases, entire branches submitted themselves to forced arbitration to the exclusion of State jurisdiction. The Japanese commercial expert Masaichiro Ishizaki has described this process for the international silk trade.[29] Many additional examples are known. The German Chamber of Commerce, in cooperation with its Danish, Finnish, Greek, Czech and Hungarian

---

[25] See on this point section 3.1.7.1.

[26] After the San Francisco catastrophe, the international insurance press reported only two cases between reinsurers and fire insurance companies (see chapter 3.1.7.3 and 3.1.7.4).

[27] Even on the level of individual States did the establishment of arbitration centres prove difficult for the interested circles in commerce and industry. In Germany, the mercantile community in Berlin had laid a cornerstone; its statute of March 2, 1820 mandated the establishment of a permanent arbitration panel. Other mercantile communities followed this example (Krause 1930, 90).

[28] Ibid., 92. The united silk dealers in the New York Silk Association agreed to binding arbitration that excluded State jurisdiction (Ishizaki 1928, 276).

[29] Ishizaki 1928, 276.

counterparts, established a general *Handelseinigungsstelle* ('commercial mediation centre'),[30] and the *Comité Maritime International* offered arbitration aid following shipping accidents and rescues from distress at sea.[31]

The plan the International Law Association had sought for a long time to create a code of international law as a foundation for international arbitration went far beyond the boundaries of individual business branches.[32] In 1912, the International Chamber of Commerce additionally proposed the establishment of arbitration panels for the settlement of private law disputes between private parties and foreign States. These projects, however, were not realised before the outbreak of World War I. For this reason, the only option open to the companies that were internationally active was to agree to the settlement of disputes through ad hoc arbitration panels by means of contract clauses. This way, however, enforceable decisions could not be achieved. The arbitration decisions were apparently nevertheless observed because a loss of face and crippling economic sanctions such as the exclusion from professional organisations impended otherwise.[33]

Altogether, the business stakeholders greatly exploited the potential for standardisation on the level of the individual States already before World War I. In international trade, the practical significance of the form contracts, standard clauses and contract formulas continued to increase considerably between and after the world wars.[34]

4.3. Tendencies in the Replacement of State Law

An additional important result of this study is the observation that the internationalisation of business was accompanied by a differentiation and internationalisation or transnationalisation of the law. Numerous different stakeholders—legislators, local authorities, companies, associations and other groups—created a multitude of novel regulations in order to enable a 'world trade' in goods, services and capital. At the same time,

---

[30] Krause 1930, 119.
[31] Koch 1999, 48.
[32] Bar and Manowski 2003, 43.
[33] The arbitration panel clauses (1912) of the *Internationaler Verband der Baumwollspinner- und Weber-Vereinigungen* ('International Federation of Cotton Spinners and Weavers') allowed, for example, for this measure.
[34] Rabel 1936, 36.

they made use of all the imaginable forms at their disposal—from form contracts to international conventions.

An internationalisation can be spoken of where the legal changes did not involve an elimination of the State legal systems. This applied, for example, to the standardisation of the railway regulations by the Berne Convention of 1890. In other fields, the formation and development of law departed from the political-institutional processes from which State law originated. Examples are once again overseas commerce and reinsurance. Here, the term 'transnationalisation' describes the origin of structures existing outside of the States more accurately.[35]

The history of the earthquake clause shows nevertheless how problematic this terminological difference can actually become in individual cases. The new contract terms and conditions were created 'transnationally' insofar as the reinsurers developed them as abstract standards regardless of the law in the individual fields of business. Their implementation, on the other hand, developed 'internationally' through painstaking implementation in each individual legal system.

The question remains as to the normative quality of the legal structures that developed more or less far removed from the political and institutional processes. Was there—in the words of the legal historian Siegbert Lammel—a 'formation of law through contracts and contract terms' (trans.)?[36] And did the differentiation of law in 'world commerce' merely lead to its fragmentation, or did a new process of integration begin, namely the origin of a new, transnational legal system? These aspects will conclude this historical classification of the international standardisation of contract terms.

4.3.1. Development of Law between Autonomy and the State's Claim to Regulation

What normative effect did the mass use of certain standard contracts, standard clauses and contract formulas have in national and international commerce? The traditional answers to this question have differed widely. They depend above all on the assumptions that are made about the origin of law and quasi-legal structures.

---

[35] Werner and Zimmermann, 'Vergleich, Transfer, Verflechtung. Der Ansatz der Histoire croisée und die Herausforderung des Transnationalen', *Geschichte und Gesellschaft. Zeitschrift für Historische Sozialwissenschaft 28* (2002), 607 *et seq.*

[36] Lammel 1993, 89 *et seq.*

The notion that private actors could create their own law was in principle an unknown concept for jurists before World War I.[37] Contemporary discourses generally regarded contract conditions as the contractual subject matter. Jurists primarily dealt with the question of the circumstances under which the standardised conditions were incorporated into individual contracts. Moreover, as of the 1870's, courts in several countries—among them Germany, France and the United States—began to examine the contents of form contracts and refused to uphold them in the case of blatant infringements of basic principles such as good faith. This monitoring of contents demonstrates a growing sensitivity to the specific problems of the nature of mass contracts. But they too remained within the framework of the contemporary theory. Perceptions of a specific quality of standardised contractual subject matter that went beyond its contractual nature only became common as of the 1920's.[38]

However, widespread regulations used in form contracts could gain recognition as legal norms through a backdoor, namely as customary law. Such recognition required that they had been used for a long period in the respective legal system and agreed with State norms—especially with the appropriate legislative and judicial practice. In this sense, the jurist William Lewis wrote in 1889 that insurance law had carried 'into modern times the character of international customary law' (trans.).[39] In principle, however, precisely the flexibility of the general conditions and terms of business—one of their largest benefits—opposed the formation of customary law. The pliability and the change in these contract terms made it difficult to qualify individual regulations as customary law. Nevertheless, from an historical perspective, a 'formation of law through contracts and

---

[37] Legal-sociological approaches such as the theory propagated by the Czernowicz Professor Eugen Ehrlich, who believed that the nucleus of the development of law was to be found 'neither in legislation nor in jurisprudence but rather in society', received almost no attention. The famous quotation derives from Ehrlich's major work, *Grundlegung der Soziologie des Rechts* 1913, 390.

[38] Important German-language contributions are: Hueck 1923, 32–118; Rosenstock-Huessy 1926; Großmann-Doerth, *Juristische Wochenschrift, 58. Jahrgang* (1929), 3447 *et seq.*; Rühl 1931; Raiser 1935.

[39] Lewis 1889, 3. Neugebauer (1990, 44) describes the insurance law contract of the nineteenth century using Goldschmidt's formulation as 'a part of the all-European "stylus mercatorum"'. Similarly: Lammel 1993, 104 and Scherner, 'Allgemeine Rechtsgrundsätze und Rechtsvergleichung im europäischen Handelsrecht des 17. und 18. Jahrhunderts', *Ius commune 7* (1978), 118 *et seq.*

contract terms' (trans.) can be spoken of. Many indices point to autonomous processes of formation of law.[40]

The economic associations drafted new business conditions in the style of legislators, gave their members room for discussion and co-ordination and published the results in their own or independent business journals. Thus, for example, the first joint contract terms and conditions were concluded by the *Verband deutscher Privat-Feuerversicherungs-Gesellschaften* ('Federation of German Private Fire Insurance Companies') in 1874. In a similar fashion, the *Internationale Transportversicherungsverband* ('International Transport Insurance Federation') developed a comprehensive body of rules and regulations for the transnational haulage industry that was established in practice and accepted by the courts. In the daily business of overseas commerce, contract terms and conditions are known that achieved quasi-legal status as well.[41] Many of these sets of clauses were—despite criticism of individual regulations—widely recognised in practice. Moreover, the users could force each other to comply with the contractual bases by threatening each other with the exclusion from the respective branch organisation.

Jurists as well began to deal with pre-formulated contract texts as if they were legislative acts.[42] Numerous court decisions and scholarly publications dealt with the interpretation of standard contracts. In 1909, the first commentary on the contract terms of the fire insurance industry was published.[43] They were and remain to this day the most important source of fire insurance law, even though the law on insurance contracts went into effect at the same time.

The beginnings of an autonomous formation of law before World War I led to conflicts. A tension between business self-determination and the

---

[40] Here it is assumed that law can in principle also originate outside of political and institutional processes. This question is even controversial today. Teubner ('Globale Bukowina. Zur Emergenz eines transnationalen Rechtspluralismus', *RJ* 15 [1996], 264 *et seq.*) provides a summary of the exemplary controversy over the existence of a *lex mercatoria*. With reference to system theory, Teubner himself (267 *et seq.*) justifies the validity of the *lex mercatoria* as a transnational legal system, but scarcely considers legal-political values, although the legal system itself provides the criteria (fairness, legal security and utility) for a normative evaluation of the emerging normative material. Hiebaum, 'Systemizität und Pluralität am Beispiel der Globalisierung des Privatrechts', *RJ* 19 (1990), 451 *et seq.*

[41] Compare the examples in the table on the international standardisation of contract conditions in section 2.3.2.

[42] This reflects its contemporary designation as *leges contractus.*

[43] Domizlaff 1914.

State's claim to regulation began to arise that was also felt in the attempts to introduce the earthquake clause internationally; in some countries such as Italy, Portugal and Spain, insurers were free to change their own contract terms and conditions. State institutions kept their distance on the question of the earthquake clause. Thus, no restrictions were placed upon the self-organisation of the business. Other states aggressively took over the power to decide upon the configuration of the contractual subject matter. In the US, the standard policies spread from state to state. In California, the accustomed balance of power between the insurance companies and their customers was even reverse: after the earthquake, it was no longer the insurers, but the insured who, through the legislative and lobbies, determined which regulations would constitute the foundation of future contracts. In Germany as well, the final decision over the contractual subject matter was exercised by the State after the establishment of the supervisory agency in 1901. No contracts could be concluded that were not based upon the contractual conditions approved by the authorities. In these countries, the scope for a dynamic development of the contractual bases by the insurers began to decline. However, this decline did not eliminate the possibility of a formation of the law through contractual practice. The validity of standard contracts could become even more pronounced through their integration into the legal system, as the example of the railway transport regulation had shown. However, the previously wide scope for business to shape law through contracts and contract terms and conditions according to their interests alone disappeared.

4.3.2. *The Genesis of a Transnational Legal System?*

In the introduction to this work, the question was raised whether the international standardisation of general business conditions between 1871 and 1914 had contributed to the development of transnational legal structures—possibly even to the formation of a *lex mercatoria*.

The term *lex mercatoria* derives from writings on commercial law in the Middle Ages and the early modern period.[44] There it referred to an independent complex of commercial law practices that originated within

---

[44] It has been detectable since the late thirteenth century. Stein 1995, 3, note 14. Among others, *law merchant* and *ius mercatorumi* are known as synonyms. Among the important early modern monographs are Malynes' *Consuetudo vel lex mercatoria* (1622, 3rd ed., 1686), Marquart's *Tractatus politico-iuridicus de iure mercatorum et commerciorum singulari* (1662) and Beawes' *Lex mercatoria rediviva* (1752, 5th ed., 1792).

the supra-regional mercantile community and became law through consensus and habitual use. Broadly formulated and widely accepted basic legal principles such as *bona fides* and *rebus sic stantibus* formed the core of this *lex mercatoria*. Their restricted substantive shaping enabled a constant adaptation to the changes in the political and economic circumstances.[45]

The term *lex mercatoria* disappeared from contemporary legal discourse around 1800.[46] A century later, they reappeared in the writings of authors such as Levin Goldschmidt—however, no longer as a description of contemporary legal phenomena, but rather as a technical term of legal history.[47]

Not until the second half of the twentieth century was the topic taken up again in legal theory.[48] European and North American jurists studying the impact of the international interweaving of western economies and the emergence of the European single market[49] on the law discovered a '*nova lex mercatoria*'.[50] However, the meaning of this notion had fundamentally changed. Besides some general legal principles and institutions,[51] internationally accepted standard contracts and clauses were seen as parts of the phenomenon. Many authors regarded them as substantive sources of law.[52]

It can, of course, not be concluded from the history of the terminology that there had not been any transnational business law in the period before World War I. Did a new independent complex of legal norms that

---

[45] Meyer 1992, 15, 69. See also Cordes, 'Auf der Suche nach der Rechtswirklichkeit der mittelalterlichen Lex mercatoria', *Zeitschrift der Savigny-Stiftung für Rechtsgeschichte* 2001, 168 *et seq.* and Galgano 2001.

[46] Trakman (1983, 113) reports on a use of the term in the English court practice of the nineteenth century, Goodwin vs. Robarts (1875) in L.R. Exch. 337 *et seq.*

[47] For example, Goldschmidt in *Vermischte Schriften* II (1901), 29 *et seq.*

[48] Schmitthoff, 'International Business Law: A New Law Merchant', *Current Law and Social Problems*, vol. 2 (1961), 129–142; Goldstajn, 'The New Law Merchant', *Journal of Business Law* 1961, 12–17; Goldman, 'Frontières du droit et „lex mercatoria"', *Archives de la philosophie et du droit* 1964, 177–192.

[49] However, the existence of a transnational commercial law as an independent legal system is still far from general recognition even today.

[50] Synonyms: among others, 'modern law merchant', 'law of the common market'. See Stein 1995, 1 *et seq.*

[51] On this point in detail, see Osman 1992; Berger 2010; Béraudo 1997.

[52] The first to state this explicitly was Bonell 1976; admittedly, he suppressed the international legitimisation of rules such as INCOTERMS. Bärmann (1977, 568) is sceptical on this point, but recognises in the 'clearly visible plenitude of form contracts [...] standard rules of international commerce'.

regulated commerce originate in business practice prior to World War I?[53] Was there perhaps a *lex mercatoria* in all periods, as many authors believe?[54]

If one merely examines the non-State part of law in the first world economy, the differences between the *leges mercatoriae* of the Middle Ages and the early modern period or the period after World War II become tangible. In fact, multitudinous norms regulating transnational commerce were created between 1871 and 1914. However, whether they actually represented an independent legal complex is very doubtful.

What did not exist, on the other hand, is easy to determine: there was neither a body of generally recognised legal principles, such as the 'old' and the 'new' *lex mercatoria* entailed, nor an international arbitration that could have developed such principles.[55] Neither the legal practice of that time nor latter-day legal historians viewed the growing transnational structures as an independent legal complex. Insofar as writers like Wilhelm Kaufmann defined the 'autonomous law of non-State international federations' (trans.) as a part of international law, they referred in the first instance to the law of the internal organisation of these federations and not to the establishment of rules that affected third parties.[56]

What remains is the contractual practice. In some branches, standard contracts and similar elements achieved a dominant position. Here, in part, processes of legal development set in. In other areas, the companies had to orient themselves more strictly on State law, but nevertheless managed to create their own contractual bases insofar as this was possible within the existing boundaries. But overall, the development did not extend beyond the mass conclusion of contracts with identical or similar contents.

---

[53] This is what a definition that is limited to the important features of the concept might look like. It adheres to the 'narrow' interpretation of a transnational commercial law that in principle excludes State law. This distinction can, of course, not always be strictly maintained. On the term 'narrow' and 'broad', including additional reference, see Stein 1995, 184 *et seq.*

[54] Trakman, 'The Evolution of the Law Merchant: Our Commercial Heritage', *Journal of the Maritime Law and Commerce* 12 (1980), 1–24 and 12 (1981), 153–182, 1 *et seq.*; part 2, 509 *et seq.*; Berman 1988, 299 *et seq.*; Berman and Kaufman 1978, 273 *et seq.*; Booysen 1992, 205.

[55] The importance of places where the communication on law takes place is especially emphasised by the representatives of system theory, for example Calliess 2002, 192 *et seq.*

[56] Kaufmann 1908, 431 *et seq.*, 439. However, Kaufmann (432) also refers to the importance of this federation law for third parties and uses the railway regulations following the Berne Convention as an example.

Thus, neither a *lex mercatoria* nor an independent transnational commercial law developed prior to 1914. The belief that there was a continuous line of tradition between the *lex mercatoria* of the early modern period up to the transnational business law of the twentieth century thus proves to be questionable.[57] The structures and sources of the older law differ too greatly from those that began to take shape anew between 1871 and 1914. Nor did the characteristic tension between the flexible, universally valid norms of the *leges mercatoriae* and the formal, nationally restricted State law develop during this period.[58]

The legal elements that originated in the world economy prior to World War I can be described as the roots of the *'nova lex mercatoria'*, for the early rudiments of a transnational business law were not completely obliterated by the war. The form contracts, the standard clauses and the contract formulas lost their significance for a while, but remained largely intact and were in part further developed after the war. They succeeded in regaining their large importance in the transnational commercial law of the late twentieth century.[59]

Moreover, some of the institutions that had promoted the international unification of the contractual bases prior to World War I resumed their activity after the war. Examples are the International Law Association[60] and the International Transport Insurance Federation.[61] The International Chamber of Commerce,[62] which among other things supported the existence of the arbitration court for international private law disputes, originated from the International Chamber of Commerce Congress in 1919.[63]

In the 1920's, numerous legal historians also began to systematically investigate the changes in contractual practice. For the first time, the autonomous development of law became an independent area of interest

---

[57] Volckart and Mangels also come to this conclusion: 'Are the roots of the modern lex mercatoria really medieval?', *Southern Economic Journal* 65/3 (1999), 427–450.

[58] Meyer 1994, 15 *et seq.*

[59] The 'grey literature' of the 1920's from the different branches of business includes a number of examples. Cf. Berger 2001, 1 *et seq.*; Stein 1996, 38, 186 *et seq.* and Voigt 1999, 23, who provides further references.

[60] Starting in 1924, the ILA developed rules for the use of the formulas in bills of sale. The development reached an important result with the Warsaw Rules for Cif Contracts of 1928 (Rabel 1936, 4).

[61] Koch 1999, 56 *et seq.*

[62] Hamm 1929, 36.

[63] Among other things, the Geneva Protocol of the League of Nations on the State Recognition of Arbitration Clauses in Commerce of 1923 was based upon an initiative of the ICC (Dietler 1935, 8).

for jurists.[64] Thus Ernst Rabel, one of the keenest observers of his time of the development of international law, concluded in 1936 'half in admiration and half in astonishment' (trans.):[65]

> World commerce has created an incredible network of clauses, contract forms and business terms and conditions. With their aid, it has built up its own legal system that has more or less liberated itself from national laws and from international private law; the more arbitrational judicature exerts its influence and adjudicates matters using other standards than those used in the public courts, the less attention they pay to all national legal provisions (trans.).[66]

In this sense, the legal-historical and legal-theoretical résumé of this work is the following: the legal structures that develop through the standardisation of the contractual conditions in the course of the industrial revolution and then in the world economy prior to World War I are principally novel. They constitute the focal points for the later 'new' *lex mercatoria*.

---

[64] Ishizaki (1928), Sforza (1929), Großmann-Doerth (1933) and Rabel (1936) made important contributions to theoretical legal scholarship.

[65] Rabel 1936, 41.

[66] Ibid., 36.

APPENDICES

TABLE OF COMPANIES INVOLVED IN THE COMPENSATION OF DAMAGES OCCURRED IN SAN FRANCISCO

The following table includes all companies involved in the compensation of San Francisco fire damages as fire and reinsurance providers and retrocessionaires and who compensated at least $25.000 or were among the important companies regardless of their share in compensations. The A. M. Best Company reports "243 insurance companies involved in the San Francisco earthquake".[1]

The information was retrieved mainly from the *ÖVZ*, *Der Versicherungsfreund* and the *Österreichische Revue für die deutschsprachige Versicherungswelt*. It originates from the US newspapers and magazines *The Coast Review*, *(New York) Insurance Press*, *Best's Report* and *Westliche Post*, from the New York insurance company *Home*, from the *London Times* and the *Economist*, from the Scandinavian and French press (*La Semaine, Nouvelle Presse libre*), from the German papers *Feuerversicherung und Feuerschutz*, *Frankfurter Zeitung, Münchener neueste Nachrichten, Deutsche Warte* and *Berliner Börsen-Courier* and from the *39th Annual Report of the Insurance Commissioner of the State of California for the year 1906* and *Whitneys Report of the special committee* [...] (*1906*).

All financial figures—except for Danish Krones—were converted into US dollars. In 1906/1907, one dollar was approximately worth 0,20 Pound sterling (£), 4,20 Mark (M), 5,10 French Francs (FRF), 3,70 Danish Krones (DKK), 4,95 Austrian Krones (C), 5,20 Italian Lira (ITL) and 2 Japanese Yen (JPY). All figures were rounded up or down to the nearest $100.

EXPLANATION OF THE ABBREVIATIONS

1. column:
* *Members of the Board of Fire Underwriters of the Pacific.*

---

[1] A. M. Best Co. 1907, 6.

2. and 3. column:

C: *in California*; SF: *in San Francisco*; ø: *average premium*.

The premium income helped find an initial estimate of the damages: 'American papers approximately estimated the current insurance sum of the individual companies in San Francisco by presuming the average insurance sum of 1¼ % for the fire-stricken part of the city. Accordingly, the […] premium income [*of the companies in the city of San Francisco*] *would have to be multiplied by 80 in order to find out the insurance status of each company. The actual damage of each* [*American*] *company is estimated at 33 ½ to 60% of the insurance sum' (trans.).*[2] *In general, it refers to gross premiums; the sources do not differentiate in this respect.*

4. column:

N.Y. agreement / yes: *approval to the suggestion to liquidate up to 75% (meeting of the 31st of May, 1906).*

N.Y. agreement / no: *disapproval, willingness to pay according to policy conditions.*

N.Y. agreement / did not participate (d.n.p.): *did not come despite invitation (the rest was not invited).*

5. column:

EC: *Earthquake Clause*; ind: *indirect damages also excluded*; FBC: *Fallen Building Clause;* no EC?: *probably no EC, but perhaps FBC;* no information: *probably FBC.*

6. column:

Percentage: *Share of the compensation of the claimed total damages or (in case of low quotas) of the amount mentioned in the policy; e.g. 75%+ or 75%– means that in general 75% of the claims were compensated, in some cases more or less.*

A: *Assets in the USA on January 1st, 1906 (according to Insurance Press; those not mentioned have less than $1 million).*

Reserves+: *enough funds, reserves, share capital, deposits for damages.*

Reserves–: *reserves etc. were not enough;* liqu.: *liquidated,* portfolio to: *total reinsurance, i.e. all contracts transferred to other companies.*

Damages: *Number of claims*

---

[2] ÖVZ 1906, 134.

Share: *as to British companies, exchange losses of the shares at the London Stock Exchange (18th–21st of April, 1906), as to German companies, exchange losses 1905–1907. All figures of losses are estimates; most of them were estimated in the summer of 1906 and might have risen by approx. a third.*

1. Fire Insurance Companies (Direct Insurers)	Current Risks (1906)	Premium Income (1905)	N.Y. Agreement	EC or FBC	Payment Behaviour and Financial Involvement
*Aachen and Munich (Aachener & Münchener, Aachen/D)	C $7,98 million; SF $3,95 million	C $130.200 (ø 1.63%) / SF $49.400	yes	FBC	75%+; share −24.5%; payment of the dividends uncertain, 1.142 damages; (A >4,7 million)
*Aetna (Hartford, Conn./USA)		SF $44.800	no	no EC?	100%; $3,13 million; (A > 16 million)
*Agricultural (Watertown, N.Y./USA)		SF $16.300	yes		75% / 98%; $765.400; (A >2,9 million)
*Alliance Ass. (London/GB)	SF $3,46 million	SF $43.700	d.n.p. (?)	EC+FBC	50% / 75% / under $500 100%; >$1,76 million
*Alliance (Philadelphia, Pa./USA)		SF $15.800	yes		98%; $1,76 million; (A >1,24 million); withdrawal from California 1906
American (Boston, Mass./USA)		SF $12.300	yes		40%; withdrawal from California 1906, portfolio to Firemen's (Newark)
*American (Newark, N.J./USA)		SF $18.900	yes		98%−; (A >6 million)
*American Central (St. Louis, Mo./USA)		SF $19.881	no	no EC?	95–98%; $1.39 million; (A >4 million)
*American Fire (Philadelphia, Pa./USA)		SF $27.600	yes		50%; early liqu., portfolio mainly to Commercial Union; (A >2,9 million)
*Assurance Company of America (N.Y./USA)					75%; early liqu., portfolio mainly to National Fire (Hartford); (A >1,0 million)
Astrœa (Sweden)					reserves lost; received

Table (*cont.*)

1. Fire Insurance Companies (*Direct Insurers*)	Current Risks (1906)	Premium Income (1905)	N.Y. Agreement	EC or FBC	Payment Behaviour and Financial Involvement
*Atlanta-Birmingham (Atlanta, Ga./USA)		SF $6.300	yes		15–25% offered; withdrawal from California 1906, portfolio to Prudential (Tazeville, Va.)
*Atlas Ass. Co. (London/ GB)	SF $3,18 million	SF $39.800	no	no EC?	98–99%; share –20 %; severely affected; 1531 damages; (A >1,9 million)
Austin Fire (Tex./USA)		SF $4.300	yes		65–85%
*Austrian Phoenix (Österreichischer Phönix, Vienna/A-H)	C $4,94 million; SF $2,44 million	C $64.300 (ø 1.3%) / SF $30.600	yes		Payment refusal; amount ca. $2 million; withdrawal from California 1906
*British American Ins. (N.Y.) / British America Ass. Co. (Toronto/CA)	SF $1,06 million	SF $13.300 (N.Y. plus $3.000 over N.Y.)	yes		85–90+%; withdrawal of both companies from California 1907; (A >1,5 million)
Buffalo German (Buff., N.Y./USA)					75–90%; (A >2,4 million)
*Caledonian (Edinburgh/ GB)	SF $3,78 million	SF $47.300	yes	FBC	75%–98%; $1,48 million
*Caledonian-American (N.Y./USA)		SF $8.800		(partly?) EC	75%–98%; $44.700; (A >1.8 million)
*California (San Francisco, Ca./USA)		SF $22.600	no	no EC?	100%; $2,55 million (or $6,05 million); after capital increase; extension of the business to the East Coast
*Calumet (Chicago, Ill./ USA)		SF $13.800	yes		Increase of the company's capital and giving the injured parties a share in it; withdrawal from California 1906
*Citizens' Fire (St. Louis, Mo./USA)		SF $17.600			98%; $148.700
Colonial Underwriters			yes		75–90%
*Commercial Union (N.Y./ USA, London/GB)	SF $3,82 million	SF $49.000 (plus $4.000 over N.Y.)	d.n.p.	EC+ FBC	50% / 75% / less than $500 100%; share –9.73%; severely affected, >$2,3 million?; (A >5 million)

Table (*cont.*)

1. Fire Insurance Companies (Direct Insurers)	Current Risks (1906)	Premium Income (1905)	N.Y. Agreement	EC or FBC	Payment Behaviour and Financial Involvement
*Concordia Fire (Milwaukee, Wis./USA)		SF $6.300	yes		75–90%; (A >1,1 million)
*Connecticut Fire (Hartford/Conn./USA)		SF $34.200	no	no EC?	98–99%; (A >5 million)
Continental (N.Y./USA)		SF $33.900	no	no EC?	100%; $2,4 million; 807 damages; (A > 16 million)
*Delaware (Philadelphia, Pa./USA)		SF $12.600	yes		60–80%; (A >1,8 million)
Donau (A-H)					$80.800
Dutchess (Poughkeepsie, N.Y./USA)		SF $14.200	yes		30%; withdrawal from California 1906, discontinuance of the business and new foundation
Eagle Fire (N.Y./USA)		SF $12.000	yes		75%; withdrawal from California 1906; (A >1,0 million)
Empire City Fire (N.Y./ USA)					$49.400
English-American Underwriters			no	no EC?	90–100%
Erste Ungarische (A–H)					$ 30.300
*Federal (Jersey City, N.J./ USA)			yes		85+%; fire insurance business discontinued, portfolio to National Fire (Hartford); (A >2,2 million)
*Fire Association (Philadelphia, Pa./USA)		SF $33.200	yes		75–95%; (A >7 million)
*Fireman's Fund (San Francisco, Ca./USA)		SF $91.400	yes		50%, rest in shares in rescue company (Firemen's Fund); $11,1 million; (A >7,23 million)
Foncière (Budapest/A-H)					$25.300
*Franklin Fire (Philadelphia, Pa./USA)		SF $20.900	yes		75–90%+
German (Freeport, Ill./ USA)		SF $52.800	yes		60%; $1,73 million(?); (A >6 million); withdrawal from California 1906, then liqu., portfolio to Royal
German (Peoria/USA)		SF $14.800	yes		50%

Table (*cont.*)

1. Fire Insurance Companies (*Direct Insurers*)	Current Risks (*1906*)	Premium Income (*1905*)	N.Y. Agreement	EC or FBC	Payment Behaviour and Financial Involvement
*German Alliance (Allianz, Berlin/D)		SF $7.400		EC	98%; share −8.5%; reserves+; (A >1,4 million)
*German American (N.Y./ USA)		SF $44.700		EC+FBC	98%; 1.812 damages; (A > 14 million)
German National (Chicago, Ill./USA)		SF $15.700	yes		60%; portfolio to Dubuque Fire & Marine (Dubuque, Iowa); (A >1,0 million)
Germania Fire (N.Y./USA)		SF $46.600	yes		75–95%; $1,80 million; (A >6 million); withdrawal from California 1906
Girard Fire & Marine (Philadelphia, Pa./USA)		SF $13.700	yes		75–80%+; (A >2,2 million)
Glens Falls (G.F./N.Y./USA)		SF $17.700	yes	(partly?) EC	90%+ $994.100; (A >4 million)
*Globe and Rutgers (N.Y./ USA)		SF $16.000	yes		75%+; (A >3,8 million)
*Hamburg-Bremen Fire (Hamburg-Bremer, Hamburg/D)	C $7,22 million; SF $1,95 million ($243.900) (SF $4,48 million?)	C $111.700 (ø 1.54%)/ SF $56.200	yes	FBC	75%; $1,58 million; reserves+; 768 damages; severe exchange losses; withdrawal from California 1906; (A >2,0 million)
*Hanover Fire (N.Y./USA)		SF $23.200	yes	(partly?) EC	75–90%; (A >4 million)
*Hartford Fire (Hartford, Conn./USA)		SF $145.800	d.n.p.		98%; net $6,1 or 11 million (?); (A > 18 million)
*Helvetia Swiss, Ins, Co. (St. Gallen/CH)	SF $1,7 million		d.n.p.	EC (ind.)	98–99%; withdrawal from California 1907
Home (N.Y./USA)		SF $39.800	d.n.p.		98–99%; $2,14 Mio; (A >21 million)
*Home Fire & Marine (San Francisco, Ca./USA)		SF $38.000	yes		(A >1,8 million); 50%, rest in shares in rescue company (Firemen's Fund); no reinsurance.
*Indemnity Fire (N.Y./USA)		SF $4.800		EC	50% / 75% / claims under $500 to 100% $25.000
Indianapolis (Indianapolis/ USA)					
Individual Underwriters			no		

Table (*cont.*)

1. Fire Insurance Companies (Direct Insurers)	Current Risks (1906)	Premium Income (1905)	N.Y. Agreement	EC or FBC	Payment Behaviour and Financial Involvement
*Insurance Co. of North America (Philadelphia, Pa./USA)		SF $53.400	yes		98%; (A >12 million)
*Law Union & Crown (London/GB)	SF $2,44 million	SF $28.000	yes		98%; >$1.37 million, 776 damages
*Liverpool, London & Globe (Liverpool/GB)	SF $4,69 million	SF $56.900	no	no EC?	100%; $4–4,4 million; share –16.98%; $4 Mio; 1.790 damages; (A >12 million)
Lloyds Underwriters (London, GB/Ca.,USA)	some major risks				max. $1 million
*London Ass. (London/GB)	SF $7 million	SF $87.700	no	no EC?	98%; share –17.57%; $5,5 million; 2.359 damages
*London & Lancashire (Liverpool/GB)	SF $5 million	SF $68.600	no	no EC?	90–100%; share –19.49%; >$2,2 million 1523 damages; A >3,2 million
Manchester Fire (Manchester/GB)	SF $445.000				98%; was already reinsured with Atlas beforehand; return of the Californian business permit for 1906
*Mercantile Fire & Marine (Boston, Mass./USA)		SF $13.000	no	no EC?	95–98%; early liqu., portfolio to American Central (St. Louis)
*Michigan Fire & Marine (Detroit, Mich./USA)		SF $7.900	yes		98%; (A >1,0 million)
Milwaukee Mechanics (Milw., Wis./USA)		SF $34.300	yes		(A >3,2 million); 70%; withdrawal from California 1906
Nassau Fire (Brooklyn, N.Y./USA)		SF $7.400	yes		70–90%
*National Fire (Hartford, Conn./USA)		SF $42.400	yes		75–90%; $2,16 million; (A >7 million)
National Union Fire (Pittsburg, Pa./USA)		SF $20.900	yes		75–90%; (A >2,1 million); withdrawal from California 1906
New Brunswick (New. Br., N.J./USA)			yes		75%
*New Hampshire Fire (Manchester/ N.H./USA)		SF $8.900	no	EC+FBC	99%; $561.000; (A >4 million); withdrawal from California 1906

Table (*cont.*)

1. Fire Insurance Companies (*Direct Insurers*)	Current Risks (*1906*)	Premium Income (*1905*)	N.Y. Agreement	EC or FBC	Payment Behaviour and Financial Involvement
New York Fire (N.Y./USA)		SF $6.900	yes		40%; withdrawal from California 1906, portfolio to New Hampshire Fire
New York Underwriters (Hartford, Conn./USA)		SF $73.400	no	no EC?	98%; $3,5 million
*New Zealand (Auckland, N.Z./USA)	SF $2,34 million	SF $29.300	no	partly EC	98%; as to EC 75–90%
*Niagara Fire (NY.)		SF $33.100	yes		98%; $1,91 million; 1.241 damages; (A >4 million)
Nordisk Brandforsikring (DK)	SF DKr 130.000				max. DKK 50.000
Nordisk Gjenforsikring (København/DK)	SF $120.000				$30.000–40.000
*North British & Mercantile (London, Edinburgh/GB)	SF $3,51 million	SF $44.600	no	FBC	98%; >$3 million; share –10%; (A >6 million)
*North German Fire (N.Y. / Norddeutsche Feuer, Hamburg/D)	C $7,87 million; SF ca. $1 million	C $109.500 (ø 1.4%) / SF $58.900 (plus $11.600 over N.Y.)	yes	EC (ind.)	Major losses; offered to compensate 30%; withdrawal from California 1906; liqu. despite reinsurance and taken over from Norddeutscher
North River (N.Y./USA)		SF $9.000	yes		75%+; (A >1,7 million)
*Northern Assurance (London/GB)	SF $4,3 million	SF $53.700			99%; share –5.06%; severely affected; $2,5 million for 912 damages; (A >3,8 million)
Northern Union				(partly?) EC	
Northwestern Fire & Marine (Minneapolis, Minn./USA)					75–85%;
Northwestern National (Milwaukee, Wis./USA)		SF $11.000	yes		98%; $592.600; (A >4 million)
*Norwich Union Fire (Norwich/GB)	SF $2,72 (4,24 million?)		d.n.p.	EC (ind.)	50% / 75% / claims under $500 to 100%; >$700.000; share –2.35%; withdrawal from California 1907; (A >2,7 million)
Nye Danske Brandforsikring (København/DK)	500.000 DKr				

Table (*cont.*)

1. Fire Insurance Companies (Direct Insurers)	Current Risks (1906)	Premium Income (1905)	N.Y. Agreement	EC or FBC	Payment Behaviour and Financial Involvement
*Orient (Hartford, Conn./ USA)	SF $4,6?	SF $14.400	no	no EC?	90–100%; >$2 million(A >2,4 million)
Österreichischer Phönix (Wien/A-H)					(is mentioned)
Pacific Underwriters (USA)		SF $20.600	yes		50%, rest in shares in rescue company (Firemen's Fund)
*Palatine Ins. Co. (London/GB)	SF $2,74 million	SF $34.200		EC+ FBC	50% / 75% / under $500 100%; >$1,7 million (A >2,3 million)
*Pelican Assurance Co. (N.Y./USA)	SF $700.000	SF $7.300	no	(partly?) EC	95–98% $400.000?
*Pennsylvania Fire (Philadelphia, Pa./USA)		SF $55.200	yes		95–98%; (A >7 million)
*Phenix (Brooklyn, N.Y./ USA)		SF $61.800	yes		75–100%; (A >8 million)
Philadelphia Underwriters (USA)			yes		90%+
*Phoenix (Hartford, Conn./ USA)		SF $28.000		EC+ FBC	75% / 98%; $1.76 million; A >8 million
*Phoenix Ass. Co. (London/GB)	SF $4,3 million	SF $53.800	no	(partly?) EC	98%; share −22.6%; $2,4 million? (A >3,4 million)
Protector Underwriters				EC+ FBC	75% / 98%
*Providence-Washington (Provedence, R.I./USA)		SF $15.800	yes		90%+; (A >3,0 million)
Providentia (Wien/A-H)					$141.400
Prussian National (Preussische National, Stettin/D)	C $8,35 million	C $80.100 (ø 0.96%) / SF $17.900	yes	FBC	75%; $260.000; share −19.4%; more insured but reinsured; (A >1,2 million)
*Queen (N.Y./USA)	$2,37 million	SF $24.100	no	no EC?	100%; >US$1,6 million (A >6 million)
*Queen City (Sioux Falls, S.D./USA)		SF $2.000	yes		75–100%
* Rhein & Mosel (Rhine & Moselle, Straßburg/D)	C $7,37 million; SF $4,77 million (f.e.R. $97.600)	C $106.400 (ø 1.44%) / SF $59.600	d.n.p.	EC+ FBC	Payment refusal, only claims under $500 to 50%; ca. $97.500; withdrawal from California 1906
Riunione Adriatica di Sicurtà (Trieste/I)					$30.300

Table (*cont.*)

1. Fire Insurance Companies (*Direct Insurers*)	Current Risks (*1906*)	Premium Income (*1905*)	N.Y. Agreement	EC or FBC	Payment Behaviour and Financial Involvement
*Rochester German (Rochester, N.Y./USA)		SF $10.700	yes		90%+; return of the Californian business permit for 1906; (A >1,6 million)
*Royal (Liverpool/GB)	SF $6,67 million	SF $83.600	no	no EC?	100%; $4,34–6,67 million; share –16.07%; severely affected; 2.283 damages; (A >8 million)
*Royal Exchange Ass. (London/GB)	SF $4,52 million	SF $56.500	yes	EC	75–95%; $2,64 million
					share –5.13% severely affected; 1.248 or 1873 damages; (A >2,2 million); withdrawal from California 1908
*St. Paul Fire & Marine (St.P., Minn./USA)		SF $18.700	no	no EC?	95–98%; (A >4 million)
Scotch Underwriters	SF $368.000		yes	(partly?) EC	75%-98%
*Scottish Union & National (Edinburgh/GB)	SF $1,75		yes	FBC	98%; $1,3 million; 500 damages; (A >5 million)
Securitas (Wien/A-H)					$141.400
Security (New Haven, Conn./USA / Topeka/CA)		SF $6.200	yes	(partly?) EC	95–98%
*Security Fire (Baltimore/ USA)		SF $7.800	yes		No payment (?); $450.000; liqu., portfolio to New Jersey Fire; (A >1,8 million)
Skandia (Stockholm/ Sweden)	SF $700.000				$644.500
Skandinavia Gjenforsikring (København/DK)	SF ca. DKK 400.000				DKK 166.700
*Spring Garden (Philadelphia, Pa./USA)		SF $9.500	yes		70%; (A >2,0 million)
*Springfield Fire & Marine (Spr., Mass./USA)		SF $26.200	no	no EC?	99%; (A >7 million)
*State Fire Ins. Co. (Liverpool/GB)	SF $1,23 million	SF $15.500	no	no EC?	95–98%; $1,25 million; 389 damages
Süddeutsche Bank (D)					
*Sun (London/GB)	SF $3,2 million	SF $40.000	no	FBC	98%; $1,65 million; share –10.71%; (A >3,1 million)

Table (*cont.*)

1. Fire Insurance Companies (Direct Insurers)	Current Risks (1906)	Premium Income (1905)	N.Y. Agreement	EC or FBC	Payment Behaviour and Financial Involvement
*Svea Fire and Life (Gothenburg/Sweden)	SF $2,07 million	C $122.400/ SF $26.000	yes	(partly?) EC	75%+; $741.200; reinsured with Aestria (Gothenburg, S)
*Teutonia (New Orleans, La./USA)		SF $5.300	no	no EC?	95–98%
*Traders (Chicago, Ill./ USA)	gut $4 ½ million	SF $58.100 (ø 1.29%)	yes		(A >3,2 million); no payments; supplementary payment ($200 per share) refused by shareholders; liqu.
*Transatlantic Fire (Transatlantische, Hamburg/D)	C $10,47 million; SF $5 million	C $150.300 (ø 1.43%) / SF $73.900	yes	FBC	Payment refusal; amount over $4 million, partly reinsured; liqu., insurance transferred to Albingia
*Union (Philadelphia, Pa./ USA)		SF $8.700			
*Union Assurance Society (London/GB)	SF $3,38 million	SF $42.300	yes		98%; $2.345.400; share –13.73%; (A >1,7 million)
*United Firemen's (Philadelphia, Pa./USA)		SF $11.000	yes		75–90%+; withdrawal from California 1906; (A >1,8 million)
United States Fire (USA)					early liqu., portfolio to American company
*Victoria (N.Y./USA)		SF $1.800	yes		98%; withdrawal from California 1906
Westchester Fire (N.Y./ USA)		SF $17.600	yes		95–98%; (A >4 million)
Westdeutsche Ver-sicherungsbank (Essen/D)					Dividend?; share –58%; $4,1 million reserve provided
*Western (Toronto/CA)	SF $1,39 million	SF $17.500	yes		85–90+%; (A >2,3 million)
Western Underwriters (USA)			yes		
Williamsburgh City Fire (Brooklyn, N.Y./USA)		SF $15.900		EC	50% / 75%; claims under $500 to 100%; (A >2,8 million)
Winchester (or Westchester)					$779.700

2. The Coast Review's overview of the shares of the direct insurers[3]	Current Risks (1906)	Premium income (1905)
4 Californian companies:	C $48.012.854	C $845.855
78 non-Californian American companies:	C $355.534.632	C $5.507.191
32 foreign companies:	C $254.507.307	C $3.930.196
Total (114 companies):	C $658.054.793	C $10.283.242

3. Figures of the New York Insurance Press from May 1906[4]	Premiums 1905	Amount of Compensation (net)	Quotient (Dollar Compensation per Dollar Premium)
49 Fire insurance companies	$1.195.789	$42.201.000	$35,30 (another increase by 15% expected)
2 Fire insurance companies	$29.676	$1.500.000	$50,55
3 Fire insurance companies	$135.509	$6.000.000	$44.28

4. Reinsurance Companies and Retrocessionaires	Current Risks (1906)	Premium Income (1905)	N.Y. Agreement	EC or FBC	Payment Behaviour and Financial Involvement
Aachener Rück (Aachen/D)					Payment of the dividend uncertain
Badische Mit- & Rückversicherungs- gesellschaft (Stuttgart/D)				EC	Reserve+
Berlinische Feuer (Berlin/D)					Reinsurance of the Aachen-Münchener. share −31,4 %; agio and profits 1906 lost; capital stock increased
Camden Fire			yes		$365.500; (A >1,6 million)
*Equitable (Providence, R.I./USA)		SF $5.800	yes		(A >1,3 million)
Erste Böhmische Rück (Prague)	"major American portfolio"				severely affected?; exchange losses; reserves $630.000; possible losses $756.000

---

[3] Manes, *Masius' Rundschau* 1906, 164. *Der Versicherungsfreund*, 1 May 1906, 2, cites information of the *Coast Review* on 105 companies.
   [4] Cited in *ÖVZ* 1906, 147.

Table (*cont.*)

4. Reinsurance Companies and Retrocessionaires	Current Risks (1906)	Premium Income (1905)	N.Y. Agreement	EC or FBC	Payment Behaviour and Financial Involvement
Globus (Hamburg/D)					involved as reinsurer
Hamburg (Hbg./D)					involved as reinsurer; Reserve+
Internationale Rück (A-H)					$25.300
Kings County			no	no EC?	return of the Californian business permit for 1906
Kölnische Rück (Cologne/D)	SF 3 million (together with Minerva)				
Minerva Retrocessions- und Rückversicherungs- Gesellschaft (Köln/D)	SF $8 million (?)				Not very high losses
Münchener Rück (Munich/D)	SF ca. $3 million				$2,7 million; Reserve+ ($13,11 million)
Schweizerische Rück (Zurich/CH)					"only moderately involved"
Süddeutsche Rück (Munich/D)	SF not very much				$25.000
Union (Philadelphia, Pa./ USA)		SF $8.700	yes		994 damages; return of the Californian business permit for 1906
Wiener Rück (Wien/A-H, reinsurer of the Hamburg-Bremer)					$282.800; dividend uncertain; exchange losses; supplementary payment for shares 30–40% and new payments planned.

TABLE OF COMPANIES INVOLVED IN THE COMPENSATION OF DAMAGES OCCURRED IN VALPARAISO

The following table includes all companies of international importance that were involved in the compensation of fire damages in Valparaiso—and also in other Chilean cities—as fire and reinsurance providers and retrocessionaires. All the information was retrieved from the *ÖVZ* and *La Semaine*. *La Semaine* also listed 21 Chilean and a number of less important European companies.[5]

All financial figures were converted into US dollars. In 1906/1907, one dollar was approximately worth 0,20 Pound sterling (£), 4,20 Mark (M) and 5,10 French Francs (FRF).

1. Fire Insurance Companies	Current Risks in Valparaiso (1906)[6]	EC oder FBC	Financial Involvement[7]
Aachener & Münchener (Aachen/DE)	$548.000	EC	$28.000
Atlas Ass. Co. (London/GB)		EC (ind.)	
Hanseatische Feuer (Hamburg/DE)	not very much	EC	ca. $73.500
Liverpool, London & Globe (Liverpool/GB)		EC (ind.)	
London & Lancashire (Liverpool/GB)		EC (ind.)	
Magdeburger Feuer	negligible rest business	EC	

---

[5] Names with no information on losses, *La Semaine*, 9 September 1906, 6 and 16 September 1906, 6.

[6] According to unproven information, values amounting to $225.42 million were insured against fire in Chile on the 31st of December, 1905, and only $3.5 million of this sum—equalling 5.6%—were reinsured.

[7] The British insurance companies expected having to pay up to $4.43 million (FRF 22.575 million); one even expected a sum as high as around $880,000 (FRF 4.5 million). Some of the British insurance companies were involved in Valparaiso with financial participations of $500,000 (£ 100,000). *La Semaine*, 25 November 1906, 7; *ÖVZ*, cited in *Feuerversicherung und Feuerschutz* 1906, 227.

Table (*cont.*)

1. Fire Insurance Companies	Current Risks in Valparaiso (1906)	EC oder FBC	Financial Involvement
Providentia (Frankfurt a.M./DE)			uncertain
Regent Fire (Glasgow/BG)			$1 million? Liqu. planned
Royal (Liverpool/GB)		EC (ind.)	

2. Reinsurance Providers and Retrocessionaires	Current Risks in Valparaiso (1906)	Financial Involvement
Aachener Rück (Aachen/DE)		$19.600
Erste Böhmische Rück		uncertain
Kölnische Rück (Köln/DE)	some 100.000 M ($24.400)	
Minerva (Köln/DE)		
Münchener Rück (München/DE)	$100.000	A in USA > $4 million
Norddeutsche Feuer (Hamburg/DE)	as reinsurance provider	moderately involved
Thuringia (DE)	as reinsurance provider	slightly involved
Westdeutsche Versicherungsbank (Essen/DE)	reinsurance provider of an English company	negligible

BIBLIOGRAPHY

BIOGRAPHICAL INFORMATION ON INDIVIDUALS MENTIONED IN THIS WORK

The following information was retrieved from different sources such as *Who is Who in Insurance* (1908), *California Blue Book or State Roster* (1907) and M. *Stolleis, Juristen* (1995).

ADLER, KARL: Austrian business lawyer. University chair in Czernowitz. Publications on commercial law, law related to bills of exchange and promissory notes and banking law.

ALCOCK, CHARLES: At the London Ass. Co. (London) until 1885 and then at Royal (Liverpool). General Manager at Royal as of 1893.

ARCOLEO, GIORGIO: Born 1850 in Caltagirone (Catania). Legal studies in Naples; writer, journalist, civil lawyer and politician. Public law teacher in Rome, then in Naples, where he also taught Italian literary studies. Died 1914.

ATWOOD, HORACE F.: Born 1850 in Boston (Mass.). In the Western Dept. for *Hamburg-Bremer* (Hamburg); as of 1879, Special Agent of the Rochester German (Rochester, N.Y.) there, as of 1880 in its Home Office; secretary of the company as of 1883.

BALDWIN, SIMEON E.: Born 1840 in New Haven (Conn.). American jurist and politician (Dem.). Justice from 1897 to 1907, Chief Justice at Connecticut State Supreme Court from 1907 to 1910, then Governor of the state.

BARZINI, LUIGI: Born 1874 in Orvieto, one of the best known journalists of Italy; mainly wrote reports on foreign countries for the *Corriere della Sera*. Died 1947.

BEDALL, EDWARD F.: Born 1839 in Essex (GB). Career as an insurer at Royal (Liverpool) in GB, CA and in the USA; president of Queen Ins. Co. of America (New York) and U.S. attorney for the Royal (Liverpool) as of 1900. President of the New York Tariff Association from 1895 to 1896, president of the New York Board of Fire Underwriters from 1896 to 1897. Member of the Committee on Clauses and Forms of the National Board of Fire Underwriters from 1906 to 1907. Publications on fire insurance.

BROCCHI, AUGUSTO: Born 1856 in Turin. Joined the *Compagnia Anonima* (Turin) in 1877; as of 1902 General Manager. Secretary of the *Concordato-Incendio Italiano* in 1907.

BRUSCHETTINI, ARNALDO: Born 1870. Jurist at the University of Naples; publications on general and specific commercial law, especially maritime law, transport law and insurance law.

BUECK, HENRY AXEL: Secretary general of the *Centralverband Deutscher Industrieller* (*CVDI*) and of the *Vereinigung der in Deutschland arbeitenden Privat-Feuerversicherungs-Gesellschaften.*

CARRIGAN, ANDREW: Vice-president of the company Dunham-Carrigan-Haden.

CERISE, GUILLAUME BARON: Born 1847 (Val d'Aoste). Worked for the insurance company *l'Union-Incendie* as of 1881; its director as of 1899; president of the *Comité de Défense du Syndicat Général des Compagnies d'Assurances à primes fixes contre l'Incendie à Paris.*

CULLINAN: Lawyer from San Francisco. Probably Eustace Cullinan, born 1876 in SF, a lawyer, businessman (Co. Cullinan & Hickey), politician (Rep.) and editorial writer of the San Francisco Bulletin.

CURTIN, JOHN BARRY: Born 1867 in Tuolumne (Ca.). Attorney at law; 1892 District Attorney; 1898 Member of the California State Senate.

CUTLER, FLETCHER A.: Californian jurist; worked as an attorney and judge in the time following the San Francisco catastrophe.

DI RENZO, VINCENZO: From 1907 until 1929 *Capo di Ufficio dell'Assunzione rischi d'incendio* of the *Compagnia di Milano.* A leading insurance clerk, Di Renzo was involved in the regulation of damages in Messina and Reggio.

DOHRMANN, FREDERICK W.: A Californian businessman, Dohrmann was involved in porcelain trade (Nathan Dohrmann Co.), hotel business (St. Francis Hotel), banking (director of the Savings Union Bank and Trust Company) etc. Co-founded the Policyholders' League in 1907.

DREW, ALEXANDER M.: Born 1857 in Stephenson County (Ill.). Jurist, called to the State Bar of California in 1888. Member of the California State Assembly as of 1902.

DUTTON, WILLIAM J.: Born 1847 in Bangot (Me.). As of 1867 employee at Fireman's Fund (San Francisco), whose president he became in 1900; also president of the Home Fire & Marine (San Francisco) as of 1896. President of the San Francisco Board of Marine Underwriters as of 1888. During some period of time president and vice-president of the Board of Fire Underwriters of the Pacific and Chairman of its Executive Committee from 1893 to 1897.

ERLE: Born 1783 in Fifehead-Magdalen, Dosset (GB). Counsel to the Bank of England for a few years and before becoming MP. Judge (justice) as of 1845. Died 1880.

EVANS, HENRY: Born 1860 in Houston (Texas). Almost continuously at Continental (New York) as of 1878; president as of 1903. Also president of the Fidelity (New York) as of 1906. From 1904 onward Chairman of the National Board of Fire Underwriters' Committee of Twenty on congested districts in cities; probably Chairman of the Finance Committee of the New York Board of Fire Underwriters 1904–06.

FADDA, CARLO: Born 1853 in Cagliati (Sardegna). Law teacher at the Universities of Macerata, Genova and—as of 1895—Naples. One of the leading Italian Romanists, he was strongly oriented towards the German Historical School; worked in various subsidiary disciplines of law. Died 1931.

FOLGER, HERBERT: Born 1858 in San Francisco. In the insurance business as of 1888; Assistant General Agent for the Pacific Coast, for the German-American (New York) and Hartford Fire (Conn.) as of 1901. President of the Fire Underwriters' Association of the Pacific from 1896 to 1897 and member of different committees.

FRIED, ALFRED H.: Born 1864 in Vienna. Book seller, journalist. Devoted pacifist; co-founder of the *Deutsche Friedensgesellschaft* in 1907. Founder and editor of various magazines such as *Annuaire de la vie internationale* (1905).

FULD, LUDWIG: Born 1859 in Mainz. Specialized in commercial and criminal law; insurance lawyer and publicist at international level. *Justizrat* as of 1906.

GAREIS, KARL: Law professor at the University of Königsberg. Publications on civil, commercial, international and colonial law.

GILLETT, JAMES N.: Born 1860 in Viroqua (Wisc.). Jurist and politician (Rep.). City Attorney in Eureka and Member of the California State Senate as of 1896; 1902 member of the US Congress; from January 1907 until 1911 Governor of California.

GOBBI, ULISSE: Born 1859 in Milan. Influential personality of Italian insurance research; Professor for political economics at the *Università Commerciale Bacconi* and at the *Reale Istituto Tecnico Superiore* in Milan.

GOLDSCHMIDT, LEVIN: Born 1828. One of the most important personalities of German commercial law. Habilitation in Heidelberg in 1855, law teacher there as of 1860. 1858 foundation of the ZHR, 1870–75 judge at the *BOHG/ROHG*, *Ordinarius* (full professor) in Berlin as of 1857, Member of the *Reichstag* (*Nationalliberale Partei*, 'National Liberal Party') 1875–97. Died 1897.

GRANT, JOSEPH D.: Probably the landowner and entrepreneur J. D. GRANT, owner of apartment houses in San Francisco.

GREELY, OTTO ETHAN: Born 1853 in Bangor (Me.). Jurist; in insurance business from 1877 onward as special agent and adjuster of the Phenix (Brooklyn, N.Y.). 1998–1999 president of the Minn. & Dak. Fire Underwriters' Assn.; 1900 president of the Fire Underwriters' Assn. of the Northwest. GREELY was sent to San Francisco as special representative and liquidator of the Phenix (Brooklyn) and at the following annual meeting of the Fire Underwriters' Association of the Northwest in Chicago reported on his experiences. Translations of his report were published in the *ÖVZ* and *ÖRev*.

GRIBEAUVAL, JEAN BAPTISTE VAQUETTE DE: Born 1715 (Amiens), French General of Artillery and weapon engineer. Career as an officer as of 1735; in 1767, he introduced a revolutionary artillery system based on mobile military divisions and standardised artillery types. Died 1789 (Paris).

GRÜNWALD (GRUENWALD), HEINRICH LEOPOLD: Born 1859 in Arad (Rumania). Grünwald was member of the executive board of the *Kölnische Rück* from 1896 to 1932 and its president from 1917 to 1932. He travelled to the USA in 1897, 1899 and 1912 in order to get to know the American insurance market.

GRUNER, ERNST: Born 1853 in Coburg (Germany). Jurist; involved in the introduction of the workers' insurance from 1887 to 1894; 1894–1902 *Vortragender Rat* in the *Reichsamt des Innern* ('Dept. of the Interior'), 1902–1914 president of the *Kaiserliches Aufsichtsamt für Privatversicherung*.

HAGEN, OTTO: Born 1865 in Landsberg (Prussia). Jurist and insurance publicist; *Landgerichtsrat* ('District Court Councillor'), as of 1907 at the *Kammergericht* Berlin ('Court of Appeal').

HARDY, EDWARD ROCHIE: Born 1862 in Detroit (Mich.). Insurance researcher and librarian. Lecturer at the School of Commerce der New York University as of 1905. Co-founded the Insurance Institute of America in 1909.

HERLITZ, KARL: Director of the Stockholm reinsurance company *Skandia* around 1906.

HAVEN, CHARLES D.: Born 1836 in New York, secretary of the Union Ins. Co. (Ca.) as of 1865; 1870–96 secretary of the Board of Fire Underwriters of the Pacific, then president. As of 1881 Resident Secretary on the Pacific Coast of Liverpool, London & Globe (Liverpool).

HOLLITSCHER, KARL V.: representative of the Co. Heckscher & Gottlieb, Berlin; also worked for the *Rossija* (St. Petersburg). Publications on reinsurance business.

HUMPHREY, RICHARD L.: secretary of the National Advisory Board on Fuels and Structural Materials of the United States Geological Survey. Humphrey was sent to San Francisco right after the earthquake had struck the city.

IVERSEN, LARS: Born 1874 in Skaarup (DK). Mathematician; initially vice-secretary of the state insurance for *Livsforsikring*, then actuary at Skandinavia.

JESSEL, SIR GEORGE: Born 1824 (London). English judge. Master of the Rolls (M.R.), i.e. president of the Court of Appeals in the House of Lords, as of 1873. Died 1881 (London).

JONES, O. G.: Prior to 1906 adjuster for Syracuse (New York). At the time of the earthquake lawyer in California. Later, an independent adjuster in San Francisco.

JORDAN, DAVID STARR: President of Stanford University at the time of the earthquake.

KAEMPF, JOHANNES: Born 1842 in Neuruppin (Brandenburg, Germany). Politician (*Fortschrittliche Volkspartei*, 'Progressive People's Party'), banker and business official. Among other things, Kaempf was *Berlin Stadtrat* ('city councillor') and member of the *Reichstag* (president of the *Reichstag* 1912–1918), president of the *Ältesten der Kaufmannschaft* of Berlin, member of the committee of the *Deutscher Handelstag* and member of the supervisory board of *Münchener Rück*.

KAHN, JULIUS: Born 1861 in Kuppenheim (Baden, Germany); in California as of 1866. Theatre actor and jurist. Rep.; member of the California State Assembly as of 1892; member of the US Congress as of 1898; repeatedly re-elected.

KAUFMANN, WILHELM: German jurist. Between 1891 and 1923, Kaufmann published various works on international law and on international non-public law of commerce.

KIDDING, I. M.: Born in 1843 in Prague; in California as of 1851; autodidact in law. Intern in a law firm for commerce law as of 1864; soon a distinguished expert on tax law; lecturer at Harvard University as of 1881 thanks to this reputation. 1902 judge at Supreme Court, died in a snow avalanche four months after appointment.

KING, L. M.: Probably the later Lyman M. King, Rep., Progressive, Californian Senator as of 1917. A San Franciscan citizen of the same name was active in the Association for the Improvement and Adornment of San Francisco around 1904.

KINNE, C. MASON: Born 1841 near Syracuse (New York). As of 1866 adjuster and agent for various companies in California, as of 1899 assistant secretary of Liverpool, London & Globe (Liverpool) San Francisco.

KISSKALT, WILHELM: jurist, consulter for *Münchener Rück* (among other things) at the time of the San Francisco catastrophe; later executive of the company.

KNEBEL-DOEBERITZ, HUGO v.: *Wirklicher Geheimer Oberregierungsrat*, member of the *Versicherungsbeirat des Kaiserlichen Aufsichtsamtes für Privatversicherung.*

LEAVITT, FRANK W.: Born 1866 in Indianapolis (Ind.). Journalist. As of 1896 member of the California State Assembly, as of 1898 of the Senate. Leavitt held various official functions before becoming Senator again in 1906.

LEMERT, CHARLES C.: Superintendent of Insurance of Ohio and president of the National Convention of Insurance Commissioners at the time of the San Francisco catastrophe.

LINDNER, B.: Director of the *Badische Rück- und Mitversicherungs-Gesellschaft* (Stuttgart, Germany) that was integrated into *Frankona* (Frankfurt a.M.). Member of the informal Earthquake Commission.

LOCK, FRANK: Born 1855 on the Isle of Wight (GB). Career in the insurance business in GB and the USA. During some period of time president of the General Adjustment Bureau and later Resident Manager for Atlas (London) in New York. Chairman of the Committee on Adjustments of the National Board of Fire Underwriters from 1906 to 1908.

LONDON, JACK: Born 1876 in San Francisco. Writer and adventurer. After the 1906 earthquake, London rode into the fire-stricken city in order to report for Collier's Magazine.

LOWDEN, WILLIAM N.: Worked at North British & Mercantile (London and Edinburgh) from 1875 to 96; afterwards Manager of the Pacific Coast Dept. for Norwich Union (Norwich). President of Fire Underwriters' Association of the Pacific 1891 to 1892.

MACKENZIE, EVAN: Founder and director of *Alleanza Società di Assicurazioni* (Genova); contact person for Lloyds of London in Italy and representative of *Münchener Rück*. Journalistic involvement in the debate on Italian insurance legislation.

MACKENZIE, ROBERT KIRKWOOD: Born 1868. Career in the insurance business in various British offices; 1892–96 Head of the foreign dept. of Royal; worked at Norwich Union from 1896 to 1905, e.g. in South Africa. Worked at State Fire (Liverpool) afterwards; as of June 1906 Foreign Superintendent. Became Sub-Manager in the process of the regulation of damages in San Francisco.

MAGALDI, VINCENZO: Born 1848. Italian national economist and social politician, Magaldi published on topics such as workers' and accident insurance. President for credits, welfare and social security, probably in the Dept. of Commerce, in 1908.

MALß (MALSS), KONRAD (CONRAD): German insurance jurist; legal adviser of Providentia (Frankfurt a.M.); founder and editor of the *Zeitschrift für das Versicherungswesen* from 1863 to 1868 that merged into *Goldschmidts ZHR*, as well as the *Zeitschrift für Versicherungsrecht* (2 volumes, 1866–1867).

MANES, ALFRED: Born 1877 in Frankfurt a.M. Dr. phil. and Dr. jur.; one of the founders of modern German insurance science. Secretary of the *Deutscher Verein für Versicherungswissenschaft* and editor of the *ZVersWiss.* as of 1902; director of the insurance department at the then existent Berlin school of commerce (*Handelshochschule*) from 1906 to 1935. Emigration to the USA due to anti-Semitic persecution by the National Socialists; Patten Lecturer at the Indiana University from 1936 to 37.

MANFREDI, PIETRO: Milan lawyer, author of various legal and historical works.

MARTITZ, FERDINAND v.: A Berlin law professor, Martitz mainly worked on public and international law.

McLAREN, SIR CHARLES BENJAMIN BRIGHT: Born 1850 in Edinburgh; Jurist (Barrister) and business official. Studied in Edinburgh, Bonn and Heidelberg (among others). From 1880 to 1885 and as of 1892 MP (Liberal); chairman of various industry conglomerates; Honorary Director of Scottish Life Ass. (Edinburgh). In the correspondence with *Schweizerische Rück*, McLaren acted as representative for Guarantee Insurance Company (probably London).

MONTESSUS DE BALLORE, FERNAND-JEAN-BAPTISTE-MARIE COMTE DE: Born 1851 in Dompierre-sous-Sauvignes. Artillery officer in San Salvador from 1881 to 1885, where he conducted earthquake studies for the first time; afterwards director of the French *École polytechnique*. Director of the *Servicio Sismológico Nacional in Santiago de Chile* at the time of the San Francisco earthquake. His major works are "Les Tremblements de Terre. Géographie Seismologique" (1906), "Bibliografia General de Temblores" (1915–1919) and "Géologie Seismologique" (1924).

MORANT, GEORGE MCKEE: 1896 founder of Fire Re (later: Kings Ins. Co.); London agent of *Norddeutsche* (Hamburg) until 1907; afterwards still Managing Director of Kings, Fire Manager of Commercial Union and Manager of Palatine (London). Also, insurance broker (G. McKee Morant & Co.), associate of Stanislas H. Haine & Co. (Antwerp) and associate of Haine & Morant (Paris).

MORROW, WILLIAM W. Born 1843 near Milton (Ind.). Served for the Union Army in the American Civil War before becoming a lawyer and politician (Rep.) in California. US Representative for California (4th District) from 1885 to 1891; judge at the US District Court (Northern District of California) from 1891 to 1897; judge at the US Court of Appeals (9th Circuit) from 1897–1922. Co-founded the American Red Cross.

OLSEN, PETER CHRISTIAN: Born 1866 in Copenhagen. Worked for various European insurance companies: *Münchener Rück* (Munich), *Allianz* (Berlin), Northern Assurance (London). Co-founded *Nordisk Gjen* in 1894 and *Nordisk Brandforsikring* (Copenhagen) in 1897, the latter of which he became manager of the reinsurance department.

OMORI, FUSAKICHI: Born 1868. Japanese seismologist. As head of the Japanese Imperial Earthquake Investigation Committee, Omori conducted research on the 1906 Californian earthquake.

OSBORN, RUSSELL W.: Manager of Pennsylvania Fire (Penns.) and publicist.

PALACHE, WHITNEY: Born 1866 in San Francisco. Worked for Hartford Fire (Conn.) as of 1890, from 1902 onward as Associate Manager. 1903 co-founder of the company Palache & Hewitt.

PARDEE, GEORGE: Born 1867 in Meadville (Penns.). Politician (Rep.). Involved in Californian fruit trade as of 1884. Member of the California State Assembly as of 1896, Californian Governor as of 1902.

PHELAN, JAMES DUVAL: Banker from San Francisco; politically and economically very active and influential in the city. Mayor from 1896 to 1901 (Dem. and Citizens' Nonpartisan); ruled in close cooperation with the Merchants' Association.

POMEROY, JOHN NORTON: Californian lawyer and law teacher; strongly supported abandoning codified civil law in favour of Common Law.

PRANGE, OTTO: Influential German insurance scientist, publicist and official of associations. Prange founded the "Deutscher Feuerversicherungs-Schutzverband" as a countercartel of small and mid-sized insured companies; its work was later expanded to all insurance branches. Author of numerous works, e.g. on insurance legislation.

PULCIFER, HARRY W.: Born 1869 in Weld (Maine). Attorney at law in Oakland; member of the California State Assembly as of 1908 (Rep.); chairman of the commission on insurance and insurance law.

RABEL, ERNST: Born 1874. Jurist, mainly at German universities. Rabel mainly focused on comparative law. After World War I, arbitration judge and judge at various institutions such as the International Court of Justice. In 1926, he founded the *Kaiser-Wilhelm-Institut für ausländisches und internationales Privatrecht* ('KWI for Comparative and international Private Law') in Berlin and the *RabelsZ* that was later named after him. From 1927 member of the *Institut für Vereinheitlichung des Privatrechts*; in this connection "Das Recht des Warenkaufes" (1936) evolved.

REDMAN, L. A.: Attorney at Law in Oakland (Ca.). Lawyer of the Policyholders' League established after the San Francisco catastrophe.

ROELLI, HANS: Swiss jurist and university professor. Among other things, he established a *VVG* draft in 1896 for Switzerland in 1896; author of a comment on the new *VVG* in 1914.

ROOSEVELT, THEODORE: Born 1858 in New York, American politician (Rep.); President of the United States as of 1901. 1906 Nobel Peace Prize for negotiating an end to the Russo-Japanese War. Rejected another nomination for President in 1908.

RUTTKE, Dr.: Director of the Prussian *Provinzial-Feuersozietät* in Posen.

SALEILLES, RAYMOND: Born 1855. French law teacher; innovatively re-organised different legal areas (such as civil law and comparative law); taught in Grenoble, Dijon and, as of 1895, in Paris. Died 1912.

SCHÄRTLIN, GEORG GOTTHARD: mathematician and scientist; lecturer at the University of Zurich and manager of the *Schweizerische Lebensversicherungs- und Rentenanstalt*. Publications on insurance matters.

SCHMITZ, EUGENE E.: Born in San Francisco; musician (violinist), trade unionist (Musicians' Union) and businessman. Mayor of San Francisco (Union Labor) in 1901. Schmitz governed in close connection to businessman Abraham "Abe" Ruef (Rep.). The Ruef-Schmitz-connection was considered a corrupt regime but survived numerous law suits and impeachment trials until 1910 thanks to the earthquake. Afterwards, both were taken to court, where Ruef was sentenced to imprisonment.

SEWELL, JOHN S.: Captain, Corps of Engineers of the United States Army. Sent to San Francisco on April 23rd, 1906 by US President Roosevelt to investigate the earthquake and fire damages.

SEXTON, WILLIAM: Born 1832 in Nova Scotia. Worked in Californian insurance business as of 1868; during certain periods of time also politician. General Adjuster of Fireman's Fund as of 1894.

SIMON, CHARLES: Born 1862. Jurist with doctorate. Vice-director of *Schweizerische Rückversicherungs-Gesellschaft* as of 1895, director as of 1900. Member of the informal Earthquake Commission. He was also known for being an alpinist, writer and humanist.

SOULÉ, FRANK: Dean of the College of civil engineering at the University of California.

SPENCER, GEORGE W.: Born 1843 in Philadelphia (Pa.). Worked for Aetna Ins. Co. (San Francisco) from 1868 to 1889 and was representative of various companies (London & Lancashire, Manchester, Caledonian, American) from 1880 to 1896; General Agent on the Pacific Coast for Aetna as of 1896 (through Boardman & Spencer).

SRAFFA, ANGELO (1865–1937): Business lawyer; professor at the universities of Turin, Parma and Milan. Numerous publications; co-editor of the *Rivista di diritto commerciale, industriale e marittimo*.

STIERLIN, EDUARD: Born 1878 in Zurich. Psychologist; Dr. med. (German doctorate in medicine, 'MD'), dissertation *Über psycho-neurotische Folgezustände bei den Überlebenden der Katastrophe von Courrières* in 1907. First assistant of Ferdinand Sauerbruch.

SULLIVAN, DENNIS T.: Commanding officer of the San Francisco Fire Department. Sullivan died on the morning of the tremors April 18th, 1906.

SUTRO, OSCAR: Founder of the Law Office Pillsbury & Sutro (1901). Worked for *Thuringia* during certain periods of time.

THIEME, CARL: Born 1854 as son of the director of *Thuringia* (Erfurt, Germany), Julius Thieme. Apprenticeship at *Thuringia*; director for the state of Bavaria as of 1871. Founded *Münchener Rück* with the support of a group of bankers, industrialists and lawyers in 1880. Co-founded *Allianz* (Berlin) in 1889/1890. Member of the informal Earthquake Commission.

THOMAS, WILLIAM: Probably Senior Partner of the Law Firm Mark L. Gerstle; around 1900 probably president of the California Water and Forest Association.

TYSON, GEORGE H.: Born 1863 in DK. Tyson worked for Fireman's Fund from 1879 to 1891, as Pacific Dept. Manager for the German Alliance as of 1897, and for Phoenix (Hartford) and New Hampshire Fire as of 1901.

UPHAM, WARREN: Born 1850 in Massachusetts. Internationally acclaimed geologist, archaeologist and etymologist (city names of Minnesota).

VAN FLEET, WILLIAM CARY: Born 1852. Jurist. Assistant District Attorney of Sacramento County (Ca.) from 1878 to 1879; member of the California House of Representatives from 1881 to 1882; director of California State Prisons from 1883 to 1884; judge at Superior Court of California from 1884 to 1892; Justice at the Supreme Court of California from 1894 to 1899. In 1907, President Roosevelt appointed Van Fleet to the US District Court, Ninth Judicial Circuit (Northern California).

VAN OMMEN: Representative of *Schweizerische Rück* in Amsterdam.

VIVANTE, CESARE: Born 1855. During a certain period of time, Vivante was considered the leading representative of commercial law in Italy. He focused on insurance law among other things. His major works are "Il contratto di assicurazione" (1890) and "Trattato di diritto commerciale" (1893–1902).

WAGNER, ADOLPH (ADOLF) H. G.: Born 1835 (Erlangen, Germany). German national economist and supporter of state socialism. From 1870 (full) professor in Berlin and temporarily president of the *Friedrich-Wilhelms-Universität* (i.e. *Humboldt-Universität*). Co-founder of the *Verein für Socialpolitik*. Died 1917 (Berlin).

WATT, ROLLA VERNON: Born 1857 in Camden (O.). Career in the insurance business in San Francisco at different companies. President of the Fire Underwriters' Assn. of the Pacific in 1894; from then on Pacific Coast Manager for Royal (Liverpool) and Norwich Union (Norwich/GB), as of 1896 for Queen (New York) instead of Norwich Union.

WEBB, ULYSSES S.: Born 1864 in W. Virginia. District Attorney in Quincy for 12 years. Californian Governor Gage appointed him Attorney General in 1902.

WEGENER, ALFRED LOTHAR: Born 1880. A German geophysicist, climatologist and meteorologist, Wegener developed the hypothesis of continental drift in 1912 ("Die Entstehung der Kontinente und Ozeane").

WHITNEY, ALBERT WURTS: Born 1870. Mathematician, economist and actuary. Whitney was considered the leading insurance scientist at the University of California. He worked for many other public and private institutions, especially in the field of fire and workers' insurance.

WOLF, E. MYRON: Born 1871 in San Francisco. Studied at Hastings Law College; practising lawyer; Californian Insurance Commissioner as of 1902.

MONOGRAPHS AND ESSAYS

A.[Alfred] M. Best Company (ed.). *Special Report upon the San Francisco Losses and Settlements / Involved in the Conflagration of April 18–21, 1906.* New York 1907.

Annual Report of the Insurance Commissioner of the State of California. San Francisco from 1868ff.

Annual report of the superintendent of insurance of the State of New York. Albany, N.Y. from 1859.

Anonymus. *U. A. / XIV: Commercial Treatises and Consular Laws / Handelsverträge und Consularrecht, XV: General Law of Insurance / Allgemeines Versicherungsrecht.* Leipzig o.J. (ca. 1912).

Alauzet, Isidore. *Commentaire du Code de Commerce,* 2nd ed., vol. 2. Paris 1868.

Arps, Ludwig. *Auf sicheren Pfeilern. Deutsche Versicherungswirtschaft vor 1914.* Göttingen 1965.

———. *Deutsche Versicherungsunternehmer.* Karlsruhe 1968.

Atiyah, Patrick Selim. *The Rise and Fall of Freedom of Contract.* Oxford 1979.

Atzpodien, Hans Christian. *Die Entwicklung der preußischen Staatsaufsicht über das private Versicherungswesen im 19. Jahrhundert unter besonderer Berücksichtigung ihres Verhältisses zum Wirtschaftsliberalismus.* Bonn 1982 (Diss.).

Bärmann, Johannes. Ist internationales Handelsrecht kodifizierbar?, in: Werner Flume et al. (ed.): *Internationales Recht und Wirtschaftsordnung. Festschrift für F. A. Mann zum 70. Geburtstag.* München 1977, 547–573.

Baker, Thomas. *La terre du réalisme: L'Esprit américain. Machinisme et standardisation. L'Opinion publique américaine.* Paris 1928.

Bament, W. A. The Story of the San Francisco Fire as Viewed from an Adjuster's Stand-point, speech at the conference of the National Association of Fire Insurance Agents, Indianapolis, Ind. (17.–19.10.1906) (reprint), in: California Institute of Technology / Center for Research on the Prevention of Natural Disasters (ed.): *Earthquakes and Insurance*. Pasadena, Ca. 1973.

Bar, Christian von / Peter Manowski. *Internationales Privatrecht*, 1st vol.: *Allgemeine Lehren*. München 2003.

Baratta, Mario. *Il grande terremoto calabro dell' 8 settembre 1905. Atti della Società Toscana di Scienze Naturali, Memorie* (1906).

——. *Carta sismica d'Italia*. 4 maps. Voghera 1901.

——. *Una pratica applicazzione degli studi sismici. Progetto di assicurazione contro i danni die terremoti*. Voghera 1899.

Bartky, Ian R. *Selling the True Time. Nineteenth-Century Timekeeping in America*. Stanford, Ca. 2000.

Beawes, Wyndham. *Lex mercatoria rediviva, or, The merchant's guide to all men in business*, 1st ed. London 1752 (5th ed. by Ths. Mortimer, 1792).

Beeching, Wilfred A. *Century of the typewriter*. Bournemouth 1990.

Bennett, Edmund Hatch. *Fire insurance cases. Being a collection of all the reported cases on fire insurance, in England, Ireland, Scotland, and America, from the earliest period to the present time*. New York / Hurd / Houghton 1872–77.

Bennett, M. L. *The Law of Railways. First American from the third London edition, with copious notes and references [by Leonard Shelford]*, 2 vol. Vernon 1855.

Bensa, Enrico et al. *Commentario al codice di commercio'*, vol. V. Milano s.l., n.d. (not until end 1909).

Berger, Klaus Peter. *The Creeping Codification of the Lex Mercatoria*. Second edition, Alphen aan den Rijn / New York 2010.

——. The New Law Merchant and the Global Marketplace, in: *The Practice of Transnational Law*. Den Haag / London / Boston 2001, 1–22.

Berz, Peter. Der deutsche Normenausschuß. Zur Theorie und Geschichte einer technischen Institution, in: Armin Adam / Martin Steglin (ed.): *Übertragung und Gesetz: Gründungsmythen, Kriegstheater und Unterwerfungstechniken von Institutionen*. Berlin 1995.

——. *08/15. Ein Standard des 20. Jahrhunderts*. München 2001 (Diss. Berlin).

Best, Alfred M. See Alfred M. Best Company.

Blaich, Fritz. *Staat und Verbände*. Wiesbaden 1979.

Blanck, Wilhelm. Die Feuerversicherung, in: Walter Rohrbeck (ed.). *50 Jahre materielle Versicherungsaufsicht*, vol. II. Berlin 1951, 161–176.

Board of Fire Underwriters of the Pacific, Co-Insurance Committee (C. F. Mullins, chairman. Report prepared by Albert W. Whitney). *Report of the Co-Insurance Committee to the Board of Fire Underwriters of the Pacific: on percentage of co-insurance and the relative rates chargeable therefor; also on the cost of conflagration hazard of large cities*. San Francisco 1905.

Boas, August. *Staatsbetrieb oder Privatbetrieb im Fernsprechwesen*. Berlin 1912 (Diss. Freiburg).

Börner, Christina. *Kodifikation des Common law. Der Civil Code von David Dudley Field*. Zürich 2000.

Bonell, Michael Joachim. *Le regole oggettive del commercio internazionale. Clausole tipiche e condizioni generali*. Milan 1976.

Bonß, Wolfgang. *Vom Risiko. Unsicherheit und Ungewissheit in der Moderne*. Hamburg 1995.

Borscheid, Peter. *100 Jahre Allianz*. München 1990.

Bousquet, Adrien. *Commentaire pratique des Règles d'York et d'Anvers es de la Règle d'Anvers 1903*. Paris 1906.

Branner, John Caspar. Earthquakes and Structural Engineering, in: *Bulletin of the Seismological Society of America*, March 1913.

Brauns, Reinhard. *Vulkane und Erdbeben*. Leipzig 1913.

Brodtbeck, K. A. *Schweizerisches Rechtslexikon*, Teil II / Nachtrag 1908. Zurich 1908.

Bronson, William. *The Earth Shook, the Sky Burned*. Garden City, N.Y. 1959, (reprinted) San Francisco 1997.

Brückner, Hermann. *Die Miete von Wohnungen und anderen Räumen nach dem Bürgerlichen Gesetzbuche*. 2nd ed. Leipzig 1902.

Brunn, Johann Heinrich von. *Die formularmäßigen Vertragsbedingungen der deutschen Wirtschaft. Der Beitrag der Rechtspraxis zur Rationalisierung*, 2nd ed. Köln / Berlin 1956.

Büchner, Franz. Die Entwicklung der deutschen Gesetzgebung über die Versicherungsaufsicht bis zum Bundesgesetz vom 31. Juli 1951, in: Walter Rohrbeck (ed.). *50 Jahre materielle Versicherungsaufsicht*, vol. I. Berlin 1951, 1–48.

California Blue Book or State Roster. Sacramento 1907.

Canguilhem, Georges. *Le normal et le pathologique*, 5th ed. Paris 1994 (1st ed. 1966).

Cesarini Sforza, Widar. *Il diritto dei privati*. Milan 1929.

Christy, B. Some lessons from the Earthquake. Discusses principally the ruin due to the fire, and how much of it could have been avoided; offering suggestions for the rebuilding of the city on a safer and improved plan, in: *Mining & Scientific Press*, April 28, 1906.

Cockerell, Hugh A. L. Combination in British Fire Insurance, in: F. Reichert-Facilides et al. (ed.). *Festschrift für Reiner Schmidt*. Karlsruhe 1976.

Cohn, Georg. *Die Anfänge eines Weltverkehrsrechts, in: Drei rechtswissenschaftliche Vorträge in gemeinverständlicher Darstellung*. Heidelberg 1888.

Coing, Helmut (ed.). *Handbuch der Quellen und Literatur der neueren europäischen Privatrechtsgeschichte*, 3rd vol.: *Das 19. Jahrhundert*; 1st part vol.: *Gesetzgebung zum allgemeinen Privatrecht*. München 1986.

——. *Europäisches Privatrecht*, vol. 2: *19. Jahrhundert. Überblick über die Entwicklung des Privatrechts in den ehemals gemeinrechtlichen Ländern*. München 1989.

Conrad, J.; Elster; W. Lexis; E. Loening. *Handwörterbuch der Staatswissenschaften*, 1st ed. (vol. 1–2). Jena 1890–1897; 3rd fully revised ed. (vol. 1–8). Jena 1909–1911.

Cramer, A. W. *Bremer Baumwollbörse 1871–1922*. Bremen 1922.

Cutrera, Alfredo. *Il commercio internazionale di frumento*. Milan 1926.

Daston, Lorraine. *Classical Probability in the Enlightenment*. Princeton 1988 (Diss. Harvard).

Deitch, Guilford Alexander. *The standard fire policy. Lectures before the Fire Insurance Club of Chicago*. Indianapolis 1905.

Deybeck, Karl (ed.). *Das Reichsgesetz über die privaten Versicherungsunternehmen vom 12. Mai 1901 [Kommentar]*. Munich 1902.

Di Renzo, Vincenzo. *Note e ricordi sullo svolgimento tecnico dell'assicurazione dei rischi d'incendio: 1895–1929*. Milan 1932.

Disconto-Gesellschaft Berlin (ed.): *Usancen der wichtigsten Großhandelsartikel*, 3rd ed. Berlin 1913.

Dohrn-van Rossum, Gerhard. *Die Geschichte der Stunde. Uhren und moderne Zeitrechnung*. München 1992.

Dollat. *Les contrat d'adhésion*. Paris 1905 (Diss.).

Domizlaff, Karl. *Der jetzige und demnächstige Feuerversicherungsvertrag: Material und Vorschläge für allgemeine Feuerversicherungsbedingungen*. Groß-Lichterfelde 1908.

——. *Die allgemeinen Versicherungsbedingungen für Feuerversicherungen, mit Erläuterungen*, 1st ed. Groß-Lichterfelde 1909; 6th ed. Berlin-Lankwitz 1914.

Dutton, Clarence E. *Earthquakes in the Light of the New Seismology*. New York 1904.

Duvinage, Angela. *Die Vorgeschichte und Entstehung des Gesetzes über den Versicherungsvertrag*. Karlsruhe 1987.

Ebel, Wilhelm. *Die Hamburger Feuerkontakte und die Anfänge des deutschen Feuerversicherungsrechts*. Weimar 1936.

Eger, Georg. *Internationales Übereinkommen über den Eisenbahnfrachtverkehr (1906–1908)*. *[Kommentar] In der Fassung des Zusatzabkommens vom 19. September 1906 und in Verbindung mit den einheitlichen Zusatzbestimmungen des internationalen Transportkomitees und mit dem Betriebs-Reglement des Vereins deutscher Eisenbahnverwaltungen, gültig vom 22. Dezember 1908.* Berlin 1909.

Ehrenberg, Victor. *Die Rückversicherung. Eine Festschrift im Namen und Auftrage der Rostocker Juristenfakultät [für Georg Beseler].* Rostock 1885.

——. *Versicherungsrecht. Systematisches Handbuch der deutschen Rechtswissenschaft,* Karl Binding (ed.), 3rd dept., 4th part, 1st vol. Leipzig 1893.

——. *Privatversicherungsrecht.* Berlin 1923.

Ehrlich, Eugen. *Das zwingende und nicht zwingende Recht im Bürgerlichen Gesetzbuch für das Deutsche Reich.* Jena 1899.

Ellsworth, W. L. Earthquake history, 1769–1989, in: R. E. Wallace (ed.). *The San Andreas Fault System, California. U.S. Geological Survey Professional Paper 1515.* 1990, 152–187.

Enciclopedia Italiana di Scienze, Lettere ed Arti, vol. 14. ed. by Istituto della enciclopedia Italiana. Rome 1936.

Enciclopedia universal ilustrada europeo-americana, vol. 51. Madrid 1926.

Encyclopedia Britannica, publ. by W. Benton. Chicago / London 1962.

Endemann, Wilhelm (ed.). *Handbuch des deutschen Handels-, See- und Wechselrechts,* vol. III: *Die Handelsgeschäfte.* Leipzig 1885.

Eucken, Walter. *Die Verbandsbildung in der Seeschiffahrt.* Munich / Leipzig 1914.

Falb, Rudolf. *Grundzüge zu einer Theorie der Erdbeben und Vulcanausbrüche.* Graz 1869.

Fire Insurance Law Chart. Summary of Special State Laws etc. ed. by Spectator Company. New York 1903.

Forstall, Richard L. *Population of States and Counties of the United States: 1790 to 1990.* U.S. Bureau of the Census. Washington, D.C. 1996.

Foucault, Michel. *Surveiller et punir. La naissance de la prison.* Paris 1975.

Frank, Ludwig. *Die bürgerlichen Parteien des Deutschen Reichstags.* Stuttgart 1911.

Freeman, J. R. *Earthquake Damage & Earthquake Insurance.* New York / London 1932.

Friedman, Lawrence M. *Contract Law in America.* Madison, Milw. 1965.

Galgano, Francesco. *Lex mercatoria.* Bologna 2001.

Galland, Jean-Pierre. *Normalisation, construction de l'Europe et mondialisation. Eléments de réflexion. Notes du centre de prospective et de veille scientifique no. 14* (March 2001).

Gareis, Karl. Handels- und Wechselrecht, in: Paul Hinneberg (ed.). *Systematische Rechtswissenschaft. Reihe Die Kultur der Gegenwart,* part II, dept. VIII. Berlin / Leipzig 1906, 92–117.

Gatta, L. *L'Italia—sua formazione, suoi vulcani e terremoti.* Milan 1882.

Gaupp, Ludwig/ Friedrich Stein. *Die Cicilprozessordnung für das Deutsche Reich, auf der Grundlage des Kommentars von L. Gaupp erl. von F. Stein.* Tübingen[8-9] 1906–1908.

Geography and History of Jamaica, 24th ed. The Jamaica Gleaner (ed.). Kingston 1995.

Gerhard, Stephan; Otto Hagen; Hugo von Knebel-Doeberitz (rev. Feuerversicherung); Hermann Broecker; Alfred Manes (ed.): *Kommentar zum deutschen Reichsgesetz über den Versicherungs-Vertrag.* Berlin 1908.

Geschäftsbericht des Kaiserlichen Aufsichtsamts für Privatversicherung für das Jahr 1908. Berlin 1909.

Geschwind, Carl-Henry. *California Earthquakes. Science, Risk and the Politics of Hazard Mitigation.* Baltimore / London 2001.

Ghisalberti, Carlo. *La codificazione del diritto in Italia 1865–1912.* Rome 1995.

Giedion, Sigfried. *Mechanization takes command: A Contribution to Anonymous History.* Oxford 1948.

Goethe, Johann Wolfgang von. *Italienische Reise.* 2nd ed., München 1988.

Golding, C. E. *A History of reinsurance with sidelights on Insurance,* ed. by Sterling Offices Ltd., compiled by C. E. Golding, 2nd ed. London 1931.

Goldschmidt, Levin. Handelsrecht. Geschichtliche Entwicklung (1892), in: *Vermischte Schriften,* 2nd vol. Berlin 1901, 29–52.

——. *Universalgeschichte des Handelsrechts (Handbuch des Handelsrechts,* vol. 1, 1st dept.— 1st ed.), Stuttgart 1864; 2nd ed., Stuttgart 1875; 3rd ed., Stuttgart 1891.

Greely, Adolphus W. *Earthquake in California, April 18, 1906. Special Report of Maj. Gen. Adolphus W. Greely, U. A., Commanding the Pacific Division, on the Relief Operations Conducted by the Military Authorities of the United States at San Francisco and other Points, with Accompanying Documents.* Washington 1906.

Gröppler, Fritz. *Die Ausdehnung der Haftung aus der Feuerversicherung auf andere Elementarschäden.* Leipzig 1910 (Diss.).

Groh, Dieter / Michael Kempe / Franz Mauelshagen. Naturkatastrophen—wahrgenommen, gedeutet, dargestellt, in: ——— (ed.). *Naturkatastrophen. Beiträge zu ihrer Deutung, Wahrnehmung und Darstellung in Text und Bild von der Antike bis ins 20. Jahrhundert.* Tübingen 2003.

Großmann-Doerth, Hans. *Das Recht des Überseekaufs*, vol. 1. Mannheim / Berlin / Leipzig 1930.

———. *Selbstgeschaffenes Recht der Wirtschaft und staatliches Recht.* Freiburg i.Br. 1933.

Gruchot, Julius Alexander. *Beiträge zur Erläuterung des deutschen Rechts.* Berlin, Neue Folge (from 1877).

Gruenwald, Heinrich Leopold / B. Lindner / Charles Simon / Carl Thieme. *Die Erdbebenklausel in den Versicherungs-Bedingungen der Feuer-Versicherungs-Gesellschaften.* s.l. 1907; along with English and French version included in: SR/FA 9.0–32/ loose material.

Hager, P. / Ernst Bruck. *Reichsgesetz über den Versicherungsvertrag nebst dem zugehörigen Einführungsgesetz vom 30. Mai 1908* [Kommentar], 1st ed. Berlin 1908; 3rd ed. Berlin 1913; 5th ed. Berlin / Leipzig 1926.

Hall, M. *Earthquakes in Jamaica—The Great Earthquake of January 14, 1907 and the After Shocks, Third Report, No. 337, Government Printing Office.* Kingston, Jamaica 1907.

Hall Caine, W. Ralph. *The Cruise of the Port Kingston.* London 1908.

Hansen, Gladys. *Who perished*, see: http://www.sfmuseum.org/perished/index.html.

Hansen, Gladys; Emmet Condon. *Denial of Disaster: Cameron and Co.* San Francisco 1989.

Hanzlik, Johann. *Die juristische Natur des Rückversicherung.* Leipzig 1911.

Hardy, E. R. *Fire insurance law; an authoritative analysis of the standard fire insurance policy.* s.l. 1913.

Harley, C. Knick (ed.). *The Integration of the World Economy, 1850–1914*, 2 volumes. Cheltenham (GB) / Brookfield (USA) 1996.

Harriman, Norman F. *Standards and Standardization.* New York 1928.

Haustein, Werner. *Das internationale öffentliche Eisenbahnrecht.* Frankfurt a.M. 1953.

Hawtrey, Ralph G. The Gold Standard from 1717 to 1914, in: Barry Eichgreen (ed.). *Monetary regime transformations* (1992), 1.

Hecker, Oskar. *Zur Gründung der Reichsanstalt für Erdbebenforschung in Jena.* Jena 1924.

Herzog, Martin. *Was Dokumente erzählen können—Zur Geschichte der Münchener Rück*, volumes I–V, along with collection of sources, volumes I–VII. München n.d.

Hickel, Erika. *Arzneimittel-Standardisierung im 19. Jahrhundert in den Pharmakopoen Deutschlands, Frankreichs, Grossbritanniens und der Vereinigten Staaten.* Stuttgart 1973.

Hirsch, Julius. *Der moderne Handel.* Tübingen 1929.

Ritter, Joachim (ed.). *Historisches Wörterbuch der Philosophie*, vol. 8. Darmstadt 1992.

Hobsbawm, Eric. *Das imperiale Zeitalter. 1875–1914*, 3rd ed. Frankfurt 1999.

Hoffman, Frederick L. *Earthquake hazards and insurance.* Chicago or New York 1928.

Hohmeister, Claudia. *Die Standardisierung von Fabrik-/Arbeitsordnungen.* Forthcoming.

Hofer, Sybille. *Freiheit ohne Grenzen? Privatrechtstheoretische Diskussionen im 19. Jahrhundert.* Tübingen (Habil.) 2001.

Hofmann, Robert. *Geschichte der deutschen Parteien. Von der Kaiserzeit bis zur Gegenwart.* München 1993.

Holden, Edward Singleton. *Catalogue of Earthquakes on the Pacific Coast 1769 to 1897.* Washington 1898.

Horwitz, Morton. Freedom of Contract and Objective Causation, in: *The Transformation of American Law* (1992), 34ff.

Hounshell, David A. *From the American System to Mass Production, 1800–1932. The development of manufacturing technology in the United States.* Baltimore / London 1985.

International Chamber of Commerce (ed.). *Standardization.* Paris 1921.

Internationaler Verband der Baumwollspinner- und Weber-Vereinigungen (ed.), *Schiedsgerichtsklauseln.* Manchester 1912.

Isaac, Martin. *Das Recht des Spediteurs.* Berlin 1928.

Ishizaki, Masaichiro. *Le droit corporatif international de la vente des soites. Les contrat-types américains et la codification lyonnaise dans leurs rapports avec les usages des autres places,* 3 volumes. Paris 1928.

Jacob, Otto. *Der Normvertrag als allgemeine Rechtsnorm.* Gelnhausen 1928 (Diss.).

Jahn, Walter. *Studien über Rückversicherung und deren Statistik.* Berlin 1912 (Diss. Munich).

Jobe, J. / H. Lachouque / Ph.-E. Cleator / D. Reichel. *Histoire Illustreé De L'Artillerie,* 2nd ed., Lausanne 1981.

Jordan, David Starr (ed.). The California Earthquake of 1906. San Francisco 1907.

Joyce, J. A. *A treatise on marine, fire, life, accident and all other insurances,* 4 volumes. San Francisco 1897.

Jung-Köhler, Evi. *Verlust und Chance.* Hamburg 1842, Hamburg 1991 (Diss.).

Kahn, Philippe. *La vente commerciale internationale.* Paris 1961.

Kegel, Gerhard. *Internationales Privatrecht.* 7th ed. München 1995.

Kempe, Michael. Von "lechzenden Flammen", "geflügelten Drachen" und anderen "Lufft=Geschichten". Zur Neutralisierung der Naturfurcht in populärwissenschaftlichen Druckmedien der Frühaufklärung, in: Franz Mauelshagen / Benedikt Mauer (ed.). *Medien und Weltbilder in der Frühaufklärung.* Augsburg 2000, 155–178.

Kennedy, E. R. Origin of the Standard Fire Insurance Policy, in: *The fire insurance contract: its history and interpretation,* comp. and ed. by, and pub. under the auspices of the Insurance society of New York. Indianapolis 1922.

Kennedy, Lawrence J. *The Progress of the Fire in San Francisco April 18th–21st, 1906. As Shown by an Analysis of Original Documents.* Berkeley (M.A. thesis) 1908.

Kenwood, Alan George / Alan Leslie Lougheed. *The Growth of the International Economy. 1820–1990,* 3rd ed. London / New York 1992.

Klapisch, Jutta. *Der Einfluß der deutschen und österreichischen Emigranten auf contracts of adhesion und bargaining in good faith im US-amerikanischen Recht.* Baden-Baden 1991.

Klein, Peter. Die Möglichkeit des Weltprivatrechts, in: *Festschrift für Ernst Zitelmann.* Munich / Leipzig 1913, 1–23.

Knipping, Franz (ed.). Das System der vereinten Nationen und seien Vorläufer, Bd. II: Vorläufer der Vereinten Nationen. 19. Jahrhundert und Völkerbundszeit, Bern / München 1996.

Koch, Arwed. *Die allgemeinen Geschäftsbedingungen der Banken—ihre rechtliche und wirtschaftliche Bedeutung und Entwicklung.* Jena 1932.

Koch, Peter. *125 Jahre Internationaler Transportversicherungsverband.* Karlsruhe 1999.

Koch, Wilhelm. *Deutschlands Eisenbahnen. Versuch einer systematischen Darstellung der Rechtsverhältnisse aus der Anlage und dem Betriebe Derselben. Zweite Abtheilung: Die den Betrieb der Eisenbahn betreffenden Rechtsverhältnisse.* Marburg 1860.

Koehne, Carl. *Die Arbeits-Ordnungen im deutschen Gewerberecht.* Berlin 1901.

Kölner Rückversicherungs-Gesellschaft (ed.). *100 Jahre Kölner Rückversicherungs-Gesellschaft,* Köln 1953

Kölnische Rückversicherungsgesellschaft (ed.) / International Insurance Monitor (publ.). *Dateline: 1897. The American Insurance Buisiness as seen by a Cologne Re Executive.* New York 1970.

Krause, Gisela. *Altpreußische Militärbekleidungswirtschaft: Materialien und Formen; Planung und Fertigung; Wirtschaft und Verwaltung.* Osnabrück 1983.

Krause, Hermann. *Die geschichtliche Entwicklung des Schiedsgerichtswesens in Deutschland.* Berlin 1930.

Kuczynski, Jürgen. *Studien zur Geschichte des Kapitalismus.* Berlin 1957.

Kurzman, Dan. *Disaster! The Great San Francisco Earthquake and Fire of 1906*. New York 2001.

Lage, Hans. *Vereinheitlichung industrieller Produktion. Probleme der Weltwirtschaft, Schriften des Instituts für Weltwirtschaft und Seeverkehr* (ed. B. Harms), vol. 38. Jena 1922.

Lammel, Siegbert. Rechtsbildung durch Verträge und Vertragsbedingungen. Vortrag gehalten auf dem deutschen Rechtshistorikertag 1990 in Nimjegen, erschienen in: Karl Otto Scherner (ed.) *Modernisierung des Handelsrechts im 19. Jahrhundert*. Heidelberg 1993, 89–117.

Larousse, Pierre (ed.). *Grand Dictionnaire du XIX. Siècle*, vol. 13, Paris 1875.

Layton, C. / Layton, E. *Who is Who in Insurance. An International Biographical Dictionary and Yearbook*. London / New York 1908.

Le Chartier, E. *Dictionnaire international des assurances. Publié en dix langues sur un plan nouveau*. Paris n.d. (ca. 1910).

Lewis, William Arthur. The Rate of Growth of the World Trade, 1830–1973, in: Sven Grassman / Erik Lundberg. *The World Economic Order. Past and Prospects*. London 1981. Lewis, James William. *Lehrbuch des Versicherungsrechts*. Stuttgart 1889.

Leydecker, Günter. *Erdbebenkatalog für die Bundesrepublik Deutschland mit Randgebieten für die Jahre 800–1994, für Schadenbeben bis 1999*. Stuttgart 2000.

Liebig, Eugen Frhr. von. *Das deutsche Feuerversicherungswesen*. Berlin 1911.

Liebowitz, Stan J. / Stephen E. Margolis. The Fable of the Keys, in: *Journal of Law and Economics 33* (April 1990), 1–21.

Lindner, C. / Fell, H. (rev.). *Reichsgesetz über den Versicherungsvertrag nebst dem zugehörigen Einführungsgesetz und dem Gesetze, betreffend Änderung der Vorschriften des Handelsgesetzbuchs über die Seeversicherung [Kommentar]*. Berlin 1909.

Link, Jürgen. *Versuch über den Normalismus. Wie Normalität produziert wird*, 2nd updated and enlarged ed. Opladen 1999.

Lobdell, Richard A. *The Jamaica Earthquake of 1907: Economic, political and policy consequences*. s.l. 1993.

Lotmar, Philipp. *Der Arbeitsvertrag*, 1st vol. Leipzig 1902.

Luhmann, Niklas. Kommunikation über Recht in Interaktionssystemen, in: ——. Ausdifferenzierung des Rechts. *Beiträge zur Rechtssoziologie und Rechtstheorie*. Frankfurt a.M. 1981, 53–78.

——. *Risiko und Gefahr. Reihe Aulavorträge, Hochschule St. Gallen für Wirtschafts-, Rechts- und Sozialwissenschaften*. St. Gallen 1990.

——. *Das Recht der Gesellschaft*. Frankfurt a.M. 1993.

Luminati, Michele. *Erdbeben in Noto*. Zurich 1995.

Lundgreen, Peter. *Standardization—Testing—Regulation. Studies in the history of science-based regulatory state (Germany / U. A., 19th and 20th centuries)*. Bielefeld 1986.

Lutz, Johann von (ed.). *Protokolle der Kommission zur Berathung eines Allgemeinen Deutschen Handelsgesetzbuches*. 9 volumes. Würzburg 1858–66.

Mac Adie, Alexander George. *Catalogue of earthquakes on the pacific coast 1897 to 1906*. Washington 1907.

Mackenzie, Evan. *Di Una Nouva Legge sulle Assicurazioni. Studio critic*. Genova 1906.

Mackenzie, Robert Kirkwood. *The San Francisco earthquake & conflagration, April, 1906. A paper read before the Insurance and actuarial society of Glasgow, 4th February, 1907*. Liverpool 1907. Typoskript (BL). Printed in: *Journal of the Federation of Insurance Institutes 10* (1907), 251–279; German translation: *Erdbeben und Brände in San Francisco im April 1905* [sic], in: *Der Versicherungsfreund*, 1 April 1907, 2*ff.*; 20 April 1907, 6*f.*; 20 May 1907, 1*ff.*; 1 June 1907, 1*ff.*; 20 June 1907, 1*f.*

Maine, Henry Sumner. *Ancient Law, 1861*. Reprint. London 1954.

Malynes, Gerard (de). *Consuetudo vel lex Mercatoria / Or the Ancient Law-Merchant / According to the essentials of traffick*. London 1622 (3rd ed. 1686).

Mancini, Pasquale Stanislao. *Della nazionalità come fondamento del diritto delle genti*. Presentation 1851 ed. by Jayme. Turin 1994.

Manes, Alfred (ed.). *Versicherungslexikon. Ein Nachschlagewerk für alle Wissensgebiete der Privat- und Sozial-Versicherung insbesondere in Deutschland, Österreich und der Schweiz*, 1st ed. Tübingen 1909.

——. (ed.). *Versicherungslexikon*, supplementary vol. Tübingen 1913.

——. (ed.). *Versicherungslexikon*. 2nd ed. Tübingen 1909.

Marquart, Johann(es). *Tractatus politico-iuridicus de iure mercatorum et commerciorum singulari*, 2 volumes. Frankfurt a.M. 1662.

Martinek, Michael. *Moderne Vertragstypen*, vol. 1–3. München 1992–1993.

Martitz, Ferdinand von. Völkerrecht, in: Paul Hinneberg (ed.). *Systematische Rechtswissenschaft. Reihe Die Kultur der Gegenwart*, part II, dept. VIII. Berlin / Leipzig 1906, 427–494.

Massard-Guilbaud, Geneviève. Introduction—The Urban Catastrophe: Challenge to the social, economic, and cultural order of the city, in: —— / Harold Platt / Dieter Schott (ed.). *Cities and Katastrophes Coping with emergency in european History / Villes et catastrophes. Réactions face a l'urgence dans l'histoire européenne*. Frankfurt (among other cities) 2001, 9–42.

Mattirolo, Luigi. *Trattato di diritto giudiziario civile italiano*, 5th ed. Turin from 1802.

Maurer, Georg Heinrich. *Über die bisherige Entwicklung der Versicherungs-Aufsicht in Deutschland*. Strasbourg 1911 (Diss.).

May, John Wilder. *The Law of Insurance, as applied to fire, life, accident, guarantee, and other non-maritime riske*, 2nd ed. Boston 1882.

McIntosh, Clarence F. *Insurance history project; a preliminary study of the early history of insurance in California and bibiliographical sources for further study*. San Francisco 1954. BL.

Meili, Friedrich. *Das internationale Civil- und Handelsrecht aufgrund der Theorie, Gesetzgebung und Praxis*. Zurich 1902.

Mercadante, Raimondo. *Messina dopo il terremoto del 1908. La ricostruzione dal piano Borzì agli interventi fascisti*. Palermo 2009.

Meschke, Jochen. *Über das Industrie-Geschäft der deutschen Feuerversicherungs-Aktiengesellschaften in den Jahren 1900–1932. Eine geschichtliche Betrachtung unter besonderer Berücksichtigung der seit 1900 verfolgten Prämienpolitik. Veröffentlichungen des Deutschen Vereins für Versicherungs-Wissenschaft Heft 54*. Berlin 1935.

Meyer, Rudolf. *Bona fides und lex mercatoria in der europäischen Rechtstradition*. Göttingen 1994 (Diss. 1992).

Meyers Konversationslexikon. 5th ed., vol. 14. Leipzig 1897.

Michel, Ulrich. *Die allgemeinen Geschäftsbedingungen als Vertragsbestandteil in der Rechtsprechung*. Tübingen 1932.

Micklethwait, John / Adrian Wooldridge. *The company*. New York 2003.

Mining and Scientific Press. *After Earthquake and Fire. A Reprint of Articles and Editorial Comment Appearing in the Mining and Scientific Press Immediately After the Disaster at San Francisco, April 18, 1906*. San Francisco 1906.

Mittelstein, Kurt. *Die Cif-Klausel*. Hamburg 1918 (Diss. Leipzig).

Mohl, Moritz von. *Die Frage von Reichs-Eisenbahnen*. Stuttgart 1876.

Municipal Report on the San Francisco Earthquake and Fire of April 1906. Published by Order of the Board of Supervisors, 1907 (Department Reports / Committee Reports / Other Municipal Reports).

Musgrave, Peter. *The Early Modern European Economy*. London 1999.

National Board of Fire Underwriters (ed.). *Pioneers of progress. National Board of Fire Underwriters, 1866–1941* (to be continued). New York 1941.

——. (ed.). *Proceedings of the annual meeting of the National Board of Fire Underwriters*. New York from 1873.

National Convention of Insurance Commissioners (ed.). *Proceedings of the annual session held at Detroit, Mich., Aug. 25–27, 1908*.

Negri, G. / A. Stoppani / G. Mercalli. *Geologia dell'Italia*. 3 volumes. Milan 1883.

Nehlsen von Stryk, Karin. *Die venezianische Seeversicherung im 15. Jahrhundert.* Ebelsbach 1986.

Neugebauer, Ralph. *Versicherungsrecht vor dem Versicherungsvertragsgesetz. Zur Entwicklung des modernen Binnenversicherungsrechts im 19. Jahrhundert. Ius commune Sonderheft Nr. 51.* Frankfurt a.M. 1990.

Nußbaum, Arthur. *Deutsches Hypothekenwesen. Ein Lehrbuch.* Tübingen 1913.

Odell, Kerry / Marc D. Weidenmier. *Real Shock, Monetary Aftershocks: The San Francisco Earthquake and the Panic of 1907. Claremont Colleges Working Papers in Economics 2001–07.* http://econpapers.hhs.se/paper/clmclmeco/2001-07.htm.

Ogburn, William F. *On Culture and Social Change. Selected Papers.* Chicago / London 1964.

Opet, Otto. *Deutsches Theaterrecht.* Berlin 1897.

Osman, Filipi. *Les principes généraux de la lex mercatoria / contribution à l'étude d'un ordre anational.* Paris 1992.

Pan, Erica Y. Z. *The Impact of the 1906 Earthquake on San Francisco's Chinatown.* New York (among other cities) 1995.

Pappenheim, Max. Die Vertragsfreiheit und die moderne Entwicklung des Verkehrsrechts, in: *Festschrift für Cohn, im Vereine mit Freunden, Schülern und Verehrern dargebracht von der Staatswissenschaftlichen Fakultät Zürich.* Zurich 1915, 291–301.

Partial recodification of the insurance laws of the State of California. Chapter 119. Assembly bill no. 456. Enacted at the session of 1907. s.l. (Sacramento) n.d. (1907). BL.

Patterson, Edwin Wilhite. *The insurance commissioner in the United States; a study in administrative law and practice.* Cambridge, Mass. 1927.

Peninou, Ernest P. / Gail G. Unzelman. *The California Wine Association and its Member Wineries, 1894–1920.* Santa Rosa 2001.

Pearson, Robin. Fire, Property Insurance, and Perceptions of Risk in Eighteenth-Century Britain, in: Geoffrey W. Clark / Gregory Anderson / Christian Thomann / Matthias Graf von der Schulenburg (eds.), *The Appeal of Insurance.* Toronto 2010, 75–106.

Petersen, Hanne / Henrik Zahle (ed.). *Legal Polycentricity: Consequences of Pluarlism in Law.* Aldershot 1995.

Pohl, Hans. *Aufbruch in die Weltwirtschaft. Geschichte der Weltwirtschaft von der Mitte des 19. Jahrhunderts bis zum Ersten Weltkrieg.* Stuttgart 1989.

Pohlhausen, Robert. *Zum Recht der allgemeinen Geschäftsbedingungen im 19. Jahrhundert.* Ebelsbach a.M. 1978 (Diss. München).

Prange, Otto. *Kritische Betrachtungen zu dem Entwurf eines Gesetzes über den Versicherungsvertrag / zugleich eine Darstellung der herrschenden Feuerversicherungspraxis.* Leipzig 1904.

——. *Die Gesetzentwürfe über den Versicherungsvertrag. Regierungsentwurf und Reichstagsvorlage [kommentierte Synpose].* Berlin 1906.

Prausnitz, Otto. *The standardization of commercial contracts in English and continental law.* London 1937.

Rabel, Ernst. *Das Recht des Warenkaufs*, vol. 1. Berlin 1936, unchanged reprints 1957 and 1964.

Raiser, Ludwig. *Das Recht der Allgemeinen Geschäftsbedingungen (1935).* Bad Homburg 1961 [reprint].

Raiser, Rolf. *Kommentar der allgemeinen Feuerversicherungsbedingungen.* Berlin 1930.

Ranft, Andreas / Stefan Selzer (ed.). *Städte aus Trümmern. Katastrophenbewältigung zwischen Antike und Moderne.* Göttingen 2004.

Rau, Heinrich. *Die Rückversicherung der Gegenwart.* Berlin 1900 (Diss. München 1899).

Rauscher, Thomas. *Internationales Privatrecht. Mit internationalem und europäischem Verfahrensrecht.* Hamburg 2002.

Reale Ufficio Geologico d'Italia. *Carta geologica d'Italia*, 2 sheets. Rome 1889.

Reatz, Carl Ferdinand. *Geschichte des europäischen Seeversicherungsrechts, 1. Theil.* Leipzig 1870.

Redfield, Isaac Fletcher. *A practical treatise on the law of railways.* Boston 1854.
Reed, Albert. *The San Francisco conflagration of April, 1906: Special Report to the National Board of Fire Underwriters' Committee of the Twenty.* New York 1906. BL.
Reisinger, Nikolaus. Das Zeitalter des Hochimperialismus—Europas Aufbruch zur Weltwirtschaft, in: Friedrich Edelmayer / Erich Landschteiner / Renate Pieper. *Die Geschichte des Europäischen Welthandels und der wirtschaftliche Globalisierungsprozess.* Vienna / Munich 2001, 207–21.
Repgen, Tilman. *Die soziale Aufgabe des Privatrechts. Eine Grundfrage in Wissenschaft und Kodifikation am Ende des 19. Jahrhunderts.* Tübingen 2001.
Report of the State Earthquake Investigation Commission (2 volumes and atlas). Vol. 1,1: Washington 1908. Vol. 1,2 by Andrew Cowper Lawson. Washington 1908. Vol. 2 (The mechanics of the earthquake) by Harry Fielding Reid. Washington 1910.
Rieber, Hans. *Das Versicherungsverhältnis nach dem badischen Gebäudeversicherungsgesetz vom 7./26. Oktober 1912 im Vergleich mit dem privaten Versicherungsrecht und der neuen preussischen und sächsischen Gesetzgebung.* Offenburg i.B. 1913 (Diss. Freiburg i.Br.).
Röttger, Rudolf. *Erdbeben.* Hamburg 1889.
Rohrbach, Wolfgang. *Versicherungsgeschichte Österreichs.* Vienna 1988.
Rohrbeck, Walter (ed.). *50 Jahre materielle Versicherungsaufsicht nach dem Gesetz vom 12. Mai 1901.* 1st volume: *Allgemeine Fragen des Versicherungsrechts und der Versicherungswirtschaft.* Berlin 1952. 2nd volume: *Entwicklung und Fortschritt in den beaufsichtigten Institutionen.* Berlin 1952. 3rd volume: *Versicherungsaufsicht im In- und Ausland;* [*Bibliographie der amtlichen Veröffentlichungen*]. Berlin 1955.
Rosenhaft, Eve. How to Tame Chance: Evolving Languages of Risk, Trust, and Expertise in Eighteenth-Century German Proto-Insurance, in: Geoffrey W. Clark / Gregory Anderson / Christian Thomann / Matthias Graf von der Schulenburg (eds.), *The Appeal of Insurance.* Toronto 2010, 16–42.
Rosenstock-Huessy, Eugen. *Vom Industrierecht. Rechtssystematische Fragen. Festgabe für Xaver Gretener zum 50jährigen Doktorjubiläum am 26.4.1926, dargebracht von der Rechts- und Staatswissenschaftlichen Fakultät der Schlesischen Friedrich-Wilhelms-Universität.* Berlin/Leipzig 1926.
Rostow, Walt Whitman. *Stages of economic growth.* Cambridge 1960.
Roth, Justus. *Über die Erdbeben.* Berlin 1882.
Ruck, Erwin. Staatliches und überstaatliches Handelsrecht, in: *Beiträge zum Handelsrecht, Festgabe für Carl Wieland,* ed. by the Faculty of Law of the University of Basel. Basel 1934, 320–333.
Rühl, Helmut. *Rechtsschöpfung durch die Wirtschaft. Rede gehalten bei der Jahresfeier der Handelshochschule Mannheim am 10. Juli 1931.* Mannheim / Berlin / Leipzig 1931.
Rürup, Reinhard (ed.). *Wissenschaft und Gesellschaft. Beiträge zur Geschichte der Technischen Universität Berlin 1879–1979.* Berlin 1979.
Said, Edward W. *Kultur und Imperialismus. Einbildungskraft und Politik im Zeitalter der Macht.* Frankfurt 1994.
Saleilles, Raymond. *De la déclaration de la volonté.* Paris 1901.
Sammlung der Versicherungsbedingungen deutscher Versicherungsanstalten, volumes 1–5. Deutscher Verein für Versicherungs-Wissenschaft (ed.). Berlin 1908–13. 1st part: *Feuerversicherung* (1908).
Sammlung von Erdbebenberichten aus der Presse (newspaper articles), Stadt- und Universitätsbibliothek Frankfurt a.M.
San Francisco Chamber of Commerce. *Annals of the chamber of commerce of San Francisco.* San Francisco 1906–1910. BL.
Sarconi, M. *Istoria dè Fenomeni del Tremoto avvenuto nelle Calabrie, e nel Valdemone nell'anno 1783 posta in luce dalla Reale Accademia delle Scienze, e delle Belle Lettere di Napoli, Atlante Iconografico.* Napoli 1784. Ristampa in facsimile, Mario Giuditta Editore. Rome-Catanzaro 1987.

Scherner, Karl Otto. *Rechtsvereinheitlichung für grenzüberschreitende Leistungen: Eisenbahnen, Banken, Versicherungen, in: Rechtsvereinheitlichung durch Gesetze—Bedingungen, Ziele, Methoden—, 5. Symposium der Kommission "Die Funktion des Gesetzes in Geschichte und Gegenwart" am 26. und 27. April 1991*, ed. by Christian Starck. Göttingen 1992, 42–80.

Schmitthoff, Clive M. International Business Law: A New Law Merchant, in: *Current Law and Social Problems*, vol. 2 (1961).

Schneiberg, Marc. *Association and Inter-firm Competition in the American Fire Insurance Industry* (paper presented at the annual meeting of the Society for the Advancement of Socio-Economics). Madison, Wisc. (July) 1999.

Scholz, Harald. *Es begann 1676. Hamburg / Geschichte / Katastrophen / Feuersbrünste / Hamburger Feuerkasse.* Hamburg 1999.

Schwartz, Gustav. *Die Allgemeinen Deutschen Spediteurbedingungen und die Speditions-Versicherung.* Berlin 1931.

Schwarz, Max (MdR). *Biographisches Handbuch der Reichstage.* Hamburg 1965.

Schwob, Georges. *Le contrat de la Corn Trade Association.* Paris 1928.

Seigneux, de / Christ. *Die Einführung eines einheitlichen Rechts für den internationalen Eisenbahnfrachtverkehr / De l'unification du droit concernant les transports internationaux par chemin de fer.* Basel 1875.

Seiler, Otto. *Die Erdbebenversicherung.* Basel 1942.

Senckpiehl, Richard. *Das Eisenbahntransportgeschäft nach deutschem Recht. Reihe Das Verkehrsrecht*, vol. 5. Berlin 1909.

Seydel, Max von. *Commentar zur Verfassungs-Urkunde für das Deutsche Reich*, 2nd ed. Freiburg i.Br. / Leipzig 1897.

Shelford, Leonard. *The Law of railways including the three general consolidation acts, 1845 and the other general acts for regulating railways in England and Ireland.* London 1845.

Sheppard, William. *The Law of Common Assurances, Touching Deeds in general: Feoffments. Gifts. Grants. Leases.* London 1669.

Sieberg, August. *Einführung in die Erdbeben- und Vulkankunde Süditaliens.* Jena 1914.

Sieferle, Rolf Peter. *Risiko als Dimension historischer Erfahrung* (Papier). St. Gallen 2004.

Smith. *A selection of leading cases in equity*, by J.I. Clark Hare and H.B. Wallace, vol. I. Philadelphia 1855.

Smith, Adam. *An Inquiry into the Nature and Causes of the Wealth of Nations (1776)*, 2 volumes. The Glasgow edition of the works and correspondence. Oxford 1976.

Sofonea, Traian. *Londra, Amburgo, San Francisco: tre sinistri storici.* Trieste 1973. Estratto dal Bollettino Generali (ott. / dic. 1972, genn. / apr. / mag. / giu 1973).

——. [*Una tragedia ancora viva nella memoria del paese:*] *1908, a Messina e Reggio Calabria la terra trema.* Trieste 1978. Estratto dal Bollettino Generali (nov. / dic. 1978).

Sombart, Werner. *Die deutsche Volkswirtschaft im 19. Jahrhundert.* Berlin 1903. 8th ed. Darmstadt 1954.

Stein, Ursula. *Lex mercatoria—Realität und Theorie.* Frankfurt a.M. 1995.

Steinberg, Ted. *Acts of God. The Unnatural History of Natural Disaster in America.* New York 2000.

Steinmetz, Willibald. *Private Law and Social Inequality in the Industrial Age. Comparing Legal Cultures in Britain, France, Germany, and the United States.* Oxford 2000.

Stierlin, Eduard. *Über die medizinischen Folgezustände der Katastrophe von Courrières (10. März 06), unter eingehender Berücksichtigung der ursächlichen Momente mit vergleichenden Beobachtungen über die Katastrophe von Hamm (12. Nov. 08) und die Erdbeben von Valparaiso (16. Aug. 06) und Süditalien (28. Dez. 08).* Berlin 1909.

Stolleis, Michael. *Innere Reichsgründung durch Rechtsvereinheitlichung, in: Rechtsvereinheitlichung durch Gesetze—Bedingungen, Ziele, Methoden—, 5. Symposium der Kommission "Die Funktion des Gesetzes in Geschichte und Gegenwart" am 26. und 27. April 1991*, ed. by Christian Starck. Göttingen 1992, 15–41.

———. *Nationalität und Internationalität: Rechtsvergleichung im öffentlichen Recht des 19. Jahrhundert.* ed. by Akademie der Wissenschaften und der Literatur (Mainz). Stuttgart 1998.

———. *Geschichte des Öffentlichen Rechts in Deutschland,* vol. 3: *Staats- und Verwaltungsrechtswissenschaft in Republik und Diktatur (1914–1945).* München 1999.

———. *Juristen. Ein biographisches Lexikon.* München 1995.

———. (ed.). *Die Bedeutung der Worte. Festschrift für Sten Gagnér zum 70. Geburtstag.* München 1991.

Story, Joseph. *Commentaries on the conflict of laws, foreign and domestic, in regard to contracts, rights, and remedies, and especially in regard to marriages, divorces, wills, successions, and judgments.* Edinburgh 1834.

Strupp, Christoph. "Nothing destroyed that cannot speedily be rebuilt"—San Francisco und das Erdbeben von 1906, in: A. Ranft / Selzer. *Städte aus Trümmern* (2004), 132–171.

Sugihara, Kaoru. Patterns of Asia's Integration into the World Economy 1880–1913, in: Wolfram Fischer / R. Marvin McInnis / Jürgen Schneider (ed.). *The Emergence of a World Economy 1500–1914.* Stuttgart 1986.

Supple, Barry. *The Royal Exchange Assurance. A history of British insurance 1720–1970.* Cambridge 1970.

Tarbell, Thomas F. *Legal requirements and state supervision of fire insurance.* New York 1927.

Teubner, Gunther. Foreword: Legal Regimes of Global Non-State Actors, in: ——— (ed.). *Global law without a state.* Dartmouth 1997, XII–XVII.

Thomas, Gordon / Max Morgan Witts. *The San Francisco Earthquake.* New York 1871 / 1980.

Tigges, Michael. *Geschichte und Entwicklung der Versicherungsaufsicht.* Karlsruhe 1985.

Trakman, Leon E. *The Law Merchant: The Evolution of Commercial Law.* Littleton, Colo. 1983.

Trebilcock, Clive. *Phoenix Assurance and the Development of British Assurance,* vol. 1: *1782–1870.* Cambridge 1985; vol.2: *The era of the insurance giants, 1870–1984.* Cambridge 1998.

Treves, Sir Frederick. *The Cradle of the Deep.* London 1908.

Vance, William Reynold. *Handbook of the law of insurance.* St. Paul, Minn. 1904.

Vec, Miloš. Standardization takes command, in: M. Kloepfer. *Technikentwicklung und Technikrechtsentwicklung* (2000), 45–55.

———. Technik oder Recht? Steuerungsansprüche in der Zweiten Industriellen Revolution, in: M. Kloepfer (ed.). *Kommunikation—Technik—Recht. Kommunikationsrecht in der Technikgeschichte* (2002), 111–138.

———. Kurze Geschichte des Technikrechts, in: Martin Schulte (ed.). *Handbuch des Technikrechts.* Heidelberg 2003, 3–60.

———. *Recht und Normierung in der Industriellen Revolution. Neue Strukturen der Normsetzung in Völkerrecht, staatlicher Gesetzgebung und gesellschaftlicher Selbstnormierung.* Frankfurt a.M. 2006 (Habil. 2004/05).

Veröffentlichungen des Deutschen Vereins für Versicherungswissenschaft, ed. by Alfred Manes. *Heft 1: Bericht über die am 12. Dezember 1902 abgehaltene wissenschaftliche Mitgliederversammlung des Deutschen Vereins für Versicherungswissenschaft,* Berlin1902. *Heft 2: Kritik des Gesetzentwurfes über den Versicherungsvertrag / Berichte und Debatten auf den Mitglieder-Versammlung des Deutschen Vereins für Versicherungswissenschaft am 10., 11. und 12. Dezember 1903.* Berlin 1904.

Visentini, Renzo. *Manuale giuridico-pratico per i periti e gli assicuratiori.* 1931.

Vivante, Cesare. *Il contratto di assicurazione,* vol. 1: *Le asssicurazioni terrestri.* Milan 1885; vol. 2: *Le assicurazioni maritime.* Milan 1890.

———. *Trattato di diritto commercial,* vol. 1. Turin 1893; vol. 2 / part 1. Turin 1894; vol. 3. Turin 1899.

Vivenzio, G. *Istoria dè tremuoti avvenuti nella provincia di Calabria Ulteriore, e nella città di Messina nell'anno 1783, e di quanto nelle Calabrie fu fatto per il suo risorgimento fino al 1787.* Naples 1788.

Vogel, Barbara. *Allgemeine Gewerbefreiheit. Die Reformpolitik des preußischen Staatskanzlers Hardenberg (1810–1820)*. Göttingen 1983.

Voigt, Rüdiger (ed.). *Globalisierung des Rechts*. Baden-Baden 1999.

Wagner, Adolph H.G. *Die Abschaffung des privaten Grundeigentums*. Leipzig 1870.

——. *Ueber Verstaatlichung der Eisenbahnen und über sociale Steuerreform. Zwei Landtagsreden des Abgeordneten Dr. Wagner (Osthavelland), gehalten im Preußischen Abgeordnetenhause am 19. und 22. Februar 1883. Nach dem amtlichen stenographischen Bericht*, ed. by Conservativen Central- Comité in Berlin. Berlin 1883.

Wenzel, Uwe. *Deregulierung, Verstaatlichung oder materielle Staatsaufsicht. Die Diskussion um das Versicherungsaufsichtsgesetz von 1901*. Steinbach (Taunus) 1990.

Westall, Oliver M. (ed.). *The historian and the business of insurance*. Manchester 1984.

Whitney, Albert Wurts. *Report of the special committee of the Board of Trustees of the Chamber of Commerce of San Francisco on insurance settlements incident to the 1906 San Francisco fire*. San Francisco (Chamber of Commerce) 1906.

Wieacker, Franz. Historische Bedingungen und Paradigmen supranationaler Rechtsordnungen, in: Bernstein, H. / U. Drobnig and H. Kötz (ed.). *Festschrift für Konrad Zweigert*. Tübingen 1981, 575–593.

Will, Heiner Karl. *Notice und Reasonableness. Instrumente der Vertragskontrolle im Common Law des 19. und 20. Jahrhunderts*. Berlin 1994.

Willis, Bailey. *Underwriting earthquake hazards; read before the 49th annual meeting of the Fire Underwriters' Association of the Pacific*. s.l. 1925.

Wolfrum, Rüdiger. International Law of Cooperation, in: Rudolf Bernhardt (ed.), *Encyclopedia of Public International Law*, vol. 2. Amsterdam 1995, 1242–1247.

Wood, Horace Gay. *A treatise on the law of fire insurance adapted to the present state of the law, English and American, with copious notes and illustrations*. Albany, N.Y. 1906.

Zedtwitz, Clemens von. *Die rechtsgeschichtliche Entwicklung der Versicherung*. Zurich 1999.

Ziegler, Otto. *Feuerversicherungsvereinigungen*. Berlin 1905.

Zink, E. *Ueber die Ermittlung des Sachverhaltes im französischen Zivilprozesse. Ein Beitrag vergleichender Studien und beleuchtender Rechtsfälle zur Umbildung des gerichtlichen Verfahrens in deutschen Landen*, 2 volumes. München 1860.

Zitelmann, Ernst. Die Möglichkeit des Weltrecht[e]s [Vortrag, 20.1.1888]. Unveränderter Abdruck der 1888 erschienenen Abhandlung mit einem Nachwort, München / Leipzig 1916; republished in: Walter Barfuß (ed.). *125 Jahre Wiener Juristische Gesellschaft*. Wien 1992, 61–71.

Zweigert, Konrad / Hein Kötz. *Einführung in die Rechtsvergleichung auf dem Gebiete des Privatrechts*, 3rd ed. Tübingen 1996.

BIBLIOGRAPHY: PERIODICALS

[*The*] *Adjuster*, San Francisco, establ. 1900.

American Journal of International Law, New York, establ. 1907.

American Journal of Sociology, Chicago, establ. 1895.

Annalen des gesam(m)ten Versicherungswesens, Leipzig, establ. 1870.

Annals of Science, London, establ. 1936.

Archiv des Völkerrechts, Tübingen, establ. 1948/49.

Archiv für bürgerliches Recht, Berlin, establ. 1888.

Archiv für Eisenbahnwesen, Berlin, establ. 1878.

Archiv für Rechts- und Wirtschaftsphilosophie, Berlin / Leipzig, establ. 1907/08.

Archiv für Rechts- und Wirtschaftsphilosophie, establ. 1907.

Archives de philosophie du droit, Paris, establ. 1931.

[*L'*]*Argus*. Journal international des assurances, Paris, establ. 1877.

Assicurazioni. Rivista di diritto, economia e finanza delle assicurazioni private, Rome, establ. 1934.

[The] Bahamas Law Reports, Nassau 1906 (only one issue).
Beiträge zur Erläuterung des deutschen Rechts. ed. by Julius A. Gruchot, Hamm / Berlin, establ. 1857.
Berliner Börsen-Courier. Modern daily newspaper for all fields, Berlin, establ. 1855.
Berliner Lokal-Anzeiger. Organ für die Reichshauptstadt, Berlin, establ. 1883.
Best's Insurance Report. Fire and Casuality. ed. by Alfred M. Best Company, New York, establ. 1899/1900.
Bollettino della Società Geografica Italiana, Rome, establ. 1868.
Bollettino della Società Sismologica Italiana, Rome, establ. 1895.
Brookings Papers on Economic Activity, Washington, D.C., establ. 1970.
Bulletin of the Seismological Society of America, El Cerrito, establ. 1911.
Business History Review, Boston, establ. 1926.
[The] Coast Review, San Francisco, establ. 1871.
Collier's Weekly. An Illustrated Journal, New York, establ. 1888.
Columbia Law Review, New York, establ. 1901.
[The] Commercial and Financial Chronicle: see Financial Chronicle.
Deutsche Juristen-Zeitung, Berlin, establ. 1877.
Deutsche Versicherungs-Zeitung. Organ für das gesammte Versicherungswesen, Berlin, establ. 1860.
[The] Economic History Review, London, establ. 1927.
[The] Economist, London, establ. 1843.
Elsner's [...]: see Repertorischer Assekuranz-Almanach.
Feuerversicherung und Feuerschutz. Zeitschrift für Versicherungstechnik und Versicherungsrecht, für Feuerschutz, Feuerlöschwesen und Unfallverhütung, Berlin, establ. 1903.
[The Commercial and] Financial Chronicle. A weekly newspaper representing the industrial interests of the United States, New York, establ. 1865.
Frankfurter Allgemeine Zeitung, Frankfurt a.M., establ. 1949.
Geschichte und Gesellschaft. Zeitschrift für Historische Sozialwissenschaft, Berlin, establ. 1975.
Gjallarhornet. Nordisk försäkringstidning, Stockholm, establ. 1891.
Hamburger Nachrichten. Morgenzeitung für Politik, Handel und Schiffahrt, Hamburg, establ. 1849.
Hamburgischer Correspondent, Hamburg, establ. 1877.
Handel und Industrie. Wochenschrift für das gesamte Wirtschaftsleben, Munich, establ. 1892.
Harvard Law Review, Cambridge, establ. 1887.
Historische Zeitung.
Insurance Monitor, New York, establ. 1883.
Insurance Press, New York.
Insurance Record [and Actuarial and Statistical Journal], London, establ. 1904.
Insurance World [and Monetary Record], establ. 1879.
Ius commune, Frankfurt a.M., establ. 1967.
Jahrbuch für Wirtschaftsgeschichte, Berlin, establ. 1960.
Jherings Jahrbücher für die Dogmatik des bürgerlichen Rechts, Jena, establ. 1857.
Journal of Business Law.
[New York] Journal of Commerce and Commercial Bulletin, New York, establ. 1893.
Journal of Legal Pluralism, establ. 1969.
Juristische Wochenschrift, Leipzig, establ. 1871.
Leipziger Zeitschrift für Handels-, Konkurs-, und Versicherungsrecht, Munich, establ. 1907.
Los Angeles Times, Los Angeles, establ. 1881.
Masius' Rundschau. Blätter für Versicherungswissenschaft, Versicherungsrecht und bemerkenswerte Vorgänge im Versicherungswesen. Neue Folge, Leipzig, establ. 1889.
Mitteilungen der Internationalen Vereinigung der Seeversicherer an ihre Mitglieder, Berlin, establ. 1912.

Mitteilungen des Jenaer Instituts für Wirtschaftsrecht, Jena, establ. 1921.
Mitteilungen für die öffentlichen Feuerversicherungs-Anstalten, Kiel, establ. 1868/69.
Monatsschrift für Handelsrecht und Bankwesen, Steuer- und Stempelfragen. ed. by Hold-heim, Berlin, establ. 1897.
Münchener Neueste Nachrichten, Munich, establ. 1887.
Neumann's [...]: see *Zeitschrift für Versicherungswesen*.
[*The*] *New York Herald*, European Edition, Paris, establ. 1861.
New Yorker Staats-Zeitung, New York, establ. 1834.
[*The*] *New York Times*, New York, establ. 1857.
Österreichische Revue, Vienna, establ. 1876.
Österreichische Versicherungs-Zeitung. Internationales Assecuranz-Organ, Vienna, establ. 1874.
Petermanns Geographische Mitteilungen [*Dr. A. Petermanns Mitteilungen aus Justus Perthes' Geographischer Anstalt*], Gotha, establ. 1879.
[*The*] *Policy-Holder*, Manchester.
Proceedings of the annual meeting of the Fire Underwriters' Association of the Pacific, San Francisco, establ. 1877.
Rabels Zeitschrift für ausländisches und internationales Privatrecht, Tübingen, establ. 1927.
Rechtshistorisches Journal, Frankfurt, establ. 1982.
Repertorischer Assekuranz-Almanach. Handbuch für den Assekuranz- und Handelsstand und für Juristen, founded by A. F. Elsner, Berlin, establ. 1867.
Representations, Berkeley, establ. 1983.
[*The*] *Review*. International insurance intelligence, London, establ. 1869/70.
Revue für Internationalismus. Multilingual publication of the Foundation of International-ism (The Hague), German edition: Leipzig, 1907.
Revue Historique de Armées, establ. 1945.
Rivista di diritto commerciale [*industriale e marittimo*], Milano, establ. 1903.
Rundschau der Versicherungen [...]: see *Masius' Rundschau*.
San Francisco Chronicle, San Francisco, establ. 1869.
[*The*] *Spectator*. A weekly review, London, establ. 1868.
The Times [*or daily universal register*], London, establ. 1788.
USGS bulletin.
Verhandlungen des Reichstags. Stenographische Berichte. Cited with information on legisla-tive period / session / volume (year).
Verhandlungen des Reichstags. Anlagen zu den stenographischen Berichte. Cited with infor-mation on legislative period / session / volume (year).
Vierteljahresschrift für Sozial- und Wirtschaftsgeschichte, Stuttgart, establ. 1903.
Wallmann's Versicherungs-Zeitschrift, Berlin, establ. 1866/67.
[*The*] *Weekly underwriter: an insurance newspaper*, New York, establ. 1880.
Westliche Post, St. Louis (USA), establ. 1857.
Yale Law Journal, New Haven, establ. 1891.
Zeitschrift der Savigny-Stiftung für Rechtsgeschichte, Vienna, establ. 1861.
Zeitschrift des Vereins Mitteleuropäischer Eisenbahnverwaltungen, Berlin.
Zeitschrift für das gesamte Handelsrecht, Stuttgart, establ. 1858.
Zeitschrift für die gesam(m)te Versicherungswissenschaft, Berlin, establ. 1901.
Zeitschrift für die gesamte Staatswissenschaft, Tübingen, establ. 1844.
Zeitschrift für die gesamte Versicherungswirtschaft, establ. 1911.
Zeitschrift für Rechtssoziologie.
Zeitschrift für Versicherungswesen. ed. von Neumann, Berlin, establ. 1877.
Zeitschrift für Völkerrecht und Bundesstaatsrecht, Breslau, establ. 1907.

INDEX